Strategic Culture, Securitisation and the Use of Force

This book investigates, and explains, the extent to which different liberal democracies have resorted to the use of force since the 9/11 terrorist attacks.

The responses of democratic states throughout the world to the September 2001 terrorist attacks have varied greatly. This book analyses the various factors that had an impact on decisions on the use of force by governments of liberal democratic states. It seeks to explain differences in the security policies and practices of Australia, Canada, France, Germany and the UK regarding the war in Afghanistan, domestic counterterrorism measures and the Iraq War. To this end, the book combines the concepts of strategic culture and securitisation into a theoretical model that disentangles the individual structural and agential causes of the use of force by the state and sequentially analyses the impact of each causal component on the other. It argues that the norms of a strategic culture shape securitisation processes of different expressions, which then bring about distinct modes of the use of force in individual security policy decisions. While governments can also deviate from the constraints of a strategic culture, this is likely to encounter a strong reaction from large parts of the population which in turn can lead to a long-term change in strategic culture.

This book will be of much interest to students of strategic culture, securitisation, European politics, security studies and IR in general.

Wilhlem Mirow has a PhD in International Relations, Center for Security Studies (CSS), Swiss Federal Institute of Technology (ETH) Zurich.

CSS Studies in Security and International Relations
Series Editor: Andreas Wenger
Center for Security Studies, Swiss Federal Institute of Technology (ETH), Zurich

The *CSS Studies in Security and International Relations* series examines historical and contemporary aspects of security and conflict. The series provides a forum for new research based upon an expanded conception of security and will include monographs by the center's research staff and associated academic partners.

War Plans and Alliances in the Cold War
Threat perceptions in the East and West
Edited by Vojtech Mastny, Sven Holtsmark and Andreas Wenger

Transforming NATO in the Cold War
Challenges beyond deterrence in the 1960s
Edited by Andreas Wenger, Christian Nuenlist and Anna Locher

US Foreign Policy and the War on Drugs
Displacing the cocaine and heroin industry
Cornelius Friesendorf

Cyber-Security and Threat Politics
US efforts to secure the Information Age
Myriam Dunn Cavelty

Securing 'the Homeland'
Critical infrastructure, risk and (in)security
Edited by Myriam Dunn Cavelty and Kristian Søby Kristensen

Origins of the European Security System
The Helsinki Process revisited
Edited by Andreas Wenger, Vojtech Mastny and Christian Nuenlist

Russian Energy Power and Foreign Relations
Edited by Jeronim Perovic, Robert W. Orttung and Andreas Wenger

European–American Relations and the Middle East
From Suez to Iraq
Edited by Daniel Möckli and Victor Mauer

EU Foreign Policymaking and the Middle East Conflict
The Europeanization of national foreign policy
Patrick Müller

The Politics of Nuclear Non-Proliferation
A pragmatist framework for analysis
Ursula Jasper

Regional Organisations and Security
Conceptions and practices
Edited by Stephen Aris and Andreas Wenger

Peacekeeping in Africa
The evolving security architecture
Edited by Thierry Tardy and Marco Wyss

Russia's Security Policy under Putin
A critical perspective
Aglaya Snetkov

Strategic Culture, Securitisation and the Use of Force
Post-9/11 security practices of liberal democracies
Wilhelm Mirow

Strategic Culture, Securitisation and the Use of Force

Post-9/11 security practices of liberal democracies

Wilhelm Mirow

LONDON AND NEW YORK

First published 2016
by Routledge
2 Park Square, Milton Park, Abingdon, Oxon OX14 4RN

and by Routledge
711 Third Avenue, New York, NY 10017

Routledge is an imprint of the Taylor & Francis Group, an informa business

© 2016 Wilhelm Mirow

The right of Wilhelm Mirow to be identified as author of this work has been asserted by him in accordance with sections 77 and 78 of the Copyright, Designs and Patents Act 1988.

All rights reserved. No part of this book may be reprinted or reproduced or utilised in any form or by any electronic, mechanical, or other means, now known or hereafter invented, including photocopying and recording, or in any information storage or retrieval system, without permission in writing from the publishers.

Trademark notice: Product or corporate names may be trademarks or registered trademarks, and are used only for identification and explanation without intent to infringe.

British Library Cataloguing-in-Publication Data
A catalogue record for this book is available from the British Library

Library of Congress Cataloging-in-Publication Data
Names: Mirow, Wilhelm, author.
Title: Strategic culture, securitisation and the use of force : post-9/11 security practices of liberal democracies / Wilhelm Mirow.
Other titles: Strategic culture, securitization and the use of force
Description: New York, NY : Routledge, 2016. | Series: CSS studies in security and international relations | Includes bibliographical references and index.
Identifiers: LCCN 2015043051| ISBN 9781138925762 (hardback : alk. paper) | ISBN 9781315683584 (ebook)
Subjects: LCSH: Strategic culture. | Strategic culture–Case studies. | National security–Decision making. | National security–Decision making–Case studies. | War–Decision making. | War–Decision making–Case studies.
Classification: LCC U21.2 .M565 2016 | DDC 355/.0335–dc23
LC record available at http://lccn.loc.gov/2015043051

ISBN: 978-1-138-92576-2 (hbk)
ISBN: 978-1-315-68358-4 (ebk)

Typeset in Bembo
by Wearset Ltd, Boldon, Tyne and Wear

Printed and bound in Great Britain by
TJ International Ltd, Padstow, Cornwall

Contents

List of figures	ix
List of tables	x
Acknowledgements	xii
List of abbreviations	xiii
Introduction	1

PART I
A comprehensive model of the use of force by the state   21

1   Ontology and causation in international relations   23

2   The theoretical model incorporating strategic culture and
     securitisation   33

3   Operationalising the theoretical model   44

PART II
Comparing strategic cultures   51

4   Formative moments, founding narratives and identity
     conceptions   53

5   Comparative cross-country analysis   78

PART III
Comparing decision processes on the use of force   103

6   Analysing British decision processes on the use of force   105

7   Analysing German decision processes on the use of force   134

8   Analysing French decisions on the use of force   162

9   Analysing Australian decisions on the use of force   181

viii *Contents*

10 Analysing Canadian decisions on the use of force   200

11 Conclusion   222

Appendix   234
Index   244

Figures

2.1	Theoretical model incorporating strategic culture and securitisation	33
2.2	The range of strategic culture and its centre of gravity	35
2.3	Shifts in strategic culture through securitisation	40
5.1	Overview of findings on strategic culture in Chapter 5	101
11.1	Overview of findings on conduciveness to securitisation	227

Tables

1.1	Overview of the Aristotelian conception of causation	31
3.1	Classification scheme for norms dimensions of strategic cultures	47
4.1	Synoptic chart of identity conceptions	74
4.2	Preliminary classification of strategic cultures	75
5.1	World Values Survey: of course, we all hope that there will not be another war, but if it were to come to that, would you be willing to fight for your country?	79
5.2	Transatlantic Trends 2007: please tell me whether you agree with the following statement: under some conditions, war is necessary to obtain justice	80
5.3	National Identity I and II (1995, 2003): how proud are you of your country's political influence in the world?	82
5.4	National Identity I and II (1995, 2003): how proud are you of your country's armed forces?	83
5.5	World Values Survey 2006/2007: people sometimes talk about what the aims of this country should be for the next ten years. On this card are listed some of the goals which different people would give top priority. Would you please say which one of these you, yourself, consider the most important? And which one the second most important?	84
5.6	Role of Government I–IV (1985, 1990, 1996, 2006): please show whether you would like to see more or less government spending on the military and defence	85
5.7	Role of Government I–IV (1985, 1990, 1996, 2006): please show whether you would like to see more or less government spending on law enforcement	87
5.8	AP-Ipsos International Poll – attitudes toward the death penalty, February–April 2007: do you favour or oppose the death penalty for people convicted of murder?	88
5.9	AP-Ipsos International Poll – attitudes toward the death penalty, February–April 2007: which punishment do you prefer for people convicted of murder?	88
5.10	AP-Ipsos International Poll – attitudes toward the death penalty, February–April 2007: if Osama bin Laden is captured, tried and convicted of being a terrorist, which punishment should he receive?	88

Tables xi

5.11 Role of Government I–IV (1985, 1990, 1996, 2006): all systems of justice make mistakes, but which do you think is worse...? 89

5.12 Role of Government I & II (1985, 1990): suppose the police get an anonymous tip that a man with a long criminal record is planning to break into a warehouse. Do you think the police should be allowed, without a Court Order, to keep the man under surveillance? 90

5.13 Role of Government IV (2006): suppose the government suspected that a terrorist act was about to happen. Do you think the authorities should have the right to stop and search people in the street at random? 91

5.14 Role of Government IV (2006): suppose the government suspected that a terrorist act was about to happen. Do you think the authorities should have the right to tap people's telephone conversations? 92

5.15 Bertelsmann Foundation "Who Rules the World?" Survey: which is the best framework for ensuring peace and stability in the world? 93

5.16 Pew GAP: please tell me if you have a very favourable, somewhat favourable, somewhat unfavourable, or very unfavourable opinion of NATO 94

5.17 Transatlantic Trends: how desirable is it that the United States exert strong leadership in world affairs? 95

5.18 National Identity Survey II (2003): please tell me if you agree with the following statement: in general, our country should follow the decisions of international organisations to which it belongs, even if the government disagrees with them 96

5.19 National Identity Survey II (2003): please tell me if you agree with the following statement: international organisations take away too much power from our country's government 97

5.20 Transatlantic Trends (2005): do you agree with the following statement: the use of military force is more legitimate when the United Nations (UN) approves it? 98

5.21 National Identity Surveys I and II (1995, 2003): how much do you agree or disagree with the following statement? For certain problems, like environmental pollution, international bodies should have the right to enforce solutions 99

A1 International military interventions since 1990 234

A2 Military expenditure in total, per capita and as percentage of GDP 237

A3 Guardian/ICM Poll of 14–16 September 2001 238

A4 "The American government requested the supply of 3,900 German soldiers for the Afghanistan crisis. Do you support, against this backdrop, the 'unrestricted solidarity' with the US, which Chancellor Schröder promised?" 240

A5 Opinion polls on the legitimacy of a US attack on Iraq 240

A6 EOS Gallup International Crisis Survey 21–27 January 2003 241

Acknowledgements

This book is based on my PhD dissertation, which has been submitted to and approved by the Center for Comparative and International Studies of ETH Zurich. The process of writing a dissertation is at times an ecstatic and exhilarating experience. At other times it is a lonely and seemingly never-ending process. Nevertheless, it is a great privilege to be engaged in it.

A fundamental prerequisite for the successful conclusion of the writing process were those who offered me their support, interest and care throughout this process and especially in the many crucial moments when these were in dire need. It is impossible for me to imagine how I could ever have reached the point of submitting it for examination without the unswerving support of numerous colleagues, friends, family members and loved ones. Each of them deserves my wholehearted gratitude. First among these, I thank my supervisor, Prof. Andreas Wenger, for having entrusted me with the task of writing a dissertation many years ago, and for having supported me with great patience and understanding throughout my pursuit of this difficult task. I would also like to thank Prof. Christopher Daase and Prof. Frank Schimmelfennig for agreeing to co-supervise and examine the dissertation. Furthermore, I thank Victor Mauer for having inspired and supported me in the early stages of the writing process. I also thank Johannes Heisig for his help and advice in trimming down the book manuscript as well as two anonymous reviewers for their constructive feedback on the book manuscript.

I owe an enormous deal of gratitude to the entire CSS crew for their fantastic support and friendship that has sustained the work on this dissertation throughout its genesis. This applies in particular to my former and current PhD colleagues Bianca Sarbu, Corinne Bara, Manuel Suter, Mark Daniel Jäger, Alrik Thiem, Marco Martini, Christoph Kaufmann, Christoph Elhardt und Sascha Langenbach. I could not have hoped for better fellows.

My friends and family, especially my parents, deserve my deepest gratitude for all their love and encouragement.

More than gratitude goes to Emmy Chow. It is difficult to express what her love and care means to me and what it meant to me over the many years that I worked on my dissertation. Suffice it to say that it showed me how incredibly fortunate I am to have her in my life and that nothing would make me happier than to spend the rest of my life with her. It is for this reason that right now I would like to ask her if she wants to marry me.

She said "yes". I am overwhelmed with joy and proud to now be able to dedicate this book to my fiancée.

Berlin, 24 October 2015

Abbreviations

ADF	Australian Defence Forces
ALP	Australian Labour Party
ANZAC	Australian and New Zealand Army Corps
ANZUS	Australia, New Zealand, United States Security Treaty
AP	Associated Press
ARD	*Arbeitsgemeinschaft der öffentlich-rechtlichen Rundfunkanstalten der Bundesrepublik Deutschland* [German association of public broadcasters]
ASIO	Australian Security Intelligence Organisation
ATA	Canadian 2001 Anti-Terrorism Act
ATCSA	UK Anti-terrorism, Crime and Security Act 2001
AUS	Australia
AWACS	Airborne Warning and Control System
BBC	British Broadcasting Corporation
BCFK	British Commonwealth Forces Korea
BCOF	British Commonwealth Occupation Force
BKA	*Bundeskriminalamt* [German Federal Criminal Police Office]
BND	*Bundesnachrichtendienst* [German Federal Intelligence Agency]
BQ	*Bloc Québécois* [Quebec Bloc]
CAF	Canadian Armed Forces
CAN	Canada
CAR	Central African Republic
CCTV	Closed-circuit television
CDU	*Christlich Demokratische Union Deutschlands* [Christian Democratic Union of Germany]
CEF	Canadian Expeditionary Force
CNN	Cable News Network
CS	Copenhagen School
CSU	*Christlich-Soziale Union in Bayern* [Christian Social Union in Bavaria]
CTV	Canadian Television Network
DEW	distant early warning line
DK	'don't know'
DM	*Deutsche Mark* (former official currency of Germany)
DOM	*Département d'outre-mer* [French Overseas Department]

xiv *Abbreviations*

DRC	Democratic Republic of Congo
DRDC	Defence Research and Development Canada
DSTO	Defence Science and Technology Organisation of Australia
EC	European Community
ECHR	European Convention on Human Rights
ECOWAS	Economic Community of West African States
EIU	Economist Intelligence Unit
EOS	EOS Gallup European Opinion Research Group
ESS	European Security Studies
EU	European Union
EUFOR	European Union Force
FAZ	*Frankfurter Allgemeine Zeitung* [Frankfurt General Newspaper]
FDP	*Freie Demokratische Partei Deutschlands* [Free Democratic Party of Germany]
FLQ	*Front de libération du Québec* [Quebec Liberation Front]
GAP	Global Attitudes Project
GB	Great Britain
GCHQ	UK Government Communications Headquarters
GDP	gross domestic product
GNP	gross national product
GSG 9	*Grenzschutzgruppe 9 der Bundespolizei* [Border Protection Group 9 of the Federal Police]
HALO	Multinational Interim Force in Haiti
IAEA	International Atomic Energy Agency
ICM	Independent Communications and Marketing Research
IEMF	Interim Emergency Multinational Force
IFOR	Implementation Force
IISS	International Institute for Strategic Studies
INTERFET	International Force for East Timor
IR	international relations
IRA	Irish Republican
ISAF	International Security Assistance Force
ISF	International Stabilisation Force for East Timor
ITN	Independent Television News
KFOR	Kosovo Force
KSK	*Kommando Spezialkräfte* [Special Forces Command]
MISAB	Inter-African Mission to Monitor the Implementation of the Bangui Agreements
MONUC	United Nations Mission in the Democratic Republic of Congo
MP	Member of Parliament
MV	motor vessel
NATO	North Atlantic Treaty Organisation
NBC	National Broadcasting Company
NDP	New Democratic Party of Canada
NGO	non-governmental organisation
NORAD	North American Aerospace Defense Command
OAF	Operation Allied Force

Abbreviations xv

OECD	Organisation for Economic Cooperation and Development
OEF	Operation Enduring Freedom
ONUCI	United Nations Operation in Côte d'Ivoire
PDS	*Partei des Demokratischen Sozialismus* [Party of Democratic Socialism]
PM	prime minister
PPP	purchasing power parity
PRT	Provincial Reconstruction Team
PS	*Parti Socialiste* [Socialist Party]
PTA	UK Prevention of Terrorism Act 2005
RAF	*Rote Armee Fraktion* [Red Army Faction]
RAMSI	Regional Assistance Mission to Solomon Islands
RECAMP	*Renforcement des Capacités Africaines au Maintien de la Paix* [Reinforcement of African Peacekeeping Capacities]
RIPA	UK Regulation of Investigatory Powers Act 2000
RPR	*Rassemblement pour la République* [Rally for the Republic]
RSL	Returned and Services League of Australia
SACEUR	Supreme Allied Commander Europe
SAS	Special Air Service Regiment
SFOR	Stabilisation Force
SIPRI	Stockholm International Peace Research Institute
SPD	*Sozialdemokratische Partei Deutschlands* [Social Democratic Party of Germany]
SZ	*Süddeutsche Zeitung* [South German Newspaper]
TNS	Taylor Nelson Sofres
TOM	*Territoire d'outre-mer* (French overseas territory)
TV	Television
UDF	*Union pour la démocratie française* [Union for French Democracy]
UK	United Kingdom of Great Britain and Northern Ireland
UMP	*Union pour un Mouvement Populaire* [Union for a Popular Movement]
UN	United Nations
UNAMIC	United Nations Advance Mission in Cambodia
UNAMIR	United Nations Assistance Mission For Rwanda
UNAMSIL	United Nations Mission in Sierra Leone
UNAVEM	United Nations Angola Verification Mission
UNEF	United Nations Emergency Force
UNIFIL	United Nations Interim Force in Lebanon
UNITAF	Unified Task Force
UNMEE	United Nations Mission in Ethiopia and Eritrea
UNMIH	United Nations Mission in Haiti
UNMISET	United Nations Mission of Support to East Timor
UNOSOM	United Nations Operation in Somalia
UNPROFOR	United Nations Protection Force
UNSC	United Nations Security Council
UNTAC	United Nations Transitional Authority in Cambodia
UNTAET	United Nations Transitional Administration in East Timor

xvi *Abbreviations*

US	United States of America
WEU	Western European Union
WMD	weapons of mass destruction
WWII	Second World War
ZDF	*Zweites Deutsches Fernsehen* [Second German Television]

Introduction

The provision of security is a state's *raison d'être* and the bottom line of its national interest. This quintessential function requires the state to defend its domestic monopoly on the legitimate use of force against both internal and external challenges. After all, for Thomas Hobbes even the most tyrannical government was preferable to the war of all against all that would naturally ensue in its absence. The power to authorise the use of force against internal as well as external threats to the state is therefore the most important power a government can wield. Consequently, questions of when states do and when they should resort to the use of force are among the oldest and continue to be amongst the most prominent fields of contestation in public as well as academic debates on international relations. Yet there still is considerable division among the theoretical approaches offered by the academic discipline of international relations (IR) to help us understand or explain state behaviour regarding the use of force.

One obstacle to more comprehensive theory building in this regard lies in theoretical approaches to the use of force not fully grasping the full nature of this social phenomenon. Too often in theoretical debates, the domestic and international applications of state force against threats are not seen as two sides of the same coin but instead, the external and internal provision of security are seen as entirely separate acts following their distinct logics. This prevents better explanation and criticism of contemporary phenomena of state security policy and practice in both their internal and external expressions.

On the basis of this insight, the present volume seeks to devise a comprehensive theoretical model that allows for improved explanations of state behaviour regarding the use of force. It proposes that the constructivist concepts of strategic culture and securitisation can be conceptualised as standing in a dialectical relationship. In this way, these concepts allow for a theoretical understanding of the dynamic interplay between the broader societal phenomenon of strategic culture and the agency of decision-making political elites. This model will be applied to an analysis of the respective security behaviour of Australia, Canada, France, Germany and the UK in three areas of post-9/11 security behaviour: the war in Afghanistan, domestic counterterrorism legislation and the war in Iraq. It seeks to explain why states such as Australia and the UK participated more readily in the wars in Afghanistan and Iraq and enacted more far-reaching counterterrorism legislation than states such as Germany and to a lesser extent Canada and France. The book will seek to disentangle the various

2 Introduction

structural, institutional, material, cultural and agential causes that contributed to the differences in behaviour that one could observe during this period. It postulates that among the various factors that contributed to each state's distinct reactions, strategic culture is a particularly important cause of the observed differences in behaviour. The following will seek to further introduce the reader to the general theme of this book, the research puzzle and research question of this book, existing approaches to such puzzles and questions, the theoretical approach proposed by this book, the potential relevance of this research as well as the structure of this book.

Extant theories of IR continue to grapple with explanations for a considerable heterogeneity that is observable in both internal and external security practices across states. This applies to liberal democracies in particular. Just as these have managed to largely resolve their internal conflicts and maintain order domestically by peaceful means, such states have also mostly managed to maintain peaceful relations between each other. Yet when confronted with substantial internal and external security challenges, and especially as the two have become increasingly intertwined in recent years, governments of liberal democracies see themselves confronted with the question of whether or to what extent these states should abandon their democratic means and principles of peaceful conflict resolution and resort to the use of force against these threats. The answers of liberal democratic states to this question vary across different states and across time.

One might argue that this variation largely comes down to the different capabilities of liberal democracies to use force when confronted by threats. After all, already in ancient Greece, Thucydides wrote in the Melian Dialogues the famous dictum that "the strong do what they can and the weak suffer what they must" (Thucydides *et al.*, 1998: 352). Large and powerful states can quite naturally be expected to react more forcefully to perceived threats in order to provide for their citizens' security. However, liberal democratic states which are of a similar size and strength in terms of their populations can also vary quite considerably in their reactions to substantial security threats. Germany and the UK, for instance, have varied quite consistently in the frequency and the intensity with which they resorted to the use of military force since 1990 (see Mirow, 2009). The heterogeneity of security policy and practice by liberal democracies thus persists across similarities in regime types and military capabilities.

Furthermore, a crucial feature of the variance in behaviour that one can observe across liberal democracies as regards their reactions to perceived existential threats lies in the relative consistency with which states differ in the extent to which they resort to the use of force both domestically and internationally. When liberal democracies come under threat both from outside and from within, they face the double dilemma of whether they should abandon the democratic principle of peaceful conflict resolution in their external relations and in their internal relations between the state and society as well as among society. They tend to take consistently similar positions regarding both dimensions of the dilemma in which they find themselves. They differ to a similar degree in the use of external, mostly military, force and in the domestic use of force or threat to use force. This suggests that there is an intrinsic quality of states besides its

Introduction 3

regime type, which impacts on the ways in which the state handles both external and internal conflicts. This intrinsic quality therefore seems to go to the heart of the state's existence. It appears be a broader societal phenomenon with strong causal effects.

Introducing the puzzle of differences in state practice after 9/11

The dramatic events of 11 September 2001 (9/11) illustrate this preliminary observation particularly pertinently. Throughout the years following these events one can observe differences across Western liberal democratic states in the extent to which these have resorted to the use of force in their security policies and practices domestically and internationally. As the target state, the United States declared a global war on terror and established an alleged nexus between rogue states, weapons of mass destruction and transnational terrorism (Rees and Aldrich, 2005). This directed its full resources towards fighting a broad range of state as well as non-state actors. But states allied to the US did not endorse the threat scenarios and follow the US lead after 9/11 in equal measure. Instead, one can observe marked differences in the degree to which states exerted force in the security policies and practices implemented following 9/11.

Some states enacted a drastic expansion of their coercive capacities in the counterterrorist legislation passed immediately after 9/11, participated readily in the initial attack on Al-Qaida and Taliban forces in Afghanistan with sizeable contingents and joined a 'coalition of the willing' to fight an alleged nexus between rogue states, weapons of mass destruction and terrorism in Iraq. Other states showed more restraint in the legislative enhancements of security institutions and their participation in the war in Afghanistan. Eventually, two years after the invocation of Article 5 of the Atlantic Charta and "an outpouring of public sympathy and government solidarity with the US", (Toje, 2008: 119) the alliance of Western liberal democracies spanning North America, Europe, Australia and New Zealand deteriorated when some states chose to abstain and in some cases even openly oppose the war in Iraq in 2003.

This remarkably differing state behaviour regarding the use of force, both internationally and domestically, within the two-year time period after 9/11 represents a broader pattern of such differences in state behaviour that is consistently observable since the end of the Cold War.

The aftermath of 9/11 is therefore a particularly interesting time period for such analyses as it was marked by exceptionally intense national security debates among liberal states. Of all the questions debated during that period, one question stood out as pivotal: when is the state's use of force legitimate? This book seeks to address the puzzle of varying answers to this question between different states at different times. The differences in the extent to which Western liberal democratic states have resorted to the use of force in their domestic and international security policies and practices since 9/11 pose the following overarching research question: why have liberal states reacted with different levels in the use of force to the security challenges that emerged in the wake of 9/11? In particular, this book seeks to explain consistent patterns of differences in the extent

4   *Introduction*

to which states resorted to the use of force in three key instances of security policy decision-making that emerged within the two years after 9/11: the war in Afghanistan, domestic anti-terrorist legislation and the Iraq War.

Introducing the theories

During the Cold War, rationalist theories have come to dominate IR as well as its subfields of security studies and foreign policy analysis. In their explanations of a state's security policy behaviour, these traditionally focus on a state's more tangible attributes such as, in the case of neorealist explanations, its power capabilities, and in the case of neoliberal explanations, the domestic as well as the international institutions within which the state operates. As was already hinted at in the introduction of this book's general theme, the empirical puzzle poses a challenge to the conventional rationalist approaches to IR such as neoliberalism or neorealism. After all, the observable differences in security behaviour after 9/11 among liberal democracies cut across groups of states with similar international institutional embedding, regime type and power capabilities. Analyses of tangible, material factors seem insufficient to fully explain this puzzle.

Furthermore, the variance of the response by democratic states to the emergence of terrorism also transgressed the divide between international and domestic state action. Yet the latter only marginally relates to theories focusing on international power structures or general political institutions. This indicates that a more intangible yet essential quality of the state plays a strong causal role among the various factors that contribute to determining the use of force.

Spurred by the abrupt end of the Cold War, the "Constructivist Turn in International Relations Theory" (Checkel, 1998) brought forth a large body of theories that seek to uncover such intangible yet seemingly powerful factors that rationalist theories appear to overlook. One of the constructivist theories' major contenders for this factor is the concept of identity. Another major contender is that of language or discourse. In relation to a growing interest in the role of identity in shaping state behaviour, the concept of strategic culture attained particular prominence within the field of security studies through the 'constructivist turn'. In brief, this concept proposes that a state's identity generates a specific relationship of that state's society to the use of force by the state. It therefore highlights the impact of culture on a state's security policy behaviour.

Despite the rising prominence of the concept of strategic culture, there is widespread disagreement over its precise nature as well as its explanatory scope and utility. Some scholars, especially those which Johnston (1995) called its 'third generation of scholarship', see strategic culture as a concept that describes the beliefs held by a state's group of individuals with the most potential influence over decisions on the use of military force. Others, especially the first and second 'generations' of strategic culture scholarship, argue that strategic culture consists of the state's actions and does not exist independently of these. Both strands of strategic culture advanced the concept significantly. But they struggle to provide explanations for differences in behaviour beyond general patterns or trends. Linking culture with specific instances of state behaviour thus remains a challenge to strategic culture research.

Furthermore, authors such as Berger (1993, 1998), Kupchan (1994), Meyer (2007), Johnston (1995, 1998) and Duffield (1998, 1999) for instance see strategic culture as a concept that describes wider societal norms, ideas and beliefs, but place more emphasis on elites as the main agents of strategic culture in their definitions of the concept while under-specifying the exact nature of this inter-relationship between elites and wider society. Since strategic culture also appears to play a role where the state acts domestically, one can assume that it has deep roots among wider society. It relates to each citizen's conception of the state they live in and derivative conceptions of how this state should behave both towards other states and the citizens themselves. Conceptualisations of strategic culture which reduce the concept to the opinions of a state's elite decision-makers on military affairs or which equate state action and culture do not fully grasp this deep-rooted, societal nature of strategic culture.

The question of where strategic culture resides therefore needs to be clarified in order to specify the role of strategic culture within the potentially dialectical and dynamic interrelationship between decision-making elites and wider society. This also entails the need for a specification of the point beyond which strategic culture has reached its explanatory limits and needs to be complemented by approaches describing separate, interrelated processes and factors at play in shaping particular instances of behaviour.

Another largely unresolved issue regarding contemporary research on strategic culture concerns its nature of change over time. Most scholars of the third generation accept the notion that strategic cultures have their formative moments or periods such as war, revolution or economic catastrophe (Lantis, 2002a: 110). But scholars increasingly came to conceive of strategic culture as a concept that can also undergo gradual, evolutionary change beyond such rare occurrences. This applies especially to those arguing that societies in Europe have incrementally converged towards a European strategic culture since the end of the Cold War (i.e. a 'convergence-hypothesis', see Biava, 2011; Cornish and Edwards, 2001, 2005; Giegerich, 2006; Howorth, 2007; Longhurst and Zaborowski, 2004; Martinsen, 2004; Meyer, 2005, 2007; Rynning, 2003; Toje, 2008) and those arguing that German strategic culture underwent gradual change, allowing the 'normalisation' of its security and defence policy since reunification (i.e. a 'normalisation hypothesis', see Harnisch and Maull, 2001; Hyde-Price, 2001; Lantis, 2002b; Longhurst, 2004; Wagener, 2006; Wilke, 2007). However, change in strategic culture cannot be sufficiently grasped by analysing the agency of strategic actors alone. Instead, the unresolved issue of evolutionary change across time within strategic culture needs to be seen in conjunction with the hitherto underspecified interaction between the structural constraints of strategic culture's wider societal base and the agency of elite actors within a strategic culture.

In sum, the overarching major challenge of strategic culture research is the challenge of meaningfully separating strategic culture from behaviour while also allowing for explorations of its impact on concrete state actions in the realm of security policy and practice. In other words, linking culture with behaviour remains the biggest challenge to researchers on strategic culture to this day. This book contends that a focus on the use of force by the state for the provision of security can help to arrive at a definition of strategic culture that clarifies its full

6   Introduction

potential as well as its delimitations, and thereby to also clarify which additional concepts need to complement strategic culture to arrive at a theoretical model allowing for explanations of variations in security policy and practice across liberal democracies.

The use of force by the state is its ultimate, most drastic and most important means to achieve its traditionally most fundamental objectives of survival, security and order. As it is thereby a state's most recognisable act, it relates to and reconstitutes the state's identity vis-à-vis the citizen particularly strongly. Identity, according to Katzenstein (1996: 6), depicts "varying national ideologies of collective distinctiveness and purpose". The collective historical experiences of a country and especially the incisive moments of its relatively recent past enable the construction of an ideology that informs its citizens about who they are and how they should act in a given situation. Identity is therefore an "inescapable dimension of being" (Campbell, 1992: 8) that is central to strategic culture. Crucially, it is an entity that is collectively shared rather than the preserve of an elite cast of decision-makers. Identity generates norms on how the state should reconstitute this identity through its actions, in particular as regards the use of force. These norms comprise a strategic culture that generates public expectations on the use of force by the state. And as Katzenstein (1996: 4) argues, "Collective expectations can have strong causal effects. Such expectations deserve close scrutiny ... for a better understanding of national security policy." In sum, because state identity concerns everyone in society, strategic culture needs to be conceptualised more as a mainstream culture.

This book therefore defines strategic culture as comprising the widely shared, identity-derived norms, ideas and beliefs about the legitimate use of force by the state for the provision of security against perceived existential threats. Strategic culture thus forms an ideational milieu which pervades in time beyond particular instances of security policy articulation and practice. In liberal democracies, it thereby generates public expectations as well as political preferences and incentives for successive instances of security policy and practice to reconstitute a particular identity. Patterns of behaviour are therefore not part of but the result of culture.

The definition locates strategic culture at the level of wider society in liberal democracies. This implies that it describes the cultural context in which this society's decision-making elites are embedded. To some extent, elite decision-makers are therefore likely to share the norms of strategic culture as they are themselves embedded in this culture and its socialisation processes. But this need not necessarily be the case because there are numerous other factors such as biographical or international socialisation processes, which shape their personal views and which factor into decisions on the use of force. However, the collective expectations, which the norms of strategic culture generate, provide certain political incentives and constraints to political actors. But neither do these incentives and constraints provide a coherent and unitary rationale for political action. After all, decisions on the use of force against perceived security threats are usually made in situations of urgency by a small group of elite decision-makers. They rarely allow for sober political cost-benefit analysis. In what ways the normative context of a strategic culture influences such decisions

Introduction 7

and in what ways the agency of this decision–making can influence its wider societal context of strategic culture needs to be analysed through another, separate analytical concept that describes the special logic that operates in such situations of urgency generated by security threats.

The increasingly prominent concept of securitisation, which stresses the power of language rather than identity, convincingly argues that state action in the realm of security is more context-independent than ordinary politics because the invocation of an existential threat gives political actors a particularly large room for manoeuvre. Yet this approach, on the other hand, goes too far in neglecting contextual factors that can still have an impact on security policy behaviour even in the face of major threats.

Securitisation addresses precisely those dynamics which are largely absent in strategic culture based explanations as well as classical approaches to security studies, as it seeks to explain how an issue is transformed by an actor into a matter of security. Based on Speech Act theory, securitisation assumes that the enunciation of security by itself creates insecurity and security policy behaviour. It is an extreme form of politicisation that enables the use of extraordinary means in the name of security (Buzan *et al.*, 1998: 23–26; Waever, 1995). Securitisation is then defined as "the inter-subjective establishment of an existential threat with a saliency sufficient to have substantial political effects". (Buzan *et al.*, 1998: 24) The success of securitisation moves depends on two factors: an internal, linguistic-grammatical factor – the speech act must follow the 'grammar of security', and an external, contextual and social factor – the 'speech actor' must hold a position of authority from which the act can be made (Buzan *et al.*, 1998: 24).

By highlighting the special repercussions of situations of threat on political action and the special role that language plays in this process, the Copenhagen School offers a thorough account of the special logic that operates in urgent security policy decisions. The approach accurately highlights that actors enjoy a particularly high degree of autonomy in such security policy making processes. But through this insight, the approach can lead to the erroneous assumption that actors can operate largely independently of context. This renders the theory vague and unclear in some respects, which has motivated several scholars to extend and amend the theory (see, inter alia, Balzacq, 2005; Boekle *et al.*, 2000; Dunn Cavelty, 2007; Huysmans, 1998; Kingdon, 2003; McDonald, 2008; Stritzel, 2007, 2014). However, most works have focused mainly on the question of how securitisation occurs. Yet a closer look at the inherent limitations of the concept suggests that a theoretical model combining strategic culture with the concept of securitisation could create synergistic effects, which also allow for explanations of when and to what extent securitisation occurs.

Specifically, there are four areas in which the limitations of securitisation theory can potentially be offset through the incorporation of securitisation processes involving the use of force into a strategic culture based model explaining national security policy and practice. These areas concern the nature of the threat, the outcomes of securitisation processes, actors' motivations, and the role of the audience.

First, since the Copenhagen School (CS) does not specify whether securitisation is context-dependent, it neglects the role played by characteristics of the

8   *Introduction*

threat subject. This renders the concept vulnerable to the same conceptual problems which the overly agency-focused second generation of strategic culture or scholars encounter. It overestimates the power of securitising actors to intersubjectively establish an existential threat through speech acts alone. Buzan *et al.* (1998) appear to assume that there is no significant variation in the mobilising potential generated by different types of threats. Strategic culture can in part fill this conceptual gap. A society's strategic culture can be considered a strong influence on the mobilising potential of specific types of threats.

This insight addresses a further deficit of securitisation theory: the question of actors' motivations. Actors' intentions are inherently inaccessible to the analyst, aside from their professed intentions. For this reason, many researchers deem it unwise to make any claims about actors' 'real' intentions. However, as Kapil Gupta (2007: 181–182) argues, if we leave out any notion of actors' intentions, securitisation runs the risk of "reducing policymaking and governance to sophisticated conspiracies". By outlining the cultural context in which actors operate the concept of strategic culture can be indicative of the normative beliefs motivating their actions. However, strategic culture cannot prove that these beliefs are in fact genuine rather than the basis of conscious calculation by decision-makers in order to ensure public support and gain political capital. But as elites are themselves embedded in this context, they are likely to genuinely share its dominant norms. In any case strategic culture reveals political constraints posed by increasing political costs as well as potential political opportunities that potentially influence their decision.

The criticism of actors' intentions thus lends itself to incorporations of the normative context into analyses of securitisation processes. This call for an incorporation of context mirrors a call from strategic culture scholars for a re-focus on the way in which agency shapes the long-term trajectory of strategic cultures (e.g. Lock, 2010). This call then receives the same criticism levelled against securitisation at this point. As Biehl *et al.* (2013: 399) point out: "Lock's call for a stronger focus on agency seems valid, but must not be mistaken for a nod towards cultural engineering." In order to relieve both approaches from potential criticisms of implicating sophisticated conspiracies or cultural engineering, these should therefore not be individually inflated but combined in acknowledgement of their respective individual limitations and mutual compatibility.

The third criticism concerns the notion of 'extraordinary measures'. Securitisation theory implies that once an issue is successfully presented as an existential threat "the actor has claimed a right to handle the issue through extraordinary means, to break the normal political rules of the game" (Buzan *et al.*, 1998: 24). However, it seems necessary to specify what is meant by 'extraordinary measures' as outcomes of securitisation processes. Rather than distinguishing between normal and extraordinary along vague criteria of existing rules and procedures by which these come about, it would be more fitting to make the distinction according to the nature of the measure. Once an issue is successfully presented as an existential threat actors can resort to measures that would be deemed illegitimate under normal circumstances. Yet the precise 'extraordinary' measure depends on the type of threat.

Such alternative conceptualisation is highly relevant to the research question of this proposal since it allows for the comparison of processes of securitisation of the same threats leading to differences in the extent to which liberal states resort to the use of force in reaction to the security issues that have emerged after 9/11. It can answer the question of why some liberal states have resorted more to extraordinary measures in the form of the use of force than others in reaction to the security issues that emerged since 9/11, both as regards the overall scope of state force invoked through all policies enacted and as regards the extent to which the use of force is invoked in individual state actions. But this requires that the concept of securitisation, to the extent that it involves the use of force, is refined from a binary conception to an understanding of securitisation as a spectrum ranging from mild securitisation involving a low intensity of force in the state measure proclaimed in reaction to the threat to strong securitisation, which involves the full scale of means at the state's disposal to use force against the declared threat.

Fourth, a crucial criticism of securitisation is its lack of attention paid to the role of the 'audience'. The Copenhagen School focuses on speech act in outlining the factors that determine a securitisation move's success. As stated before, it argues that an issue is likely to take on societal salience or be included in the security agenda when an actor holding a position from which an authoritative claim about security can be made utilises the "grammar of security" in his speech act to portray an issue as an existential threat requiring extraordinary measures as the only way out (Buzan *et al.*, 1998: 31–33). Yet actors in similar positions of authority in different countries may present the same security issue in different ways, and thereby engender different reactions. There seem to be different 'grammars of security' delimiting what is considered legitimate state action across countries.

In a similar vein, Thierry Balzacq (2005: 173) argued that "...language has an intrinsic force that rests with the audience's scrutiny of truth claims, with regard to a threat, made by the speaker." Speech act and actors' discursive authority, the facilitating conditions of securitisation processes, cannot explain the outcomes of securitisation alone. These two factors are not the only ones determining whether an audience 'accepts' the security arguments presented by securitising actors. But if we can obtain a clear picture of the norms and collective expectations engendered by a society's strategic culture we can also establish which security arguments are more likely to find resonance than others, provided that these involve the use of force. This may hold the key to the puzzle of varying securitisation processes in response to similar security threats. As Matt McDonald (2008: 571) argued:

> Put simply, in developing a universal framework for the designation or construction of threat through speech acts the Copenhagen School ultimately downplays the importance of contextual factors – such as dominant narratives of identity – that condition both patterns of securitization and the broader construction of security.

This book therefore suggests that the outcome of securitisation processes depends on the extent to which the speech act employed by actors with the authority to voice security concerns 'hits the nerve' of the audience. The ways

10   *Introduction*

and substance of actors' enunciations of security need to be in line with the characteristics of the audience that needs to accept the securitisation move. If speech acts employ "frequently used idioms or phrases", which can "cue certain repertoires of behaviour", (Johnston, 1995: 51) they resonate with the audience. This can explain variances in securitisation processes across countries and this shows why securitisation approaches and strategic culture 'need each other' to make theoretically more powerful assertions about state behaviour. Their combination specifies the respective roles played by elites and the public in security policy decision-making processes involving the use of force.

The key insight derived from the securitisation approach for the purposes of the research question addressed here is that the use of force by the state is usually decided upon in situations of urgency and threat, which generate a special logic that the approach can describe. However, at first glance this contradicts the key insight from the strategic culture approach, which is that different societies can have different conceptions of the legitimate use of force by the state and thereby react differently in similar situations. However, one can understand the role which a strategic culture anchored among wider society can play despite the special logic that operates in situations of heightened insecurity when securitisation regarding the use of force by the state is understood in a new and different way. It needs to be conceived of not merely as a binary of securitisation and non-securitisation but as a spectrum ranging from mild securitisation involving a low intensity of force used by the state to strong securitisation involving the full intensity of force at the state's disposal

Introducing the theoretical model

The main problems with each of these two approaches, which are an overly elite-centric conception of strategic culture and an overly context-independent conception of securitisation, are symptomatic of a wider problem with many constructivist approaches to security studies. This is the problem of a conflation of the respective causal roles played by structure, including culture, and agency. By itself, strategic culture treats agency as epiphenomenal while securitisation treats its underlying cultural or other structural influences as epiphenomenal. And when either concept sees both structure and agency as appearing simultaneously, i.e. as being co-constitutive, it risks becoming a tautological explanation of behaviour.

Such conflations make it impossible to assess the causal impact of culture on agency and vice versa. It also prevents a consideration of the causal effects of other, more tangible factors relative to cultural causes of state behaviour. But when seeking to explain differences in the behaviour of two states of different strength, size and types of government, one cannot attribute these differences to culture or the language employed by agents alone. This conflation is therefore problematic because it does not allow for individual factors to be disentangled and their causal impact to be assessed one by one. However, when both concepts are acknowledged for being essentially a structural and an agential component, respectively, these can be seen as factors that each play an important role at different stages of a process leading to a particular instance of state action.

Introduction   11

In this way, they can also be seen as standing in a dialectical relationship in which each alternately influences the other.

This book therefore proposes that a theoretical model designed to explain differences in the use of force by the state understood in its entirety, i.e. its internal and international dimensions, against perceived threats to national security necessitates a reconceptualisation of strategic culture as a broader concept describing widespread public conceptions on the legitimate use of force by the state rather than a concept restricted to descriptions of the views of an elite caste of military or defence experts and decision-makers. This, on the other hand, necessitates an explanation of the causal interlinkages between the mass phenomenon of specific strategic cultures and individual acts of security policy decision-making, which makes the concept of strategic culture highly compatible with securitisation. Thus enhancing and combining these two theoretical approaches into a theoretical model on the behaviour of liberal democracies regarding the use of force can then, in turn, allow for more comprehensive explanations of the security policies and practices of liberal democracies. Furthermore, it allows for an assessment of the causal strength of strategic culture relative to other, non-ideational, structural factors that potentially have an impact on state action.

A dialectical, 'morphogenetic' ontology accommodating both structural and actor-centric factors as well as an expanded notion of causality as devised by the 'critical realism' approach to philosophy of science and Archer's (1998, 1995) works in particular, provides the necessary ontological and epistemological underpinnings of this theoretical model. In a nutshell, this school of thought argues that one should adopt a deeper and broader notion of causality that stands in an Aristotelian rather than a Humean tradition. It posits that causes are ontologically real as long as these bring about 'real world' effects. It then distinguishes between different types of causes that be divided into conditioning and activating causes of social action. The former relates to structure or culture, the latter relates to agency. Based on this understanding of causation, one can then analytically separate structure from agency and sequentially analyse their mutual causal effects.

Archer proposes to distinguish between three phases within sequences of interaction between structure or culture and agency. These are termed 'structural conditioning', 'agential social interaction' and 'structural elaboration'. This book sees strategic culture as a conditioning cause of state action alongside power capabilities and institutions. These operate during the phase of structural conditioning, which means that they are pre-existent to agency. Culture thus operates on the level of structure but must not be conflated with other conditioning causes since it has very distinct properties, especially regarding its malleability.

Triggering events or 'policy windows', such as the emergence of an acute threat, then combine with securitising agents to provide the activating causes of state behaviour regarding the use of force. During securitisation processes, these actors and strategic culture then socially interact as securitisation processes generate resonance among wider society in the form of debates taking place, inter alia, in parliament, the media and 'on the street'. Crucially, strategic culture

12   *Introduction*

not only potentially conditions whether securitisation processes will take place or not but they can also condition the particular expression of securitisation processes. The different expressions of securitisation can range from mild securitisation, which maintains restraint in its invocation of means to use force, to strong securitisation, which propagates the mobilisation of the state's full resources.

When securitising agents act in line with strategic culture, which is the most likely scenario, they achieve positive resonance and thereby maintain strategic culture, also during the phase of structural elaboration. This is termed 'morphostasis'. If securitisation processes act contrary to a strategic culture's most widely shared norms, they achieve a change in strategic culture during the phase of structural elaboration and bring about 'morphogenesis'. Depending on how far actors deviate from the norms of a strategic culture, they can either sway their audience into adopting new cultural beliefs, or they alienate their audience and generate a backlash of strategic culture in the opposite direction of the agency. This theoretical model is illustrated in Figure 2.1 (see Chapter 2).

The research aim of this book is to assess to what extent strategic culture can account for the differences in particular instances of state practice across states that form the research puzzle and question of this book. It is assumed that it had a significant impact on these particular variances in post-9/11 security behaviour by being an important conditioning factor on securitisation processes.

Introducing the cases

As mentioned before, the time period selected for the empirical investigation of securitisation processes and their resonance needs to ensure that policy windows and focusing events as potential triggers of securitisation processes present themselves to all states in equal measure. The post-9/11 era was marked by a particularly powerful focusing event creating a number of policy windows, either by itself or in combination with other events or indicators. It allowed for the establishment of a nexus of security threats primarily driven by the US, which linked transnational terrorism with rogue states and weapons of mass destruction. The period after 9/11 was one in which liberal states saw themselves confronted with violent danger. There were ample policy windows. Yet some states identified more necessity to use force within this period than others. Some states opened policy windows more widely than others.

In order to empirically examine the validity of the theoretical model outlined above, this book will test this model on the basis of three crucial post-9/11 security policy decisions – the wars in Afghanistan and Iraq as well as domestic anti-terror legislation – in five countries chosen as case studies: Australia, Canada, France, Germany and the UK.

The five countries are chosen as case studies because of the comparability of Australia and Canada as well as France, Germany and the UK in terms of their material and institutional properties, which stands in contrast to stark differences in behaviour within these two groups of states as regards the domestic and international use of force by the state. To illustrate these differences, Table A1 (see Appendix) lists all major military interventions of the five countries since 1990 alongside the troop size of each intervention. Each instance of intervention is

Introduction 13

shaded according to the robustness of the actual mandate with which the mission was equipped. A lighter shade of grey indicates a traditional peacekeeping mission with a low degree of combat activity. A darker shade of grey indicates that the intervention had a more robust mandate to also enforce peace terms or other interests of the intervener, if necessary, and a black background indicates that the intervention can be characterised as warfare.

The list shows that differences within the two-year post-9/11 period only represent a larger pattern of differences that persists not least since 1990. For instance, Australia engaged in combat activities from a very early stage onwards in both the wars on Afghanistan and Iraq. In contrast, Canada abstained from the war in Iraq and played only a minor role in the initial invasion of Afghanistan but plays a strong role in peacebuilding and combat operations in Afghanistan under ISAF. The two countries also display roughly the same frequency of interventions since 1990. But the size and mandates of individual interventions reveal significant differences. While Australia and Canada intervened with similar frequency, Australia's interventions are generally larger in size and more robust in their mandates, especially as regards interventions in its vicinity and US-led campaigns such as the Iraq War or ISAF.

As regards France, Germany and the UK, one can observe a significant difference between Germany and the other two countries, both as regards frequency and as regards scale and intensity. As Table A1 shows, Germany has intervened with increasing frequency since 1990 but remains below the levels of its two European counterparts. France, on the other hand, displays a significantly higher frequency in its interventions but many of these stem from its near-continuous military engagement in Africa, which has transformed from short-term unilateral interventions based on mutual defence treaties to multilateral, UN-mandated interventions since the 2000s. In contrast to these two nations, the UK's record of military interventions is characterised by a high degree of involvement in large-scale, combat intensive missions. This becomes particularly apparent in its sizeable contributions to large-scale, US-led operations such as the Gulf War, Operation Allied Force, Operation Enduring Freedom, ISAF and the Iraq War. Thus, while Germany and Canada consistently display restraint in their military record, Australia, France and especially the UK display a high frequency as well as a high intensity in their use of military force.

Domestically, one can discern a similar picture in the analyses of counterterrorist legislation enacted after 9/11. While Canada and especially Germany have shown restraint in the wording and the stipulations of their anti-terrorism laws, e.g. regarding detention and surveillance powers; Australia, France and the UK by contrast expanded the state's coercive powers extensively in their adoption of new anti-terror laws. This is in line with the previous observation of Canada and Germany showing more restraint in the frequency, intensity and scale with which these states resort to the use of force abroad. It is this coherent picture of stark differences in state behaviour cutting across similarities in institutions and power capabilities between the five countries that will form the explanatory subject of this book.

The selection of these five countries as case studies is guided by a consideration of whether these states are comparable and allow for the relative control of

14 *Introduction*

the other structurally conditioning factors that can explain the variety of their national security policy and practice. There needs to be relative similarity in their potential power capabilities, their democratic institutional systems and their international institutional embedding.

When comparing the potential power capabilities of the five states on the basis of their populations, territories and gross domestic products (GDPs) one can discern similarities between Australia and Canada as well as between France, Germany and the United Kingdom. The former two consist of vaster territories as well as smaller populations and economies than the latter three, making up a fourth to a third in each bilateral relation. Since military power capabilities should be proportional to a state's score in these material attributes under neorealist logic, the comparison of actual power capabilities and consequently the conversion of potential into actual power should therefore occur similarly within two groups of countries: Australia and Canada as small-to-medium powers and France, Germany and the UK as medium-to-great powers. Furthermore, although all states experienced population and economic growth since 1990, these were strongest in Australia, followed by Canada. The same applies to their total and per capita GDP. Their military power should therefore also have grown the strongest since 1990.

In order to compare the translation of potential into actual power capabilities, Table A2 (see Appendix) shows data for total and per capita military expenditure as well as military expenditure as a percentage of the country's total GDP in current prices and five year intervals since 1985. It reveals several "paradoxes of unrealised power" (Baldwin, 1979). For example, despite a smaller population and lower total GDP, one can discern a consistently widening gap between Australia's and Canada's per capita military expenditures and their military expenditures as a percentage of GDP since 1985. Australia's per capita military expenditure was almost twice that of Canada and the highest of all five countries in 2010. And in 2005, it assigned twice as much of its GDP to defence as Canada.

Another notable gap between potential and actual capabilities can be identified when comparing figures for Germany with those for the UK and France. Despite Germany's larger population and higher GDP both per capita and in total, France and the UK consistently outspent Germany not only in terms of military expenditure per capita but also in total military expenditure, except for 1995, when Germany spent more than the UK in total. In this comparison one can also discern a widening gap since the end of the Cold War. By 2010, the UK spent over 70 per cent more than Germany on defence per capita. The UK also displayed the highest figures of military expenditure as a percentage of GDP before it converged with France and Australia by the mid-2000s and then rose to the highest rank again by 2009.

Overall, this analysis revealed that there are significant differences between the five states in their translation of potential into actual power projection capabilities. These cut across similarities in geographic size, population and economic strength, and they persist beyond the Cold War. In fact, the 'unrealised power paradox' of states translating their potential into actual capabilities to varying degrees shows that the analysis of power capabilities partially adds to the

Introduction 15

puzzle of this book and therefore cannot stand alone as an explanation to it. The selection of these five countries therefore allows for an insightful comparison of the impact of strategic culture on state behaviour.

Regarding the five states' domestic institutional configuration, various democracy indicators such as Freedom House's *Freedom in the World Index* or the Economist Intelligence Unit's (EIU) *Democracy Index* show that all five countries are similarly democratic in nature. However, as the EIU points out, France's presidential political system may have some more deep-seated democratic deficits, which need to be taken into account when assessing the various factors that lead to different security policies and practices after 9/11 (Economist Intelligence Unit, 2010: 16). This aside, there are no differences in polity that could potentially explain differences in state behaviour.

Regarding the membership of international security institutions, the five states are largely embedded in the same institutional structure. With the exception of Australia all states are NATO Member-States. France withdrew all of its armed forces from NATO's military command in 1966 and only reintegrated them into NATO command structures in 2009, but it remained a NATO Member-State throughout this time. Australia is a member of another military alliance – the Security Treaty between Australia, New Zealand and the United States of America (ANZUS or ANZUS Treaty). Although the treaty is less strongly worded than the North Atlantic Charter it also obliges Australia to assist in the defence efforts of the other two parties to the treaty in the case of an attack in the region.

Aside from these defence treaties the EU also binds together France, Germany and the UK in defence affairs through its Common Security and Defence Policy. Lastly, the Organisation for Security and Cooperation in Europe provides extensive non-military instruments for security cooperation between Canada, France, Germany and the UK. Despite some differences, all five states are firmly embedded in the Western security architecture. Differences in defence and security policy behaviour can therefore not entirely be attributed to different international institutional configurations. Furthermore, as the case of Australian involvement in Afghanistan and Iraq shows, some states show more commitment and eagerness in US-led military operations after 9/11 despite weaker legal and institutional ties to the US than some NATO-members. As with the other two factors previously assessed, one can therefore conclude that international institutional configurations are insufficient by themselves to explain the puzzle to be addressed by this book.

Introducing the research methodology and aims

In order to address this empirical phenomenon, this book will proceed in two research steps. Based on the ontological and epistemological assumptions briefly outlined above, this book will adhere to an eclectic and pragmatic methodology in which the different components of the theoretical model will be analysed through methods that best fit the research purpose for each component, irrespective of the method's research paradigm, as long as their results are meaningfully translatable, as will be outlined in Chapter 2.

16   *Introduction*

The first research step, conducted in Chapters 3–5, will turn to a comparative analysis of each state's strategic cultures. These will be elaborated on the basis of literature on identity conceptions and cross-country comparative opinion polls on public attitudes towards the use of force by the state. On the basis of these findings one can then formulate assumptions about the conditioning effects of the structural factors on the agency triggered in response to policy windows that presented themselves to all five states in relatively equal measure in the two years after 9/11.

The second research step involves a comparative within-case analysis of the securitisation processes and their resonance regarding three crucial state decisions of the post 9/11 period – participation in Operation Enduring Freedom (OEF), anti-terrorism legislation and the war in Iraq. This analysis will examine whether strategic culture conditioned securitisation processes, and hence these received positive resonance or whether dissonance initiated a process of structural elaboration that resulted in the morphogenesis of strategic culture. This analysis will be conducted on the basis of content and discourse analyses of public speeches, parliamentary debates and print media commentaries as well as specific public opinion polls.

Overall, this book seeks to contribute to theory building among the various constructivist approaches to IR. In particular, it seeks to advance strategic culture-based approaches to security studies and thereby contribute to a better understanding of historical as well as contemporary state practice by liberal democracies regarding the use of force. It builds on an earlier work of the author on strategic culture (see Mirow, 2009), which established that strategic culture is an important factor in explaining differences in the frequency and intensity with which states resort to the use of military force that are otherwise similar in their potential military strength and in being liberal democracies. The book seeks to expand this and other such works of the 'third generation' of scholarship on strategic culture by placing the concept firmly among wider society rather than elites, and seeing it as one, albeit particularly important, component among many within a larger theoretical framework.

By taking a step back, acknowledging its inherent limitations and combining it with securitisation into a comprehensive theoretical framework the book seeks to establish a theoretical link between strategic culture and decisions on state behaviour in the realm of national security. This hopefully allows for a better understanding of the wider process of the evolution of a society's beliefs about the necessity and legitimacy of the state using force to provide security and order domestically and internationally. It also allows for answers to questions of when securitisation processes occur and to what extent or degree these occur in a given situation.

Specifically, by focusing on decisions over domestic counterterrorist actions as well as military operations abroad, this book will advance conceptualisations of strategic culture as well as of securitisation as it will specify the scope, role and relevance of culture in decisions on the use of force. This will shed more light on the interaction between the public and elites in security policy decision-making processes. Empirically, the book will allow for a better understanding of a liberal state's national security policy behaviour in times of perceived insecurity. The book will thereby also seek to contribute to a better understanding of the precise

Introduction 17

causes of the deterioration of the transatlantic relationship since 9/11 and the differences in strategic culture that inhere in the alliance to this day.

Finally, the empirical insights gained through the theoretical framework proposed here potentially allow for more refined criticisms of historical and contemporary state practice regarding the use of force. It highlights that one needs to scrutinise both the actions of governments and the underlying norms of a society that condition these actions. By contributing to a better understanding of the process by which societies and their respective leaderships constantly re-evaluate the legitimacy and efficacy of state force for the provision of security, it is the author's hope that ultimately the book also contributes in some way to more peaceful international relations.

The road ahead is divided into three parts and ten chapters. In Part I, this book will outline the theories and methods used in this book. The first chapter will discuss literature on strategic culture and securitisation, while the second chapter explains in detail how these should be combined into a theoretical framework. Chapter 3 then outlines the research methodology and strategy. Part II then turns to the first research step of this book. It analyses and compares each state's strategic culture in detail. Chapter 4 elaborates the origins and foundations of each strategic culture as well as likely expressions of contemporary norms on the use of force within each strategic culture on the basis of secondary literature. Chapter 5 then tests these assumptions through international public opinion polls in a cross-country comparative analysis. Part III then turns to the comparative case studies of securitisation processes and their resonance in three instances of post-9/11 security policy decision-making. Chapters 6 to 10 analyse British, German, French, Australian and Canadian securitisation processes regarding the war in Afghanistan, domestic counterterrorism legislation and the war in Iraq. The Conclusion then briefly outlines the empirical findings and discusses both the theoretical and empirical insights gained.

Bibliography

Baldwin D (1979) "Power Analysis and World Politics". *World Politics*, 31(2), 161–194.

Balzacq T (2005) "The Three Faces of Securitization: Political Agency, Audience and Context". *European Journal of International Relations*, 11(2), 171–201.

Berger TU (1993) "From Sword to Chrysanthemum: Japan's Culture of Anti-Militarism". *International Security*, 17(4), 119–150.

Berger TU (1998) *Cultures of Antimilitarism: National Security in Germany and Japan*. Baltimore: JHU Press.

Biava A (2011) "The Emergence of a Strategic Culture within the Common Security and Defence Policy". *European Foreign Affairs Review*, 16(1), 41–58.

Biehl H, Giegerich B and Jonas A (eds) (2013) *Strategic Cultures in Europe: Security and Defence Policies Across the Continent*. Wiesbaden: Springer.

Boekle H, Nadoll J and Stahl B (2000) *Identität, Diskurs und vergleichende Analyse europäischer Außenpolitiken: Theoretische Grundlegung und methodische Vorgehensweise*. Project on the Comparative Analysis of Foreign Policies in Europe ('PAFE') Working Paper, Trier: Universität Trier, Available from: www.phil.uni-passau.de/fileadmin/group_upload/61/Theoretische_Grundlegung_und_methodische_Vorgehensweise.pdf (accessed 28 January 2014).

18 Introduction

Buzan B, Waever O and Wilde JD (1998) *Security: A New Framework for Analysis*. New York: Lynne Rienner Publishers.

Campbell D (1992) *Writing Security: United States Foreign Policy and the Politics of Identity*. Minneapolis: University of Minnesota Press.

Checkel JT (1998) "The Constructivist Turn in International Relations Theory". *World Politics*, 50(2), 324–348.

Cornish P and Edwards G (2001) "Beyond the EU/NATO Dichotomy: The Beginnings of a European Strategic Culture". *International Affairs (Royal Institute of International Affairs 1944–)*, 77(3), 587–603.

Cornish P and Edwards G (2005) "The Strategic Culture of the European Union: a Progress Report". *International Affairs*, 81(4), 801–820.

Duffield JS (1998) *World Power Forsaken: Political Culture, International Institutions, and German Security Policy after Unification*. Palo Alto, CA: Stanford University Press.

Duffield JS (1999) Political Culture and State Behavior: Why Germany Confounds Neorealism. *International Organization*, 53(4), 765–803.

Dunn Cavelty M (2007) *Cyber-Security and Threat Politics: US Efforts to Secure the Information Age*. CSS Studies in Security and International Relations, Milton Park, Abingdon, Oxon; New York: Routledge.

Economist Intelligence Unit (2010) *The Economist Intelligence Unit's Index of Democracy*. London: The Economist Intelligence Unit Ltd., Available from: www.eiu.com.

Giegerich B (2006) *European Security and Strategic Culture: National Responses to the EU's Security and Defence Policy*. Baden-Baden: Nomos.

Gupta K (2007) "The State of Securitization Theory: A Review of 'The Politics of Insecurity'". *Whitehead Journal of Diplomacy and International Relations*, 8(1), 181–183.

Harnisch S and Maull H (2001) *Germany as a Civilian Power?: The Foreign Policy of the Berlin Republic*. Manchester: Manchester University Press.

Howorth J (2007) *Security and Defence Policy in the European Union*. Basingstoke: Palgrave Macmillan.

Huysmans J (1998) "Security! What Do You Mean? From Concept to Thick Signifier". *European Journal of International Relations*, 4(2), 226–255.

Hyde-Price A (2001) "Germany and the Kosovo War: still a Civilian Power?" *German Politics*, 10(1), 19–34.

Johnston AI (1995) "Thinking about Strategic Culture". *International Security*, 19(4), 32–64.

Johnston AI (1998) *Cultural Realism: Strategic Culture and Grand Strategy in Chinese History*. Princeton: Princeton University Press.

Katzenstein PJ (ed.) (1996) *The Culture of National Security*. New York: Columbia University Press.

Kingdon JW (2003) *Agendas, Alternatives, and Public Policies*. New York: Longman.

Kupchan C (1994) *The Vulnerability of Empire*. Ithaca: Cornell University Press.

Lantis J (2002a) "Strategic Culture and National Security Policy". *International Studies Review*, 4(3), 87–113.

Lantis J (2002b) "The Moral Imperative of Force: The Evolution of German Strategic Culture in Kosovo". *Comparative Strategy*, 21(1), 21–46.

Lock E (2010) "Refining Strategic Culture: Return of the Second Generation". *Review of International Studies*, 36(3), 685–708.

Longhurst K (2004) *Germany and the Use of Force*. Manchester: Manchester University Press.

Longhurst K and Zaborowski M (2004) "The Future of European Security". *European Security*, 13(4), 381–391.

Martinsen PM (2004) "Forging a Strategic Culture: Putting Policy into the ESDP". *Oxford Journal on Good Governance*, 1(1), 61–66.

McDonald M (2008) "Securitization and the Construction of Security". *European Journal of International Relations*, 14(4), 563–587.

Meyer CO (2005) "Convergence Towards a European Strategic Culture? A Constructivist Framework for Explaining Changing Norms". *European Journal of International Relations*, 11(4), 523–549.

Meyer CO (2007) *The Quest for a European Strategic Culture: Changing Norms on Security and Defence in the European Union*. London: Palgrave Macmillan.

Mirow W (2009) *Strategic Culture Matters – a Comparison of German and British Military Interventions Since 1990*. Forschungsberichte Internationale Politik, Berlin: Lit Verlag.

Rees W and Aldrich RJ (2005) "Contending Cultures of Counterterrorism: Transatlantic Divergence or Convergence?" *International Affairs*, 81(5), 905–923.

Rynning S (2003) "The European Union: Towards a Strategic Culture?" *Security Dialogue*, 34(4), 479–496.

Stritzel H (2007) "Towards a Theory of Securitization: Copenhagen and Beyond". *European Journal of International Relations*, 13(3), 357–383.

Stritzel H (2014) *Security in Translation: Securitization Theory and the Localization of Threat*. London: Palgrave Macmillan.

Thucydides, Strassler RB and Crawley R (1998) *The Landmark Thucydides: a Comprehensive Guide to the Peloponnesian War*. New York: Simon & Schuster.

Toje A (2008) *America, the EU and Strategic Culture: Renegotiating the Transatlantic Bargain*. Abingdon: Taylor & Francis.

Waever O (1995) "Securitization and Desecuritization". In: Lipschutz RD (ed.), *On Security*, New York: Columbia University Press, pp. 46–86.

Wagener M (2006) "Normalization in Security Policy? Deployments of Bundeswehr Forces Abroad in the Era Schröder, 1998–2004". In: Maull H (ed.), *Germany's Uncertain Power: Foreign Policy of the Berlin Republic*, Basingstoke: Palgrave Macmillan, pp. 79–92.

Wilke T (2007) *German Strategic Culture Revisited: Linking the Past to Contemporary Germany Strategic Choice*. Forschungsberichte Internationale Politik, Berlin: Lit Verlag.

Part I

A comprehensive model of the use of force by the state

1 Ontology and causation in international relations

The Introduction stressed that it is possible to reconcile strategic culture and securitisation by employing what resembles a moderately constructivist, positivist methodological worldview, which posits that culture and social structure is inherently malleable but nevertheless it is possible to draw inferences about their current constitution while at the same time accounting for how these can evolve. But this assumption requires solid justification through a discussion of perspectives on the nature of causation in IR, which is the subject of this chapter.

Structure and agency in IR

By combining strategic culture as a contextual variable and securitisation as a process- or agency-centred approach, the proposed theoretical model necessarily encounters a structure-agency problematique that beset international relations to a considerable degree not least since Wendt's (1987) publication of "The Agent-Structure Problem in International Relations Theory." This problematique addresses the question of ontology or of basic assumptions about the nature of social reality. In this publication's aftermath, scholars debated whether analyses of international relations should be conducted more on the basis of a structuralist or on the basis of an individualist ideal type-ontology (cf. Hollis and Smith, 1990). As these terms indicate, those adhering more to structuralist ontologies tend to emphasise that structures such as institutions determine the behaviour of social actors, while those adhering to individualist ontologies tend to emphasise the free will or rationality of individual social actors as bases for examining social phenomena. The former became a principal ontology in IR by underpinning its dominant theories such as neorealism and institutionalism during the Cold War. This had arguably been helped by the relative stability of the Cold War (Checkel, 1998) and the popular prominence of the academic discipline of economics in contrast with political science or other social sciences.

In any case, the end of the Cold War also marked an increase of scholarly interest within IR in reflections on the ontological underpinnings of its dominant theories. This was preceded by similar, wider reflections on the philosophy of social sciences in general within the field of sociology as advanced by Giddens, which in turn drew on centuries-old debates within this field of the philosophy of science between 'classics' such as John Stuart Mill, Emile Durkheim and Max Weber (Durkheim and Lukes, 2006; Giddens, 1979; Mill,

24   *Model of use of force by the state*

1858; Weber, 1949). Driving this increased interest in ontological questions was the aforementioned 'constructivist turn' in IR. This turn marked the beginning of a search for an ontological compromise since both ideal-type ontologies by themselves came to be regarded as deeply insufficient for theoretical accounts of global politics. The search for "deterministic 'causes' and universal, non-contingent, law-like regularities" (Jasper, 2014: 10) on the part of adherents to structuralist ontologies rendered their theories "to be understood as reducing states to mere rule-followers ... so downplaying states' agential abilities to 'do otherwise'" (Hagmann, 2010: 76). A fully individualist ontology, on the other hand, would amount to little more than an account of individual actions or choices, which is scarcely compatible with the notion of 'theory'. A theory based on either ontology alone thus rather resembles a bird trying to fly with only one wing. Constructivists within IR therefore set out to theorise on the basis of a dialectical ontology "that weds both structural and agential factors into one framework" (Hagmann, 2010).

The dissatisfaction experienced by many scholars of IR in the late 1980s and 1990s with theories based on structuralist ontologies, be they accompanied by positivist or interpretivist epistemology, mirrors the criticisms levelled against the overly static and structural conceptions of strategic culture, especially among its third generation, as well as the overly agency-focused and context-independent conceptions of securitisation addressed in the Introduction. An explanation of state behaviour based solely on culture conceived of as collective norms, be they attained through positivists' analyses of purportedly objective facts or through interpretations of social interaction, reduces social actors such as the state to normative automatons, or "cultural dopes", as Giddens (1979: 52) fittingly argued. Inversely, securitisation can be argued to adhere to an overly agency-centric ontology.

Together with these ontological reflections, a momentous epistemological debate also entered IR scholarship from wider developments among the social sciences. After all, reflections on the nature of things in the social world (i.e. ontology) need to go hand in hand with reflections on how one can come to know things about the social world (i.e. epistemology). This epistemological debate ran between the aforementioned positivist or 'explaining' and the interpretivist or 'understanding' camps of social science philosophy (see Geertz, 1973; and Checkel, 1998, respectively). Suffice it here to portray this debate as one between positivists adhering to a 'homo oeconomicus' conception of social actors on the one side, and interpretivists or reflexivists (also known as post-positivists) on the other, who adhere to a 'homo sociologicus' view of social actors. The former acts in a unitary way based on objective rationality that can be decoded and thereby lead to the positive accumulation of knowledge about behaviour within the social world, while the latter acts within an intersubjec-tively constructed system that needs to be understood first in order to under-stand the action in question. For interpretivists, any social knowledge then only pertains to the system in which it occurred, and which is inherently in flux. The constructivist attempts in IR to devise a dialectical ontology favoured an inter-pretivist epistemology just as structuralist theories such as realism or liberalism tend to favour a positivist epistemology.

Ontology and causation in international relations 25

Wendt (1987, 1992, 1994, 1995) was one of the leading figures in this constructivist drive for new theoretical approaches to IR which can offer dialectical ontological underpinnings that can overcome the structure-agency dichotomy. He drew from Giddens' (1979, 1984) earlier, similar work within sociology on 'structuration theory' and devised the concept of 'co-constitution', which stipulates that structure and agency must be welded into one so that one can take 'snapshots' of the properties of the social system that one seeks to understand. As Hagmann (2010: 78) puts it: "Special to constitution ... is both the conflation of structure and agency into one single and non-separable entity and the static kinds of analyses that this conflation permits." Wendt thus offered a dialectical ontology, which sees structure and agency as recursively and instantaneously involved in co-constituting social reality. Simply put, through analytical 'snapshots' of things as they are in the social world, the analyst can deduce the way in which this world works and the way in which the action captured by this 'snapshot' keeps the social world working the way it works.

Again, there are critiques of this 'co-constitution', or 'structuration' approach, which mirror those levelled against the shortcomings of the first two generations of strategic culture as well as securitisation. A key criticism levelled against these approaches lies in their – albeit deliberate – conflation of structure and agency. This, alongside their wholesale rejection of positivism, makes it impossible to separate cause from effect and to study the relative impact of structure on agency, and vice versa, as well as the conditions under which one takes precedence over the other. Yet this distinction would be necessary if one was to conceive of the two as standing in a dialectical relationship (Archer, 1995: 87; Carlsnaes, 1992: 258; Hagmann, 2010: 79, 2013: 434). Furthermore, the interpretations about social phenomena derived through 'snapshot' observations of structure and agency wielded into one preclude inferences about the temporal dimension of these. As Taylor (1993: 124) put it: "To conflate structure and action is to rule out from the start the possibility of explaining change in terms of their interaction over time." These two criticisms can be applied in equal measure to conceptions of strategic culture such as those of the second generation, which conflate the respective roles of elite decision-making and cultural constraints.

As the above showed, the proposed solutions which IR scholars advanced in search of a 'dialectical exit' from the structure-agency problematique again encountered criticisms which mirror those levelled against different conceptions of strategic culture and securitisation. An approach to this problematique advanced by the 'critical realism' approach to the social sciences as advanced by the sociologist Margaret Archer (Archer, 1988, 1995), meanwhile, lends itself to combining both approaches in order to mutually offset their respective limitations, as was argued before, and stipulates underlying ontological and epistemological assumptions that can advise researchers to forge such a combination.

Morphogenesis and causality in critical realism

Within the field of the philosophy of social sciences, Archer (1988) was particularly influential in addressing the structure-agency problematique as well as the

26   Model of use of force by the state

culture-agency problematique. Crucially, Archer (1988: 6) sought "to bring the analysis of culture on par with that of structure" and suggested that "the two can be analysed in very similar generic terms". In order to address both related problematiques, she does not reject the need to develop a dialectical ontology but seeks to further develop Giddens' attempts. For this purpose, she draws from the work on 'critical naturalism' by philosophical 'realists' within the philosophy of social science, often called critical realists, and Roy Bhaskar in particular (see Bhaskar, 1975, 1998; Harré and Madden, 1975). In brief, this school of thought rejects the 'Humean' notion of causality that has dominated not only philosophy but also common understandings of the term 'causality' for the last three centuries. This notion reduces causality to 'push and pull' factors and implies determinism, objectivity and laws (see Kurki, 2006: 189–201). Critical realists, by contrast, revert to an 'Aristotelian' notion of causality, which offers both a broader and deeper understanding of the concept. They accept that causes can be unobservable in the 'real world', i.e. intangible, but reject that these are therefore not real, as long as they bring about 'real world' effects. As will be elaborated later on, this concept of 'cause' is thereby both more complex and more 'common-sensical' because they are more in line with causal assumptions that one makes in everyday life.

The implications of this development in the philosophy of the social sciences of the late 1970s for IR theory, and foreign policy analysis in particular, were discussed by Carlsnaes (1992), who specifically referred to Archer's works, and Kurki (2006), amongst others, (see Dessler, 1991; Patomäki and Wight, 2000; Patomäki, 2002; Wendt, 1999) and have recently gained ground within IR through the related concept of 'pragmatism' (e.g. see Bauer and Brighi, 2008; Franke and Weber, 2012; Hamati-Ataya, 2012). Critical realist ideas have been applied in research within the field of security studies inter alia by Jasper's (2014) pragmatist analysis of nuclear non-proliferation policy in Switzerland and Libya as well as by Hagmann's (2010) analysis of contemporary French, German and Swiss security and foreign policy.[1] Although Archer applies the critical realist school of thought to the structure-agency problematique specifically with a view of this as a problematique that is also bound to plague almost any cultural researcher as it parallels a culture-agency problematique, it has not yet garnered attention within strategic culture research, at least to the author's knowledge.

Strategic culture, securitisation and the culture-agency problematique

In *Culture and Agency*, Archer makes the distinction between a 'Cultural System' and 'Socio-cultural life', which she equates to the difference between the *parts* of culture, which are an ideational matter, and the behaviour of the *people* who bear this matter. Although the two do not exist independently of each other, they are analytically separable and this is essential for exploring in what ways one affects the other. She argues:

> Clearly the Cultural System and the Socio-Cultural life do not exist or operate independently of one another; they overlap, intertwine and are mutually influential. But this is precisely the point, for I am *not* asserting

Ontology and causation in international relations 27

dualism but rather the utility of an analytically dualistic approach, the main recommendation for which is the very fact that it allows this interplay to be explored.

(Archer, 1988: xix)

With regards to the use of force by the state, this distinction matters all the more since decisions on the use of force are made by a minuscule group of people but in the name of the entire nation. This makes the question of their interaction all the more relevant. The main implication of this analytical distinction is that culture has an autonomous role to play in social theory. While Archer (1988: xi) asserts that culture and structure are not entirely the same and should not be "clamped together in a conceptual vice, doing violence to our subject matter by eliding the material and the ideational aspects of social life", she argues that culture and structure raise "identical difficulties" in social science, "and the method by which these can be resolved turns out to be exactly the same".

In her criticism of attempts to address the identical difficulties which both face with regards to agency, Archer distinguishes between three logically possible ways in which theorists conflate structure and agency or culture and agency. Each relate to the theorist's choice of ontology, as discussed above. Those adhering to a more structuralist ontology tend to treat agency as epiphenomenal, i.e. inert, and engage in 'downwards conflation', while those who adhere to a more individualist ontology treat structural factors as epiphenomenal and thereby engage in 'upwards conflation'. Giddens' and Wendt's attempts to construe a dialectical ontology, meanwhile, conflated the two mid-ways, which she refers to as 'central conflation' (Archer, 1995: 81–89). The first two types imply that their 'reductionist' ontologies lead to one-dimensional theories and therefore provide unsound ontological bases for theorising. The third, however, does not imply that a dialectical ontology is flawed per se, since structure and agency are indeed mutually constitutive. It merely implies that the two should not be temporally and conceptually moulded into an instantaneous interplay so that the 'parts', i.e. culture or structure, can only be analysed when they instantiate themselves through 'people', or agency. This would amount to "sinking" rather than "linking" culture and agency, as it leads to non-causal analyses (Archer, 1988: xiv). Archer compared this to trying to look at two sides of the coin at the same time. Put differently: "By enjoining the examination of a single process in the present tense, issues surrounding the relative independence, causal influence and temporal precedence of the components have been eliminated at a stroke" (Archer, 1995: 93–94).

Once again one can discern the resemblances between these three categories of conflation and the problems inherent in the strategic culture and securitisation approaches discussed above. Schematically, the first generation of strategic culture can be argued to have conflated structure and culture by intermixing ideational factors and material factors such as power into a 'conceptual vice', besides also conflating the resulting flawed conception of structure upward. The second generation, meanwhile, moulded culture and agency into one, thus engaged in 'central conflation'. The third generation then sought to separate culture from behaviour but thereby engages in 'upward conflation' that precludes causal

28 *Model of use of force by the state*

explanation in the absence of an agency-counterpart. Narrowing the focus on a select group of elites with a potential influence on decisions does not offer a way out of this conundrum since this, in turn, conflates the norms of decision-makers with the strategic culture of a society, which amounts to little more than conflating their agency with culture. Securitisation, on the other hand, can either be seen as treating context as epiphenomenal, thus conflating downwards, or as engaging in central conflation, when context is seen as incorporated into the concept but only as it instantiates itself through securitisation processes. On their own, both concepts are therefore inherently vulnerable to criticisms of either reducing politicians to "cultural dopes" (Giddens, 1979: 52) or of nodding towards notions of "sophisticated conspiracies" (Gupta, 2007: 181–182) or "cultural engineering", (Biehl *et al.*, 2013: 399) or to the criticism of providing tautological arguments. Hence, neither strategic culture nor securitisation alone can explain differences in the use of force by states pursuant to 9/11.

Through this journey from debates confined to the concepts of strategic culture and securitisation themselves to wider debates within IR to wider debates within the philosophy of social science back to debates about the concepts themselves, one can discern that the fundamentals of these debates resemble each other to an astoundingly large degree. What remains is the realisation that any conceptual expansion or refinement of the concepts themselves offers no remedy to their inherent ontological flaws. Both concepts instead need to be acknowledged for what they are, i.e. a largely structural and a largely agential account, respectively. This fosters the realisation that the third generation of strategic culture needs another 'agency-wing' in order to fly, and that securitisation represents a promising candidate in this regard. But these need to be embedded in a sound dialectical ontology that allows for each to be separated analytically and sequentially. This can be achieved by applying Archer's (1988, 1995) morphogenetic approach.

Morphogenesis and morphostasis

In order to analytically separate structure from agency so as to allow for analyses of their mutual causal effects, Archer proposes to distinguish between three phases within sequences of interaction between structure or culture and agency. These are termed 'structural conditioning', 'social interaction' and 'structural elaboration'. Their cyclical reoccurrence forms the basis of an ontology that is both dialectical and sequential. Each sequence can either lead to morphogenesis, a term first coined by Walter Buckley (1967: 58) and defined as "those processes which tend to elaborate or change a system's given form, structure or state", or lead to morphostasis, which by contrast refers to "those processes in a complex system that tend to preserve the above unchanged" (Archer, 1995: 75). Put differently, a cycle of these three phases can either change the culture or leave it unchanged. The approach thus offers "a genuine method of conceptualizing how the interplay between structure and agency can actually be analysed over time and space" (Archer, 1995: 15). It rests on the propositions that "structure necessarily pre-dates the action(s) leading to its reproduction or transformation" and that "structural elaboration necessarily post-dates the action.

Ontology and causation in international relations 29

sequences which gave rise to it" (Archer, 1995: 15). In a first step, researchers should therefore analyse the properties of the structure or culture in question, a second analytical step then addresses action within this structure and a third step involves assessing the effects of this action on the structure. The three phases are logically sequential but not temporally exclusive. There can be overlap between them.

This approach to culture–agency interaction is both simple and compelling because it allows for a reconciliation of the popular notion that a state's identity is shaped by war with strategic culture's central proposition that culture also conditions war. It allows for a cultural analysis of differences in the use of force by states without failing to recognise that the use of force is an important catalyst for cultural change, i.e. structural elaboration. Such ontological clarification is therefore of fundamental necessity before proceeding to use strategic culture as a base for theoretical explanations of differences in the use of force after 9/11. In very crude terms, this approach will be adopted through the sequence of strategic culture, securitisation and resonance. But before proceeding to outline how this morphogenetic approach will be applied to a comprehensive theoretical model explaining the use of force through strategic culture and securitisation, it is necessary to outline the epistemology that this critical realist ontology entails. After all, a causal model cannot be outlined before the notion of 'cause' is specified.

Causality in critical realism

Applying the dialectical and sequential ontology of critical realism to one's research requires that one is aware of the distinct conception of the notion of 'cause' on which this ontology rests. After all, critical realism rejects the reductionist ontologies of structuralism and interpretivism and the dialectical ontology of interpretivism. Yet each of these ontologies pertains to specific epistemologies that are not necessarily compatible with the ontology advanced by critical realism. The positivist epistemology that commonly underpins structuralist ontologies favours the discovery of universal, law-like contingencies as well as reductionism and parsimony (Jasper, 2014: 10). It therefore cannot accommodate claims of causal relationships between entities as intangible and incalculable as culture and discourse.

On the other hand, as Kurki (2006: 189) put it: "The so-called reflectivist 'constitutive' theorists have maintained that causal analysis is neither a necessary, nor a desirable aim in understanding world politics." Yet causal analysis as such is a prerequisite for explorations of the sequential interaction between structure or culture and agency. As mentioned before, critical realism therefore also rejects the interpretivists' wholesale rejection of positivism. The approach sees both strands of epistemology as flawed because they either endorse or reject an overly narrow conception of 'cause' as advanced by David Hume. Instead, it advocates a return to an Aristotelian notion of causality that is more complex but also more accommodating of causal claims and assumptions that are made intuitively and casually in every-day life. Only this notion of causality enables the conception of Archer's morphogenetic ontology.

30   *Model of use of force by the state*

Critical realism offers a deeper notion of causality through two propositions. Firstly, it proposes that we accept causes as ontologically real even if they are physically unobservable, as long as these have a 'real world' effect, i.e. bring about an observable event. In order to comprehensively explain why something happened, one therefore needs to establish theoretical frameworks that can conceptualise real yet unobservable causes (Kurki, 2006: 202). Second, the school of thought proposes that the social world consists of open systems in which it is near-impossible to fully isolate and test individual causal mechanisms, but this should not discredit claims of relative causal power. As Kurki (2006: 202) puts it: "the central focus of causal analysis is not the analysis of isolated independent variables (through statistical methods), but rather understanding the complex interaction of a variety of different kinds of causal factors (through the building of conceptual frameworks)."

This deeper understanding of causality results from a broader conception of causes offered by Aristotle's philosophy of causation. In brief, this philosophy entails that "contrary to what Hume, the empiricists and even many philosophical realists assume, 'causation is not a single, monolithic concept'" (Kurki, 2006; she quotes from Cartwright, 2004), hence one needs to appreciate the various types of causation and understand their various interactions in order to acquire knowledge about the social world. There are four main types of causation, which can be grouped into conditioning and activating causes. The former group contains material and formal causes; the latter contains efficient and final causes. Material causes refer to "the passive potentiality of concrete matter", (Hagmann, 2010: 94, 2013: 438) such as power capabilities, while formal causes refer to "the structure or 'internal relations' that give meaning and being to things" (Hagmann, 2010: 94, 2013: 438), and can thus be either cultural or other structural causes such as institutions. Efficient causes, meanwhile, refer to causes that incite a result, such as the appearance of a danger. Final causes, lastly, refer to the professed intentions, motivations or reasons that "make things happen" or in other words, they refer to "that, for the sake of which" something is done (Hagmann, 2010: 94; Kurki, 2006: 208). This can be, for example, actors' enunciation of threat and invocation of exceptional measures through securitisation.

To illustrate the difference between these four causes one can also use the analogy of a person sitting on a chair in a room filled with wood. Once another person enters the room, bringing food, the person assembles a three-legged table and then eats the food from that table. This table then has four causes. A material conditioning cause is the presence of wood in the room. A formal conditioning cause is the negative prior experience of eating from a wobbly four-legged table. An efficient activating cause is the other person bringing food, while a final activating cause is the act of assembling the table. Conditioning causes are thus specific to agency in that they condition and empower an action while activating causes are specific to agency since they activate and instantiate an action. An overview of the four causes as described by Kurki (2006: 207–210) is provided in Table 1.1 below, which is based on the table used by Hagmann (2010: 94, 2013: 438), with the addition of a brief general description for each type of cause instead of an explanation of its focus in the third row:

With this ontological and epistemological luggage, we can proceed to the details of the theoretical model in the next section. To summarise the 'story so

Ontology and causation in international relations 31

Table 1.1 Overview of the Aristotelian conception of causation

Category	Type	Description	Ontological position
Conditioning causes	Material causes	Passive potentiality of concrete matter	Structure: conditions and empowers
	Formal causes	Gives meaning and being to things	
Activating causes	Efficient causes	Incites a result	Agency: activates and instantiates
	Final causes	Makes things happen	

Source: Kurki (2006: 207–210); Hagmann (2010: 94, 2013: 438).

far', there are differences in the extent to which liberal democracies used force after 9/11, which appear to be coherent regarding their domestic and international application. These hold the key to realising the precise empirical confines of strategic culture. The underspecified elite–public relationship within the concept, in turn, holds the key to the precise conceptual limitations of the concept. The lack of a specification of contextual factors in securitisation theory holds the key to its complementarity to strategic culture as a structural concept, and vice versa. Archer's concept of morphogenesis as well as the ontological and epistemological propositions of critical realism hold the key to the realisation of how the two can be put in relation to each other.

Note

1 I am indebted to both, who are colleagues from the Centre of Security Studies at ETH Zurich and exponents of the 'Zurich School', for bringing this body of thought to my attention, and especially to Jonas Hagmann for having introduced me to Archer's works.

Bibliography

Archer MS (1988) *Culture and Agency: The Place of Culture in Social Theory*. Cambridge: Cambridge University Press.

Archer MS (1995) *Realist Social Theory: The Morphogenetic Approach*. Cambridge: Cambridge University Press.

Bauer H and Brighi E (2008) *Pragmatism in International Relations*. Abingdon: Routledge.

Bhaskar R (1975) *A Realist Theory of Science*. London; New York: Verso.

Bhaskar R (1998) *The Possibility of Naturalism: A Philosophical Critique of the Contemporary Human Sciences*. Abingdon: Routledge.

Biehl H, Giegerich B and Jonas A (eds) (2013) *Strategic Cultures in Europe: Security and Defence Policies Across the Continent*. Wiesbaden: Springer.

Buckley WF (1967) *Sociology and Modern Systems Theory*. Upper Saddle River, New Jersey: Prentice-Hall.

Carlsnaes W (1992) "The Agency-Structure Problem in Foreign Policy Analysis". *International Studies Quarterly*, 36(3), 245–270.

Cartwright N (2004) "Causation: One Word, Many Things". *Philosophy of Science*, 71(5), 805–820.

Checkel JT (1998) "The Constructivist Turn in International Relations Theory". *World Politics*, 50(2), 324–348.

32   Model of use of force by the state

Dessler D (1991) "Beyond Correlations: Toward a Causal Theory of War". *International Studies Quarterly*, 35(3), 337–355.

Durkheim E and Lukes S (2006) *The Rules of Sociological Method: and Selected Texts on Sociology and Its Method*. Aldershot: Palgrave Macmillan.

Franke U and Weber R (2012) "At the Papini Hotel: On Pragmatism in the Study of International Relations. *European Journal of International Relations*, 18(4), 669–691.

Geertz C (1973) *The Interpretation Of Cultures*. New York: Basic Books.

Giddens A (1979) *Central Problems in Social Theory: Action, Structure, and Contradiction in Social Analysis*. Oakland: University of California Press.

Giddens A (1984) *The Constitution of Society: Outline of the Theory of Structuration*. London: John Wiley & Sons.

Gupta K (2007) "The State of Securitization Theory: A Review of 'The Politics of Insecurity'". *Whitehead Journal of Diplomacy and International Relations*, 8(1), 181–183.

Hagmann J (2010) *Insecurity Communities: Contested Constructions of Security and Foreign Politics in Contemporary France, Germany and Switzerland*. Geneva: Graduate Institute of International and Development Studies.

Hagmann J (2013) "Representations of Terrorism and the Making of Counterterrorism Policy. *Critical Studies on Terrorism*, 6(3), 429–446.

Hamati-Ataya I (2012) "Beyond (Post)Positivism: The Missed Promises of Systemic Pragmatism". *International Studies Quarterly*, 56(2), 291–305.

Harré R and Madden EH (1975) *Causal Powers: a Theory of Natural Necessity*. Oxford: Blackwell.

Hollis M and Smith S (1990) *Explaining and Understanding International Relations*. Oxford: Oxford University Press.

Jasper U (2014) *The Politics of Nuclear Non-Proliferation: A Pragmatist Framework for Analysis*. Abingdon: Routledge.

Kurki M (2006) "Causes of a Divided Discipline: Rethinking the Concept of Cause in International Relations Theory". *Review of International Studies*, 32(02), 189–216.

Mill JS (1858) *A System of Logic, Ratiocinative and Inductive: Being a Connected View of the Principles of Evidence and the Methods of Scientific Investigation*. London: Harper & Brothers.

Patomäki H (2002) *After International Relations: Critical Realism and the (Re)construction of World Politics*. Hove: Psychology Press.

Patomäki H and Wight C (2000) "After Postpositivism? The Promises of Critical Realism". *International Studies Quarterly*, 44(2), 213–237.

Taylor M (1993) "Structure, Culture, and Action in the Explanation of Social Change". In: Booth WJ, James P and Meadwell H (eds), *Politics and Rationality: Rational Choice in Application*, Cambridge: Cambridge University Press, pp. 89–131.

Weber M (1949) *Methodology of Social Sciences: Max Weber*. New York: Transaction Publishers.

Wendt A (1992) "Anarchy Is What States Make of It: the Social Construction of Power Politics". *International Organization*, 46(2), 391–425.

Wendt A (1994) "Collective Identity Formation and the International State". *American Political Science Review*, 88(2), 384–396.

Wendt A (1995) "Constructing International Politics". *International Security*, 71–81.

Wendt A (1999) *Social Theory of International Politics*. Cambridge University Press.

Wendt AE (1987) "The Agent-Structure Problem in International Relations Theory". *International Organization*, 41(3), 335–370.

2 The theoretical model incorporating strategic culture and securitisation

In order to accommodate the potential causes of differences in post-9/11 security policy and practice, this book proposes a theoretical model that contains a combination of three conditioning and two formal causes that are placed into a sequential and interactive framework. As conditioning factors, the model sees potential power capabilities as material causes and international as well as domestic institutions as formal causes of the material and ideational structure that logically pre-dates the agency leading to the use of force. Strategic culture, which accounts for the collective norms on the use of force, provides a formal conditioning cause in the shape of a conditioning culture which logically pre-dates agency. This culture must not be conflated with other intangible structural factors such as institutions. Nevertheless, the conditioning factors are to some extent interrelated. Through the selection of cases with similar institutions and power capabilities, this book will seek to allow for a primary focus on differences in strategic culture rather than power or institutions. Policy windows then serve as triggering events or 'efficient causes', which logically pre-date securitisation processes. These are seen as the 'formal causes' of action in which actors

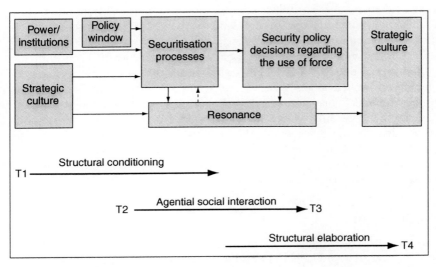

Figure 2.1 Theoretical model incorporating strategic culture and securitisation.

34 *Model of use of force by the state*

determine what the threat constitutes and how to encounter it. These two causes initiate a period of agential social interaction between securitisation actors and the strategic culture of their audience as expressed in the resonance to the securitisation move.

After the securitisation move culminates in a security policy decision regarding the use of force, this resonance continues through structural elaboration and eventually transforms into a strategic culture that is either changed through morphogenesis or preserved through morphostasis. Figure 2.1 graphically depicts an overview of the complete theoretical model incorporating strategic culture and securitisation.

The central proposition of this theoretical model is that the higher a society's cultural proclivity to deem the use of force for the provision of security justified, the more likely it is for securitising actors to invoke the extensive application of force in the security policy and practice enacted following a specified triggering event. As will be elaborated later on, strategic cultures will be classified across five different but interrelated dimensions of norms regarding the use of force by the state into four crude categories of proclivities to use force, which are ordered along a spectrum ranging from a low to a high proclivity. These categories are labelled 'passive', 'reactive', 'proactive' and 'aggressive/suppressive'. Securitisation, meanwhile, is not understood in its orthodox way as strictly a binary concept that either occurs or does not occur, as it has been proposed before and as will be elaborated below. Once an issue on one's political agenda passes a threshold between being recognised as a risk or another type of danger to being recognised as an existential threat, it passes a threshold from being politicised to being securitised. As regards the use of force within the resultant countermeasure, this then opens a spectrum ranging from mild to strong securitisation.

We can then assume that, depending on the classification of strategic culture across the four categories of normative proclivities to use force, agents engage in either a milder or a stronger securitisation process. Passive and reactive strategic cultures lend themselves to milder securitisation processes while proactive and aggressive/suppressive strategic cultures lend themselves to stronger securitisation processes. The outcomes are differences in the extent to which states resort to the use of force within their security policy and practice across both domestic and international policy domains, especially within the post-9/11 'war on terror'-period. However, in any given society security is most likely a field of contestation. Individuals may have numerous and overlapping identities. Strategic culture can therefore only be seen as an ideational source of national predispositions that delimits the range of possible actions and outlines the political costs involved in deviating from the core of strategic culture. It still leaves room for the agency of decision-making elites in determining concrete outcomes of decision processes. The chapter will now turn to each of its theory components.

Strategic culture

Strategic culture is defined here as comprising the widely shared, identity derived norms, ideas and beliefs about the legitimate use of force by the state for the provision of security against perceived existential threats. Strategic culture thus forms an ideational milieu which pre-dates particular instances of security policy articulation and practice. In liberal democracies, it thereby generates public expectations as well as political preferences and incentives for instances of security policy and practice to reconstitute a particular identity. However, in the pluralistic societies of modern liberal democracies there is a wide distribution of vastly divergent norms generated by multiple and overlapping group identities. The inherent heterogeneity of political opinions in pluralistic societies poses a challenge to the argument that a coherent strategic culture conditions security policy and practice.

However, national identity relates particularly strongly to conceptions of how the state should behave regarding the use of force, both domestically and internationally. This is the distinguishing feature of strategic culture over other cultural concepts in the social sciences. Strategic culture can therefore structurally condition the distribution of normative proclivities towards the use of force across the basic compositions of political, gender, age, regional and other sub-identities that can be found in pluralistic societies. In other words, strategic culture conditions the composition of diverging political opinions regarding the use of force in liberal democracies. Strategic cultures can therefore be considered relatively distinct and coherent, at least from a comparative perspective. They form a range of norms on the use of force within a spectrum between low and high proclivity to use force. This range has a 'centre of gravity' consisting of the most widely shared expressions of norms within strategic culture, and margins which gradually fade along the spectrum. This conceptualisation is graphically illustrated in Figure 2.2.

Alternative structural conditioners

It is argued here that one should not refrain from causal analyses and allegations only because a drive for parsimony, regularity and determinism cannot be fully satisfied. Nevertheless, as the discussion of philosophical underpinnings of social science above also showed, one must beware of endorsing mono-causal explanations, especially when invoking a concept as academically contested as culture. Instead, one must identify the various types of causes and their complex interaction. Strategic culture can therefore only be seen as one – albeit important – structural conditioner among many that might contribute to the observed differences in outcomes. Within the theoretical model proposed here, power and institutions are proposed as two other important 'structural conditioners'. Through the selection of states with similarities in both for the case studies, it will be attempted to control for their relative impact to the extent possible. But this does in no way imply that their causal effects are fully controlled for.

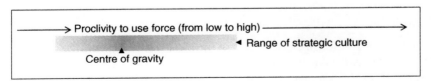

Figure 2.2 The range of strategic culture and its centre of gravity.

36 Model of use of force by the state

The relative similarities in power capabilities and institutions in the cases analysed show strategic culture to be the most important structural cause of the observed differences in the use of force. Furthermore, power capabilities and institutions causally interact with strategic culture and are therefore to some extent co-determined by different strategic cultures. But this does not imply uniformity in the relative causal impact of each across the different instances of the use of force, especially as regards domestic policy domains involving the use of force, in which strategic culture arguably has less explanatory power. The following will therefore spell out the details of the two additional conditioning causes as well as their interaction with strategic culture and their varying relative impact across different policy domains.

Power capabilities

From a realist perspective, differences in power capabilities matter a great deal for explaining differences in security policy and practice where these would otherwise not be expected. And not only potential power capabilities matter for explaining differences in military practice, but also the actual capability to deploy troops to remote locations at a given moment, or 'out of area capabilities' – especially so in the post-Cold War era. Furthermore, a country's actual military capabilities might affect intergovernmental dynamics in joint military operations, i.e. explicit demands by the US regarding particular military contributions affected liberal states' behaviour after 9/11. However, in cases of variance in security policy and practice since 9/11 as well as corresponding variance in actual power capabilities despite similarities in potential power capabilities, the "paradox of unrealised power" remains (Baldwin, 1979: 163). Differences in the extent to which liberal states chose to translate potential into actual power capabilities thereby add to the question of differences in behaviour rather than resolving it. Furthermore, the coherence in states' differences in behaviour across domestic and international security policy domains, as is the case in the research puzzle of this book, shows that strategic culture and securitisation can have a similar effect on externally and domestically directed state actions, the latter of which operates more independently of external demands and military capabilities. It is therefore assumed that in some decisions on military deployments a state's extant capabilities played a role but overall this structural conditioning cause plays a minor role within the theoretical framework among states with similar potential power capabilities. Inversely, the more states differ in their potential power capabilities, the more the causal impact of strategic culture on differences in behaviour needs to be seen in relation to the causal impact of power capabilities as a structurally conditioning material cause.

Institutions

From a liberal institutionalist perspective, there is a need to differentiate between different democratic constitutions of liberal states when analysing why some have showed more readiness to employ force in domestic and international counterterrorist operations. Some countries have shorter political processes and

Strategic culture and securitisation   37

less direct public or parliamentary control instituted for the authorisation to deploy military force or changes in the legal framework for domestic counterterrorist operations. However, the question remains why some states choose to officially leave decisions to use military force to the executive while others constitutionally require extensive parliamentary control over the armed forces. An analysis of underlying norms on the legitimate use of force can shed light on the extent to which differences in legal authorisation requirements in decisions regarding a state's use of force are a cause of differences in security policy and practice or to what extent these reflect differences in such collectively held norms on the use of force.

Furthermore, since strategic culture is conceptualised as a primarily societal and contextual factor, its impact is conditional upon the state being democratically constituted and hence potentially responsive to the public realm. This opens up a spectrum of the relative magnitude within which strategic culture potentially conditions securitisation and thereby influences security policy decisions. Arguably, it ranges from perfect democracy to perfect totalitarianism. The more democratic a state, the less autonomous are its elites or central decision-makers even in the realm of security policy decision-making, and hence the more strategic culture matters. Another potential structuring cause of differences in the use of force can be found in international institutional configurations. When states have different international institutional affiliations, there are different legal and normative demands and constraints imposed by these, which can then potentially condition state behaviour.

Furthermore, as argued in the introduction to Part I, from an institutionalist perspective a state's embedment in international security institutions matters in determining states' resort to the use of force since institutions reduce uncertainty but also legally oblige states to mutual defence in the case of institutionalised alliances. However, different degrees of involvement by states within the same or similar international institutional embedments can indicate that beyond a state's membership of an alliance, its degree of involvement within this alliance is cross-determined by strategic culture.

Variations across policy domains

One cannot expect a uniform impact of strategic culture as an explanatory factor on all types of national security policy and practice. This applies especially to policy domains in which existential threats to security emanate from both outside and within states, and in which the distinction between national, transnational and international threats becomes increasingly blurred. As the range of threats has diversified since the end of the Cold War, so have the means to counter them. It is therefore necessary to specify in which policy domains the predominating impact of strategic culture is most likely to be observable.

As discussed before, strategic culture is most commonly associated with grand strategy (Lantis, 2002: 88). Interstate warfare arguably constitutes the most extreme form of the use of force by the state, and so the assumption that distinct historical experiences have burned themselves into collective memory and thus shaped specific role conceptions and identity-derived norms which

38   *Model of use of force by the state*

influence security policy behaviour is strongest in the realm of interstate warfare. Yet especially with the rise of transnational terrorism on the global security agenda, the question arises if the concept is also applicable to other types of security policy behaviour that do not involve lethal physical force directed at targets outside the state.

In the case of counterterrorism a substantial body of literature seeks to explain idiosyncrasies in Western liberal democracies' counterterrorist policies on the basis of prior encounters with political terrorism. Wenger and Zimmermann (2006) for example have argued that "the heterogeneity in national and international responses to terrorism reflects diverging threat perceptions and differences in perspectives on the question of effectiveness versus legitimacy in counterterrorism that go back to the rise of political terrorism during the Cold War" (see also Foley, 2010). This suggests that domestic counterterrorist policies emanate from a domestic normative context which may to some degree have origins which differ from those of domestic norms on the deployment of military force.

This is not to say that there is no overarching norm context guiding decisions on the use of force against perceived threats to national security both domestically and internationally. Debates weighing the use of lethal force abroad for the sake of national security against peace may take the same shape as debates weighing restrictions on civil liberties and coercive measures within the state against civil liberties. Both address conceptions of the legitimate use of force by the state. But as the latter is less direct and largely about a state's internal affairs, strategic culture can be expected to have a lesser impact on it. The domestic use of force by the state determines how it will be seen largely by its own citizens whereas its use abroad also exposes the state's action internationally (for a general discussion of this theme, see Campbell, 1992; and Connolly, 1991). And a state action involving the direct use of lethal force by the state is more contentious than one involving the threat of potentially coercive force by the state domestically. Therefore, the higher the amount of force is involved in a state action and the more this state action is directed at the external environment, the more the state's identity will be at stake and strategic culture will have an impact on this state action.

Policy windows

I do not argue that strategic culture triggers securitisation processes but that it determines the margins within which morphostasis occurs. This raises the question of how securitisation processes get started. In other words, what is the efficient cause of the use of force by the state against existential threats? There are many potential threats that governments could react to, but only some are given attention while others are ignored (Kingdon, 2003: 90–115). How does one of the many potential threats a government could react to get propelled onto the security agenda? How does the use of force by the state come into consideration? While there is a plethora of literature citing innumerable factors in this regard, this proposal will single out two concepts borrowed from agenda-setting theory as developed by Kingdon (2003) as particularly helpful: focusing events and policy windows. Kingdon argues that suboptimal conditions, which are pervasive in society, need to be identified as serious problems by governments for these to act upon them. This can happen through one or a combination of the following factors: more or less systemic *indicators* signifying that there is a problem, formal and informal *feedback* through, e.g. systematic monitoring and evaluation studies or complaints and, most applicable to the field of security policy, *focusing events* such as crises, disasters or the personal experience of policymakers. One or a combination of these creates policy windows. Once a problem is identified, it creates an opportunity to move an issue from a governmental agenda or a broader pool of policies that are considered by a government onto a decision agenda, or issues that gain the attention of the highest levels of government.

These policy windows are the starting point of securitisation processes. They emerge as a result of focusing events or indicators and allow securitising actors to identify an issue as a threat requiring a decision on its alleviation. The more visible a focusing event, the more such policy windows it can create and the wider are the policy windows. It then depends on decision-makers at the highest levels of government to open these policy windows and initiate securitisation processes or to keep such policy windows closed. In its extreme form, this would amount to ignoring an immediate and existential threat. Among countries with strong mutual affiliations, such as Western liberal democracies, securitisation in one country can then have spillover effects generating policy windows in other countries. If an issue is identified as a threat and moved onto the decision agenda in another country, the question arises whether it also constitutes a threat in one's own country. Securitisation actors thus also determine to what extent they want to follow the example of other states in opening policy windows for securitisation processes and, ultimately, extraordinary measures such as the use of force.

Securitisation and resonance

The agency of deciding on the use of force then takes place within securitisation processes. These are the final cause of the use of force. They inherently reduce the decision to a very small group of decision-making elites who derive this special authority from the situation of urgency generated by the recognition of an existential national, transnational or international threat. Hence securitisation is defined as "the intersubjective establishment of an existential threat with a saliency sufficient to have substantial political effects" (Buzan *et al.*, 1998: 24). These securitisation processes can be analysed within the decision processes leading towards either the use of force or the non-use of force. At first, these need to be referred to as decision processes because without knowledge of the outcome, i.e. whether actors indeed established an existential threat with a saliency sufficient to have the substantial effect of the state resorting to the use of force, the analysis cannot presuppose that the process indeed constitutes securitisation. In capturing this restriction to a small group of relatively autonomous actors, even in liberal democracies, of decision processes on the use of force by the state against perceived existential threats due to the situation of urgency, securitisation grasps the distinguishing feature of decision processes on the use of force.

40 Model of use of force by the state

The securitisation approach accurately captures this distinguishing feature but the Copenhagen School then went too far in assuming that the process therefore becomes nearly devoid of any structural or contextual component. Instead, one should conceive of securitisation as a process that cannot only vary between non-securitisation and securitisation, but also between mild and strong securitisation. The difference between mild and strong securitisation processes lies in the extent to which they prescribe the use of force. It can vary from the prescription of non-military and non-coercive alternatives such as mediation or the prescription of a 'token force' for primarily symbolic purposes to the prescription of the full-scale mobilisation of the country's resources into a total war.

Within this process, actors stand in agential social interaction with their audience, which consists of society at large. Depending on the structural conditioning of an analytically pre-existing strategic culture, a securitisation process either achieves positive resonance or negative resonance, which will also be referred to as dissonance. If the actors position the securitisation process at the centre of gravity of strategic culture they are likely to achieve widely positive resonance and maintain or reproduce strategic culture, thus generating morphostasis. If they deviate from the centre of gravity but stay within the confines of strategic culture at large, they can still achieve positive resonance that establishes their action as a justified innovation of agency. Actors can convince their audience of the merits of adopting new norms by justifying their actions on the basis of a changing external environment such as new demands by allies, changing global norms, a changing geostrategic environment such as the end of the Cold War, or the demonstration of hitherto undetected, innovative norms that can be absorbed by existing strategic culture. In this case, the actor can come to be regarded as 'leading the country into a new direction', and thereby achieve a shift in strategic culture, i.e. morphogenesis. This ideal-type process is illustrated in Figure 2.3.

If the actor positions the securitisation process too far away from the centre of gravity of a strategic culture, the actor generates 'dissonance'. This means that the actor alienates their audience. Society experiences a loss of trust in the norm advanced by the respective decision-making actor. This produces a 'backlash' among the audience, i.e. society, towards the norms that stand in contrast to this behaviour perceived as demonstrably unfavourable. This shift in strategic culture is then another form of morphogenesis. Such shifts can occur in both directions along the spectrum of proclivity to the use of force. Actors can not only alienate their audience through overly 'hard' securitisation processes but also through overly 'mild' ones that come to be regarded as insufficient to meet the society's security needs, for instance.

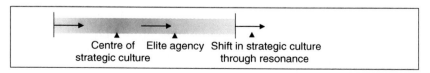

Figure 2.3 Shifts in strategic culture through securitisation.

Strategic culture and securitisation 41

Both forms of morphogenesis can also come about as a consequence of endogenous change in strategic culture e.g. through demographic dynamics or other changes to the basic constellation of identities and norms within a pluralistic society. If the actors' securitisation process adopts a position that pertains to the centre of gravity of strategic culture prior to its endogenous change, i.e. of a society's 'old' strategic culture, the actors can find themselves in dissonance with the current strategic culture. Political elites and the public are thus perpetually and sequentially engaged in either maintaining or shaping strategic culture in an ongoing, dynamic relationship.

Securitisation and resonance occur in parallel and constitute a phase of agential social interaction between securitisation and strategic culture. But the resonance continues into the phase of structural elaboration, which goes beyond the point at which securitisation culminates in a final decision. Through the resonance within securitisation processes, actors can be motivated to change their opinion and, correspondingly, the securitisation process. But this is rare and unlikely. After all, the distinguishing attribute of securitisation processes, as opposed to politicisation, is the autonomy of their agency generated by the situation of urgency in the face of threat. Insecurity professedly requires fast and determined decisions and actions. For this reason, the arrow leading from the box labelled 'resonance' to the box labelled 'securitisation' in Figure 2.1, above, is drawn as a dashed line. This is, however, not to deny that another conditioning formal cause in the shape of democratic constitutions interacts with securitisation at this point. In some countries, decision-makers face more legal requirements to receive formal approval by parliament or other democratic institutions. Hence, in some countries this line is less 'dashed' than in others. As discussed above, these legal requirements, in turn, causally interact with strategic culture.

Strategic culture nevertheless conditions securitisation processes by constituting the culture from which securitisation actors are drawn and which securitisation actors possess some knowledge of by virtue of their profession. National identity, after all, forms part and parcel of political leadership. A complete disregard for the norms which this identity generates is highly unlikely to lead to electoral success in liberal democracies. Decision-making elites are therefore likely to be aware of, and share, the norms of a strategic culture to some degree. At least, this awareness conditions actors insofar as it also entails awareness of the possible personal consequences, i.e. political costs and opportunities or incentives, of the respective positioning of a securitisation process within the distribution of the norms of a strategic culture along a scale ranging from low to high proclivity to the use of force.

However, these elites can take positions deviating from strategic culture's most widely shared cognitive elements, its centre of gravity, as these are exposed to various other external and internal influences. Domestically, these may include inter-bureaucratic pressures as well as the relative ideological disposition of particular elite personalities and political parties in power. But most importantly, the security policy decision-makers are most exposed to international influences. Elite socialisation, the demands of partners and allies as well as the higher exposure to information about the international environment can create

42   Model of use of force by the state

cognitive dissonance between the cognitive environments of consistency-seeking culturally embedded elites and their operational environment. By employing the right 'grammar of security', which is here understood as language that appeals to the existing norms of a strategic culture, from an appropriate position of author-ity, securitising actors can then invoke securitisation processes in order to reconcile external with domestic pressures and conflicting norms within a stra-tegic culture. We can therefore generally expect securitisation processes to be within the broad parameters of strategic culture or, in rare cases, to produce consequences which discernibly affect the collectively shared norms among wider society.

This resonance continues beyond decisions on the use of force and into the period of structural elaboration. Changes to a strategic culture through securiti-sation processes do not necessarily occur in concurrence with the securitisation process itself and any such concurrent changes can also be reverted at a later stage. Such deferred structural elaboration can occur through events that shed new light on the premises on which the respective decision rested when it was made. This can be the absence of a promised 'quick victory' or 'surgical warfare' and the appearance of casualties instead, or the discovery of the material absence of the professed threat itself. Since the later appearance of such factors is only to some extent predictable concurrent to the securitisation process, their full impact is deferred.

Conclusion: potential relevance of the theoretical model

The theoretical framework can potentially explain how societies organised into modern, liberal democratic states come to decide on what constitutes the legiti-mate use of force by the state through a dialectical interplay between decision-making actors and society at large. The question of the causal impact of structure relative to that of agency as well as its related question of the causal impact of culture relative to that of agency is one that has preoccupied the social sciences for centuries. It is as yet not fully resolved within the field of international rela-tions and its subfield of security studies. This theoretical model proposes that the use of force by the state for the provision of security against perceived threats, irrespective of whether this force is applied domestically or abroad, has a particu-larly strong cultural cause with very specific attributes and conditioning powers.

The concept of strategic culture can allow for a sound understanding of the importance of this cultural cause relative to other situational, material and insti-tutional causes factoring into decisions on the use of force. On the other hand, the agency of a state's leadership constitutes another, final, cause of the use of force by the state. The securitisation approach accounts for why this agency is a specifically important cause of the use of force relative to other policy decisions taken through ordinary political processes within normal circumstances. By themselves, these two approaches seemingly contradict each other.

If the two concepts are combined into a comprehensive theoretical framework, which is placed within a morphogenetic, sequentially dialectical ontology and epi-stemology, they can retain the promise to provide explanations for specific deci-sions on the use of force. This allows for an exploration of how the state comes to a decision on who should be captured or killed in the name of its people. It is through this attribution that the question inescapably concerns every citizen. The theoretical framework should therefore be of interest not only to those engaged in the drafting and exercise of security policy but also to the keen and critical observer of security policy who, within a liberal democracy, indirectly but inevitably also partakes in the state's practice of using force to capture or kill.

Bibliography

Baldwin D (1979) "Power Analysis and World Politics". *World Politics*, 31(2), 161–194.

Buzan B, Waever O and Wilde JD (1998) *Security: A New Framework for Analysis*. New York: Lynne Rienner Publishers.

Campbell D (1992) *Writing Security: United States Foreign Policy and the Politics of Identity*. Minneapolis: University of Minnesota Press.

Connolly WE (1991) *Identity, Difference: Democratic Negotiations of Political Paradox*. Ithaca, NY: Ithaca Press.

Foley F (2010) "Norms, Threat Perceptions, and the Development of British and French Operations Against Islamist Terrorism". Conference paper presented at the International Studies Association Annual Conference 2010, New Orleans, USA.

Kingdon JW (2003) *Agendas, Alternatives, and Public Policies*. New York: Longman.

Lantis J (2002) "Strategic Culture and National Security Policy". *International Studies Review*, 4(3), 87–113.

Wenger A and Zimmermann D (eds) (2006) *How States Fight Terrorism: Policy Dynamics in the West*. Boulder, Colo.: Lynne Rienner Publishers.

3 Operationalising the theoretical model

How to operationalise this theoretical model and which methods to apply? Akin to the underlying ontology and epistemology, which lends itself to a more pragmatic research approach that transcends qualitative and quantitative as well as interpretivist and positivist research paradigms, this book will also proceed within a pragmatist research methodology and strategy. This implies that each causal element as outlined in Figure 2.1 up until security policy decisions regarding the use of force will be operationalised and analysed within research methods pragmatically tailored to the specific causal components. These research methods are a qualitative comparative analysis of strategic culture and comparative case studies mainly involving discourse analyses of securitisation processes and their resonance.

The research strategy consists of two analytical steps. The first analytical step involves a detailed analysis of each country's strategic culture. The second research step turns to the phase of agential social interaction and analyses the interplay between agency through securitisation and strategic culture through resonance. The following will describe these analytical steps in more detail by describing the operationalisation of strategic culture, securitisation and resonance.

Operationalising strategic culture

The first analytical step turns the cross-country comparative analysis to strategic culture as the potentially most important structurally conditioning formal cause of differences in post-9/11 state behaviour. By placing this analytical step after the analyses of power, institutions and behaviour, one can assess to what extent differences in strategic culture are coherent with differences in behaviour where the other structural conditioners are similar. The section on operationalising strategic culture below will elaborate the methods and indicators used for this analytical step.

The ideational matter that is strategic culture will be elaborated for each country in two steps. Firstly, dominant identity conceptions emanating from formative moments and founding narratives as well as the norms these engender will be identified through secondary literature. This indicator will serve as a basis for a general description of the relevant strategic culture. It allows for the formulation of assumptions about strategic cultures that are then tested through another indicator. The aim is to assess the extent to which one can discern a

Operationalising the theoretical model 45

coherent, dominating identity conception rather than several competing notions, and to describe such identity conceptions. The analysis will identify these and trace their internalisation, instrumentalisation and contestation throughout each country's history. This analysis then allows for assumptions about four key aspects of each country's identity narratives and conceptions: their key formative moments or founding myths as well as the emanating dominant conceptions of the country's power status and international role, the role of the state in the provision of security and the role of international institutions and the law regarding the provision of security. For the last aspect, the table allows itself to reach a judgement on whether the role conception that emanates from the respective dominant identity conception comes closer to resembling a 'Hobbesian' or a 'Kantian' identity. These categories refer to the political philosophies of Thomas Hobbes and Immanuel Kant. They describe whether the said country tends to see itself more as an actor that seeks to maximise and rely on its own capabilities for power projection in an inherently anarchical world or as an actor that values consensus building, international institutions and international law in a world that progresses towards institutional order. A synoptic chart will compare and contrast the findings for each country within these four elements.

Having systematically analysed identity conceptions one can then make assumptions about the norms and collective expectations these are these likely to generate regarding the use of force along the different norms dimensions in which strategic culture will be classified. Meyer (2007: 23), Kirchner and Sperling (2010: 12), and Dalgaard-Nielsen (2006: 36) produced useful typologies of the major norms dimensions that make up a strategic culture. They are, however, imperfect for the purposes of this book as they only capture norms dimensions regarding the state-external use of force. The typology used in this book is a modified version of the typology used by Meyer (2007: 23). It is outlined in Table 3.1 on page 47.

As in Meyer (2007: 23), the typology contains four norms dimensions which each express a propensity to the use of force by the state. They are therefore placed along a scale of a state's proclivity to use force. The first norms dimension is most expressive of such proclivity while the other three dimensions are largely derivatives of this first norms dimension. It is therefore most relevant to systematic comparisons of strategic culture and its explanatory relevance for differences in behaviour. This norms dimension uses the more explicit label "Norms regarding range of modes of the use of force by the state that are considered legitimate" instead of "Goals for the use of force", as Meyer (2007: 23) labelled it. It also uses different, more specific expressions for this norms category. Instead of Meyer's (2007: 23) second values dimension "The way in which coercive means are used", which I considered too overlapping with the first dimension, this book will use a new category which captures norms on the domestic use of force for the provision of security, with its own expressions. Although this modified typology is still rather crude, it can serve as a guide to categorise empirical findings and sketch out key differences between strategic cultures.

At its most general level, the typology classifies the norms of a strategic culture into four categories of proclivity towards the use of force, each confined in between two of five demarcations along a spectrum of proclivity towards the

46   *Model of use of force by the state*

use of force that ranges from the demarcation of proclivity to complete passivity, as the lowest extreme end of the spectrum, through the demarcations of reactiveness, proactiveness and robustness to the highest extreme end of complete aggressiveness or oppressiveness, which is however incompatible with liberal democracy. The spans of proclivity within two consecutive demarcations form the four crude categories of strategic culture: passive-reactive, reactive-proactive, proactive-robust, robust-aggressive/oppressive (see Table 3.1, opposite).

Through the prior analysis of the four key aspects of each country's identity conceptions one can formulate assumptions about their strategic culture's position within these four categories and along the five norms dimensions. In rough terms, it will be assumed that the more 'Kantian' the identity conception, the higher are the proclivities towards the use of force of norms within a strategic culture assumed to be. One can then assess the validity of the assumptions on differences in strategic culture generated on the basis of prior analyses of identity conceptions. This will be done for the most part on the basis of comparative public opinion polls. These polls will serve to assess the extent to which the narratives portrayed in the literature have retained traction among wider society throughout the time frame covered by the polls and beyond. Because the analysis turns to comparative cross-national opinion polls at this stage, it will then address each norms dimension rather than each country in turn.

Regarding these polls, certain caveats are in order. Firstly, their utility is disputed in the social sciences due to the necessarily small size of their representativeness. Although this book will only use weighted polls provided by reputable polling institutions, they only represent the opinions of around a thousand individuals from states of up to 80 million inhabitants. Furthermore, although strategic culture logically pre-dates agency, this book will also use opinion polls conducted after the time period under analysis. This is because there are not many public opinion polls that indeed pre-date this time period. The working assumption is that they are still indicative of relative differences in strategic culture that have by and large also existed prior to 9/11. Overall, public opinion polls are used in this book for lack of a better alternative of discerning relative differences in norms regarding the use of force across states.

Operationalising securitisation and resonance

The second analytical step will turn to the phase of agential social interaction between agents acting within securitisation processes and strategic culture acting through the audience. This step will therefore assess whether strategic culture can indeed be said to have a discernible conditioning impact on securitisation processes and their outcomes. How to analyse this interplay between strategic culture and securitisation within the phase of agential interaction? For this purpose, this book will turn to individual country case studies of the three major decision processes of the post-9/11 period: the war in Afghanistan, domestic counterterrorism measures and the war in Iraq. The countries under analysis are Australia, Canada, France, Germany and the UK. Since the immediate effect of resonance on securitisation is limited, we can analytically and sequentially separate the two. For each country and each instance of security policy

Table 3.1 Classification scheme for norms dimensions of strategic cultures

Norms dimension	Proclivity to use force, ranging from passive (lowest) to aggressive/oppressive (highest)			
Norms regarding range of modes of the use of force by the state that are considered legitimate	Passive to reactive (e.g. territorial defence and reaction to immediate threat)	Reactive to proactive (e.g. peacekeeping and peace enforcement)	Proactive to robust (e.g. humanitarian intervention; reaction to indirect threat; pre-emptive war)	Robust to Aggressive/oppressive (e.g. war for power, ideological and material interests; expansionism)
Norms regarding competences of the state in providing security to citizens	No acceptance of infringements on civil liberties for the provision of security	Low level of acceptance of infringements on civil liberties for the provision of security	High level of acceptance of infringements on civil liberties for the provision of security	Acceptance of rigid and repressive controls, low level of civil liberties
Preferred modes of international cooperation	Armed and unarmed neutrality	Afiliation with alliances/organisations	Affiliation with particular states	Unilateralism
Domestic and international authorisation requirements	High domestic, high international	High domestic, low international	Low domestic, high international	Low domestic, low international

Note
Includes content presented in Table 2 of Meyer, 2007: 23.

48   *Model of use of force by the state*

decision-making, we will therefore first look at the securitisation process and assess to what extent this was structurally conditioned by strategic culture.

Cues about the effects of strategic cultural constraints and enablers as well as the securitisation process' relative position within these are provided by the nature and the scope of the securitisation process. Regarding the nature of a decision process, one can employ discourse analysis in order to analyse the language and metaphors employed by securitising actors in crucial statements and speeches for justifying either a more 'mild' or a more 'strong' position. These can indicate whether this position draws from references to established norms on the use of force or whether it is presented as an action requiring new modes of thought. It can indicate to what extent strategic culture structurally conditioned the 'milder' or 'stronger' securitisation action by supplying discursive resources for the legitimisation of the respective securitisation move. Such resources can be found in the framings and frequently used idioms, phrases, analogies and metaphors that draw from dominant identity conceptions and norms.

The scope of securitisation processes indicates the extent of structural conditioning by strategic culture as it discloses the time and effort which securitising actors dedicated to establishing the threat and to invoking the countermeasures. It thereby indicates to what extent strategic culture lends itself to a certain decision regarding the use of force. It can be discerned through examining the time that lapsed between the opening of a policy window and the first establishment of the securitisation process. The scope will also be analysed on the basis of whether securitising actors passed the decision through more ordinary policy channels such as multiple parliamentary committees following extensive debate and involving a broader range of actors, or whether the government's highest ranking executives could make the decision more expeditiously and autonomously, utilising more extraordinary policy channels such as specific executive powers reserved for emergency measures. The former constitutes a broad scope of the securitisation process, which in turn indicates a relatively mild securitisation process. This should correlate with a strategic culture containing norms with a low proclivity towards the use of force by the state, while the latter indicates the opposite. Since to some extent these decision processes take place behind closed doors, this section will need to rely on official documents, scholarly literature and public statements by the executive as well as journalistic accounts in order to obtain information on the sequence of events. In this regard, the disclaimer also once again applies that the scope in the sense of policy channels used is only fully comparable across countries to the extent that there are similar constitutional legal requirements for authorising the use of force.

Yet crucially, in liberal democracies the references to the pre-existing norms of a strategic culture contained in securitisation discourse must indeed appeal to those pre-existing norms of the audience, i.e. wider society, if it is said to have a discernible impact on behaviour. One must therefore assess whether these frames and symbols actually appealed to the audience or not. The question is whether the securitising actors thought they adhered to strategic culture, or whether they really did. In addressing this question, one can assess to what extent securitisation adhered to the confines of strategic culture and thereby generated positive resonance and to what extent new norms advanced by the securitisation move could

Operationalising the theoretical model 49

be accommodated by the pre-existing strategic culture. This can provide retrospective clues about the relative explanatory relevance of strategic culture as a 'formal cause', i.e. a conditioning factor of securitisation processes leading to differences in the use of force after 9/11. It therefore has direct implications for the answer to the research question of this book.

Therefore, the book will turn to crucial parliamentary debates, print media commentaries and public opinion polls on the specific policy in question, where available, in order to assess the securitisation move's resonance among wider society. This can reveal to what extent the milder or stronger securitisation process appealed to existing norms, values and beliefs of different segments of the audience and therefore achieved resonance or whether it stood in conflict with those and therefore received dissonance. For strategic culture to be said to be a major formal cause of the respective country's distinct post-9/11 behaviour, countries with a strategic culture containing norms with a higher level of inclination towards the use of force should also generate positive resonance in reaction to strong securitisation moves resulting in decisions to use force extensively, and vice versa. This assumption applies to the composition of opinions across the entire range of audience segments analysed in this section, which range from parliamentarians to the media and ultimately the general public at large. This extensive, multilayered analysis is required in order to establish to what extent strategic culture structurally conditioned the debate as a whole across the many segments of a pluralistic society.

In crucial parliamentary debates, the scope and nature of parliamentarians' reactions to the securitising actors' discourse will be analysed in much the same way as their speeches and statements were previously analysed. The analysis will be conducted on the basis of the key arguments on the respective decision of all parties represented in parliament, and by assessing the arguments and language employed by each party's lead MP weighted by the size and importance of the party. In addition, the position of other MPs who contributed statements in a debate will be ascertained through their statements.

The second step involves analysing the resonance of the securitisation process in the media. This part will analyse opinion-expressing print media content in the form of commentaries, editorials and opinion pieces relevant to the respective decision in the crucial months leading up to the decision and shortly after it was made. It will select three newspapers for each country in order to have a broad spectrum of popular opinions represented in the media. Besides the two most renowned quality newspapers of the political centre-left and centre-right, each country's newspaper with the highest circulation, which in most cases is a tabloid newspaper, will also be analysed. The inclusion of tabloid newspapers will allow for further assessment of the assumption that the wider public normally shares a distinct strategic culture in which elites are embedded and which elites at least cannot afford to ignore in view of future decisions or elections. In order to maximise their high circulation rates and dominant position in the market, tabloid newspapers must recognise and adhere to the norms, beliefs and ideals contained in this strategic culture, besides actively shaping it to the degree possible. Thereby tabloid newspapers can allow for a good assessment of the theoretical assumptions on the interplay between elites and the broader public that takes place during securitisation processes.

50 *Model of use of force by the state*

The method by which the articles will be analysed will also be that of a simple content analysis. With the help of the online database Lexis Nexis all opinion-expressing articles containing either the terms Afghanistan and war, terror and law, or Iraq and war, will be filtered out of the three selected newspapers for each country within the selected time frame or they will be filtered out manually in archives when these are not accessible electronically. The opinion expressed in each article will be ranked along a scale ranging from strongly supportive, moderately supportive, uncommitted and moderately critical to strongly critical. Each article, meanwhile, will be treated as one content unit, even if individual sentences or paragraphs within it express divergent opinions. Articles that weigh various and differing arguments for and against the respective decision before coming to a conclusion will be categorised as moderately supportive or critical. If, on the other hand, the main focus of the article lies in elaborating the author's own arguments with none or only little space allocated for discussing diverging opinions, it will be categorised as strongly critical or supportive. All articles will then be compiled in a table listing their date, author, title and rank, before the main arguments presented in each newspaper will be summarised in order to establish the newspaper's dominant position in resonance to the decision and to assess the cohesion of this resonance with the norms of its country's strategic culture.

The third part will then turn to specific public opinion polls in order to ascertain the general public's resonance to the securitisation move. These will only be polls that ask respondents about their support or opposition towards the specific policy in question. The polls will have to be conducted by professional public opinion research institutions using weighted and representative samples. The analysis will present and analyse the results of all relevant surveys as well as their disaggregation by gender, political orientation and age, to the extent possible.

The wider structural elaboration phase will not be examined in detail in this book because it has no direct bearing on the research question. It will only be briefly addressed through analyses of the trajectory over the last few decades of the ways in which states resorted to the use of force against major threats as well as the evolution of their identity conceptions and, to the extent that they are available, public opinion polls indicative of norms on the use of force by the state. On this basis, an 'outlook' beyond the cases will be provided in the conclusion of each case study.

Bibliography

Dalgaard-Nielsen A (2006) *Germany, Pacifism and Peace Enforcement.* Manchester: Manchester University Press.

Kirchner EJ and Sperling J (eds) (2010) *National Security Cultures: Patterns of Global Governance.* London; New York: Routledge.

Meyer CO (2007) *The Quest for a European Strategic Culture: Changing Norms on Security and Defence in the European Union.* London: Palgrave Macmillan.

Part II

Comparing strategic cultures

4 Formative moments, founding narratives and identity conceptions

The aim of this chapter is to derive an image of each country's strategic culture individually through a systematic elaboration of formative moments, founding myths and the identity conceptions these are likely to emanate from secondary literature. This will form the basis for assumptions on the expressions each country is likely to take in the four norms dimensions of strategic culture.

Australian formative moments, founding narratives and identity conceptions

Visitors to Australia often notice the large number of war museums scattered throughout the country. It is one of the many general observations frequently made, from which one might get the superficial impression that war and the provision of security play a particularly strong role in the Australian mindset. After all, as outlined in the introduction, Australian security policy and practice, both internationally and domestically, is marked by a high degree of activism towards the provision of security and the display of power. And despite its remote geographic location Australia frequently fought wars throughout its relatively short history alongside the UK and the US in regions as distant from Australia as the Middle East or Europe.

A salient element in the identity conception underpinning these behavioural characteristics is the ANZAC legend (Bloomfield and Nossal, 2007: 296; McDonald, 2010; Nourry, 2005). The involvement of the Australian and New Zealand Army Corps (ANZAC) in the First World War, especially in the Gallipoli Campaign, is commemorated every year with a national holiday and is often regarded as the moment of birth of Australian and New Zealand nationhood. Paradoxically, the Gallipoli Campaign also constitutes one of the worst defeats of the British Empire in the First World War. Out of a nation of 5 million, 60,000 Australian soldiers lost their lives in this campaign (Dennis and Grey, 2008: 36). But it is precisely this high level of sacrifice that has rendered this campaign so legendary and central to Australian identity. Furthermore, this first action of a solely Australian military unit became stylised as having revealed an Australian 'national character': on the battlefield Australians showed themselves to be "innocent and fit; stoical and laconic; irreverent in the face of hidebound authority; naturally egalitarian and disdainful of British class differences" (Manne, 2007). It thereby associates the ideal Australian type with white males

54   *Comparing strategic cultures*

possessing a fighting spirit and emphasises norms of comradeship and self-sacrifice for the country as well as its traditional allies or the Empire. The ANZAC legend therefore entails that the Australian national character became identifiable and passed its 'baptism of fire' and proved itself in the eyes of the world with the Gallipoli campaign. It put Australia on the world map in the eyes of its allies and enemies alike.

The new national holiday 'ANZAC Day' was introduced first by individual states and territories, and then throughout the country in 1925 (Bridge, 2008: 34). It was therefore initially a public sentiment that became gradually institutionalised. Eventually, ANZAC Day became more important than Australia Day, the official and more manufactured national holiday on 26 January. Under the auspices of the Returned and Services League of Australia (RSL), the day consists of dawn services at war memorials followed by parades, speeches and further services at 11 a.m. In the afternoon, the mood generally turns more celebratory, which is aided by the start of the football season as it "produces a heady brew of sport and patriotism" (Bridge, 2008: 34). Considering the origins and process of ANZAC Day one can therefore speak of a tradition which has grown and is being carried in a bottom–up fashion. It establishes a clear link between Australian national identity and warfare in a mixture of commemoration and celebration.

The course taken by the tradition of ANZAC Day over the last century reveals to what extent the Australian populace amended, challenged or marginalised the ANZAC legend's position in Australian identity conceptions. In this regard, it is noticeable that despite a diminishing population of veterans, Anzac Day has experienced a revival since the late 1980s. Not only did the marches open up to relatives of veterans but they also became more inclusive as groups of Aboriginal, Vietnamese, Greek and other communities' veterans joined the march (Bridge, 2008: 36). As a result, the march has remained the same in size or even grown despite fewer returned servicemen and women, while Dawn Service attendances and television audiences have surged (Bridge, 2008: 36). Moreover, ANZAC Cove on the Gallipoli peninsula in Turkey became "an ever more popular *rite de passage*" for Australian backpackers, which even posed problems in traffic control (Dennis and Grey, 2008: 426).

However, in part this resurgence of the ANZAC tradition took a slightly different form from its more right-wing conservative and Empire-laden origins. Since the 1970s a new narrative challenged the traditional one by asserting that although the Gallipoli Campaign did display typically Australian characteristics and its soldiers fought bravely, it also demonstrated Australia's subservience to Britain, which basically used Australians as cannon fodder throughout the First World War. In the Second World War, on the other hand, Australia had its real baptism of fire as it had to defend its own country for the first time. Since then, however, it replaced its subservience to the UK with subservience to the US until the Vietnam War occurred, and Australians realised the need to pursue a more independent course (see Dennis and Grey, 2008: 41–42). Through this new narrative, the traditional stylisation of the ANZAC myth along with Australia's support for the Vietnam War, the relative indifference of prior Australian governments towards atrocities committed by the Suharto regime in Indonesia, the Howard government's strong support for the 'war on terror', a restrictive asylum policy, social exclusion of the

Moments, narratives and identity conceptions 55

aboriginal population and a sceptical stance towards international climate policy can therefore be said to have come under increasing scrutiny in recent years (Burke, 2008: 6). This new narrative is not universal but more representative of the left in Australia. But even this modified, more left-wing version of the ANZAC narrative shares with the more conservative one a widespread notion that war brought forth and continues to shape Australian identity as a state which does not shy away from the use of force and which embodies a hands-on, independent minded and resolute national character.

Accompanying and nurturing the ANZAC legend, the notion of 'invasion anxiety' also plays a central role in the Australian identity conception. After all, before the ANZAC campaign occurred, the Australian colonies experienced apprehension towards invasion or war involving Britain throughout the nineteenth century during the so-called 'colonial war scares'. One can therefore depict Australian history essentially as the story of a Western civilisation:

> established on a hitherto unknown continent in the southern ocean (...) by an anxious cultural and strategic imagination marked by the overwhelming presence of the Other: a "presence" crucial to a political subjectivity in which the individual and collective might be fused into a potent psychological totality.
>
> (Burke, 2008: 47–48)

This suggests that historical narratives of European immigrants struggling to populate and control a vast landmass together with corresponding perceptions of separateness from the geographical neighbourhood play a major role in Australian identity. They create a sense of vulnerability which emanates norms conducive to the use of force as an effective means to counteract a broad range of acutely perceived threats.

Australian identity conceptions therefore appear to engender a strategic culture pertaining to a relatively high proclivity to the robust and proactive use of force as well as a strong normative attachment to its alliances with the English-speaking world. Domestically, this sense of vulnerability and remoteness can be expected to lead to norms supportive of the state taking up a strong role in the provision of security both externally as well as domestically and at the interface between the domestic and the international, especially regarding immigration policy. Lastly, the relatively strong normative proclivity towards the robust use of force and the strong role afforded to the state in the provision of security can be expected to entail norms demanding relatively low domestic and international authorisation requirements for the use of force by the state. However, the caveat also applies here that a normative counter current conveying a stronger aversion towards US leadership and interventionism has gained in strength over the last two decades. But the traditional narrative is continuously strong. The often mentioned 'invasion anxiety' coupled with the traditionally high regard for the armed services are likely to award the state with a relatively high level of trust regarding its decisions over the use of force domestically and internationally, although in this regard the counter current of increased scepticism towards the state's conventional security practices has most probably achieved significant inroads over the last few decades.

56   *Comparing strategic cultures*

Canadian formative moments, founding narratives and identity conceptions

The year 2012 marks the 200-year anniversary of the War of 1812. Throughout the country ceremonies, parades, speeches and exhibitions at national historic sites commemorate this 32-month conflict between the United States and the British Empire as well as its allies. The reason why this war is considered so crucial for Canadian identity formation lies in its embodiment of several characteristics that are today considered distinctly Canadian as well as distinguishing features between Canada and the United States. Crucially, the war is believed to have forged unity among the highly disparate groups inhabiting a thinly populated, vast and rugged territory on which the British sought to create a mirror-state north of its rebellious colonies (Stoddard, 2012). These groups included British colonial settlers, native Canadian 'First Nation' tribes, disaffected French Catholics and refugee crown loyalists as well as black slaves fighting for the British in return for their freedom. Expecting an easy victory and to be greeted as liberators, American troops trying to take advantage of this disunity were soundly defeated by British regulars, colonial militia and First Nation warriors (Granatstein and Oliver, 2010: 463). But the significance of this story does not lie in the resounding defeat that these troops afforded the American forces. Throughout the bicentennial commemorations, episodes of the war such as the infamous 'Burning of Washington', an attack on Washington which resulted in the burning of the White House and other buildings, or an unsuccessful invasion attempt of New Orleans, receive scant attention. Instead, the significance of the War of 1812 lies in the romanticised image it can create of Canada as a country that opposed slavery and white Anglo–Saxon domination but instead cherished diversity, multilingualism and multiculturalism (Johnson and Joshee, 2007: 22–23).

In addition to the War of 1812 the myth of the 'Benevolent Montie', as the Royal Canadian Mounted Police is commonly referred to, is also conducive to the image of Canada as a peaceful, tolerant, inclusive and diverse nation. The myth is based on the story of Canadian westward expansion and the corresponding subjugation of native Canadians at the end of the nineteenth century, which is said to have taken place with less bloodshed and more benevolence than in the US (MacKey, 2002: 1). The story of Canada's justice and tolerance towards its minorities is therefore used to create a national identity that stresses forbearance and moderation in the use of force in a drive for a harmonious relationship with – but also difference and distance from – its powerful southern neighbour. This, in turn, gave rise to the idea of Canadians as an 'unmilitary people' (Dawson, 1989). There was not the same sense of colonial inferiority and longing for recognition within the Empire as in Australia. While Canada fought enthusiastically alongside the allies in the First and Second World Wars there was also contestation between English Canadians and French Canadians over Canada's role within the Empire (Nossal, 2004: 505). As a consequence, the highly successful Canadian campaigns of the First World War did not lead to national jubilation but to the Conscription Crisis of 1917 and to a general war fatigue as well as diminishing imperial sentiment, also among English Canadians (Nossal, 2004: 512).

Moments, narratives and identity conceptions 57

During the interwar period, Canada's historical experiences with its idiosyncratic cultural and geographic set-up therefore brought forth a more measured attitude towards the use of force by the state. But the achievement of full independence in 1931 and the rise of Hitler, which fewer and fewer Canadians viewed with indifference, brought about the search for a more proactive role in world affairs (James and Kasoff, 2008: 252; Nossal, 2004: 512). Having been instrumental in several key battles of the Second World War, Canada emerged more powerful and firmly embedded within NATO as a significant partner of the Western alliance in the early Cold War years. But this did not automatically translate itself into the complete abandonment of notions of moderation in the use of force and cosmopolitanism from Canadian identity conceptions. Instead, successive Canadian governments innovatively forged a distinct role for Canada in world affairs. This role was directed by five principles of Canadian diplomacy laid out by Foreign Minister Louis St Laurent in 1947: "a regard for the maintenance of the country's unity, a commitment to political liberty, respect for the rule of law, recognition of forces of good and evil, and a willingness to accept international responsibilities". The last principle was particularly important, since St Laurent also argued that "Canada's security is to be found in a firm structure of international organisation" (cited in James and Kasoff, 2008: 252–253). A firm commitment to multilateralism and peacekeeping therefore stood at the heart of this new role conception. Culminating in the so-called 'Golden Era of Canadian diplomacy' 1945–1957, the 'Benevolent Mountie' myth gradually translated itself into a Canadian identity as a benevolent middle power highly involved in international organisations, diplomacy and peacekeeping all over the world besides being a reliable NATO partner during the Cold War.

This mythical 'Golden Era of Canadian diplomacy' is embodied by Lester Pearson, a former Canadian senior diplomat, foreign minister from 10 September 1948 to 20 June 1957 and prime minister from 22 April 1963 to 20 April 1968. While foreign minister Pearson became strongly involved in the early years of the UN and NATO, which culminated in the award of a Nobel Peace Prize in 1957 in acknowledgement of his role in defusing the Suez Crisis through the UN. Due to this role he is said to have invented peacekeeping (Fraser, 2005; Hillmer, 1994; O'Connor and Vucetic, 2010). Due to complaints by the Egyptians that some of the Canadian peacekeepers' uniforms were too indistinguishable from British uniforms, the Canadian army introduced a more distinctly Canadian uniform during its deployment to Suez. And while Pearson was prime minister his government also introduced the first distinctly Canadian flag and adopted an official national anthem (Granatstein, 2002: 347). This suggests that the 'Golden Era' may have been instrumental in further fostering a Canadian national identity.

In the following decades peacekeeping can indeed be said to have become a part of Canada's identity. According to several authors the role of a behevolent middle power and the world's peacekeeper allowed successive Canadian governments to further build on the 'Benevolent Mountie' myth and project this image internationally in order to strengthen a national identity in the face of its multiple challenges to national unity (Thomsen and Hynek, 2006). As the Canadian Senate Standing Committee on Foreign Affairs reported in 1993, peacekeeping

58   *Comparing strategic cultures*

became the "sole military activity that Canadians fully support". (Canadian Department of National Defence, 1997). Hogg (2003: 534–536) thus argues that today the Canadian public still measures every action undertaken by Canada abroad against the achievements of this 'Golden Era'.

Massie (2009: 637–638) notes that Canadian internationalism, including the idea that peacekeeping is or should be a core element of Canadian security policy and practice, also had major repercussions in the 2000s. Regarding Afghanistan, it led to a gradual shift in political rhetoric to frame the mission as a nation-building intervention as it became increasingly unpopular. Especially the Conservative government, which came to power in 2006, put greater emphasis on 'rebuilding', 'stabilisation', human security and the non-military dimensions of the mission rather than 'retaliation' and 'war' (Boucher, 2008; Massie, 2009: 638). But also the liberal Prime Minister Jean Chrétien, who famously opposed Canadian involvement in the war in Iraq, often expressed his belief in peace-keeping over war-fighting (O'Connor and Vucetic, 2010: 541). Lloyd Axworthy, Chrétien's second foreign minister, further stepped up the traditional internationalism in Canada's foreign policy by embracing the concept of 'human security' (O'Connor and Vucetic, 2010: 540). A landmines ban, the International Criminal Court and a global environmental regime were celebrated in Canada not only because they were promoted by Axworthy and his team, but also precisely because they were opposed by the United States. In a drive for difference and distance, peacekeeping became a convenient tool to shape a distinct national identity.

However, peacekeeping as a tool to forge a national self-image may be an overly simplistic description of the underlying identity motives driving Canadian security policy and practice. After all, the current Conservative government under Prime Minister Stephen Harper does not afford peacekeeping missions a great priority in its security policy. The need for a common national purpose to stem the tide of separatism and to garner national distinctness may have reached its zenith long ago or may have been an intellectual artifice from the outset. The events of 11 September 2001 may have contributed to a re-evaluation of the necessity of a continuously strong Canadian engagement in global peace support operations, as polls taken shortly after 9/11 showed that Canadians now felt closer to Americans (Sasikumar and Kitchen, 2009: 159). The image of a 'helpful fixer' and 'honest broker' may gradually fade and become replaced by a more conventional image of a reliable US ally and NATO partner. But the wave of post-9/11 solidarity also subsided soon after the event. By the end of 2002 a new poll showed that already one-third fewer than the year before started to see Americans as like family or best friends, and 57 per cent of Canadians showed concern about losing their independence to the US (cited from Sasikumar and Kitchen, 2009: 159–160). This indicates that a national identity that affords a certain measure of difference and distance continues to have some appeal in Canada.

This dominant identity conception may consequently result in norms containing a slight relative aversion towards the use of military force beyond its reactive use for peacekeeping and peace enforcement activities. A normative change occurred towards less aversion to an American style of foreign and security policy than could be found at the end of the 1990s. Nevertheless, in their entirety the norms contained in Canadian strategic culture regarding the range of modes of the legitimate use of force by the state can still be classified as 'reactive to proactive', though more proactive.

This relative aversion towards the more robust use of force as well as the relatively widespread appreciation of the Canadian population's diverse character, which in part stem from a drive for a distinct identity in the face of Canada's powerful southern neighbour, most probably translates itself into a high normative regard for civil liberties protected by the rule of law and restraint in the domestic use of force by the state. This drive for difference and distance diminished somewhat in the wake of post-9/11 solidarity but also faded soon thereafter. Canadian strategic culture is therefore assumed to contain norms bearing a low level of acceptance towards infringements on civil liberties for the provision of security.

Several Canadian governments showed strong dedication to the advancement of institutions promoting and facilitating multilateral efforts to preserving peace and security in an attempt to forge a common identity in a relatively young and diverse nation bordering a powerful and potentially overshadowing nation to the south. This is likely to translate itself into durable norms supporting a strong attachment to multilateral organisations and alliances as well as the rule of law in the conduct of security provision domestically and internationally.

Similarly, Canadian identity can be expected to generate a strategic culture containing norms supportive of moderately high domestic and international authorisation requirements for the use of force. The traditional emphasis on diversity, multiculturalism, multilateralism and diplomacy contained in Canadian identity implies that there is a high regard within Canadian strategic culture for state practices involving force to be subjected to an extensive body of legislation and deliberation.

French formative moments, founding narratives and identity conceptions

The high degree of activism that can be observed throughout the French Fifth Republic's security policy and practice reflects two relatively constant motives in French foreign policy: the promotion of national *grandeur* and the pursuit of an elevated global status or *rang* (Treacher, 2003: 2). These motives can be traced back to several formative moments in French history ranging from the aspirations of French bishops to recreate the Roman Empire; the legacy of Louis XIV; the French Revolution and the Napoleonic Wars to the *Force de Frappe* and de Gaulle's presidency, which have all forged a national identity that grants the state a particularly central position. Lacking a distinct ethnicity or geography and forged together by force and marriages, France has always required a strong central authority to resist its 'inherent centrifugal forces' (Treacher, 2003: 9). This requirement translated itself into the self-stylisation of the central state authority as possessing the sacred mission to overpower religious and feudal divisions between its subjects in order to forge these together as a people. In France, the state therefore preceded the nation (Jenkins, 1987; Treacher, 2003: 8).

60 *Comparing strategic cultures*

Under the reign of Louis XIV, perfecting and glorifying centralised state control already became France's trademark. In theory, the French Revolution of 1789 and the rise of Napoleon Bonaparte then transferred this glory to the entire people, thus promoting them from subjects to citizens. The introduction of a new centralised bureaucracy in which political power was now supposed to be based on merit rather than possession created a mythology which defined being French on the basis of being privileged to be a citizen of this state. And through the introduction of conscription every citizen became implicated in the defence of the revolution's propagated achievements, thus further tying the citizen and the state together and placing the military as well as the use of force at the centre of French identity. For the remainder of the nineteenth century this mythology rendered the French government a strong claim to authority, both domestically and internationally. The perceived universality of the ideals and values which the revolution engendered drove the pursuit of *rang* and *grandeur* in France's imperial endeavours especially during the reign of Napoleon III. After all, French colonies were officially part of France or at least closely attached to France. The idea of a *mission civilisatrice*, the mission to spread those universal ideals and values, was the declared aim of French colonialism. The state's claim to greatness, both before its people and towards other peoples, as well as the state's claim to global influence, are therefore firmly embedded in the mythology of traditional French identity conceptions. Logically underpinning this claim to greatness is a claim to a high level of control and authority by the state, which necessarily needs to be backed up by the use of force – both domestically and internationally.

But the twentieth century brought with it another series of formative moments that fundamentally challenged this traditional narrative. The defeat in the Franco-Prussian War 1870–1871 already sent shockwaves throughout the country as it constituted a severe loss not only of territory but also of *rang* and *grandeur*. Although France could recover these territorial losses with the First World War, its victory came at an enormously high cost and left behind a significant war-fatigue. Furthermore, the legacy of Verdun left behind an army doctrine of a highly defensive nature that sought to ensure the future inviolability of France's borders through an elaborate system of fortifications rather than more mobile and offensive arrangements (Kier, 1999: 43). This doctrine turned out to be ineffective against the German onslaught in the Second World War. After only four weeks France suffered a complete military collapse in 1940, which was followed by a moral collapse embodied by the widespread collaboration with the occupiers under the Vichy-regime of Marshal Pétain (Meyer, 2007: 51). This military and moral collapse stood in stark contrast to the traditional narrative of the French state being exceptional and therefore enjoying extra powers conferred upon it by its citizens. It can therefore be said to have sparked a significant identity crisis. According to Christoph Meyer the events of 1940 remain "the single most important event shaping French strategic culture" (Meyer, 2007: 51).

The significance of 1940 does not only lie in the national humiliation suffered by the military defeat but also in the moral collapse suffered by collaboration. The latter was particularly demoralising as it caused deep divisions bordering a civil war within French society. It is for these reasons that Jeanneney (1995: 24)

Moments, narratives and identity conceptions 61

described Vichy and the collaboration as "the dominant trauma affecting French politics". The difficulty in overcoming the trauma of collaboration and division in 1940 is exemplified by a statement by former French President George Pompidou, who even in 1972 exclaimed:

> Must we forever perpetuate the bloody wounds of our national discord? Has not the time come to draw a veil over them, to forget those days when the French did not love each other, tore each other to pieces, even killed each other?
>
> (quoted from Jeanneney, 1995: 20)

After all, the traditional narrative places particular emphasis on national unity as a core element of post-revolutionary France. In this narrative, *rang* and *grandeur* are bestowed upon the state through the universality of the revolutionary ideals which the state embodies. The nation therefore prides itself in its unity that stems from unanimous consent for those ideals. From the literature, one can largely discern two rival and alternating consequences of this trauma. One consequence was a defiant revival of the traditional narrative based on exceptionalism and evoking *rang* and *grandeur* with the de Gaulle era, another consequence was a continuous search for a more inclusive and multilateral role conception to replace the traditionally asserted exceptionalism. The latter was facilitated by the post-1940 minor traumata of Dien Bien Phu 1954 and Algiers 1958. It came to full fruition with the student protests of 1968.

One immediate reaction to France's defeat was a reversal in its foreign policy approach towards Germany. After the US and the UK dismissed radical plans to completely dismantle the German state in light of the Soviet threat after 1945, high ranking civil servants such as Robert Schuman and Jean Monnet were instrumental in devising schemes to overcome mutual fears and enmities through economic and institutional integration (Meyer, 2007: 51). This new approach gradually disbanded a centuries-old Franco-German rivalry that nourished French feelings of natural superiority over Germany. At the same time, France experienced domination and humiliation by its Anglo-Saxon allies during the Second World War; and with the UK again during the Suez Crisis. This reinforced suspicion towards these allies, which were colloquially known as 'la perfide Albion', but given the circumstances France had no choice but to closely cooperate with the US and the UK during the war and in its aftermath. These experiences fundamentally challenged notions of exceptionalism, *rang* and *grandeur*. The French state itself was also in worse shape after the war. The constitution of the Fourth Republic gave primary authority to the National Assembly and produced a long and confusing sequence of short-lived governments that were unable to bestow the state with authority both domestically and internationally. Adding to this, military defeats in wars of decolonisation in Vietnam 1946–1954, notably the battle of Dien Bien Phu 1954, and Algeria 1954–1962 further weakened France's standing and undermined the state's claims to *grandeur* and *rang*.

But, as Treacher (2003: 14) noted, "French political elites have demonstrated a remarkable capacity to retain a claim to greatness for their country even in the

62   *Comparing strategic cultures*

face of apparently total defeat". When a new constitution inaugurated the Fifth French Republic in 1958 and Charles de Gaulle became its first president, the state became a highly unitary and centralised actor again, which set the stage for efforts to reshape collective memory and reconstruct French identity along more traditional lines. The office of the presidency received unprecedented powers, with security policy becoming its near-exclusive preserve. This institutional change combined with the charismatic agency of de Gaulle revived the traditional themes of France being a nation born out of both centralistic splendour and revolution, which was naturally inclined to be highly protective of the state's achievements and therefore wary of the emergence of new hegemonies in the light of the wars of the past. In consequence, French political elites acquired enough momentum to pull out of NATO's integrated military command in 1966 and, most importantly, to acquire its own independent nuclear capabilities, the so-called *Force de Frappe*, in 1960. De Gaulle's 'politics of grandeur' (Kolodziej, 1974) have thus sparked a major revival of traditional French identity conceptions that stress a centralised state actor, independence of action and an elevated international status.

It is remarkable that the high level of popular support enjoyed by de Gaulle's presidency upon his restoration of *rang* and *grandeur* did not fade significantly over the succeeding decades. Aside from a strong student protest movement in 1968, there have been no serious calls to revise the constitution in order to reduce the level of authority afforded to the presidency, and neither has there been a strong pacifist and anti-nuclear movement, despite significant such movements in neighbouring countries in the 1980s (Treacher, 2003: 16, 21). But the end of the Cold War demonstrated that retaining *rang* and *grandeur* required an emphasis on national independence to be replaced by the now more viable alternative of greater cooperation and integration with principle partners and institutions (Treacher, 2003: 3). One instrument was to become a champion of peace support operations on behalf of the UN, and a second instrument was to forge an autonomous European security and defence identity, "obviously to be guided from Paris, that would be in a position to promote and defend Europe's (read French) interests" (Treacher, 2003: 3–4). France's traditional identity conception based on the legacy of the revolution, combined with the legacy of de Gaulle's revival of these traditional revolutionary notions of exceptionalism, appear to continue to shape and drive French security policy, although in different and adapted guises.

Dominant French identity conceptions are shaped by the legacy of the French revolution, defeat and humiliation during the Second World War and a restoration of national pride and self-confidence during the presidency of de Gaulle. Altogether, these founding myths and formative moments contain a great deal of idealism regarding the state and the values of freedom and democracy on which it rests. Norms contained in French strategic culture are therefore likely to carry high levels of support for robust military interventions as long as these are conducted on humanitarian grounds or in defence of democracy and civil liberties. At the same time, especially given the humiliating experience of collaboration and occupation during the Second World War as well as the aversion towards the 'perfide Albion' that emerged during that time, one can expect these norms to stop short at similarly robust interventions that lack a clearly defensive, idealistic or humanitarian motive as this would not reconstitute French identity. This renders a clear categorisation of French strategic culture within this norms category more difficult. On the one hand, norms support robust intervention; on the other hand, they are likely to exclude modes of the legitimate use of force by the state such as reactions to an indirect threat or pre-emptive war. French strategic culture is therefore classified as in between proactive and robust, but more on the proactive side.

Regarding the use of force by the state domestically, one can also discern a strong sense of pride in the civil liberties enjoyed and provided by the French state while at the same time the high regard for the institution of the state as such and a high rate of preoccupation with the provision of security that is imbued in French identity conceptions implies that norms within French strategic culture also afford the state significant autonomy in the practice of security provision. But this indicates that there is the potential for a normative divergence between elites and the general population rather than the presence of overall norms supporting major infringements on civil liberties. Popular norms on the competences of the state in providing security to citizens are expected to contain low levels of acceptance of infringements on civil liberties for the provision of security.

Regarding preferred modes of cooperation this chapter asserted that French identity conceptions have transformed since the end of the Cold War away from seeing the preservation of independence of action as a central element of French identity towards pursuing the traditional claim to greatness or *rang* and *grandeur* by embracing multilateralism and championing the cause of multilateral institutions such as the UN and the EU. This goes along with a traditional distrust of American leadership within the Western security architecture. One can therefore expect norms within French strategic culture to favour affiliations with organisations and alliances rather than affiliations with particular states alone.

The high regard for the institution of the French state and especially the presidency that is contained in French identity conceptions is also likely to express itself in French strategic culture containing norms carrying low domestic authorisation requirements for the use of force. The same does, however, not necessarily apply regarding international authorisation requirements. The recent trend away from the pursuit of independence of action towards the embracing of multilateralism is rather likely to translate itself into norms of high international authorisation requirements within French strategic culture.

German formative moments, founding narratives and identity conceptions

The trajectory of German security policy and practice since the end of the Cold War shows signs of both continuity in its preference for multilateral diplomatic means over the exercise of military force, especially when not sanctioned by the UN Security Council, and a growing adaptation in its behaviour to that of other countries of similar size, power capabilities, domestic regime type and international institutional embedding. Whether scholarly emphasis is placed on the

64 *Comparing strategic cultures*

process of a growing normalisation in Germany's security policy or on Germany's continued exceptionalism in the form of an exercise in restraint is ultimately a matter of preference and perspective. When depicting this trajectory, one can point to signs of both – a gradual process of increased vigour when comparing German security policy across time and continued restraint when comparing it to that of other similar countries such as France and the United Kingdom. It is relatively certain, however, that the trajectory of German security policy did not live up to many rationalist and popular predictions that were made about Germany's future role in Europe around the time of reunification.

Many scholars, especially from the neorealist camp, brought forth prognoses of a more unstable era under multipolarity that would fall behind the relative stability and security the world could enjoy under bipolarity. In this vein, some predicted Germany would abandon its commitment to European integration and assume a more assertive stance and a more self-centred or 'normal' great power role (Longhurst, 2004: 7). Predictions of Germany acting as a great power and upheaving the established balance of power were not confined to the scholarly world. One only needs to recall the reservations displayed by Margaret Thatcher and François Mitterrand throughout the process of German reunification. According to Helmut Kohl's memoirs Thatcher even exclaimed at an EC summit in December 1989: "We've beaten the Germans twice. Now they're back" (Kohl, 2005: 1013).

As it turned out, such prognoses and fears of Germany abandoning its commitment to European integration and multilateralism and instead pursuing a more assertive, nationally focused security policy did not materialise, as the trajectory of German military interventions abroad since 1990 shows. This makes a study of German strategic culture all the more pertinent. It is necessary to find out if and how a mindset formed that still reverberates today. The task of this section is therefore to derive the historico-mythological origins of those patterns of behaviour. In the German context identifying the most significant formative moment of Germany's contemporary identity conception is a relatively straightforward exercise. The experience of total and utter defeat coupled with widespread testimonies of death, destruction and the worst atrocities imaginable at the end of the Second World War can hardly be matched in intensity and must have deeply engrained itself in the collective consciousness and psyche. Thus, the *Stunde Null*, Germany's "zero hour", "the total physical, moral and psychological devastation and trauma that prevailed in Germany at the close of the Second World War" (Longhurst, 2004: 26), is widely regarded as the key formative moment of its identity conception (Conrad and Stumm, 2004: 46; Hoffmann and Longhurst, 1999; Longhurst, 2004: 25–28; Meyer, 2007; Wilke, 2007). However, this moment did not instantly bring about contemporary German identity conception but only initiated the process of its construction, internalisation, instrumentalisation and modification.

An early indication that the *Stunde Null* experience indeed brought about a new German identity conception can be seen in the general absence of resentment towards allied policies of demilitarisation in the early years of the Federal Republic (see Longhurst, 2004: 26–28). Articles 4, 24, and 26 of the Basic Law of 1949 stipulate that no one may be compelled against his conscience to render war service involving the use of arms; allow the Federal Republic to enter a system of mutual collective security; and declare unconstitutional acts disturbing the peaceful relation between nations, especially to prepare for aggressive war. Not only the inclusion of such checks and balances, which directly related to Germany's past, into the constitution of the new German state, but also their strict and narrow interpretation that dominated West German security policy and practice until the 1990s shows that the experience of the Second World War and the Third Reich constructed a new West German identity that was diametrically opposed to militarism and the use of force for purposes other than self-defence.

In fact, at its inception the Federal Republic did not have its own army. Only as allied demands for a German defence contribution in the face of a Soviet threat grew and it became increasingly clear that the Adenauer government's objectives of achieving full sovereignty and international rehabilitation as well as solid security guarantees from the West could not be realised without meeting those demands, West Germany rearmed in 1956. Ironically, it was not the period of disarmament and demilitarisation but the process of rearmament that met discord and controversy in Germany.

It must be noted that the Adenauer administration did not share the pacifism and drive for neutrality of its SPD opposition but instead shared the anti-communist, hawkish sentiments of its US counterpart to a large extent. However, both the German government and the opposition shared a determination to pursue a radical break with Germany's militaristic past in the design of its new armed forces in the post-war years. All in all, the strong reactions towards rearmament, the difficult and protracted process by which it came about and the manifold precautions instilled to prevent a resurgence of militarism show that *Stunde Null* brought about a completely new German identity conception that based itself on constitutionalism and the ideal type of a Western liberal democracy that overcame its demons of the past in the shape of totalitarianism and expansionism. This lent itself to a strategic culture that emphasised democratic control of the armed forces rather than militarism and a strong role of the army in society; adherence to international institutions and law rather than power politics; and strong alliance commitments rather than self-assertiveness.

The 1968 movement and its early 1980s neo-counterpart had a decidedly anti-militaristic cause and made explicit references to the Third Reich. It can therefore be said to have sustained and internalised the Adenauer era's aversions to Germany's militaristic past both to succeeding generations and to a broader popular level. The 1968 student movement in Germany was distinct from its Western counterparts in its additional accusation towards the establishment of harbouring former Nazi officials and covering the Nazi past with a veil of silence. There was thus a call for a more explicit decry of the country's recent past that went beyond institutional reform and policy changes but also translated itself into the promotion of a new self-understanding brought about by an open, vocal and uncompromising rejection of the recent past. The peace protests against the NATO Double-Track Decision in the early 1980s further indicate a growing internalisation of a new national identity based on national history in an unorthodox sense of 'learning from failure' by generations beyond those who

66 *Comparing strategic cultures*

suffered the immediate consequences of the war. In East Germany oppositional movements hosted by the Protestant church mainly centred on the themes of environmental degradation and disarmament. This indicates that aside from official state propaganda, which propagated socialism as the only true form of vindication from the ills of fascism for Germany, many shared this identity and culture of remembrance that took shape in the West in the post-war period.

A 1985 speech by Federal President Richard von Weizsäcker concurs with this assumption by elevating the notion of memory to Germany's *raison d'état*. Rather than drawing uncritically on national history as a source of national identity, the Federal Republic nurtured the concepts of constitutional patriotism (*Verfassungspatriotismus*) and memory of the Holocaust and the Second World War as a special responsibility. When several notable German historians and sociologists debated the singularity of the Holocaust and the role it should play in German identity in the so-called *Historikerstreit* of 1986/87, this identity conception became scrutinised. The outcome of this debate remains a subject of dispute. But 12 years later the influential journalist Josef Joffe drew a favourable review of this identity in a landmark editorial (Joffe, 1998). Conradt (2008: xi) summed it up thus:

> Indeed, as Josef Joffe has pointed out, the intensive and extensive examination of Germany's tragic past and, of course, above all the responsibility of Germans for the Holocaust, has been and continues to be a vital part of the Federal Republic's identity and a major reason for Germany's six decades of peaceful and positive relationships with its neighbours in Europe and the larger world community.

With the end of the Cold War and reunification several challenges to the continuity of this identity conception emerged. Calls for a more affirmative national identity grew after reunification restored the nation-state, the right to which some West German politicians and intellectuals had long denied the German people in view of its history (Buras and Longhurst, 2004: 21).[1] One indication of intellectual calls for a reconceptualisation of national identity came with a debate sparked by a speech by the novelist Martin Walser on 11 October 1998, in which he criticised the instrumentalisation of collective memory and Auschwitz in particular (see Muller, 2000: 244–253). This posed a fundamental challenge to orthodox conceptions as it purported a memory-based national identity to serve self-interested motives of moral superiority as a justification of military passivity relative to power status and capabilities. Hitting a sensitive nerve, the debate thus exemplified tensions between those who were concerned about the potential for a nationalist backlash inherent in reunification and sought to maintain the status quo on the one hand and those who advocated for a more assertive stance towards identity, patriotism, nationhood and the past. The latter position translated itself into the advocacy of a more proactive security policy behaviour in line with the new geopolitical situation in which Germany now found itself. Growing efforts to expand European integration into the realm of security policy and to forge a common European identity facilitated this position. After reunification and especially in the light of the tragedies which

Moments, narratives and identity conceptions 67

occurred in Bosnia, Kosovo and elsewhere in the 1990s, an identity based almost entirely on memory risked becoming a no longer valid excuse for impassivity to an increasing number of Germans.

What can be concluded from this analysis is that the notion of memory as the German *raison d'état* and the Basic Law rather than conventional pride in national history were nurtured as the foundations of German post-war identity across party lines and generations, and thereby retained their role long after the end of the Second World War. Initially institutionalised as a result of a combination of external and domestic forces by the drafters of West Germany's new constitution and the first post-war government, this identity was gradually internalised by wider society. Consequently traditional conceptions of power status and role in the international security environment contain an aversion to militarism, unilateralism and leadership as well as preferences for restraint in the use of armed force, and non-confrontational, multilateral approaches to security matters.

Domestically, Germany's identity and the formative moments from which it emerged translate into conceptions of the state as being as much of a potential threat to security as being its guarantor. Therefore, the armed forces and other state organs with the mandate to execute state violence are seen as having to be firmly integrated into society and subjected to political control and deliberation. Acts of state violence tend to be seen as necessary evils rather than heroic acts. And *Stunde Null* implies as much an aversion to militarism as to totalitarian control of the state over its citizens. All in all, traditional German identity and role conceptions tend to adhere to an identity in which consensus building, international institutions and international law rather than the projection of and reliance on one's own power capabilities are cherished by political and intellectual elites as well as the general public.

Regarding norms within German strategic culture on the range of modes in which the use of force by the state is considered legitimate one can expect a general aversion to use force for purposes other than self-defence (or allied) defence, which has, however, increasingly eroded in the 1990s in low-intensity and more humanitarian-motivated missions. German strategic culture can thus be said to have developed from a state of complete amilitarism after 1945 to passivity by embracing norms supporting the defence of NATO territory after rearmament in 1957 and to reactiveness through the encapsulation of norms also supporting peacekeeping and peace enforcement in the course of the 1990s. In sum, although a shift in norms regarding legitimate ends and means for the use of force occurred especially in the last 20 years, German strategic culture retained its general aversion towards state violence and thereby its relative antimilitaristic distinctness. It therefore pertains to the reactive to proactive category.

Domestically, *Stunde Null* most likely translated itself into an aversion towards totalitarian state control as much as towards militarism. Hence, norms will have developed that support a strict limitation of state powers and competencies in exercising the use of force domestically in order to provide security. However, police tasks will not be as much scrutinised as military affairs since identity and culture do not express themselves as strongly in state behaviour directed towards the internal rather than the external because identity needs to reconstitute itself against an 'other', an external entity. In this case the 'other' is the citizen vs the

68   *Comparing strategic cultures*

'state' as essentially restricted to the government rather than the 'state' understood as encapsulating the entire society whose identity is being reconstituted against another state as a whole, as outlined in Chapter 1. Nonetheless, these norms are expected to have a discernible impact on German state behaviour regarding the domestic components of counterterrorist legislation enacted after 9/11.

These basic characteristics of German identity conceptions are also likely to generate norms on preferred modes of international cooperation that contain an aversion to unilateralism and leadership. Instead, the credo borne out of the post-war period is likely to generate strong normative attachments to multilateralism, the rule of international law, including the supremacy of the UN Security Council, and consensus-building both domestically and internationally. Given that the US plays an important role in the notion of Germany's liberation from the Third Reich, its significantly more assertive style of leadership in international security affairs bears the potential for strong normative attachments to Western defence structures under US leadership to clash with the other equally strongly pronounced elements of German strategic culture.

The general aversion towards the use of force and especially the determination to fully integrate the armed forces into society and to subject it to civilian political control that displayed itself in the rearmament debates of the late 1940s and early 1950s is likely to reverberate and express itself in enduring high domestic and international authorisation requirements. Comprehensive checks and balances regarding the armed forces coupled with a new sense of patriotism based on institutions and legal frameworks rather than glories of the past are likely to ensure that the legal requirements placed into the Basic Law regarding the domestic and international authorisation requirements will remain important elements in debates over the use of force and will continue to be narrowly interpreted.

British formative moments, founding narratives and identity conceptions

It is common knowledge in the UK that the last time England was invaded dates back to 1066, and that Britain has not lost a major war since the American War of Independence. It is equally common knowledge that the British Empire, at its apogee in the late nineteenth century spanned one-fifth of the world's surface and one-fourth of its population (Cain and Hopkins, 2001). But one might see an even more impressive feat of this historical record in the economic achievements of this era. As the country that witnessed the invention of the steam engine on its soil and consequently as the first country in the world to experience industrialisation, Britain pioneered modern economic growth and spread it throughout the world. To illustrate, Britain's relative share of world manufacturing output stood at 19.9 per cent in 1860, making it the world's largest economy, while that of the world's second largest economy, France, only amounted to 7.9 per cent in that year (Self, 2010: 15). One might think that this imperial legacy bears the potential to provide a coherent narrative installing a strong sense of pride in UK citizens and providing a clear idea of what it means to be British as well as what Britain's role in the world entails. And yet, while

Moments, narratives and identity conceptions 69

identity itself is already elusive enough a concept, British national identity is particularly complex and multilayered. Its imperial legacy exists alongside a narrative of relative decline since the early twentieth century. Furthermore, British national identity is composed of and challenged by the local identities of England, Scotland, Wales and Northern Ireland.

English local identity plays a special role in this regard. It can be seen as the core of British identity that superimposed itself on the other local identities. For Krishan Kumar, for example, England first created an 'inner empire' on the British Isles by achieving dominance over Scotland, Wales and Ireland. This inner empire then created a far more extensive 'outer empire' (Kumar, 2003). But both the inner and the outer empire had "raw English power operating as the irreducible cultural core of the British political unit" (Hadfield-Amkhan, 2010: 12). Therefore one can see "all the major events and achievements of national life as English" (Kumar, 2003: 2; quoted from Hadfield-Amkhan, 2010: 12). From this perspective, classical English attributes such as a strong Protestant work ethos, entrepreneurship, competitiveness, bravery and cheerfulness can be seen as first having first won over tribal England's tumultuous past itself, then over its immediate vicinity on the British isles and ultimately over large parts of the world through colonisation and the spread of industrialisation. This narrative conveys an image of the state as a crucial enabler of these attributes coming to full fruition. A primary task in this regard is the provision of security. The state had to maintain order domestically and defend British commercial interests and exploration globally but beyond that, private enterprise drove Britain's industrial and territorial ascent. At the same time, the vast and expansive social hierarchy and inequality which the empire and industrialisation created relied on a powerful state with the capacity to effectively maintain order. The legacy of the empire therefore entails a traditional identity conception that supports a strong state with the power to display its influence globally in order to defend freedoms of navigation and trade, as well as the power to display its influence domestically in order to maintain a rigid class structure on which its rise to power relied.

The decline of the empire and the rise of rival powers in Europe naturally challenged this imperial identity conception. Emerging new norms of self-determination, emancipation, universal suffrage and human rights fundamentally undermined both the concept and practice of imperialism and of the rigid class structure brought about by industrialisation. At the same time, Britain's economic hegemony declined as other powers caught up and eventually overtook British manufacturing output by the turn of the nineteenth century (Self, 2010: 15). The First World War then brought home the bitter realisation that as other European powers gain in strength the costs of balancing potential rivalling hegemons and the costs of meeting aggression have risen exponentially. The ongoing tradition of Remembrance Day, also known as Poppy Day, demonstrates the profound effects which the mass casualties of this war had and continue to have on the British psyche. The rituals of this day display an image of war as a tragic fact of life rather than an entirely heroic affair. In the weeks leading up to Remembrance Day large segments of society as well as virtually all influential public figures wear artificial 'remembrance poppies' sold by the Royal British Legion, a veterans' charity organisation, as a brooch or in their buttonholes. The poppy,

70 *Comparing strategic cultures*

which grows widely in the border region between Belgium and France, serves as a reminder of battlefields such as Verdun, where all sides suffered immense casualties during the First World War. It now symbolises the sacrifice of all former and current British servicemen and women. While the gratitude towards these expressed in this ritual does continue to instil some sense of heroism in warfare, it also conveys the message that war not only involves glory but also great tragedy. The fact that the senseless slaughter which the First World War constituted for all European powers is so vividly remembered in the UK therefore shows that it represents a break from the jingoistic days of imperialism towards a more measured imagination of war in contemporary Britain.

However, Chamberlain's policy of appeasement towards Hitler, nourished by the interwar years' war fatigue, and Britain's victorious emergence from the Second World War is remembered at least as vividly as the ordeal of the First World War. Even today, former Prime Minister Neville Chamberlain's policy of appeasement towards Hitler finds such widespread condemnation that the terms 'appeasement' and 'Munich', in reference to the location where the infamous Munich Agreement was signed in 1938, are almost swearwords which hardly any public figures arguing in support of war or intervention fail to mention in debates. His successor Winston Churchill's firm stance against Nazism and his wartime leadership, on the other hand, have earned him such a strong legacy that a 2002 television poll conducted by the British Broadcasting Corporation (BBC) for its television show *The 100 Greatest Britons* revealed that participating viewers chose Churchill to rank in first place on a list of 100 people whom they considered the greatest Britons in history (BBC News, 2002). This victory therefore had the profound long-term effects of reviving Britain's role conception as a key actor in maintaining global order as well as of restoring confidence in the state and its armed forces to meet whatever challenges this role may entail.

Yet at the same time the events of the late 1940s and 1950s did not allow the British public to bask in post-war glory for a very long time. While Churchill is considered the greatest Briton of all time today, he was voted out of office immediately after having delivered victory in 1945. The election of Churchill's successor Clement Attlee, who pursued a decidedly reformist agenda with strong socialist elements, indicates that there was a desire to break with the imperialist past and the rigid social hierarchies, and to focus on urgent domestic economic problems instead. Under the slogan "cheer Winston, vote Labour", the Labour party's promise of social reform and the establishment of a welfare state afforded it a landslide victory. At the same time, decolonisation accelerated and culminated in the independence of India in 1947, which was considered the 'crown jewel' of all colonies. There was therefore an increasing shift away from imperial affairs and towards collective security in Europe within the Cold War context and as a junior NATO partner of the US. The very last attempt to play out an old imperial role conception and to act independently from the US occurred with the Suez War of 1956. It resulted in a humiliating defeat, the resignation of Anthony Eden as prime minister and a striking rebuke by President Eisenhower of the US at the United Nations (Rothwell, 1957). As one British defence official remarked in an interview in 2005: "Suez had a profound effect on a generation as it marked the retreat from empire and the realisation that we cannot go it alone without the Americans" (quoted from Meyer, 2007: 49). Not least since Suez, the legacy of ascent and heroism, worldwide influence and order maintained through robust state control at home and globally therefore alternates with and is increasingly counteracted by a narrative of decline, imperial overstretch, global resistance to colonial oppression and social emancipation at home all demanding fundamentally new foundations of British identity.

For the remainder of the Cold War this oscillation between sober management of relative economic and military decline along with strict maintenance of the 'special relationship' with the American superpower on the one hand and clinging on to the last vestiges of an independent superpower role on the other hand. The latter arguably manifested itself most prominently with the Falklands War of 1982. The Argentine invasion of the Falklands was generally not portrayed in material terms as the product of failed deterrence but in highly ideological terms as a blatant and unexpected invasion of sovereign British island territory (Hadfield-Amkhan, 2010: 158). The images of a British flotilla victoriously returning to Portsmouth and being greeted with utmost fanfare by great masses of spectators chanting "Rule, Britannia!" conjured up an identity that instils a strong sense of pride and confidence in the state's ability to provide security that is expressed almost with defiance towards the empire's decline, or, in other words, "an identity preoccupied with retaining the trappings of international seniority while learning to operate in an increasingly interdependent world" (Hadfield-Amkhan, 2010: 135). Despite being deeply unpopular because of her economic policies by the end of her first term, Margaret Thatcher won the general election in 1983 by a wide margin, which is largely credited to the patriotic fervour with which she conducted the Falklands War and with which she celebrated its victory (Self, 2010: 65–66).

This quasi-revival of imperial glory did not entirely outlast the 1980s but only represented a buffer between the 'politics of decline' that dominated the 1950s, 1960s and 1970s (Gamble, 1994) and the 'politics of identity' that ensued after the end of the Cold War, as identified by Schnapper (2011). As the privileged status within the Western alliance, which the 'special relationship' with the US afforded the UK throughout the Cold War now lost further relevance without the Soviet threat, it was not only Britain's position vis-à-vis Europe and the US that underwent increasing scrutiny, but also British identity itself became questioned in the light of immigration as well as English, Scottish and Welsh identities (Schnapper, 2011: 48–49). When in 1997 Tony Blair became the first Labour Prime Minister since 1979, he sought to reconcile imperial legacy and decline by highlighting the cosmopolitan character that the past has left Britain with, which imbued it with a global outlook, as well as a seniority and moral high grounds that allowed it – if not rather compelled it – to punch above its weight in the conduct of its security policy. A record of five wars during Blair's premiership was the result. In an election campaign speech in 1997 he summed up his approach towards a new British identity conception with these words:

> The Britain in my vision is not Britain turning its back on the world – narrow, shy, uncertain. It is a Britain confident of its place in the world, sure of itself, able to negotiate with the world and provide leadership to the

72 *Comparing strategic cultures*

world.... Century upon century it has been the destiny of Britain to lead other nations. That should not be a destiny that is part of our history. It should be part of our future. We are a leader of nations or nothing.

(quoted from Kampfner, 2004: 3)

Although the dubious grounds on which Blair justified the war on Iraq brought irreparable damage to his premiership's legacy, it did not bring about a fundamental change in this identity conception towards isolationism and anti-militarism, as the interventions in Libya and Mali under the Conservative premiership of David Cameron suggest.

Britain's imperial legacy has therefore not entirely disappeared from the British public's psyche. While at its zenith in the late nineteenth and early twentieth century, the empire allowed for the forging of a cohesive British identity but with the end of the Second World War, despite victory, its decline heralded the end of a period in which this British identity was unquestioningly accepted. As Britain had to manage its inevitable decline in the coming decades, it adopted at times an anxious and defensive posture that mirrored uncertainty over its identity and rightful place in the world. In the post-Cold War decades it then forged a new identity as a pivotal US ally that cherishes entrepreneurship and free trade, still possesses a certain seniority that allows it to play a significant role going beyond countries of similar size and economic strength – at least to the extent that its budget allows, and that cherishes the multiculturalism that stems from its imperial past. All in all, one can assume that the identity narrative which emerged in the UK over the nineteenth and twentieth centuries instilled a strong sense of confidence and pride in the state's capacity to provide for the security of its citizens, and at times also those of other nations through the exercise of force.

One can therefore assume that the norms contained in British strategic culture, regarding the range of modes of the use of force by the state that are considered legitimate, support robust state actions including humanitarian interventions, reactions to indirect threats and pre-emptive wars. British strategic culture therefore presumably pertains to the proactive to robust category.

Domestically, this long and proud record of policing the seas, the empire and the British Isles during tumultuous periods of industrialisation and war can also be expected to result in British strategic culture containing norms regarding the competencies of the state in providing security to its citizens entailing a relatively high level of acceptance of considerable infringements on civil liberties in compromise for the provision of security.

The notion of seniority contained in dominant British identity conception also bestows a pivotal role in international security provision to the British state. The most visible way in which this expresses itself is the special relationship with the world's superpower which the UK claims for itself. One can therefore assume that British strategic culture contains norms allowing for affiliations with particular states to potentially take precedence over affiliations with organisations, institutions or even alliances in certain circumstances.

Lastly, this general proclivity towards the use of force is also likely to translate itself into norms within British strategic culture favouring short and expeditious authorisations of the use of force in order to allow for swift and decisive action

Moments, narratives and identity conceptions 73

leading to higher chances of success. One can therefore assume that there are norms favouring low domestic authorisation requirements. The eagerness to display one's seniority internationally as well as the strong dedication to US leadership within the Western security architecture is also likely to translate itself into relatively low international authorisation requirements for the use of force.

Overview of preliminary classifications

As is hardly surprising, this chapter could identify that just as every nation considers its own history as unique, it has a unique repertoire of formative moments, myths and founding narratives at its disposal which, taken together, can build a fairly coherent identity conception and narrative underlying the state in its active provision of security. But while these repertoires are unique, varied and elusive, they allow for the discernment of certain patterns once one no longer shies away from analytical simplification and generalisation. On the basis of the individual country analyses that have been conducted in this chapter, the table below therefore summarises the four key aspects of each country's identity narratives and conceptions, as discussed in this chapter.

It shows that overall, the identity conceptions and narratives that are present and dominant in Australia, France and the UK form a group of more 'Hobbesian' countries whereas Canada and Germany can be classified as more 'Kantian' actors. However, this categorisation does not imply complete exclusivity between and homogeneity within these groups. Regarding the first group, this applies to France in particular. Its championing of institutions such as the UN, the EU and human rights, which increasingly sat alongside a certain independent-mindedness in its pursuit of *rang* and *grandeur* in recent years implies that it contains more 'Kantian' elements in its identity conception than Australia and the UK do. In the case of the second group, the strong aversion towards militarism that is imbued in the German 'Stunde Null' concept implies that it differs in key respects from the more politically constructed legacy of anti-militarism in Canada.

Based on the analysis of identity conceptions, the assumptions made in this chapter for possible expressions of individual strategic cultures within their respective norms dimensions are summarised in Table 4.2. As in Table 4.1, it lists each norms dimension and its possible expressions alongside a spectrum ranging from a low to a high proclivity to use force. The country initials are placed in bold within each category at the point along this spectrum where the norms dimension is likely to have its centre of gravity (see Table 4.2). This exercise seeks to illustrate the position each country's strategic culture is assumed to have relative to other countries as well as its position along the spectrum of each norms dimension. It shows that while one cannot cluster the countries into distinct groups at this stage, one can discern a relatively coherent picture in the countries' relative position to each other. In most dimensions, Germany is located to left of the other countries, the UK and Australia are to the right and France and Canada assume a position in the middle. At this stage, one can therefore discern a pattern that mirrors the findings on capabilities and institutions, security policy and practice, and identity conceptions.

Table 4.1 Synoptic chart of identity conceptions

	Formative periods and founding myths	Conceptions of power status and international role	Role of state in provision of security	Role of international institutions and law
Australia	ANZAC-myth, East Timor, Tampa-affair	Proactive role to counterbalance geographic remoteness of traditional allies	High rate of preoccupation by the state in provision of security	Stronger reliance on own capabilities/'Hobbesian identity'
Canada	War of 1812, 'Golden Era' of Canadian diplomacy"	Proactive but non-coercive role in drive for difference from North-American neighbour	Role of state equally seen as ensuring individual liberties are upheld and security is provided	Strong adherence to international law and institutions/'Kantian identity'
France	French Revolution, German invasion in 1940 and occupation during the Second World War, de Gaulle-Presidency	Independent-mindedness, pursuit of *rang* and *grandeur* imply conception of elevated power status and important international role	High rate of preoccupation by the state in provision of security	Strong adherence to international institutions and high regard for international law in pursuit of providing counterweight to Anglo-Saxon dominance, 'Hobbesian' identity with strong 'Kantian' elements
Germany	'Stunde Null', liberation from Hitler, Basic Law, reunification, Srebrenica	Aversion to militarism, unilateralism and leadership; restraint in the use of armed force; multilateralism	State force potential threat to individuals' security, therefore subject to extensive public control and deliberation	'Kantian' identity, strong adherence to international institutions and law
UK	Empire and decline, the First World War and poppies, victory in the Second World War	Special relationship with US implies important role, seniority implies high degree of power	State plays highly important and active role in provision of security	Stronger reliance on own capabilities/'Hobbesian identity'

Table 4.2 Preliminary classification of strategic cultures

Norms dimension	*Proclivity to use force, ranging from passive (lowest) to aggressive/oppressive (highest)*			
Norms regarding range of modes of the use of force by the state that are considered legitimate	Passive to reactive (territorial defence and reaction to immediate threat)	Reactive to proactive (plus peacekeeping and peace enforcement) D → CAN	Proactive to robust (plus humanitarian intervention; reaction to indirect threat; pre-emptive war) F → UK, AUS	Robust to aggressive/oppressive (plus war in pursuit of power, ideological and material interests; expansionism)
Norms regarding competences of the state in providing security to citizens	No acceptance of infringements on civil liberties for the provision of security D →	Low level of acceptance of infringements on civil liberties for the provision of security → F, CAN	High level of acceptance of major infringements on civil liberties for the provision of security → UK, AUS	Acceptance of rigid and repressive controls, low level of civil liberties
Preferred modes of international Cooperation	Armed and unarmed Neutrality	Affiliation with alliances/organisations D, F, CAN →	Affiliation with particular states UK, AUS	Unilateralism
Domestic and international authorisation requirements	High domestic, high international D → CAN →	High domestic, low international F →	Low domestic, high international	Low domestic, low international → AUS, UK

Note

1 Arguably the most prominent example being the famous novelist Günter Grass (see Grass 2009).

Bibliography

BBC News (2002) "Churchill Voted Greatest Briton". *BBC*, 24 November, Available from: http://news.bbc.co.uk/2/hi/entertainment/2509465.stm (accessed 11 February 2013).

Bloomfield A and Nossal KR (2007) "Towards an Explicative Understanding of Strategic Culture: the Cases of Australia and Canada". *Contemporary Security Policy*, 28(2), 286.

Boucher JC (2008) "Selling Afghanistan". *International Journal*, 64(3), 717–733.

Bridge C (2008) "ANZAC Day". 2nd edn. In: *The Oxford Companion to Australian Military History*, Melbourne: Oxford University Press, pp. 32–37.

Buras P and Longhurst K (2004) "The Berlin Republic, Iraq, and the Use of Force". *European Security*, 13(3), 215–245.

Burke A (2008) *Fear of Security: Australia's Invasion Anxiety*. Cambridge University Press.

Cain P and Hopkins T (2001) *British Imperialism: 1688–2000*. 2nd edn. London: Pearson.

Canadian Department of National Defence (1997) "Peacekeeping: Concepts, Evolution, and Canada's Role". *Report of the Somalia Commission of Inquiry*, Available from: www.dnd.ca/somalia/vol. 1/v1c10e.htm#83 (accessed 19 December 2012).

Conrad B and Stumm M (2004) *German Strategic Culture and Institutional Choice: Transatlanticism and/or Europeanism?* Trierer Arbeitspapiere Internationale Politik, Trier: Trier University.

Conradt DP (2008) *The German Polity*. Boston: Cengage Learning.

Dawson PF (1989) Canadian Military Mobilization. *Armed Forces & Society*, 16(1), 37–57.

Dennis P and Grey J (2008) *The Oxford Companion to Australian Military History*. 2nd edn. Melbourne: Oxford University Press.

Fraser G (2005) "Liberal Continuities: Jean Chrétien's Foreign Policy, 1993–2003". In: Cooper AF and Rowlands D (eds), *Canada among Nations 2005: Split Images*, Montreal: McGill-Queen's Press – MQUP, pp. 171–186.

Gamble A (1994) *Britain in Decline: Economic Policy, Political Strategy and the British State*. 4th edn. Basingstoke: Palgrave Macmillan.

Granatstein JL (2002) *Canada's Army: Waging War and Keeping the Peace*. 1st edn. Toronto: University of Toronto Press.

Granatstein JL and Oliver DF (2010) *The Oxford Companion to Canadian Military History*. Oxford: Oxford University Press.

Grass G (2009) *Als der Zug abfuhr: Rückblicke auf die Wende*. Goettingen: Steidl.

Hadfield-Amkhan A (2010) *British Foreign Policy, National Identity, and Neoclassical Realism*. Rowman & Littlefield Publishers.

Hillmer N (1994) "Peacekeeping: Canadian Invention, Canadian Myth". In: Granatstein JL and Akerman S (eds), *Welfare States in Trouble: Historical Perspectives on Canada and Sweden*, North York: Swedish-Canadian Academic Foundation, pp. 159–174.

Hoffmann A and Longhurst K (1999) "German Strategic Culture in Action". *Contemporary Security Policy*, 20(2), 31–49.

Hogg W (2003) "Plus Ca Change – Continuity, Change and Culture in Foreign Policy White Papers". *International Journal*, 59(3), 521–536.

James P and Kasoff MJ (2008) *Canadian Studies in the New Millennium*. Toronto: University of Toronto Press.

Jeanneney JN (1995) "The Legacy of Traumatic Experiences in French Politics Today". In: Flynn G (ed.), *Remaking the Hexagon: The New France in the New Europe*, Boulder, CO: Westview Press.

Moments, narratives and identity conceptions 77

Jenkins B (1987) "Nation, Nationalism and National Identity in France since 1789: Some Theoretical Reflections". In: Bridgford J (ed.), *France: Image and Identity*, Newcastle upon Tyne: Newcastle upon Tyne Polytechnic Products.

Joffe J (1998) "Erinnerung als Staatsräson". *Süddeutsche Zeitung*.

Johnson L and Joshee R (2007) *Multicultural Education Policies in Canada and the United States*. Vancouver: University of British Columbia Press.

Kampfner J (2004) *Blair's Wars*. New edition. New York: Free Press.

Kier E (1999) *Imagining War: French and British Military Doctrine between the Wars*. Princeton, MA: Princeton University Press.

Kohl H (2005) *Erinnerungen: 1982–1990*. Munich: Droemer.

Kolodziej EA (1974) *French International Policy Under De Gaulle and Pompidou: The Politics of Grandeur*. 1st edn. Ithaca: Cornell University Press.

Kumar K (2003) *The Making of English National Identity*. Cambridge: Cambridge University Press.

Longhurst K (2004) *Germany and the Use of Force*. Manchester: Manchester University Press.

MacKey E (2002) *The House of Difference: Cultural Politics and National Identity in Canada*. Toronto: University of Toronto Press.

Manne R (2007) "The War Myth That Made Us". *The Age*, 25 April, Available from: www.theage.com.au/news/robert-manne/the-war-myth-that-made-us/2007/04/24/1177180648069.html (accessed 25 October 2011).

Massie J (2009) "Making Sense of Canada's 'Irrational'International Security Policy: A Tale of Three Strategic Cultures". *International Journal*, 64(3), 625–645.

McDonald M (2010) "'Lest We Forget'": The Politics of Memory and Australian Military Intervention. *International Political Sociology*, 4(3), 287–302.

Meyer CO (2007) *The Quest for a European Strategic Culture: Changing Norms on Security and Defence in the European Union*. London: Palgrave Macmillan.

Muller JW (2000) *Another Country: German Intellectuals, Unification, and National Identity*. New Haven: Yale University Press.

Nossal KR (2004) "Defending the 'Realm': Canadian Strategic Culture Revisited". *International Journal*, 59(3), 503–520.

Nourry D (2005) "Body-Politic (National Imaginary): 'Lest We Forget … Mateship (Empire) Right or Wrong'". *Continuum: Journal of Media & Cultural Studies*, 19(3), 365–379.

O'Connor B and Vucetic S (2010) "Another Mars–Venus Divide? Why Australia said 'Yes' and Canada said 'non' to involvement in the 2003 Iraq War. *Australian Journal of International Affairs*, 64(5), 526–548.

Rothwell JJ (1957) "Eisenhower, Eden and the Anglo-American 'Special Relationship' During the Suez Crisis". *Department of State Bulletin*, 36(917), 83–87.

Sasikumar K and Kitchen V (2009) "Canada (En)Counters Terrorism: U.S.-Canada Relations and Counter-terrorism Policy". *Terrorism and Political Violence*, 21(1), 155–173.

Schnapper P (2011) "New Labour, Devolution and British Identity: The Foreign Policy Consequences". In: Daddow OJ and Gaskarth J (eds), *British Foreign Policy: The New Labour Years*, Basingstoke: Palgrave Macmillan, pp. 48–62.

Self PR (2010) *British Foreign and Defence Policy Since 1945: Challenges and Dilemmas in a Changing World*. Basingstoke: Palgrave Macmillan.

Stoddard G (2012) "War of 1812: Violence, Glory and Canadian-ness". *BBC News Magazine*, 19 June, Available from: www.bbc.co.uk/news/magazine-18497113 (accessed 14 December 2012).

Thomsen RC and Hynek N (2006) "Keeping the Peace and National Unity: Canada's National and International Identity Nexus". *International Journal*, 61(4), 845.

Treacher A (2003) *French Interventionism: Europe's Last Global Player*. Aldershot: Ashgate Publishing Ltd.

Wilke T (2007) *German Strategic Culture Revisited: Linking the Past to Contemporary Germany Strategic Choice*. Forschungsberichte Internationale Politik, Berlin: Lit Verlag.

5 Comparative cross-country analysis

Public opinion surveys can provide a rough idea about the extent to which different conceptions of the legitimate use of state force can indeed be identified amongst the general public or, in other words, the extent to which alleged thought patterns can be identified to hold traction over the last decade. The data collected and presented in tables of the percentages of respondents per answer to each question represents the best available data to the author's knowledge for measuring differences and similarities in those norms that strategic cultures consist of over the last decades. They are collected from data sets on international public opinion such as the Transatlantic Trends survey by the German Marshall Fund, the World Values Survey (2015), the Role of Government and National Identity surveys by the International Social Survey Programme, and the Global Attitudes Project by the Pew Research Center. These data sets utilise weighted opinion polls attained through telephone interviews conducted by professional market research companies such as Taylor Nelson Sofres (TNS), the GfK Group and ACNielsen.

There are some unavoidable problems associated with mass public opinion surveys. First, they only represent a sample of 500 to 2,500 individuals' opinions in countries with populations of 20 million to 80 million. There are therefore issues of representativeness as well as issues of sampling error, question wording and several other practical difficulties that can introduce error or bias into the findings. Second, the financial and human resources needed to collect this type of data imply that by necessity the author needs to rely on pre-existing data. The survey questions do therefore not always relate directly to the research needs in each dimension of norms but sometimes these are only indirectly relevant. Several opinion polls are also relevant for multiple dimensions of norms, in which case they will be displayed only once in the first norms category to which they relate while they will be referred to again within the text on the subsequent relevant dimension. The surveys also do not always cover all five countries and most contain data collected sporadically rather than in yearly intervals. It is therefore more problematic to make precise assertions for some countries and time periods than it is for others. Ultimately, the data can only be analysed *ex post facto* based on the questions, years and countries available in the polls. Nevertheless, the wealth of surveys available provides a useful tool for cross-examining the claims made in the previous chapters based on identity conceptions as described in the literature.

Comparative cross-country analysis 79

Norms regarding modes of the use of force by the state that are considered legitimate

This category of norms is the most essential one for describing a strategic culture as it goes to the heart of a state's proclivity to use force. It circumscribes the extent to which a state is likely to be willing to exercise military force. The opinion poll data used here either directly relates to different modes of the use of force or it indirectly establishes respondents' views on the use of force for different purposes by prompting questions on various aspects of national pride.

Overall, the available mass public opinion survey data directly relevant to this category of norms tend to confirm the assumptions elaborated above. Table 5.1 shows that there is an 8 per cent to 11 per cent lower rate of willingness to fight for one's country among respondents in Canada as well as an even wider gap between the rates in France and especially Germany compared with those in Australia and the UK, with the notable exception of the latest survey results for the UK. These show a sharp drop since the previous survey in 1990, which

Table 5.1 World Values Survey: of course, we all hope that there will not be another war, but if it were to come to that, would you be willing to fight for your country? (in %)

Willingness to fight for country		No	Yes	Don't know/ refused	Not applicable
Australia	2005/2006	34.0	61.4	4.6	–
	1999/2000	–	–	–	–
	1995	23.2	68.9	7.9	–
	1990	–	–	–	–
	1981/1982	23.1	68.4	–	8.5
Canada	2005/2006	34.8	53.2	12.0	–
	1999/2000	30.1	60.1	9.7	–
	1995	–	–	–	–
	1990	26.5	56.4	17.2	–
	1981/1982	31.6	57.3	11.0	–
France	2005/2006	33.3	52.3	7.3	7.2
	1999/2000	35.2	48.2	16.6	–
	1995	–	–	–	–
	1990	27.6	53.7	18.7	–
	1981/1982	45.9	41.9	12.1	–
Germany (1981/82: West Germany only)	2005/2006	50.7	30.3	19.0	–
	1999/2000	40.2	32.4	27.5	–
	1997	43.7	42.9	13.3	–
	1990	39.7	34.8	25.6	–
	1981/1982	41.4	34.8	23.8	–
United Kingdom	2005/2006	31.6	50.4	9.0	9.0
	1999/2000	–	–	–	–
	1995	–	–	–	–
	1990	22.6	67.9	9.4	–
	1981/1982	27.0	62.9	10.1	–

Source: World Values Survey, 2015.

80   *Comparing strategic cultures*

could be a result of war fatigue caused by the height of the Iraq War. France, meanwhile, does indeed assume a position in the middle ground together with Canada, although the percentages of willingness to fight in war are significantly lower than Canada's in all years except for 2005/06. Germany consistently displays by far the lowest rate of willingness to fight for one's country in case of war throughout the years covered by this survey.

Also, Table 5.2 shows that when it comes to obtaining justice, the UK displays a distinctly high rate of support for the use of force compared with both Germany and France, despite a gradual decline of support also for this statement throughout the 2000s. From 2003 to 2007, support for this claim among respondents in the UK declined from 74 per cent in 2003 to 59 per cent in 2007 while it declined from 39 per cent to 25 per cent in France and from 39 per cent to 21 per cent in Germany.

So far the polls show that norms on the use of force contained in Australian and British strategic culture tend to support a broad range of modes, in line with previous findings, despite a trend running through the 2000s of diminishing support. And despite a large volume of literature suggesting a process of

Table 5.2 Transatlantic Trends 2007: please tell me whether you agree with the following statement: under some conditions, war is necessary to obtain justice (in %)

	France	Germany	UK
Agree strongly 2007	6	6	23
2006	9	6	22
2005	7	7	23
2004	9	7	33
2003	12	12	35
Agree somewhat 2007	19	15	36
2006	22	20	42
2005	21	22	41
2004	24	24	36
2003	27	27	39
Disagree somewhat 2007	26	28	16
2006	32	31	14
2005	33	25	14
2004	28	30	13
2003	28	25	10
Disagree strongly 2007	47	50	21
2006	36	43	18
2005	37	45	16
2004	37	38	14
2003	32	35	13
DK/[REFUSAL] 2007	2	1	4
2006	1	1	4
2005	1	1	5
2004	2	1	4
2003	1	1	3

Source: German Marshall Fund, 2007.

Comparative cross-country analysis 81

normalisation in German security policy and practice alongside its strategic culture the available data consistently shows lower levels of support for the use of force by German respondents compared with those of the other four countries. Despite the changes which have occurred in the post-reunification phase, German strategic culture retained its distinct aversion towards the use of force.

These differences in strategic culture within this norms category become clearer when analysing polls that do not present a specific purpose for the use of force or a specific threat to respondents but that instead ask about certain role conceptions that relate to the use of force for different purposes. After all, the norms of a strategic culture also impact upon the way in which a threat is established through securitisation processes. Questions concerning a state's identity can therefore indicate which norms within a strategic culture determine the range of modes in which the use of force is considered acceptable by operating at the stage before the threat or objective is clearly established.

For example, Table 5.3 shows that when asked about their pride in their country's political influence in the word, Canadian respondents showed the most pride in this form of state behaviour, with an average of around 70 per cent replying that they felt proud in 1995 and 2003. This is followed by France with 59 per cent in 2003, and Australia, Germany and the UK averaging at around 51 per cent to 52 per cent.

When asked about their pride in their countries' armed forces on the other hand, Australian and the UK's respondents affirmed feelings of pride in 1995 and 2003 with averages of 79 per cent and 83 per cent respectively, while Canadian respondents only averaged 60 per cent, followed by France with 49 per cent in 2003 and Germany with 25 per cent in 1995 and 2003 (see Table 5.4). This shows that while respondents from Australia and the UK show strong levels of pride in their armed forces but less so in their country's political influence in the world, Canadian and to a lesser degree also French respondents show less pride in their armed forces but high levels of pride in their countries' political influence in the world. Canada displays particularly distinct levels in this regard. Meanwhile, German respondents display exceptionally low levels for both aspects of national pride.

Overall, one can see from these surveys that there is a pattern of Australia and the UK showing a generally supportive attitude towards the robust use of force while respondents from Canada and France occupy a middle ground and especially German respondents generally do not show much support beyond the reactive use of force.

Competences of the state in providing security to citizens

This dimension of norms is reflective of the previous dimension but addresses its domestic aspects particularly strongly. Again, two forms of opinion poll data will be utilised. The bundle of opinion polls addresses conceptions of the role of the army as a mirror of norms concerning the role of the state in the provision of security. Table 5.5 addresses various popular conceptions of the role of the state in society. Especially the first and the second optional answers pitch two opposing conceptions of a modern liberal democracy against each other. Seeing strong defence forces rather than a high level of economic growth as a top priority for

Table 5.3 National Identity I and II (1995, 2003): how proud are you of your country's political influence in the world? (in %)

	Australia		Germany-West		Germany-East		UK		Canada		France	
	2003	1995	2003	1995	2003	1995	2003	1995	2003	1995	2003	1995
Very proud	8.5	5.2	7.1	9.5	3.0	9.2	9.5	7.6	13.2	21.4	7.6	–
Somewhat proud	44.5	44.5	41.9	44.3	46.5	45.3	43.5	40.6	54.9	50.6	51.8	–
Not very proud	27.5	39.3	32.1	28.5	35.2	27.3	28.5	32.4	22.1	15.1	19.1	–
Not proud at all	8.5	3.8	7.3	7.6	6.6	5.6	7.8	7.4	3.4	3.8	6.7	–
Can't choose	8.1	5.2	11.1	8.1	7.1	10.9	8.1	9.4	6.0	6.4	8.5	–
NA	2.9	2.1	0.6	2.0	1.6	1.8	2.5	2.6	0.3	2.8	6.3	–
Sample size	2,183	2,438	850	1,282	437	612	873	1,058	1,211	1,543	1,669	–
Very proud and somewhat proud combined	53.0	49.7	49.0	53.8	49.5	54.5	53.0	48.2	68.1	72.0	59.0	–

Source: GESIS Leibniz Institut für Sozialwissenschaften, 2003.

Table 5.4 National Identity I and II (1995, 2003): how proud are you of your country's armed forces? (in %)

	Australia		Germany-West		Germany-East		UK		Canada		France	
	2003	1995	2003	1995	2003	1995	2003	1995	2003	1995	2003	1995
Very proud	39.5	26.6	3.6	4.7	1.6	4.1	49.6	44.1	27.2	18.5	12.0	–
Somewhat proud	42.5	49.2	24.7	21.0	22.9	18.3	35.2	37.2	37.9	36.1	37.3	–
Not very proud	9.0	16.0	35.5	30.3	37.5	31.9	6.3	6.7	21.1	21.9	16.5	–
Not proud at all	2.8	2.9	15.4	26.7	20.8	26.0	2.4	4.0	8.7	14.8	10.0	–
Can't choose	3.8	4.0	19.5	15.5	15.8	17.8	4.9	5.7	4.8	6.5	17.6	–
NA	2.3	1.4	1.2	1.9	1.4	2.0	1.6	2.3	0.4	2.1	6.6	–
Sample size	2,183	2,438	850	1,282	437	612	873	1,058	1,211	1,543	1,669	–
Very proud and somewhat proud combined	82.0	75.8	28.3	25.7	24.5	22.4	84.8	81.3	65.1	54.6	49.3	–

Source: GESIS Leibniz Institut für Sozialwissenschaften, 2003.

84   *Comparing strategic cultures*

Table 5.5 World Values Survey 2006/2007: people sometimes talk about what the aims of this country should be for the next ten years. On this card are listed some of the goals which different people would give top priority. Would you please say which one of these you, yourself, consider the most important? And which one the second most important? (in %)

Aims of country: first choice	France	UK	Canada	Australia	Germany
A high level of economic growth	40.4	37.8	49.0	53.9	62.8
Strong defence forces	7.0	12.0	5.7	12.8	2.2
People have more say about how things are done	40.4	43.2	38.9	30.2	30.9
Trying to make our cities and countryside more beautiful	12.2	7.0	6.3	3.2	4.1

Aims of country: second choice	France	UK	Canada	Australia	Germany
A high level of economic growth	28.9	31.6	31.5	24.0	23.9
Strong defence forces	12.1	17.3	14.2	27.8	6.5
People have more say about how things are done	33.6	31.0	33.9	31.9	48.9
Trying to make our cities and countryside more beautiful	25.4	20.1	20.3	16.2	20.7
Strong defence forces first and second combined	19.1	29.3	19.9	40.6	8.7

Source: World Values Survey, 2015.

the country implies a more individualistic rather than a collectivist conception of the nation–state in which security should be the key concern of the state while economic welfare should be achieved through the business of private individuals. This, in turn, implies a more accepting attitude towards the domestic as well as the international use of force by the state for the provision of security, as it is considered the state's principal function. As the table shows, Germany assigns the lowest percentage to its defence forces amongst all five countries, while the UK and especially Australia assign these the highest percentage and Canada and France once again assume a position in the middle ground.

Differences in preferences regarding the allocation of one's country's priorities also show that the differences in the levels of pride accorded to the country's armed forces identified earlier were not influenced by current levels of resource allocation by the government or the army's perceived performance but that these are indeed indicative of norms regarding both the range of modes in which the use of force is deemed acceptable and regarding the state's competences in the provision of security. This is also shown in Table 5.6. If levels of pride in the armed forces are influenced by levels of military spending and the corresponding performance and size of the armed forces rather than differences in strategic culture, one would expect respondents from those states which have lower levels of per capita military expenditure to desire an increase in military spending and vice versa. Yet as Table 5.6 shows, when asked whether respondents prefer military expenditure to increase, decrease or remain the same, there is no discernible negative correlation between the lower and higher levels of

Table 5.6 Role of Government I–IV (1985, 1990, 1996, 2006): please show whether you would like to see more or less government spending on the military and defence (in %)

Country	Year	Spend much more	Spend more	Spend the same as now	Spend less	Spend much less	NA, refused	Can't choose, don't know	Sample size
Australia	1985	18.9	25.3	35.3	12.0	5.0	3.5	0	1,528
	1990	5.3	19.6	34.4	28.4	11.3	0.7	0.3	2,398
	1996	7.4	18.6	47.3	19.7	4.3	2.3	0.3	2,151
	2006	4.4	19.3	50.4	14.4	5.6	4.5	1.3	2,781
Canada	1996	1.4	6.4	29.1	33.2	25.3	2.6	1.9	1,182
	2006	8.7	32.4	36.0	11.9	5.7	1.4	4.0	933
France	1996	2.1	5.0	25.8	33.0	31.3	2.1	0.8	1,312
	2006	1.6	6.5	39.4	29.9	16.3	4.6	1.7	1,824
Germany	1985	1.5	4.4	29.6	31.4	29.5	1.2	2.4	1,048
	1990	1.4	2.9	12.7	30.9	49.1	1.5	1.4	2,812
	1996	1.8	5.2	22.6	35.3	30.7	0.6	3.8	3,470
	2006	2.7	8.4	31.1	34.1	18.4	1.5	3.7	1,643
UK	1985	4.9	12.1	42.9	23.3	12.2	2.7	2.0	1,530
	1990	2.1	6.3	41.3	31.7	14.0	2.5	2.1	1,197
	1996	3.1	14.3	44.9	22.9	8.4	3.8	2.6	989
	2006	8.6	20.5	42.3	16.1	6.3	3.3	2.8	930

Source: GESIS Leibniz Institut für Sozialwissenschaften, 2006.

86   *Comparing strategic cultures*

military expenditure discussed in the introduction and preferences for increases or decreases. In Australia, which has a significantly higher level of military spending than Canada, preferences for increased military expenditure average at around 30 per cent whereas in Canada, these average at around 25 per cent, although the two values available differ significantly, with 7.8 per cent desiring more spending in 1996 and 41.1 per cent doing so in 2006. Respondents from France and the UK, which have both higher absolute and proportional military expenditure rates than Germany, prefer increases in military expenditure with averages of 15 per cent and 18 per cent, while in Germany only 7 per cent do so on average. Preferences for decreased military expenditure, on the other hand, are particularly high in Germany, Canada and France. This is in line with the expectation that popular norms on the competences of the state in providing security to citizens contain relatively low levels of acceptance of infringements on civil liberties for the provision of security in these states.

Table 5.7 shows that similar differences can be discerned when it comes to preferences regarding resource allocation for state capacities to provide security domestically, although the differences are less stark. Respondents from Australia and the UK preferred increases in government spending on law enforcement by an average majority of 65 per cent and 54 per cent respectively while respondents in Canada, Germany and France desired more spending on law enforcement by averages of 42 per cent, 35 per cent and 43 per cent respectively. This shows that regarding norms on competences of the state in the provision of security one can assume higher levels of acceptance of infringements on civil liberties in the UK and Australia than in Canada, France and Germany.

The second group of indicators used for this dimension of norms consists of polls on popular attitudes towards various security measures by the state. Tables 5.8 to 5.10 show the results of opinion polls on capital punishment. This issue prompts respondents with the question of whether the state's domestic coercive powers over its citizens should extend into issuing death sentences. In this regard, the results also reflect the pattern discerned earlier insofar as Germany displays consistently lower levels of support for the death penalty, while the UK displays the highest levels of support followed by Canada and France in Table 5.8 and Table 5.9 while the results are very similar in all three countries in Table 5.10. Therefore, the data tends to confirm assumptions generated in the previous chapter that there are low levels of acceptance of infringements on civil liberties for the provision of security in Germany, while there are high levels of acceptance in the UK and slightly lower levels of acceptance in Canada and France.

Table 5.11 shows the results of an opinion poll enquiring on respondents' attitudes towards the provision of security in a similarly abstract way. It asked respondents, whether it is worse to convict an innocent person or to let a guilty person go free. Once again, a similar pattern can be discerned among the results as before but once again the differences between countries are more marginal. In all five countries the majority of respondents agreed on the more liberal position that it is worse to convict an innocent person. And in all countries except France one can also observe a trend towards the more conservative attitude that it is worse to let a guilty person walk freely. But on average, the rate of conservative attitudes is highest again in the UK with 24 per cent and Australia with 23 per cent followed

Table 5.7 Role of Government I–IV (1985, 1990, 1996, 2006): please show whether you would like to see more or less government spending on law enforcement (in %)

Country	Year	Spend much more	Spend more	Spend the same as now	Spend less	Spend much less	NA, refused	Can't choose, don't know	Sample size
Australia	1985	21.1	43.6	28.3	2.2	0.7	4.0	0	1,528
	1990	13.4	53.7	27.3	3.8	0.5	0.9	0.4	2,398
	1996	18.2	47.0	29.8	1.9	0.1	2.8	0.2	2,151
	2006	18.8	45.3	29.1	1.5	0.5	4.0	0.6	2,781
Canada	1996	6.7	25.9	51.9	10.4	1.5	2.2	1.4	1,182
	2006	9.5	42.0	39.3	4.2	0.6	0.9	3.4	933
France	1996	10.2	26.9	46.5	8.1	4.4	2.5	1.4	1,312
	2006	9.0	23.2	48.8	9.4	3.9	4.3	1.2	1,824
Germany	1985	8.4	20.0	58.6	7.0	1.1	1.9	3.0	1,048
	1990	11.1	30.3	41.9	10.1	2.5	1.7	2.3	2,812
	1996	22.4	37.8	31.3	4.4	0.9	0.5	2.8	3,470
	2006	12.2	30.7	45.8	6.6	1.2	1.0	2.6	1,643
UK	1985	8.4	29.9	51.7	4.2	1.8	2.4	1.7	1,530
	1990	10.2	38.3	44.4	3.2	0.4	2.3	1.3	1,197
	1996	20.4	50.3	23.1	1.3	0.5	3.0	1.4	989
	2006	15.4	44.3	32.2	2.4	0.6	3.5	1.6	930

Source: GESIS Leibniz Institut für Sozialwissenschaften, 2006.

88   *Comparing strategic cultures*

closely by Canada with 21 per cent. In Germany and France conservative attitudes are relatively low with averages of 18 per cent and 17 per cent respectively.

When it comes to the surveillance of known criminals, however, respondents from Australia, Germany and the UK did not differ significantly in their responses, as Table 5.12 shows. When asked whether the police should be allowed to detain a man with a long criminal record suspected of breaking into a warehouse, respondents from Australia, the UK and Germany agreed by averages of 91.5 per cent, 90 per cent and 89 per cent, respectively.

When asked about whether the police should be afforded random stop and search powers in the case of a suspected imminent terrorist act, differences among respondents resurface, as Table 5.13 shows. In the UK, 73 per cent supported this, followed by Australia with 53 per cent, Germany with 50 per cent, Canada with 36 per cent and France with 18 per cent.

Table 5.8 AP-Ipsos International Poll – attitudes toward the death penalty, February–April 2007: do you favour or oppose the death penalty for people convicted of murder? (in %)

Country	Oppose	Favour	Not sure
Canada	52	44	5
France	52	45	3
Germany	62	35	2
United Kingdom	45	50	5

Source: Ipsos MORI, 2007.

Table 5.9 AP-Ipsos International Poll – attitudes toward the death penalty, February–April 2007: which punishment do you prefer for people convicted of murder? (in %)

Country	Long term prison sentence	Life without parole	Death penalty	Not sure
Canada	20	51	25	3
France	22	55	21	3
Germany	27	59	11	3
United Kingdom	19	44	34	3

Source: Ipsos MORI, 2007.

Table 5.10 AP-Ipsos International Poll – attitudes toward the death penalty, February–April 2007: if Osama bin Laden is captured, tried and convicted of being a terrorist, which punishment should he receive? (in %)

Country	Long term prison sentence	Life without parole	Death penalty	Not sure
Canada	8	45	42	5
France	5	53	38	4
Germany	10	60	26	4
United Kingdom	6	48	40	5

Source: Ipsos MORI, 2007.

Comparative cross-country analysis 89

Table 5.11 Role of Government I–IV (1985, 1990, 1996, 2006): all systems of justice make mistakes, but which do you think is worse…? (in %)

Country	Year	Convict innocent person	Let guilty person go free	NA, refused	Can't choose, don't know
Australia	1985	71.3	21.2	7.5	0
	1990	64.5	20.7	1.8	13.0
	1996	64.6	21.8	2.6	11.0
	2006	59.5	26.5	3.5	10.5
Canada	1996	61.6	18.2	1.4	18.8
	2006	58.8	23.4	1.5	16.3
France	1996	73.5	17.3	1.7	7.5
	2006	75.8	16.0	3.0	5.2
Germany	1985	76.3	13.2	0.4	10.1
	1990	65.2	18.1	2.0	14.7
	1996	66.8	15.4	0.9	16.9
	2006	61.8	20.3	1.1	16.9
UK	1985	66.7	20.3	0.7	12.4
	1990	61.4	19.1	0.4	19.0
	1996	56.2	26.9	1.2	15.7
	2006	52.2	29.1	0.6	18.1

Source: GESIS Leibniz Institut für Sozialwissenschaften, 2006.

When asked about their opinion on wiretapping suspected terrorists in 2006, respondents from the UK alongside Australian and French respondents took a more conservative attitude than Germany, with 72.8 per cent, 74.5 per cent and 73.8 per cent, respectively (see Table 5.14). In Germany and in Canada respondents supported wiretapping by a slightly lower percentage of 65.2 per cent and 57.5 per cent, respectively.

It is noticeable that once again, French attitudes at times fluctuate between extreme ends in the polls. Support for civil liberties is expressed most strongly in polls on more abstract positions while considerable support is also lent to potential infringements in civil liberties in polls on more concrete state measures for the provision of security. This may reflect both a potential norms conflict between allegiance to and admiration for the institution of the French state on the one hand and a traditional championing of civil liberties on the other as well as a disconnect between policy-making elites and the general public in France. German positions are again generally less conservative than in other countries although there are some notable exceptions in this section. Australian and British positions are once again generally more conservative than in the other countries although Canadian positions at times converged with Australian and British positions in this section. Poll results may well have been influenced by recent events surrounding the time at which fieldwork was conducted, especially in the UK, which was the target of terrorist acts itself after 9/11. Yet for the UK polls also reveal more conservative attitudes when it comes to more general questions or fieldwork conducted prior to 9/11. All in all, the above opinion polls suggest that there are more conservative and less liberal attitudes on state security

Table 5.12 Role of Government I & II (1985, 1990): suppose the police get an anonymous tip that a man with a long criminal record is planning to break into a warehouse. Do you think the police should be allowed, without a Court Order, to keep the man under surveillance? (in %)

Country	Year	Definitely allowed	Probably allowed	Probably not allowed	Definitely not allowed	NA, refused	Can't choose, don't know	Sample size
Australia	1985	72.8	16.0	2.6	3.3	5.4	0	1,528
	1990	49.1	45.0	3.3	1.6	0.7	0.3	2,398
Germany	1985	69.6	25.5	2.2	1.7	0.3	0.8	1,048
	1990	48.0	34.8	8.2	5.3	0.7	3.0	2,812
UK	1985	68.9	21.2	3.3	4.5	1.2	0.9	1,530
	1990	61.7	28.8	2.8	4.8	0.6	1.3	1,197

Source: GESIS Leibniz Institut für Sozialwissenschaften, 2006.

Table 5.13 Role of Government IV (2006): suppose the government suspected that a terrorist act was about to happen. Do you think the authorities should have the right to stop and search people in the street at random? (in %)

Country	Definitely should have right	Probably should have right	Probably should not have right	Definitely should not have right	Can't choose	NA	Sample size
Australia	22.8	29.8	23.1	19.3	1.8	3.1	2,781
Canada	11.1	25.2	27.8	28.8	5.7	1.4	933
France	6.4	12.0	25.0	51.9	1.7	3.0	1,824
Germany-West	19.8	31.1	28.1	15.7	4.3	0.9	1,112
Germany-East	19.6	29.4	25.8	22.0	3.0	0.2	531
UK	35.6	37.7	13.2	7.8	3.1	2.5	930

Source: GESIS Leibniz Institut für Sozialwissenschaften, 2006.

Table 5.14 Role of Government IV (2006): suppose the government suspected that a terrorist act was about to happen. Do you think the authorities should have the right to tap people's telephone conversations? (in %)

Country	Definitely should have right	Probably should have right	Probably should not have right	Definitely should not have right	Can't choose	NA	Sample size
Australia	36.7	37.8	13.3	7.4	1.9	2.9	2,781
Canada	20.5	37.0	20.9	15.8	4.9	1.0	933
France	39.2	34.6	12.5	9.5	1.9	2.4	1,824
Germany–West	30.1	39.8	15.5	9.5	4.3	0.7	1,112
Germany–East	26.4	34.1	18.8	17.5	3.0	0.2	531
UK	32.8	40.0	13.5	7.3	3.8	2.6	930

Source: GESIS Leibniz Institut für Sozialwissenschaften, 2006.

Comparative cross-country analysis   93

measures in Australia and the UK than in France, Germany and Canada. This suggests that in line with the assumptions spelled out in the previous chapter, norms on competences of the state regarding the provision of security to its citizens allow for a higher level of acceptance of infringements on civil liberties for the provision of security in Australia and the UK than in the other three countries. However, in this normative dimension the differences are not as strongly pronounced as in the previously analysed dimensions, which is also in line with the prior assumption that there will be more similarities in norms that relate to domestic state security measures more strongly.

Norms regarding international cooperation

This dimension of norms concerns preferred modes of international cooperation. Its possible expressions range from armed and unarmed neutrality to unilateralism. Identity and role conceptions that generate norms allowing for the frequent and robust use of force are also likely to generate norms allowing the state to operate more independently of international laws and institutions in cooperation with individual allies or even completely autonomously. Inversely, strategic cultures containing norms demanding a very measured approach to the use of force domestically and internationally, that is subject to extensive legislation, are also likely to contain norms that generate preferences for more multilateral law–based and institutionalised modes of international cooperation. This dimension of norms is therefore likely to be largely reflective of the first two dimensions. Survey data is more readily available for this dimension. Unfortunately, however, many of these do not include Australia and Canada.

Table 5.15 indicates that German respondents display a strong belief that a system led by the United Nations is the best way to ensure peace and stability in the world, while French and especially British respondents are more ambiguous and torn between preferences for UN multilateralism and power politics. Unilateralism and bipolarity on the other hand are largely rejected by all three countries. To the question within which framework peace and stability in the world can best be achieved 67 per cent of German, 45 per cent of French and 47 per

Table 5.15 Bertelsmann Foundation "Who Rules the World?" Survey: which is the best framework for ensuring peace and stability in the world? (in %)

Country	Year	A system led by the United Nations	A system led by a balance of regional powers	A system led by a single world power	A system led by two world powers	Don't know/no answer
France	2007	43	36	5	4	12
	2006	46	34	5	4	11
Germany	2007	66	20	6	4	4
	2006	68	21	4	3	4
UK	2007	47	44	6	3	–
	2006	47	40	3	2	7

Source: Bertelsmann Stiftung, 2007.

94 Comparing strategic cultures

cent of British respondents answered "a system led by the United Nations", whereas 42 per cent in the UK, 35 per cent in France and only 21 per cent in Germany on the other hand answered "a system led by a balance of regional powers". Notably, of all nine countries addressed by the survey German respondents were most in favour of UN multilateralism.

Table 5.16 shows that an average of 62 per cent in the UK, 69 per cent in France and 64 per cent in Germany had a favourable opinion of NATO between 2009 and 2012. This also shows that support for the transatlantic alliance is strong in all three countries. However, averages of 30 per cent of respondents from France and Germany also had an unfavourable opinion of NATO, while only 17 per cent did so in the UK. This suggests that while support for NATO is strong in all three countries, support for the transatlantic alliance polarises opinion more in Germany and France than it does in the UK.

But contrary to common belief Germany and the UK do not differ significantly over their views on the transatlantic partnership with the US. French respondents, meanwhile, are largely unsupportive of US leadership in world affairs. On average, 38 per cent of respondents in France, 51 per cent in Germany and 59 per cent in the UK stated that the US exerting strong leadership in world affairs would be desirable, as Table 5.17 shows. However, sentiments of attachment to the US have weakened steadily in all three countries between 2002 and 2008. In 2002 48 per cent of French, 68 per cent of German and 72 per cent of British respondents deemed it desirable that the US exerts strong leadership in world affairs. In 2008 these figures were reduced to 28 per cent in France, 39 per cent in Germany and 48 per cent in the UK. In 2009, figures rebounded to 52 per cent in France, 65 per cent in Germany and 64 per cent in the UK. All in all, the findings confirm prior assumptions that German strategic culture contains strong normative attachments to multilateralism as well as to the Western, US-led security architecture, which bears the potential of the

Table 5.16 Pew GAP: please tell me if you have a very favourable, somewhat favourable, somewhat unfavourable, or very unfavourable opinion of NATO (in %)

Country	Year	Very favourable	Somewhat favourable	Somewhat unfavourable	Very unfavourable	Don't know/ no answer
France	2012	8	59	21	10	1
	2011	10	60	23	7	1
	2010	6	62	24	7	2
	2009	12	59	20	7	1
Germany	2012	8	57	26	4	5
	2011	6	54	29	4	7
	2010	7	50	27	6	9
	2009	14	59	18	4	5
UK	2012	15	47	13	4	20
	2011	17	46	12	5	20
	2010	18	42	12	5	24
	2009	22	41	11	6	21

Source: Pew Research Center Global Attitudes Project, 2012.

Table 5.17 Transatlantic Trends: how desirable is it that the United States exerts strong leadership in world affairs? (in %)

Country	Year	Very desirable	Somewhat desirable	Somewhat undesirable	Very undesirable	Neither or both equally	Don't know/refused
France	2012	10	46	29	14	0	1
	2011	9	39	31	18	1	2
	2010	9	37	35	16	1	2
	2009	10	42	27	15		5
	2008	4	24	41	27	1	3
	2007	5	23	39	25	2	6
	2006	5	25	39	26		5
	2005	4	24	44	25		3
	2004	1	23	43	30	1	2
	2003	2	25	43	27		3
	2002	10	38	33	15	0	4
Germany	2012	11	50	30	8	1	1
	2011	8	52	28	8	1	2
	2010	8	51	33	6		3
	2009	10	55	25	8		1
	2008	5	34	43	16	1	2
	2007	5	33	43	16	1	2
	2006	5	39	40	14	1	2
	2005	5	35	42	17	1	1
	2004	3	34	44	16	2	2
	2003	4	41	37	13	3	2
	2002	11	57	21	6	3	2
UK	2012	20	42	20	12	2	5
	2011	20	46	17	10	2	5
	2010	22	52	14	7	2	2
	2009	16	48	19	11	2	3
	2008	14	34	27	19	1	5
	2007	14	36	26	17	2	5
	2006	12	36	28	17	1	6
	2005	17	36	24	17	2	4
	2004	16	38	23	14	2	6
	2003	15	40	24	14	3	4
	2002	28	44	18	7	1	2

Source: German Marshall Fund, 2007.

96 Comparing strategic cultures

two coming into conflict. In the UK on the other hand, the preference for strong leadership of the US or to some extent also the EU as well as strong attachment to NATO outweigh the normative attachment to UN multilateralism. In France, preferences for EU leadership are strongest among all three options while support for US leadership in security affairs is lowest and suffered heavily during the Bush years.

Although there is little information available on attitudes towards preferred modes of international security cooperation in Australia and Canada, Table 5.18 suggests that the differences between the UK on the one hand and France and Germany on the other are to some extent also present between these two countries. Table 5.18 shows that on the controversial question of whether their country should follow decisions of international organisations even if their own government disagrees with the decision, respondents from all countries replied negatively. However, respondents from the UK and Australia showed the lowest levels of support for this claim with 23 per cent and 26 per cent respectively. In Canada, 31 per cent of respondents were in support, in Germany 32 per cent were in support and in France 40 per cent agreed to this.

Likewise, Table 5.19 below shows that when prompted with the statement that international organisations take away too much power from the national government, only 29 per cent of Canadian and 30 per cent of German respondents agreed while 38 per cent of Australian, 45 per cent of French and 52 per cent of British respondents agreed. The responses from European countries are most likely reflective of opinion towards the EU's legislative authority. The high rate of disagreement in the UK is therefore most likely reflective of widespread Euroscepticism as well as a preference for affiliations with particular states or alliances rather than more institutionalised and legislated forms of multilateral cooperation. In France, the result probably reflects its traditionally strong independent-mindedness and aspirations for an own leadership role, as identified earlier. However, Table 5.18 also showed that support for abiding with rules of international organisations even in the case of disagreement was also strongest in

Table 5.18 National Identity Survey II (2003): please tell me if you agree with the following statement: in general, our country should follow the decisions of international organisations to which it belongs, even if the government disagrees with them

	Australia	Germany-West	Germany-East	UK	Canada	France
Agree strongly	3.6	3.5	3.7	1.9	3.6	10.1
Agree	22.2	24.6	29.5	21.4	27.7	28.8
Neither agree nor disagree	31.1	26.1	25.2	32.6	27.8	23.2
Disagree	30.7	25.2	22.7	31.5	30.6	20.4
Disagree strongly	4.9	4.9	4.8	2.9	2.7	7.7
Can't choose	5.9	14.9	13.0	7.7	6.7	4.8
NA	1.7	0.7	1.1	1.9	1.0	5.1
Sample size	2,183	850	437	873	1,211	1,669

Source: GESIS Leibniz Institut für Sozialwissenschaften, 2003.

Comparative cross-country analysis 97

Table 5.19 National Identity Survey II (2003): please tell me if you agree with the following statement: International organisations take away too much power from our country's government (in %)

	Australia	Germany-West	Germany-East	UK	Canada	France
Agree strongly	9.2	4.8	4.6	15.3	6.9	15.9
Agree	29.5	25.4	24.5	37.1	22.3	29.4
Neither agree nor disagree	31.1	23.6	23.1	27.1	35.8	23.4
Disagree	20.6	25.9	25.6	12.3	24.1	17.4
Disagree strongly	2.1	4.2	3.0	0.5	1.4	4.1
Can't choose	5.6	15.4	17.8	6.1	8.7	5.1
NA	2.0	0.6	1.4	1.6	0.9	4.7
Sample size	2,183	850	437	873	1,211	1,669

Source: GESIS Leibniz Institut für Sozialwissenschaften, 2003.

France. This may indicate a potential schism present in norms on preferred modes of international cooperation present in French strategic culture between aspirations for one's own lead role in international affairs in lieu of US leadership on the one hand and demands for a more law-abiding conduct of international politics. Although the difference between Canadian and Australian respondents is only marginal, it is in line with the differences in levels of pride in one's country's military and in its political influence in the world identified above, which suggest that in contrast to Australian strategic culture, Canadian strategic culture contains more of a normative attachment to affiliations with international organisations or alliances rather than with particular states.

While the polls suggest that norms on international cooperation in the UK and in Australia are more supportive of affiliations with particular states or alliances rather than international cooperation that is tightly regulated and governed by international organisations and international law, the inverse can be said about Germany and Canada. Norms in French strategic culture, meanwhile, appear to embrace the rule of international law and multilateral institutions such as the UN and the EU alongside Germany. There also appears to be a general distrust of American leadership within the Western security architecture. At the same time, one can discern a normative attachment to autonomy in the conduct of international cooperation. Norms within French strategic culture therefore appear to favour affiliations with organisations and alliances rather than affiliations with particular states alone, yet paradoxically they also support an independent course in pursuit of a more pronounced leadership role in international affairs.

Norms on international and domestic authorisation requirements

This dimension of norms concerns norms regarding democratic control mechanisms governing the use of force. Surveys indicating expressions in this dimension are both scarce in general and mostly exclusive of Australia and Canada.

98 Comparing strategic cultures

However, expressions in this norms category derive from the above norms dimensions particularly strongly since strategic cultures with higher proclivities to support the use of force by the state are also likely to demand less authorisation requirements for its use and vice versa. Conclusions for this norms dimension can therefore also be drawn on the basis of the prior analyses on the other three norms dimensions above.

The first poll results in this category surprise at first as they seem to disconfirm prior assumptions on German strategic culture placing strong emphasis on multilateralism and the UN. As Table 5.20 shows, 74 per cent and 76 per cent of French and British respondents agreed with the statement that the use of force was more legitimate with UN approval, while only 60 per cent of German respondents did. This shows that while respondents from all countries value UN approval, fewer respondents from Germany agreed that it renders more legitimacy to the use of force by the state. This might be due to differences in the first norms dimension: Germans are less inclined to deem the use of force legitimate than the other two countries, with or without UN approval.

As a more indirect indicator of expressions in this norms dimension, Table 5.21 takes an inverse perspective and asks respondents whether international bodies should have the right to authorise state measures to tackle global problems, in this case environmental pollution. It shows that French respondents are most supportive of this statement with an average of 81 per cent, followed by 79 per cent in Germany, 71 per cent in Canada, 66 per cent in the UK and 63 per cent in Australia. This suggests that in line with prior findings in the above norms dimensions and discussions of identity conceptions, international organisations are afforded more normative authority in Canada, France and Germany than in the UK and Australia.

The polls indicate the presence of norms demanding high international authorisation requirements in Germany and relatively lower international authorisation requirements in the UK while French respondents showed themselves to be supportive of a strong role for international institutions in governing state measures to tackle global problems while they also appeared to demand high international authorisation requirements, although to a lower degree than German respondents. Respondents from Australia and Canada took slightly different positions over whether international organisations have the authority to impose solutions for global problems. One can therefore assume that in line with

Table 5.20 Transatlantic Trends (2005): do you agree with the following statement: the use of military force is more legitimate when the United Nations (UN) approves it? (in %)

	France	Germany	UK
Agree strongly	34	23	41
Agree somewhat	40	37	35
Disagree somewhat	14	24	13
Disagree strongly	11	15	7
Don't know/refused	1	2	5

Source: German Marshall Fund, 2007.

Table 5.21 National Identity Surveys I and II (1995, 2003): how much do you agree or disagree with the following statement? For certain problems, like environmental pollution, international bodies should have the right to enforce solutions (in %)

	Australia		Germany-West		Germany-East		UK		Canada		France	
	2003	1995	2003	1995	2003	1995	2003	1995	2003	1995	2003	1995
Agree strongly	16.1	25.0	22.6	37.4	16.9	40.2	20.4	25.6	22.2	32.5	42.3	–
Agree	45.4	40.0	51.5	44.3	56.3	48.4	42.8	44.0	43.4	42.9	38.2	–
Neither agree nor disagree	16.1	12.6	9.4	6.2	12.4	3.4	17.6	15.1	14.9	10.6	7.7	–
Disagree	13.5	15.2	7.1	5.2	7.1	2.8	11.0	8.6	12.0	8.7	4.0	–
Disagree strongly	3.6	5.0	1.6	1.8	0.9	0.7	0.8	0.9	3.1	1.9	2.0	–
Can't choose	3.0	0.4	7.3	3	5.3	3.3	4.7	4.2	3.8	2.2	1.7	–
NA	2.2	1.9	0.5	2	1.1	1.3	2.6	1.5	0.7	1.1	4.1	–
Sample size	2,183	2,438	850	1,282	437	612	873	1,058	1,211	1,543	1,669	–

Source: GESIS Leibniz Institut für Sozialwissenschaften, 2003.

100 *Comparing strategic cultures*

the assumptions made in the previous section, Canadian strategic culture contains norms demanding slightly higher international authorisation requirements than Australian strategic culture. This is also suggested by the findings in the prior norms dimension on preferred modes of international cooperation.

Summarising and synthesising the findings

By and large, the opinion polls analysed could confirm the pattern identified in the prior analysis of identity conceptions. As Australian identity conceptions appeared to engender a strategic culture pertaining to a relatively high proclivity to the robust and proactive use of force as well as a strong normative attachment to its alliances with the English-speaking world, despite a trend away from this traditionally strong attachment in recent years, opinion polls also suggested that the proclivity to use force domestically and internationally is higher than in other countries, notably Canada. Canadian identity conceptions, meanwhile, suggested that there is a strong normative attachment to the US and NATO on the one hand but there is also the element of a drive for difference and distance that feeds on the notion of an anti-militaristic history. This was taken to suggest that there is less of a proclivity to use force than in the UK and Australia. The analysis of opinion polls also showed that while there are indications of a convergence over the last ten years between Australian and Canadian positions towards the use of force, there are also discernible differences that constitute a critical mass for different security policies and practices among the two members of the extra-European 'Anglosphere'.

Among the three European countries, the analysis of identity conceptions showed that French identity is likely to generate norms allowing for the robust use of force only for a certain range of modes and up to a certain degree, although its political class is given considerable leeway in its actual decisions, especially regarding domestic state security measures. Opinion polls could confirm that there is strong normative support for a relatively heavily armed state with robust deterrence and defence capabilities but there is little support for the more controversial and intractable applications of state force at home and abroad. As for Germany, both the analysis of identity conceptions and the analysis of opinion polls could identify a consistently lower proclivity towards the use of force in its strategic culture. The opposite applies to the UK, as the analyses could show. It displayed consistently higher values in support of the use of force at home and abroad.

Despite extensive discussions of a convergence between European strategic cultures, especially on the part of German strategic culture, the analysis of opinion polls could find no indications of a continued 'normalisation' in Germany in the 2000s. Although this unavoidably simplifies the complexity inherent in each strategic culture, the findings for each norms category are aggregated into one estimated value for each country and are displayed graphically for the purpose of illustrating these findings in Figure 5.1. Each bar represents the strategic culture of one of the five countries. Darker shades of grey indicate where the centre of gravity of each strategic culture is assumed to be located on an aggregated scale of strategic cultures' proclivity to use force ranging from complete passivity (low) to complete aggressiveness/oppressiveness (high), based on the analyses conducted in this chapter. It displays the UK

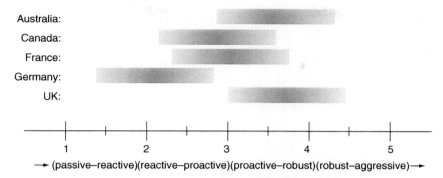

Figure 5.1 Overview of findings on strategic culture in Chapter 5.

slightly to the right and Australia slightly to the left of each other within the 'proactive to robust'-category, which indicates their strategic cultures to contain a moderately high proclivity to the use of force. France and Canada on the other hand are placed slightly to the right and the left of the 'proactive' demarcation, while Germany is placed slightly to the left of the 'reactive' mark.

All in all, the findings in this part suggest that the strategic cultures analysed contain significant differences in their proclivities to use force, both internationally and domestically. The findings showed that while norms in Australian and British strategic cultures contain a relatively high proclivity towards the use of force, both domestically and internationally, Canadian and French strategic cultures rather take a position in the middle ground while German strategic culture shows a distinctly lower proclivity to the use of force, despite indications that since 1990 German strategic culture changed towards a slightly higher proclivity. From this analysis one can assume that the reservations towards the use of force as well as potential tensions between elites and the public in Germany and to some degree also France and Canada condition agency in a way that they are likely to lead to comparatively milder securitisation processes in those countries, while debates in Australia and the UK are likely to run alongside stronger securitisation efforts resulting in more robust security measures taken both domestically and internationally.

While elites in Germany and to a lower extent also in Canada and France have to reconcile stronger tensions between domestic cultural constraints and external demands by allies and partners, this problem will probably not present itself to the same degree in Australia and the UK. This is likely to lead to more protracted, reactive debates involving lower resonance with the public in these three countries. Furthermore, one can assume that in response to the policy window of 9/11 the relative magnitude of state force contained in both domestic and international state measures differs in accordance with the identified differences in strategic culture. Their respective strategic cultures are likely to generate collective expectations for more measured state actions in Canada, France and Germany while those of Australia and the UK display expectations of the more robust use of force in state action.

102   *Comparing strategic cultures*

Bibliography

Bertelsmann Stiftung (2007) "Who Rules the World?" Available from: www. bertelsmann-stiftung.de/fileadmin/files/BSt/Presse/imported/downloads/xcms_bst_ dms_23371_23372_2.pdf (accessed 9 August 2015).

German Marshall Fund (2007) "Transatlantic Trends". Available from: http://trends. gmfus.org/ (accessed 9 August 2015).

GESIS Leibniz Institut für Sozialwissenschaften (2003) "GESIS – ISSP: National Identity". Available from: www.gesis.org/en/issp/issp-modules-profiles/national-identity/ (accessed 9 August 2015).

GESIS Leibniz Institut für Sozialwissenschaften (2006) "GESIS – ISSP: Role of Government". Available from: www.gesis.org/en/issp/issp-modules-profiles/role-of-government/ (accessed 9 August 2015).

Ipsos MORI (2007) "Death Penalty – International Poll." Available from: www.ipsos-mori.com/researchpublications/researcharchive/163/Death-Penalty-International-Poll.aspx (accessed 9 August 2015).

Pew Research Center "Global Attitudes Project (2012) Spring 2012 Survey". Available from: www.pewglobal.org/category/datasets/2012/?download=27361 (accessed 9 August 2015).

World Values Survey (2015) WVS Database. Available from: www.worldvaluessurvey.org/wvs.jsp (accessed 9 August 2015).

Part III

Comparing decision processes on the use of force

6 Analysing British decision processes on the use of force

Norms contained in British strategic culture are conducive to short, rather swift and clear-cut securitisation processes resulting in robust and decisive action domestically as well as internationally, hence 'stronger' securitisation processes. On the basis of these findings, one can therefore assume that the decision to use force in all three instances analysed in this chapter was taken comparatively swiftly by a small circle of elites centred at the highest level of government authority through policy channels available to this elite in extraordinary circumstances. Parliament, the media and the public are likely to take a comparatively supportive stance towards these decisions. To some extent, this is likely to be co-determined by extra-cultural factors such as a parliamentary and electoral system that is unlikely to produce governments which need to rely on coalition partners as well as a media landscape that is traditionally vocal in its opinion pieces.

The three main parties represented in the British House of Commons are the left-of-centre Labour Party, the right-of-centre Conservative Party and the social-liberal party Liberal Democrats. Aside from these major three parties, there are several regional parties represented in the House of Commons. Between 2001 and 2003, these were the left-leaning Plaid Cymru party from Wales, the left-leaning Scottish National Party, the Social Democratic and Labour Party from Northern Ireland, left-leaning Sinn Féin of Northern Ireland, the more conservative Ulster Unionist Party of Northern Ireland, and the also conservative Democratic Unionist Party of Northern Ireland. At the time of the attacks, the ruling Labour Party was still somewhat divided between reformist elements labelled as New Labour on the one hand, which largely comprised the government and the party's higher echelons of power, and remaining adherents to Old Labour on the other, which were mostly found on the back benches of Parliament. Although Labour faced the opposition of two major parties in government, opposition towards the government's decisions to use force was most likely to come from the Labour back benches themselves.

Analysing the British decision process regarding the use of force in Afghanistan

The first decision to be analysed is the British decision to use force in Afghanistan. As it represents the most immediate and the most drastic action taken in response to 9/11, it is also likely to represent one of the most heavily securitised

106   *Comparing decision processes on use of force*

instance of security policy decision-making analysed in this chapter. The process occurred at a time when the New Labour government under Tony Blair already displayed a highly proactive agency in security policy and practice regarding humanitarian interventions in Kosovo in 1999 and in Sierra Leone in 2000.

Alongside the US, British air, naval and ground forces and assets took part in the initial allied attacks on Taliban and Al Qaeda forces in Afghanistan supporting the Northern Alliance from the first day of the attacks on 7 October 2001 onwards. Two Royal Navy submarines launched cruise missiles against Taleban and Al Qaeda targets, and Special Forces fought on the ground alongside their US counterparts. Subsequently, the UK played a lead role in establishing and maintaining the International Security Assistance Force (ISAF), which it did until 2014.

The decision to use force in Afghanistan

The relatively short time frame of the decision to launch strikes therefore lasts from 11 September 2001 as the triggering event to the first strikes on 7 October 2001. Blair saw a necessity for the use of force immediately after the triggering event. On 14 September 2001 he stated before parliament that the form of terrorism witnessed through 9/11 now represented an existential threat, since it demonstrated the perpetrators' capability of killing without discrimination and their willingness to "go further and use chemical, biological, or even nuclear weapons of mass destruction" (House of Commons, 2001a: 606). He then immediately established a link between the terrorist threat and a conventional, Westphalian threat by state actors in claiming that "We know, also, that there are groups of people, occasionally states, who will trade the technology and capability of such weapons" (House of Commons, 2001a: 606). Consequently, he stated the necessity to use extraordinary measures in the shape of military force against this existential threat: "It is time that this trade was exposed, disrupted, and stamped out. We have been warned by the events of 11 September, and we should act on the warning" (House of Commons, 2001a: 606).

Although the attacks took place in the US, Blair squarely implicated the UK on grounds of self-defence on the basis of the number of British citizens having died, as well as alliance solidarity and wider implications of the attacks having been attacks on fundamental beliefs and values. On 16 September Blair then openly stated for the first time that Britain and the US were at war with terrorism. In an interview held at Downing Street, which was broadcast in the US for CNN, he declared:

> Are we at war with the people who committed this terrible atrocity? Absolutely.... It is a war between the civilised world and fanaticism. We must put together a broad-based coalition to hound these people down and bring them to justice.
>
> (Webster *et al.*, 2001)

Blair's relatively bellicose remarks, with their frequent references to history as having taught the imperative to use force in certain circumstances, show that Blair's language relates to British strategic culture's specific identity and role

Analysing British decision processes 107

conceptions on the legitimate use of force by the state. In his television address issued the night before the beginning of the attacks on 6 October 2001, Blair stated that "we know that sometimes to safeguard peace we have to fight. Britain has learned that lesson many times before in our history" (Full transcript of Blair's remarks: *New York Times*, 2001). Blair's personal aversion of 'appeasement', which he adopted as a result of the West's inertia during the Bosnian War, is framed here as the product of British historical narratives. The decision to go to war was framed as something that was not optional but imperative, since extraordinary circumstances demand extraordinary measures.

Not only the time frame and the language employed in this securitisation process, but also its nature in terms of the actors and policy channels involved, suggest that it mirrored the characteristics of British strategic culture. According to an online article by *Guardian* journalists Ewen MacAskill and Michael White, the decision to deploy forces was taken almost single-handedly by then Prime Minister Tony Blair (also see Kampfner, 2004: 59; MacAskill and White, 2001; and Williams, 2006: 49, who share this assessment). According to the journalistic sources of MacAskill and White, which admittedly are only comprised of anonymous "White Hall planners" as well as "some ministers, MPs, officials and journalists", Blair only held two cabinet meetings, both of which were reportedly devoid of debate. Blair practiced a 'presidential style' of decision-making and did not consult widely before taking the decision.

The proactivity, autonomy and swiftness with which Blair acted are also discernible in his international agency after 9/11. According to Jason W. Davidson, Blair was convinced that the UK's special relationship with the US afforded him the unique opportunity to influence US policy before it was fully formed. Proactivity would therefore allow for a decisive British imprint on the allied reaction to 9/11 (Davidson, 2011: 106–107). Blair therefore sought to maximise his influence in Washington by persistently asking for British forces to take part in the attacks from the first day onwards, according to journalist John Kampfner (2004: 129). Aware of the British public's concern with the Bush administration's propensity for unilateralism, a key objective in this maximisation of influence over US policy was to forge as broad a coalition as possible and to seek the – at least tacit – approval of as many international actors as possible.

Blair's proactive engagement with the Bush administration then allowed him to assume a lead position within the coalition against terror, which in turn allowed Blair to forge this coalition in his way and thereby pre-empt an entirely unilateral approach by the US through engaging in intense shuttle diplomacy from 19 September onwards (Williams, 2006: 50). This shows that the decision to use military force against Al Qaeda and Taliban targets in Afghanistan reportedly did not follow express demands by the US but Blair proactively pushed this decision and led the UK to war almost single-handedly. This proactive and autonomous agency on both the domestic and the international level, which centred almost exclusively on the top executive of the UK government, and which took place in a comparatively short time frame, shows that the British securitisation process after 9/11 constitutes a relatively strong securitisation process which is in line with the relatively high proclivity towards the use of force previously identified in British strategic culture.

108   *Comparing decision processes on use of force*

Resonance of the decision to use force in Afghanistan

These words and actions of the immediate aftermath of 9/11 in the UK so far displayed the characteristics of British strategic culture. But in order to fully establish a link between strategic culture and the securitisation process, it is still necessary to assess how the public and other influential actors received these words and actions. Fortunately, there was some debate in Parliament and extensive commenting across the media in the run up to the first strikes, despite the short time frame of the decision to use force in Afghanistan. Several public opinion polls by Gallup and ICM also provide data on the wider public's reception to this decision.

In a special session of the House of Commons convened three days after the events of 9/11, the leader of the largest opposition party, the Conservatives, mostly echoed Blair's statements and expressly concurred with them. Iain Duncan Smith reiterated Blair's references to the UK's normative attachment to the transatlantic alliance based on narratives of common historical experiences as well as references to fundamental values being under attack. He also supported President Bush's description of 9/11 as an act of war:

> I have absolutely no hesitation in giving the prime minister my party's full support for his immediate pledge to stand shoulder to shoulder with our strongest friends and allies in the United States. Together, we must ensure that the perpetrators are hunted down and brought to justice, as he said.
>
> (House of Commons, 2001a: 607)

Speaking on behalf of the Liberal Democrats, which are traditionally a more pacifist party, Charles Kennedy also fully associated his party "with the proper sentiments that have been expressed so well by the prime minister and by the new leader of the Conservative Party" and reaffirmed that "this House stands shoulder to shoulder in full support of our American cousins" (House of Commons, 2001a: 610). He also stated that "It seems almost inevitable that there will be some sort of military response at some point" involving British service people (House of Commons, 2001a: 610). Blair's language regarding the UK's close ties with the US and the need for military action thus largely resonated with the leaders of the two main opposition parties, which suggests that reflects a strategic culture in which both are embedded.

These three statements were followed by a series of short questions and statements from other MPs as well as longer statements by Foreign Secretary Jack Straw and Defence Secretary Geoffrey Hoon. Although at this point the use of military force in Afghanistan was not explicitly put to debate and the main objective of all statements was to express sympathy to the American people and the relatives of the lost ones, most statements also commented on the prospect of military intervention either explicitly or implicitly. Of these, the vast majority out of the 43 MPs who made comments through statements or questions supported the prime minister's pledge to fully support the US in reacting to this event by military means. Three MPs voiced major reservations about the prospect of military action in general or in Afghanistan in particular, and one MP

Analysing British decision processes 109

voiced his personal disdain for President Bush. These MPs can be attributed to the 'Old Labour' camp. Their comments reveal a general disdain for the use of military force abroad and US foreign policy more generally, which may stem from the anti-imperialist roots of their party. Their negative assessment of the UK's policy towards Iraq over the preceding ten years also played a major role in informing their opposition towards an invasion of Afghanistan. All other MPs either supported any US-led military action outright or voiced their support but also mentioned certain caveats. The debate therefore revolved not as much around whether terrorism should be fought by military means but how it should be fought by military means and which emphasis these should be given relative to other measures that need to be taken to prevent future terrorist incidences.

Overall, this debate mirrors prior findings on UK strategic culture. A consensus quickly emerged on the general legitimacy of military force in the given situation. The only strong opposition came from a very small minority of Labour MPs who can be attributed to the 'Old Labour' camp and who share a tradition and an identity of being 'anti-establishment', i.e. strongly critical towards emerging political consensus in many other respects. All others shared the consensus that the UK had a special role to play given its special relationship, both in preventing the US from overreacting and going down a unilateral path and in augmenting the military firepower dedicated to the fight against terrorism. This consensus was often backed by direct references to historical experiences that underpin the relatively high proclivity towards the use of force that characterises contemporary British strategic culture. Many MPs referred to the experiences of terrorism in Northern Ireland,[1] appeasement in the run up to the Second World War,[2] the Falklands War, the allegedly premature end of the Gulf War and the UK's determination during the Korean War, which were all invoked to emphasise the importance of the UK proactively engaging threats in a determined, decisive and forceful manner, as it had done throughout its history[3] (House of Commons, 2001a).

These characteristics are also noticeable in the next crucial debate on the use of force in Afghanistan, which took place in the British House of Commons on 4 October 2001. As plans for military action now became clearer, this debate was more focused on the specific decision to use military force against Al Qaeda and Taliban forces in Afghanistan. The debate was marked by a great deal of unanimity. At its onset, Blair informed the House of evidence of Osama bin Laden and Al Qaeda being behind 9/11 and of the Taliban regime in Afghanistan providing the necessary means of a safe haven. He also revealed that the US already responded positively to his discussions with the Bush administration over concrete plans for a British involvement in military actions in Afghanistan. In the question and answer session that followed Blair's statement, the leader of the Conservative opposition once again gallantly concurred in a longer statement. He also revealed his anticipation of unanimity in the remainder of the debate in stating:

> So today we should reaffirm our single and collective purpose in this House. No excuses can be made, no justification sought and no help offered to those who would carry out such deeds. Simply put, let right be done.
>
> (House of Commons, 2001a: 678)

110   *Comparing decision processes on use of force*

Charles Kennedy, the leader of the Liberal Democrats, also made clear from the outset that his party fully supported the government's efforts to "root out international terrorism" (House of Commons, 2001a: 680). Once again, therefore, the leaders of the three biggest parties represented in the UK Parliament agreed on the government's course of action regarding the use of military force. However, in line with his party's traditionally more pacifist stance, Kennedy's statement also showed that his party took a more critical, albeit fully supportive, stance towards the plan to use military force in Afghanistan. Kennedy raised several points of particular importance to his party that he wished to clarify with the prime minister. He stressed the "overarching need to work within the broad framework of the United Nations" especially regarding "the strength of the evidence against bin Laden" in order to "reassure world opinion about the justice of impending military action" and he emphasised that advanced planning was needed to deal with the humanitarian crisis already unfolding and with the potential political and humanitarian consequences of removing the Taliban from power (House of Commons, 2001a: 680–682).

Other MPs overwhelmingly supported the decision to use military force as made autonomously by executive, with strong emphasis, especially from the political left, that it needs to be international and take into account humanitarian aspects, as well as strong emphasis mostly from the political right that the UK needs to act robustly in support of its valued key ally and that domestic aspects of counterterrorism also need to be taken into consideration. Labour MP Gerald Kaufman summed up this consensus by stating:

> Sometimes, there is a sanctimony about expressions of unity in the House, but on this occasion what has been said on both sides of the House has been completely sincere, is utterly necessary and should hearten the Government and the international coalition in the action that they are rightly planning to take.
>
> (House of Commons, 2001a: 703)

On 1 November 2001, the House of Commons therefore held an official vote on Britain's participation in Operation Enduring Freedom (OEF) which the government won by 373 to 13 votes (Davidson, 2011: 110). This parliamentary resonance therefore shows that across the political spectrum in the UK one can discern the effects of a widely shared strategic culture containing norms that are conducive to the use of force in a robust but proportionate and targeted way, in close cooperation with key allies, and under the directorate of those in the highest echelons of the executive. This mirrors the findings on British strategic culture identified in Chapter 5.

It will now be evaluated whether the impact of a distinct and widely shared strategic culture on the British decision to use force in Afghanistan through the resonance of this securitisation move can also be discerned in the media. The three newspapers selected for analysis in this section are *The Times*, the largest and most established centre-right newspaper in the UK with a circulation of approximately 713,000, the centre-left the *Guardian* which has a circulation of approximately 400,000 and the biggest tabloid newspaper, the Murdoch-owned

Analysing British decision processes   111

Sun with a circulation of 2,400,000 (as of January 2013). These newspapers were scanned for opinion pieces relating to debates over military action in response to 9/11 between 12 September and 12 October 2001.

The Times featured 35 commentaries on the decision to use force within this time period. The large majority were strongly or moderately supportive of the decision. In this analysis, only four articles were categorised as moderately critical, one as strongly critical and another one article as neutral. The other 29 articles were classified as either moderately or strongly supportive. Most of these print commentaries called for united support by public opinion in Britain, in other Western democracies and in the Muslim world for the American-led fight against terrorism by military means. Many were also critical of moderating voices within the UK, accusing these of appeasement. Most of the criticism therefore addressed a perceived over-intellectualisation and inaction by more left-wing figures in other media as well as in politics. There was even a considerable amount of impatience with the US acting not soon enough and allies not showing enough support during the limbo-phase before the 7 October attacks (see, for example, Righter, 2001). A strong belief in the necessity and Britain's capability to fight terrorism effectively through military force can be found particularly succinctly in Michael Gove's commentary titled "This is war, and it will demand our steel" from 18 September 2001:

> It is in the nature of terror that it can never be eradicated altogether … but it can be driven back inch by inch, as Britain has proved from Kenya to Malaysia. And if we do not? Then the West consents to its own suicide, more slowly, but just as surely, as any of the bombers determined on our destruction.

In *The Guardian* on the other hand, commentaries were considerably more mixed and multifaceted, but became more conciliatory and supportive of the US's and Blair's drive for military action against the Taliban and Al Qaeda in Afghanistan and elsewhere towards the advent of military strikes, although strong criticism resurfaced immediately after the launch of the first strikes. Of the 40 opinion pieces that were found in the period between 12 September and 12 October 2001, 20 could be considered critical of the decision, of which ten were strongly critical, while 19 expressed support of the decision, seven of which did so in strong terms. Critics and supporters therefore held each other in balance. Commentators such as Richard Norton-Taylor (2001) Hugo Young (2001) and Martin Woollacott (2001) voiced early fears in the *Guardian* that the US would overreact and ignore US policies in the Middle East that played into the hands of extremists. Arguably, George Monbiot was the most fervent critic of the impending decision to use force in Afghanistan, arguing that "The governments of Britain and America are using the disaster in New York to reinforce the very policies which have helped to cause the problem" and that "Dissent is most necessary just when it is hardest to voice" (Monbiot, 2001).

Yet the closer the start of military action came, the more conciliatory were the *Guardian*'s comments. Self-critical of traditional left-wing stances, Polly Toynbee for instance wrote that "old fixed attitudes towards the US and many

112 Comparing decision processes on use of force

other nations need to be suspended" since the enormity of recent events may evoke "fundamental recalibrations of old positions" (Toynbee, 2001). This echoes the sentiments of many *Guardian* commentators. Despite a more critical inclination towards US foreign policy an increasing number struck conciliatory tones at the Bush administration in the aftermath of 9/11. Yet also at this stage not all *Guardian* commentators shared this conciliatory stance towards those in favour of full-scale military action. Fervent critics such as George Monbiot, Peter A. Hall, Mike Marqusee, Madeleine Bunting and Seumas Milne maintained the line that US plans for military action were driven by a desire for retaliation and constituted another act in a series of ill-fated US interventions, advocating for a diverse and not always fully spelt-out array of non-military alternatives.

But on 8 October, the day after the first strikes against the Taliban were launched, a lead article in the *Guardian*'s online edition titled "The World at War" showed itself to be strongly supportive of Blair's decisions. It also mentioned the need for a comprehensive strategy in which non-military means accompany military action, but concluded:

> Much of the world remains deeply sceptical about this campaign, to put it mildly. Naturally, also, many will fear that its goals are unachievable. Nevertheless, judged by his words last night, Mr Bush understands these truths much better than some of his critics have given him credit for.... It is now for the US military and their allies to put those words into action. Nothing in the world is more important right now than that they succeed.
>
> (*Guardian*, 2001a)

These lines best sum up the general stance of those other *Guardian* commentators such as Tim Garden, Hugo Young, Martin Woollacott and Polly Toynbee in the month following 9/11. While roughly half of all *Guardian* commentators maintained their critical stance towards military action until its launch and beyond, the other half backed Blair's efforts in light of the extraordinary circumstances of 9/11's immediate aftermath, despite the *Guardian*'s traditionally critical stance towards US military action and war-rhetoric.

All of the 23 opinion articles analysed in the *Sun*, meanwhile, were hugely bellicose and supportive of war. The Sun's opinion pieces specifically pointed out Blair's positive image in the US and the gratitude he received there for his decisiveness in backing Bush. At the same time, the Sun was very careful to point out that this was not a war against Islam. Against the backdrop of caution towards xenophobia and religious hatred all other commentaries fully focused on praising the US's and the UK's leadership under Bush and Blair as well as stoking up patriotic sentiments in awe of the US's and the UK's military capabilities. These sentiments were coupled with criticisms bordering ridicule of the political left in both countries as well as the more cautionary leadership of European allies. On 15 September, for example:

> This is the A-team of world politics. If Clinton were still president, America would be saddled with the likes of the hopeless Al Gore or the unimpressive

Analysing British decision processes   113

Madeleine Allbright ... Bush will do exactly what is right for America and the world.

(*Sun*, 2001b)

The article then went on to express doubts about other European allies' commitment to impending military operations against terrorism: "Can we rely on our EU and NATO partners to do the same? The world will be watching the deeds of France, Germany and Italy over the coming days..." (*Sun*, 2001b).

Broad public support for military action in Afghanistan against Taliban and Al-Qaeda targets can also be identified in the weighted opinion polls conducted after 9/11. A Gallup poll on 14 and 15 September revealed that 79 per cent of British respondents compared to 73 per cent of French and 53 per cent of German respondents agreed that their country "should take part in military actions against terrorists with the United States", after having been informed that "Some countries and all NATO member states have agreed to participate in any military action against the terrorists responsible for the attacks or against those countries harbouring the terrorists" (Gallup International poll of 14/15 September 2001; see Gordon, 2001; and archived version by Canadian Centres for Teaching Peace Inc., 2001). Likewise, an Ipsos MORI poll also reveals that nearly three quarters of all respondents backed a British involvement in military action, which gradually subsided to two-thirds of all respondents by November 2001. These general public opinion polls therefore show that there was strong public support for military action against terrorist organisations and countries harbouring them immediately after 9/11 as well as throughout the three months following 9/11.

A *Guardian*/ICM poll of 14–16 September 2001 offers more disaggregated data on public support for military action immediately after 9/11 (see Appendix, Table A3). It shows that two in three respondents backed the use of military force against terrorist organisations, and 59 per cent supported military action against countries harbouring terrorists. Some 63 per cent were also prepared to see British troops, ships and planes take part in such military strikes. Only 14 per cent rejected a military response outright. Respondents did not, however, embrace the prospect of a long, drawn-out war with similar enthusiasm. Only 49 per cent supported military action against state sponsors of terrorism "if it meant that the United States and NATO (including the UK) got into a war" (ICM Research/*Guardian*, 2001: 2). Public support for the government's decision to firmly back the US in its military endeavours after 9/11 also expressed itself through strong approval rates of both Blair's close cooperation with the US in the days after 9/11 and of the way President Bush dealt with the crisis. Only 14 per cent thought that during the crisis Blair "has got too close to the Americans" while 76 per cent thought he got the relationship "about right" (ICM Research/The Guardian, 2001: 2). Some 76 per cent also thought Bush handled the aftermath of 9/11 "very well" or "quite well" (ICM Research/*Guardian*, 2001: 2).

Table A3 (see Appendix) also shows that these strong approval rates for the Blair government's course of action applied to respondents of all party orientations, age groups and genders. Labour and Conservative voters were equally in favour of seeing military attacks on countries that harbour terrorists, and there

114　*Comparing decision processes on use of force*

was even greater support among Labour voters (76 per cent) than Conservatives (69 per cent) for military strikes against terrorist organisations. However, as could be expected, Liberal Democrat voters were more sceptical, with only 59 per cent backing military strikes. Interestingly, the young showed themselves to be more belligerent than the old, with 74 per cent of 25-to-34-year-olds supporting military action compared with 60 per cent of over-65s. Women also turned out to be a lot less inclined towards military action and war than men, with only 58 per cent supporting military action against terrorists and only 43 per cent doing so if it meant that the UK "got into a war" (Travis, 2001). Overall, however, the resonance was widely positive, which suggests that the securitisation move and its resultant decision to use force took place solidly within the margins of British strategic culture. The *Guardian* was right to comment on its poll results on 18 September that although "Poll results like these always need an accompanying health warning" since "at such times, people want to pull together and to feel they are saying the right thing", a mood which "could change further down the line", there was "no disputing the bottom line. On this one, Tony Blair is definitely speaking for Britain" (*Guardian*, 2001b).

Analysing the British decision to introduce counterterrorist legislation after 9/11

The previous chapter suggested that those norms of the strategic cultures under analysis that concern the domestic use of force for the provision of security have quite similar expressions to norms concerning the use of force in general, including the use of military force. One can therefore assume that strategic culture nonetheless provides a structurally conditioning formal cause to differences in expressions of post-9/11 state behaviour regarding the use of force within the domestic policy domain, even though this cause is likely to be less strongly pronounced in this domain than in the two other, more externally-oriented policy domains. In the case of British strategic culture, these norms are conducive to comparatively strong securitisation processes regarding domestic counterterrorism legislation.

The UK government's domestic response to 9/11 came in the shape of the Anti-Terrorism, Crime and Security Act 2001 (ATCSA). With the introduction of this package of counterterrorist legislation, the UK government sought to prevent the occurrence of terrorist acts and to fight terrorist activities in the UK. However, only one year before, the New Labour government passed the Terrorism Act 2000 "intended to be the last word on anti-terrorism powers and procedures for the foreseeable future", according to Liberty (House of Lords Constitution Committee, 2009: 77). Since the Terrorism Act 2000 already afforded the state far-reaching new coercive powers for the fight against domestic terrorism, the ATCSA's main focus lay in compensating for the perceived shortcomings of existing legislation and the Terrorism Act 2000 in particular.

Nonetheless, the ATCSA represents a comparatively far-reaching piece of emergency legislation. It introduced a pre-charge detention of up to 28 days, which is by far the longest possible period of arrest without formal pre-trial

Analysing British decision processes 115

confinement in all five countries analysed in this book. Another key security concern which the act addressed was the government's inability to deport foreign nationals suspected of terrorism because the European Convention on Human Rights did not allow for the forced deportation of these individuals to their countries of origin, as they were likely to face torture or the death penalty due to these countries' poor human rights records. The government, seeing itself faced with suspected terrorists that could neither be prosecuted nor deported, created new provisions that allowed for the indefinite detention of foreign nationals deemed a threat to national security. After Parliament passed the Act it continued to be the subject of debate among judges, legal experts and civil right groups until its replacement by the Prevention of Terrorism Act 2005.[4] Its centrepiece is the derogation from Article 5(1) of the European Convention on Human Rights (ECHR), which spells out the right to a fair trial and to liberty unless convicted, on grounds of there being a state of emergency after 9/11.

The executive decision to introduce counterterrorist legislation after 9/11

Relative to the depth and scale of the ATCSA, the time frame within which it was enacted can also be considered extraordinary. The decision to introduce tough new laws to fight terrorism at home came within days of 9/11. In the first parliamentary debate after 9/11 on 14 September 2001, Blair already signalled his intention to introduce new anti-terrorism laws by announcing that "We need to look once more, nationally and internationally, at extradition laws and the mechanisms for international justice..." (House of Commons, 2001a: 606). In an interview with BBC reporter David Frost in the BBC's *Breakfast with Frost* programme on 30 September, Blair then announced to "bring forward a package of measures for the House of Commons" in the next four to six weeks that would include measures to "speed up the laws on extradition", "to make sure that our asylum process is not abused by terrorists" and measures to prevent Bureau de Change from laundering money for terrorists (Frost, 2001). Frost asked further about "that surprising remark" by Lord Justice Woolf "that human rights take precedence over protecting the lives of people from terrorists and so on", adding: "you don't believe that, do you?" (Frost, 2001). Blair replied: "No I think our first duty has got to be to protect our citizens.." (Frost, 2001). This interview exemplifies how the media, and by that extent the wider public, brought the issue of far-reaching new anti-terrorism legislation to the government's attention as a matter of course. And when the media pressed the issue on the government, it concurrently saw the issue as a matter of course.[5]

Charged with developing draft legislation on this matter, Home Secretary David Blunkett laid out the details of his first draft bill before the House of Commons on 15 October. Blunkett underlined his belief in a broad consensus about the need for swift action when he stated: "I think that we all accept that there is a compelling need for more effective powers to exclude and remove suspected terrorists from our country" (House of Commons, 2001b: 924). At this stage he still expressly believed that derogation might not be necessary, but he already signalled that:

116 *Comparing decision processes on use of force*

it may well be necessary, using article 15, to derogate from article 5 of the European convention. That would allow the detention of foreign nationals whom we intend to remove from the country, and who are considered a threat to national security.

(House of Commons, 2001b: 924)

In this first government statement on new anti-terrorism laws before the House of Commons one can therefore recognise that Blunkett thought of their intro-duction as much as a matter of course for the UK as did Blair and, at least to their minds, as did most other MPs.

This firm stance on the state's coercive anti-terrorism capacities also revealed itself during the ATCSA's parliamentary passage. Blunkett officially introduced the first bill to the House of Commons on 12 November 2001. The day before, Blunkett issued the so-called "Human Rights Act 1998 (Designated Derogation) Order 2001" (Blunkett, 2001). This executive order would come into force on 13 November 2001 and cease to be effective after 40 days unless both Houses of Parliament approved it within this time frame. With this derogation order, Blunkett effectively declared a state of emergency in the UK, which allowed the government to immediately detain terror suspects without trial and indefinitely. He was allowed to do so without prior parliamentary approval on the basis of a so-called 'statutory instrument', which is the UK's legal format for secondary legislation, or in other words, laws that the government can enact on the basis of other laws. In this case, the government interpreted Article 15(1) of the ECHR to allow the government to disregard Article 5(1) of the ECHR as incorporated into British law through the Human Rights Act 1998, which spells out the right to be brought before a court following arrest, and the right to liberty unless con-victed. Article 15(1) of the ECHR allows for such derogations in cases of "public emergency threatening the life of the nation" and the government claimed that after 9/11 the UK faced a terrorist threat amounting to such a public emergency. Since the derogation order would automatically lapse after 40 days should Parliament not pass it into law, one can assume that Blunkett also issued the order with the intention to speed up the process of parliamentary approval to his draft bill. It shows that the government had little hesitation to invest itself with extraordinary coercive powers on the basis of a proclaimed emergency situation after 9/11.

On 19 November the House of Commons held its first official debate on Blunkett's bill. Already in this session, the majority of MPs voted to approve the government's derogation order (House of Commons, 2001d: 147). In his opening statement, Blunkett justified his actions on the grounds that "Circum-stances and public opinion demanded urgent and appropriate action after the 11 September attacks on the World Trade Centre and the Pentagon" (House of Commons, 2001d: 22). Ultimately, Parliament abandoned the government's plans to turn incitement of religious hatred into a new criminal offence. It also added several 'sunset clauses' to the bill, which ensured that unless Parliament or the highest court of appeals regularly reviewed and reapproved its most contro-versial elements, such as the detention provisions, these would automatically expire after a certain period. Aside from this the final product largely resembled

Analysing British decision processes 117

the government's original plans. The ATCSA received royal assent on 14 December 2001. Five days later, the first foreign nationals were interned under the act (Anti-Terrorism, Crime and Security Act 2001, 2009).

Resonance of the decision to introduce counterterrorist legislation after 9/11

In contrast to decisions on military intervention overseas there is considerably more room for discussion in decisions over domestic anti-terrorism legislation. The state action under debate does not constitute soldiers being sent overseas to engage enemies but it involves passing legislation on the basis of which a wide array of domestic law-enforcement agencies act in a multitude of different ways against a diverse set of actors and threats, some of which are more immediate and others of which are more potentially present. The structural conditioning power of strategic culture is therefore less pronounced in this policy domain. But the resonance in parliament, the media and public opinion can nevertheless be expected to reflect a discernible conditioning impact in the shape of a strategic culture that is relatively permissive of far-reaching state measures involving the domestic use of force, and especially coercion, for the provision of national security.

The complexity of an anti-terrorism bill inherently inflates the scope of debates as it automatically generates more questions over details to be addressed by Parliament. This section will therefore focus on the most crucial parliamentary debates. It will also focus on the most contentious issues of derogation and indefinite detention as these reflect the main arguments provided for and against the government's planned domestic actions against terrorism, which revolved around the issue of balancing civil liberties with security from terrorist attacks. Despite the large volume of this debate one can discern a coherent preference for robust laws which potentially compromise on civil liberties but professedly allowed for more determined state action against residents of the UK involved in terrorist activity.

On 4 October, MPs generally welcomed Blair's announcement that "In the next few weeks, the Home Secretary intends to introduce a package of legislation" on new state anti-terrorism powers (House of Commons, 2001a: 675). Leader of the Opposition Iain Duncan Smith commented on this by declaring that "In the context of 11 September we will certainly give our support to whatever measures are justified and we will scrutinise them in the usual way", adding that the ECHR ought not to prevent the Home Secretary from deporting individuals dangerous to national security (House of Commons, 2001a: 677). The leader of the Liberal Democrats, Charles Kennedy, also offered Blair his party's general support. He stated that "any forthcoming legislation must meet two tests" (House of Commons, 2001a: 680). It must exclusively concern the fight against terrorism and it must not "compromise civil liberties to such an extent that the terrorist is seen to win by default". He also supported an extension of existing discrimination laws to include religion and he expressed that "we will certainly support moves on extradition..." (House of Commons, 2001a: 680), adding later that "Surely it is not beyond our wit to fashion a system that is both fair and expeditious" (House of Commons, 2001a: 706). One

118 *Comparing decision processes on use of force*

can therefore discern that at this stage Blair and Blunkett were right to assume that most other primary political actors in the UK saw the adoption of new anti-terrorism powers after 9/11 as much as a matter of course as they did.

On 19 November, in the first debate after Blunkett introduced his bill into Parliament one week earlier, there was considerably more protest, especially among Labour back-bench MPs. The debate over whether Parliament should proceed with the bill and whether it should accept the government's derogation order lasted from 3.30 p.m. to midnight. A key concern and criticism for many MPs, including Conservative MPs, was that they were not given enough time to review the bill before it was put to debate in the House of Commons, which gave the impression that the government intended to rush it through Parliament. Others mostly from the Labour and Liberal Democrats camps complained that the UK was as much unique among the state parties to the ECHR as it was wrong to declare a state of emergency threatening the life of the nation, since, as Labour MP Mark Fisher argued, "We saw people flocking to early showings of 'Harry Potter', and others doing their Christmas shopping. We also saw the trains at least trying to run on time. The life of this nation is not at risk" (House of Commons, 2001d: 76). The vociferous and frequent criticisms coming mostly from the Labour back benches required the Home Secretary to defend his position robustly and repeatedly. Other Labour MPs often came to his assistance. Labour MP Kevin Hughes, for example, asked Blunkett:

> Does my right hon. Friend find it bizarre – as I do – that the yoghurt and muesli-eating, *Guardian*-reading fraternity are only too happy to protect the human rights of people engaged in terrorist acts, but never once do they talk about the human rights of those who are affected by them?
>
> (House of Commons, 2001d: 30)

Tellingly, the Conservative opposition largely concurred with this position. It mostly criticised the clauses on incitement of religious hatred as a restriction of free speech and the lack of mechanisms for regular parliamentary or judicial review of the provisions i.e. through so-called 'sunset clauses'. But the issue of indefinite detention based on derogation from Article 5 of the ECHR was criticised from the other direction. Shadow Home Secretary Oliver Letwin reiterated his argument that the UK should renegotiate its support for the ECHR altogether in order to be in a position to deport known terrorists irrespective of the human rights situation in the country to which they are to be deported (House of Commons, 2001d: 50). On the question over how to deal with terrorism suspects who can be neither put to trial nor deported to their countries of origin, the Conservative Party proposed the even more drastic measure to permanently opt out from that clause of the ECHR which bans deportations of suspects to countries in which they might face certain death.

Likewise, the Home Affairs Spokesperson for the Liberal Democrats, Simon Hughes, voiced his party's general support for the bill on the grounds that it rightly contained "additional powers to deal with terrorists" and "an emergency timetable to put those powers into statute within days" (House of Commons, 2001d: 56). However, this support was conditional on provisions for regular parliamentary

Analysing British decision processes 119

review and re-enactment. The parties thus aligned with the government's strong securitisation process on the basis that established norms allowed for exceptionally coercive state practice given the urgent need for action against a major threat.

It is therefore not entirely surprising that, despite the vocal criticism of mostly Labour back-benchers and the lively debate that took place in this session, the votes taking place at the end of the session all turned out decisively in the government's favour. The House of Commons accepted the motion to carry the bill forward into Committee stage by 460 votes in favour and only seven votes opposed, four of which came from Labour MPs and three from Conservative MPs, while all Liberal Democrat MPs alongside a few Labour and Conservative MPs did not cast their vote (House of Commons, 2001d: 115). The motion to approve the derogation order from Article 5(1) of the ECHR, meanwhile, passed with 331 votes in favour and 74 opposed. All 47 Liberal Democrat MPs present at the debate and 15 Labour MPs voted against the derogation order while only five Conservative MPs cast their vote, two of whom voted in favour and three against the motion (House of Commons, 2001e: 440). A very similar voting pattern emerged on 21 November 2001, when the House of Commons approved a clause by which the Home Secretary can issue a certificate against individuals he reasonably believes to be a risk to national security and reasonably suspects to be a terrorist as well as a clause allowing for the indefinite detention of those suspects without charge (House of Commons, 2001e: 406–407). One can therefore see that although the bill stirred controversy in the House of Commons, the main opposition either voted alongside the government or abstained but it did not stand in the way of drastic new anti-terrorism legislation in the UK after 9/11.

Outright opposition came from Labour back-bench MPs and at some stages from the Liberal Democrats, who argued that the actual situation of danger did not legitimise the government's conscious suspension of human rights standards in its practice of indefinite detention. Other MPs either argued that the government's approach was balanced with regards to human rights or, in the case of many Conservative MPs, that the government should go further in neglecting human rights concerns in order to allow for the more effective provision of security through enhanced deportation powers. This largely positive parliamentary resonance indicates that a strategic culture carrying norms conducive to far-reaching coercive domestic powers of the state underlay the securitisation process, which generated the new legislation and its resonance.

Since the issue of domestic anti-terrorism legislation is not as newsworthy as that of warfare, at least from a journalistic perspective, there were also fewer commentaries on this issue in the press. *The Times* featured 12 articles on this issue between 12 September and 13 December 2001, most of which strongly supported an extension of domestic governmental powers for anti-terrorism. In fact, there are strong indications that *The Times'* comments pressed the government into action on this issue. The short commentary of 15 September titled "Still a Haven – Terrorists Are still Using London to Plot Evil Overseas" answered to Blunkett challenging *The Times* the previous day on the BBC's *Today* programme to supply details of *The Times*'s repeated charge laid against him that Islamic militants were still active in Britain (*The Times*, 2001). In the commentary, *The Times* replied that "Despite fine promises and emergency

120   *Comparing decision processes on use of force*

legislation, Britain is still home to hundreds of extremists who have made this country one of the centres for the violent transnational network that inspired and encouraged the barbarism in New York and Washington" (*The Times*, 2001). Blunkett then quoted these exact words from *The Times* on 19 November in order to justify the speed and scope of his anti-terrorism bill (House of Commons, 2001d: 25). Not all commentaries then welcomed the proposals put forward by Blunkett, but commentators Mick Hume and Michael Gove also warned of civil liberties being curtailed. But two thirds of all commentaries on this issue that could be identified supported the proposed legislation, all but one even strongly so. It is also notable that the frequent commentaries on this topic written collectively by *The Times* consistently supported the bill. One can therefore speak of *The Times* as one of the chief proponents of the anti-terrorism legislation implemented in the UK after 9/11.

Of the 13 articles identified in the *Guardian*, on the other hand, only one article can be categorised as supportive of new anti-terrorism legislation in the UK. Of the other 11 articles, seven are classified as strongly critical. The *Guardian* revealed its critical stance towards anti-terrorism legislation already at the outset of the ensuing debate. Already in late November and early October, before details of proposed new legislation were known, the newspaper argued in generic terms that emergency legislation enacted in response to terrorist events threatens to erode civil liberties rather than providing more security. Although some articles then lauded the restraints and safeguards which especially the House of Lords has managed to impose on the legislation, most articles became more critical the more details about the proposed legislation emerged.

In the *Sun*, meanwhile, two articles can be considered moderately critical, one moderately supportive and the other five strongly supportive of the government's introduction of new anti-terrorism legislation. Initially, the commentaries focused on the terrorist threat to the UK and the need for stronger government powers to remove individuals deemed terrorists. One commentary even threatened that "The Government would NEVER EVER be forgiven by voters if a terror attack was carried out here by people who had enjoyed our hospitality" ("Last Hours"; *Sun*, 2001a). Overall, the *Sun* first urged the government to introduce new anti-terrorism laws and then endorsed the government's efforts at acquiring these new powers.

Opinion polls indicate that the general public largely supported the government's new anti-terrorism powers acquired after 9/11. This is in line with prior findings on norms regarding the domestic use of force by the state prevalent in the UK, which suggests that the domestic securitisation process of 9/11 in the UK resonated positively with the wider population due to a strategic culture that supports such robust expansions of state power to counter perceived terrorist threats.

Analysing the British decision process regarding the use of force in Iraq 2003

Chapter 5 concluded that the 'proactive-robust' nature of British strategic culture may include the pre-emptive use of force against perceived threats in the

Analysing British decision processes 121

range of modes of the use of force that is considered legitimate. These norms derived from an identity conception of a country with the necessary seniority and confidence to play an active and positive role in actively reshaping the world for the better alongside the US, as its most valued and powerful ally as well as with the support of strong international institutions and laws. In the case of the run-up to the Iraq War, these characteristics can be assumed to have informed its country's executive in initiating a strong, swift and persuasive securitisation process which receives positive resonance from most segments of the population and which results in a large-scale contribution to the US-led war effort. The UK indeed contributed the largest troop contingents beside the US. Yet the ease with which the government could persuade the UK Parliament, the media and the public of its case for war as well as the extent of their consent or discontent remains a subject of debate to this day, as do the merits of the Blair and Bush governments' decision as such. This section will show that the UK's securitisation process in the run-up to the invasion of Iraq in March 2003 as well as its resonance in parliament, the media and the public at large mirrors the pre-existent characteristics of British strategic culture as identified in Chapter 5. However, the process also demonstrated the limits of state actions which this strategic culture is able to support since actors positioned themselves precariously close to these boundaries.

The decision to use force in Iraq

The UK government's decision to go to war with Iraq alongside the US cannot be broken down to one particular point in time but it proceeded rather like a sequence of events operating like a funnel of choices that gradually narrowed in on the option to go to war against Iraq. Since the Gulf War 1990–1991 the UK pursued a policy of containment towards Saddam Hussein's regime in Iraq in order to protect parts of the Iraqi population, the region and ultimately the world at large from the continuing threat which the UK still saw the regime to pose. The US drove this policy in tandem with the UK, and the UN Security Council sanctioned the policy, which rested on regular UN weapons inspections, sanctions and a no-fly zone enforced by the US and the UK through air force (Bluth, 2004).

The events of 9/11 alerted many policymakers in the US and the UK to what they perceived as a combined threat of rogue states, WMD (weapons of mass destruction) and terrorism (Bluth, 2004; Davidson, 2011). While they may have alerted the neoconservatives within the Bush administration the most, Blair also stated during a judicial inquiry in July 2003 that with 9/11 he saw a need to realign his mind-set towards this perceived combination of threats and he decided he had "to deal with this because otherwise the threat will grow" (quoted from Bluth, 2004: 874). Reportedly, Bush announced his decision to go to war in April 2002, during a meeting with Blair on his ranch in Crawford, Texas (Kampfner, 2004: 167). There are reports that the British government's decision to participate in the Iraq War rested largely with Blair, and that he settled on the need for the UK to support a US-led war to change the regime in Iraq also by April 2002, in preparation to and during his meeting with Bush in

122 *Comparing decision processes on use of force*

Texas, where the two spent a lot of time in private (Bluth, 2004: 875; Kampfner, 2004: 168). One can therefore claim with relative certainty that the combined triggering events of 9/11 and the US government's subsequent determination to move from containment to regime change by force provided the impulse for the British government's decision.

Furthermore, there are reports that Blair passed the ultimate point of no return on this decision at the end of February 2003. By this time it became increasingly clear that the Security Council would not pass a UK-sponsored draft resolution explicitly authorising the use of force against Iraq. According to Blair's leading biographer Anthony Seldon, Bush then gave Blair the opportunity to withdraw his country's offer to participate in the war but Blair refused (Davidson, 2011: 134; Seldon *et al.*, 2008: 161). On 10 March the French president publicly removed any last doubts about his intention to veto a resolution authorising the use of force in Iraq. Nonetheless, on 17 March Blair asked the House of Commons for support for his government's decision to disarm Iraq by force. One can therefore assume that the time frame of the British government's decision to use military force in Iraq lasts from late March and early April 2002 to February 2003 and that the decision rested with the highest authority of the British executive. As presumed, these scope characteristics – the relatively early moment at which Blair jumped on the US-driven campaign for war and the autonomy with which he acted in this regard – are in line with the characteristics of a strategic culture with a moderately high proclivity towards the use of force favouring short and swift decision procedures.

However, within this time frame one can observe a high frequency of instances in which the Blair government attempted to establish the case for war to the British public. The British government could therefore not easily securitise a threat of Saddam Hussein to his own people, the region and the world at large, including the UK and its allies. Especially in contrast to the American context, this required repeated efforts in the UK. These efforts also differed in their nature from their American counterparts. The securitisation moves placed more emphasis on the premise of an existential threat which Saddam posed to humanity at large rather than of an imminent threat to national security (Bluth, 2004). At the end of Blair's visit to Texas he declared in a speech that since 9/11:

> we must be prepared to act where terrorism or weapons of mass destruction (WMD) threaten us.... Not just in Afghanistan but elsewhere. If necessary the action should be military and again, if necessary and justified, it should involve regime change.
>
> (Blair, 2002)

Already then he referred to the British interventions in Kosovo, Sierra Leone and Afghanistan, adding that "Britain is immensely proud of the part our forces have played and with the results but I can honestly say the people most pleased have been the people living under the regime in question" (Blair, 2002).

The British government published two documents which formed the cornerstone of Blair's securitisation efforts: the 24 September 2002 document "Iraq's Weapons of Mass Destruction: The Assessment of the British Government",

Analysing British decision processes 123

commonly known as the September Dossier, and the 3 February 2003 briefing document "Iraq – Its Infrastructure of Concealment, Deception and Intimidation", commonly known as the Iraq Dossier (UK Government, 2002, 2003). Both documents outlined details of the government's claim regarding the threat of Iraqi WMDs. The first document, commonly known as the 'September Dossier', contains the notorious claim that Iraqi WMDs could be deployed within 45 minutes of an order to do so. On the day of its publication the House of Commons convened to discuss its contents. In the first statement of this debate, Blair argued: "We know, again from our history, that diplomacy not backed by the threat of force has never worked with dictators and never will" (House of Commons, 2002b: 5). These interlinkages of humanitarian arguments, with WMD-threat claims and references to British history bestowing the UK with a leadership role in international affairs, form the essence of Blair's securitisation process in the run-up to the Iraq War as well as his general world view and the main tenets of British strategic culture.

Amid growing scepticism of the documents' validity, Blair passionately reiterated his case for the war to the House of Commons one last time on 18 March, and two days later the invasion began. In his statement, he spoke at length about the Munich Agreement of 1938 and the importance of pre-emption in tumultuous times, before reiterating his threat case (House of Commons, 2003c: 767–768). Behind the scenes, reportedly, the Labour Party's inner circle spent the whole day meeting pre-categorised wavering MPs in their private rooms in the Houses of Parliament in order to present them with arguments which were tailor-made to appeal to their specific category (Kampfner, 2004: 306–307).

Resonance of the decision to use force in Iraq

Just as the securitisation process leading up to the Iraq War covered a relatively wide time span and revealed efforts of an intense nature, so its resonance could be found in public debates throughout the period in which the decision was under discussion. It involved a wide array of actors, stirred up heated exchanges and revealed deep divisions over this subject.

Already in the House of Commons debate on 24 September 2002 the frontlines in the parliamentary debates over the Iraq War became discernible. After Blair's statement, Iain Duncan Smith, as the Leader of the Opposition, supported Blair in seeing Saddam Hussein as "a threat to Britain's national security and the wider international order" (House of Commons, 2002b: 7). However, he based his arguments more on the immediate threat to the UK by claiming that Saddam had the means, the mentality and the motive to strike against Britain, since Iraq was "self-sufficient in biological weapons" and 3,900 British service personnel were "in range of the missiles that Saddam possesses today" (House of Commons, 2002b: 7–8). The opposition Conservatives therefore signalled early on that they supported the government's course (see also Davidson, 2011: 142; Riddell, 2004: 203).

Even the leader of the Liberal Democrats, Charles Kennedy, granted the government at this stage that "There is, of course, general consensus that Iraq constitutes a grotesque, amoral regime, and that that must be dealt with" (House of

124 *Comparing decision processes on use of force*

Commons, 2002b: 9). But he also demanded that the House of Commons would get to vote before any military action begins and that the UN had absolute supremacy over this issue, thus asking Blair to resists calls for precipitate action. Kennedy also spoke of regime-change as an "ill-defined" notion, warning that it would set "a dangerous precedent in international affairs" (House of Commons, 2002b: 10). Nevertheless, his statement signalled that under certain conditions the Liberal Democrats might also support a war against Iraq.

The real danger for the government, however, came from the Labour party's own ranks. The prime minister spoke for one and a half hours during the parliamentary recall and he took 25 interventions. After this question and answer session, Labour MP Tam Dalyell asked the Speaker of the House Michael Martin to allow for a vote on the motion "That this House declines to support a war against Iraq using the royal prerogative unless it has been authorised by both the United Nations Security Council and a motion carried in this House" (House of Commons, 2002b: 24). After the speaker rejected his request, the House of Commons held a so-called Adjournment debate, which is a debate on an open issue. Although this debate did not entail a vote, several members held a vote anyway and 64 MPs symbolically voted against the government's motion "That the House do now adjourn", while six voted in favour (House of Commons, 2002b: 154). Of all 64 votes cast against the motion, 63 votes came from Labour MPs and MPs from Labour's smaller party-affiliates while one vote came from the Liberal Democrats (House of Commons, 2002b: 155). The debate revealed the risk of an unholy alliance between back-benchers from all major parties of the House of Commons forming if the government decided to pursue military action without express authorisation by the United Nations.

The government faced an even bigger rebellion by Labour MPs during a debate on 26 February 2003. Only three months earlier, on 25 November 2002, 30 Labour MPs alongside all Liberal Democrat MPs and ten MPs from smaller parties voted in favour of a motion which would require a second, more explicit Security Council resolution besides Resolution 1441, before military action could be taken (House of Commons, 2002c: 129). Although the motion was defeated by 451 to 83 votes, it revealed a core of 30–40 Labour back-benchers opposed to the war. This time, Labour MP Chris Smith tabled a cross-party motion to add the line "but finds the case for military action against Iraq as yet unproven" at the end of the main motion broadly supporting the government's plans to disarm Iraq by force (House of Commons, 2003c: 285). At the end of a heated six hour debate, a majority of 393 MPs rejected the motion to declare the case for war to be as yet unproven, while 199 supported it (House of Commons, 2003c: 363).

The situation in the House of Commons deteriorated even further for the government when Robin Cook, the Labour government's current Leader of the House of Commons and Foreign Secretary until June 2001, resigned from his cabinet post on 17 March 2003 in protest of the Iraq War. On the evening of his resignation, he read out a Personal Statement before the House of Commons. As Foreign Secretary he had access to much of the same undisclosed intelligence which Blair now claimed to indicate the presence of a clear threat and consequently a case for war. But "to gasps" (Kampfner, 2004: 300) Cook now stated that:

Analysing British decision processes   125

Iraq probably has no weapons of mass destruction in the commonly understood sense of the term.... It probably still has biological toxins and battlefield chemical munitions, but it has had them since the 1980s.... Why is it
now so urgent that we should take military action to disarm a military capacity that has been there for 20 years, and which we helped to create?

(House of Commons, 2003a: 727–728)

Cook thus diametrically challenged the government's securitisation case the
night before Blair asked the House of Commons for approval of its decision to
go to war without a second UN resolution.

On 18 March, consequently, the outcome of that day's debate was far from
certain. Before Blair delivered his statement, the Speaker announced that he had
received another motion from Labour MP Chris Smith, which deemed the case
for war as not yet established (House of Commons, 2003c: 779). Reportedly,
before the debate began there were rumours of 160 to 200 Labour MPs who were
inclined to vote for the 'rebel cross-party amendment' (Kampfner, 2004: 307–309).
After Blair delivered his statement, Iain Duncan Smith made clear from the outset
that 'the official opposition' would vote with the government (House of
Commons, 2003c: 774). He also made clear that his party's support did not derive
from concerns for human or regional security but because Saddam posed a "direct
threat to our national security" and therefore it was "in the British national
interest" to go to war (House of Commons, 2003c: 775). The government's threat
claims therefore still resonated strongly with most Conservatives. Labour MP Peter
Kilfoyle then officially moved the rebel motion. He did not accuse the government of being disingenuous but of being wrong in its judgement. While he did
not deny that Britain faced a terrorist threat he denied that Saddam had the capability to attack Britain (House of Commons, 2003c: 780). Speaking for the Liberal
Democrats, Charles Kennedy also justified his party's opposition to the war mainly
on grounds of being unconvinced of "the causal link between the Iraqi regime, al-
Qaeda and September 11" (House of Commons, 2003c: 781).

Yet many MPs, first among them the Conservatives, thought that opposition
to the war precluded moral support to the British troops. This moral support
was, however, widely regarded as a general moral obligation since nearly all pro-
nouncements of criticism were accompanied by the declaration of deep-seated
respect for the armed forces irrespective of an ultimate decision. Ironically,
Conservative MPs supported the government's motion most fiercely throughout
the debate. Their foreign affairs spokesperson William Hague, for example,
argued that "in some of the opposition to the Government's stance there is a
hint of appeasement" (House of Commons, 2003c: 790). But he not only
attacked other MPs but also criticised other countries, most notably France, for
shirking their responsibilities, thus leaving it to the US to provide for their
security. These arguments highlight the sizeable prevalence of pre-existent identity conceptions of the UK as a country that accepts its international responsibility for the provision of security. The derivative norms underpinned the
government's securitisation efforts.

Altogether, the debate lasted for seven and a half hours and entailed 354
impassioned speeches, which revealed deep divisions cutting across party lines.

126   *Comparing decision processes on use of force*

But the government won both votes by large majorities. The first vote on the cross-party rebel amendment was defeated by 396 votes to 217 (House of Commons, 2003c: 902). A sizeable 138 Labour MPs voted for the amendment, but with 245 Labour MPs opposing it, this only constituted 36 per cent of the Labour votes. Besides all 53 Liberal Democrats, 15 Conservative MPs as well as 11 MPs from smaller parties also voted for the rebel amendment. The result for the government's main motion looked similar. 254 Labour MPs and 146 Conservative MPs supported the motion, defeating its opponents by 412 to 149 votes. Some 84 Labour MPs voted against it alongside two Conservative MPs, all Liberal Democrats and ten MPs from smaller parties (House of Commons, 2003c: 907). Although Blair ultimately had to rely on Conservative votes and over one-third of all MPs voted against the government's line, he could secure a comfortable parliamentary majority for his actions.

Altogether, the House of Commons held six votes before the invasion of Iraq, all of which supported the government. The last vote revealed a vociferous, sizeable and growing opposition to the war, especially after it became clear that there would not be another UN resolution. But this opposition did not trigger a no-confidence vote or significant cabinet defections. This shows that the parliamentary resonance to Blair's securitisation move in the run-up to the Iraq War was divided but mostly positive. Many MPs were not convinced of the seriousness of the threat, many firmly believed that the United Nations should have the final say over the use of force and that the United States should not dictate UK policy, and many believed that Iraqi disarmament could still be achieved by peaceful means. However, the majority, including the government, expressed their belief in Britain's historical vocation as a force for good in the world, which had to maintain its role as the US's most faithful ally in order to maximise its influence, expressed their belief in the government's threat claims, and concurred that these necessitated extraordinary means by which the threat is to be dealt with.

The intense debates which took place in the House of Commons therefore show that the success of a securitisation move does not only depend on the right language and position of authority of its proponent, but it is also determined by the cultural propensities of its audience. The more conducive the norms contained in the audience's strategic culture are to the securitisation move, the more widely it is likely to resonate positively with its audience and the more likely it is to succeed. Yet the more the securitisation move approaches the limits of what the norms of its audience's strategic culture can support, the stronger the share of negative resonance becomes. In the case of British parliamentary debates on the Iraq War, the government moved perilously close to the tipping point where negative resonance overwhelms positive reception of the securitisation move.

In the month leading up to the Iraq War, between 20 February and 20 March 2003, *The Times* expressed their commentators' opinions in at least 46 opinion pieces. Of these, this analysis identified 23 to be strongly supportive of the use of force in Iraq, while 15 were identified as moderately supportive, three as moderately critical and five as strongly critical. This suggests that contrary to Meyer's (2007: 99–100) claims about *The Times*' commentaries in the

Analysing British decision processes 127

run-up to the Iraq War, a large majority of opinion pieces showed little caution towards war but endorsed the government's position and criticised its domestic as well as its international opponents rather than the Blair government or the US. Editorialists such as Mary Ann Sieghart, Michael Gove, Anatole Kaletsky and Peter Riddell as well as several collective opinion pieces by *The Times* praised Blair's courage to stand up for his conviction alongside the US despite fierce domestic and international opposition, and Blair's use of his influence in the US to make the Bush administration seek UN approval. A large number of articles, especially those from Ben Macintyre, William Rees-Mogg, Anatole Kaletsky, James Bone and those written collectively, were also highly critical of the French government's and Mr Blix's behaviour. Aside from some critics, most editorialists in *The Times* thus took the same position as the Conservative Party and backed the government's decision to use military force as a decision that upheld British norms on the legitimate use of state force and the country's proper role in the world.

The editorial line of the *Guardian*, on the other hand, was unequivocal in its staunch opposition to war. Of the 44 articles identified to have expressed an editorial opinion on the issue in the month leading up to the war, 32 were deemed strongly critical, ten to be moderately critical and only two commentaries were deemed moderately supportive and strongly supportive, respectively. The two supportive commentaries were guest commentaries by former Labour cabinet minister Peter Mandelson and by US President Bill Clinton. Mandelson criticised the French position in the Security Council and Clinton called for trust in Blair's threat claims (Clinton, 2003; Mandelson, 2003). But all in-house editorialists and all other guest commentaries, on the other hand, dismissed the government's case for war as illegal, illogical, unjustified and incompatible with norms on the UK's role in the world as well as on the global order in which this role is to be played out.

The *Sun*, on the other hand, threw itself behind the government's case for war with full fervour. All 20 commentaries in the *Sun* identified in the period under analysis strongly supported the government. It grossly amplified the government's threat claims and manifestly presented the government's case for war not only in its editorials but also in its regular reporting long before the time period under analysis. For example, its front-page headline after the publication of the September Dossier on 25 September read "He's got 'em. let's get him, PM warns on Saddam." On the inside of the paper an article then carried the headline "Brits 45 mins from doom" (*Sun*, 2002a, 2002b). While the paper swung its full support and all its rhetorical resources behind the Bush and Blair governments, it also scorned at those within the UK and internationally who opposed these governments' actions. On 21 February, the *Sun* distributed free copies in Paris in which Chirac was decried as a 'worm' in French on the front page. Similarly, after Cook's resignation, the *Sun* described him as a 'quitter'. Their drastic nature shows that parts of the British tabloid not only resonated positively with the government's securitisation efforts but it can even be said to have actively amplified these. This would have incurred the newspaper great risks of a large-scale loss in readership if its editors could not be sure of the appeal this would have among its readership base. This indicates that the UK's

128   *Comparing decision processes on use of force*

strategic cultural context provided for the overwhelmingly positive resonance which the government's securitisation move received in British tabloids.

During the heated and at times acrimonious debates over the Iraq War both sides to the debate have at various times cited various polls to claim to have public opinion on their side. But due to the intense debate that took place over a relatively long period, polling companies conducted a particularly high number of polls before and during the Iraq War, which asked a wide range of different questions covering an extensive range of issues related to the Iraq War. It is therefore difficult to draw general inferences from individual polls alone as it is difficult to derive a comprehensive picture of public opinion encapsulating all available polling data. Furthermore, not all polling companies release the full polling data available. Luckily, Everts and Isernia (2005) as well as Everts (2007) made much of this polling data publicly available. Based on the subsequent analysis of available polling data, this section can come to the conclusion that the British public saw Iraq as a threat but was generally divided over the issue of war with Iraq in general. A clear majority was supportive of a war with explicit UN authorisation but opposed to war without it. Immediately after the war started public opinion swung around to support the war nonetheless.

The polling data generally indicates that British public opinion supported the government's claim that Iraqi WMDs posed a threat before the start of the war. On the issue of British military force in Iraq, public opinion in the UK was generally divided before the war started. Polling data related to general opposition or support of the war shows no clear majority either in favour or opposed to the war. An international Pew Research poll conducted on 2–10 November 2002 showed that 47 per cent each favoured and opposed Britain "joining the US and other allies in military action in Iraq to end Saddam Hussein's rule" (Pew Global Attitudes Project, 2002; sample size: 965). A Gallup International poll of January 2003 reveals a similar picture. Asked whether Britain should support it "if military action against Iraq goes ahead", 44 per cent said it should and 41 per cent said it should not (Everts, 2007: 182; quoted after Goot, 2004: 242).

However, as it became increasingly unlikely that the Security Council would provide another explicit mandate for the war, a majority opposed the war even in questions not mentioning UN mandate and WMD issues.

When polls raised the issue of UN authorisation in the question, one can observe a clear majority in favour of military action with and opposed to military action without UN authorisation. At the same time, the Gallup International survey of January 2003 found that "if the UN Security Council decides on a military intervention in Iraq", 78 per cent thought the UK should participate in it (EOS Gallup Europe, 2003: 9). But even on the issue of UN authorisation, the poll data is not completely in accordance. A YouGov poll for the BBC, for example, found out that in mid-March 2003 76 per cent thought the UK should commit troops if the Security Council decided to launch military action and only 18 per cent thought it should not, but if a majority of the Security Council supported the use of force against Iraq yet "one or two countries use their power of veto", 54 per cent still thought the UK should commit troops (YouGov/ BBC, 2003). At the same time, paradoxically, 70 per cent thought France was

Analysing British decision processes 129

wrong to block any resolution threatening military action against Iraq (YouGov/ BBC, 2003). Furthermore, 61 per cent considered that it would be justified "that our country participates in a military intervention in Iraq if the Iraqi regime does not cooperate with United Nations inspectors", according to the Gallup International poll of January 2003 (quoted in Everts, 2007: 183). Once military action started, however, one can observe a sharp increase in approval ratings for British military action in Iraq. The data therefore indicates that although the government ultimately managed to sway divided public opinion and rally the public behind its cause, it encountered a high degree of scepticism towards the claims on which it rested its securitisation move throughout the run-up to military action in Iraq.

Conclusion and outlook

This chapter showed that the sequentially dialectical interplay between securitis- ing actors, chiefly among these Tony Blair, and the 'proactive-robust' strategic culture of British society followed a largely coherent pattern across the three instances of decisions on the use of force. In all three instances, British strategic culture provided a conditioning formal cause and the Blair government's securi- tisation agency a final cause of the relatively extensive and robust use of force against the perceived threats of the post-9/11 period. In all three instances, the government acquired largely positive resonance and thus reconditioned British strategic culture through morphostasis. In other words, since the government's actions largely adhered to pre-existing norms and public expectations, they had no immediate impact on strategic culture in the form of a backlash or a shift.

However, the degree of positive resonance varies across the cases. In the case of the securitisation process leading to the Iraq War, dissonance among the audi- ence already reached a critical level, as the parliamentary debates, media com- mentaries and public opinion polls show. The British government's move to securitise a threat of Iraqi WMDs, triggered by 9/11 and the Bush administra- tion's early determination to set course on the removal of Saddam Hussein in early 2002 was ultimately successful. But the intense efforts required by the gov- ernment to present its case and the intense scrutiny and scepticism on the side of the audience already demonstrated significant strain on the carrying capacity of British strategic culture.

The eventual non-existence of Iraqi WMDs, hence new information about the retrospective absence of an immediate threat, as well as the heavy casualties incurred during British post-war stabilisation and anti-terrorism efforts in Iraq are likely to have had a deferred conditioning effect on British strategic culture during the extended period of structural elaboration. One can therefore expect some morphogenesis towards a less 'robust' strategic culture through a loss of trust and alienation from the pre-war British political leadership having caused a re-evaluation of extant norms of British strategic culture among wider society. As Chapter 5 showed, one can discern declining rates of British public support for the use of force in public opinion polls across the later 2000s.

A possible expression of this effect can arguably be identified in the defeat of a House of Commons bill intended to authorise the UK to join US-led military

130   *Comparing decision processes on use of force*

strikes against Syria on 30 August 2013 by 285 to 272 votes (BBC News, 2013). Also, after the UK launched a military intervention in Libya alongside coalition in March 2011, an Ipsos MORI poll taken in April showed that only half of the respondents supported the military action (Ipsos MORI/Reuters, 2011). And yet it is telling that it would be the UK that poses the question of an armed intervention in Syria and gets involved in military action in Libya from the outset. It is also telling that the allegations of Edward Snowden about an extensive US-run global surveillance programme stirred an international uproar that was followed up on by allegations of an even more ambitious such programme run by the British Government Communications Headquarters (GCHQ) (Harding, 2014). Hence, there probably remains an element of truth in what the then-British Foreign Secretary Lord Palmerston implied when he stated before the House of Commons in 1832: "I will not talk of non-intervention, for it is not an English word" (quoted from Ridley, 2013: 156–157).

Notes

1 See statements by MPs Michael Ancram, Conservative; Peter Mandelson, Labour; Ian Paisley, Democratic Unionist Party; John Battle, Labour; Bernard Jenkin, Conservative (House of Commons, 2001a).
2 See statements by MPs Iain Duncan Smith, Conservative; Bernard Jenkin, Conservative; Gordon Marsden, Labour (House of Commons, 2001a).
3 See statements by MPs Patrick Cormack, Conservative; Menzies Campbell, Liberal Democrat; Julian Brazier, Conservative; George Galloway, Labour; Bruce George, Labour; Julian Lewis, Conservative (House of Commons, 2001a).
4 For an August 2002 opinion of The European Council's Commissioner for Human Rights, Mr Alvaro Gil-Robles, charged with overseeing the implementation of the ECHR, on the ATCSA's derogation, see (Gil-Robles, 2002). For the December 2004 judgement of a House of Lords judicial committee (the 'Law Lords') specially convened to decide on the legality of the Act's derogation (see House of Lords, 2004).
5 Another such exemplary media statement can be found in an interview with Home Secretary David Blunkett televised on 11 November 2001 on the London Weekend Television channel, in which he reportedly stated: "We could live in a world which is *airy fairy, libertarian*, where everybody does precisely what they like and we believe the best of everybody *and then they destroy us*" (emphasis added, quoted from Wintour, 2001).

Bibliography

Anti-Terrorism, Crime and Security Act 2001 (2009) *Guardian*, 19 January. Available from: www.guardian.co.uk/commentisfree/libertycentral/2009/jan/13/anti-terrorism-act (accessed 6 May 2013).
BBC News (2013) 'MPs' vote halts UK action over Syria'. BBC, 30 August. Available from: www.bbc.co.uk/news/uk-politics-23892783 (accessed 23 February 2014).
Blair T (2002) Full text of Tony Blair's speech in Texas. *Guardian Online*, 8 April. Available from: www.theguardian.com/politics/2002/apr/08/foreignpolicy.iraq (accessed 10 August 2013).
Blunkett D (2001) The Human Rights Act 1998 (Designated Derogation) Order 2001. *2001 No. 3644*. Available from: www.legislation.gov.uk/uksi/2001/3644/made (accessed 30 July 2013).
Bluth C (2004) The British Road to War: Blair, Bush and the Decision to Invade Iraq. *International Affairs*, 80(5), 871–892.

Analysing British decision processes 131

Canadian Centres for Teaching Peace Inc. (2001) Gallup International poll on terrorism in the US. Available from: www.peace.ca/galluppollonterrorism.htm (accessed 23 July 2013).

Clinton B (2003) "Trust Tony's Judgment". *Guardian*, London, 18 March.

Davidson JW (2011) *America's Allies and War: Kosovo, Afghanistan, and Iraq*. New York: Palgrave Macmillan.

EOS Gallup Europe (2003) International Crisis Survey. Available from: www.paks.uni-duesseldorf.de/Dokumente/International-Crisis-Survey_Rapport-Final.pdf (accessed 16 August 2013).

Everts P (2007) *Public opinion on 'Iraq': International Comparative Polls and Countries Outside USA (up to August, 2004)*. Leiden: Leiden University, Department of Political Science. Available from: http://media.leidenuniv.nl/legacy/Poll%20Data%20War%20against%20Iraq%20(outside%20the%20US).pdf (accessed 16 August 2013).

Everts P and Isernia P (2005) "The War in Iraq". *Public Opinion Quarterly*, 69(2), 264–323.

Frost D (2001) BBC Breakfast with Frost Interview: Prime Minister Tony Blair MP 30 September 2001. *BBC Breakfast with Frost*, London: BBC One. Available from: http://news.bbc.co.uk/2/hi/programmes/breakfast_with_frost/1571541.stm (accessed 29 July 2013).

Gil-Robles A (2002) Opinion of the Commissioner for Human Rights, Mr Alvaro Gil-Robles, on certain aspects of the United Kingdom 2001 derogation from Article 5 of the European Convention on Human Rights. European Council, Commissioner for Human Rights, Available from: https://wcd.coe.int/ViewDoc.jsp?id=980187&Site=C ommDH&BackColorInternet=FEC65B&BackColorIntranet=FEC65B&BackColorLo gged=FFC679 (accessed 25 July 2013).

Goot M (2004) "Introduction: World Opinion Surveys and The War in Iraq". *International Journal of Public Opinion Research*. Available from: http://psycnet.apa.org/psycinfo/2004-16961-001 (accessed 13 August 2013).

Gordon PH (2001) "NATO after 11 September". *Survival*, 43(4), 89–106.

Guardian (2001a) "The World at War". *Guardian Online*, 8 October. Available from: www.guardian.co.uk/world/2001/oct/08/afghanistan.terrorism39 (accessed 19 July 2013).

Guardian (2001b) "Two Nations, One View: Public Opinion Rallies Behind the US". *Guardian*, 18 September.

Harding L (2014) "Writing The Snowden Files: 'The Paragraph Began to Self-Delete". *Guardian*, London, 20 February. Available from: www.theguardian.com/books/2014/feb/20/edward-snowden-files-nsa-gchq-luke-harding (accessed 24 February 2014).

House of Commons (2001a) *Hansard*, 4 October 2001. The United Kingdom Parliament, Available from: www.publications.parliament.uk/pa/cm200102/cmhansrd/vo011004/debindx/11004-x.htm (accessed 1 July 2013).

House of Commons (2001b) *Hansard*, 14 September 2001. The United Kingdom Parliament. Available from: www.publications.parliament.uk/pa/cm200102/cmhansrd/vo010914/debindx/10914-x.htm (accessed 1 July 2013).

House of Commons (2001c) *Hansard*, 15 October 2001. The United Kingdom Parliament. Available from: www.publications.parliament.uk/pa/cm200102/cmhansrd/vo011015/debindx/11015-x.htm (accessed 30 July 2013).

House of Commons (2001d) *Hansard*, 19 November 2001. The United Kingdom Parliament. Available from: www.publications.parliament.uk/pa/cm200102/cmhansrd/vo011119/debindx/11119-x.htm (accessed 30 July 2013).

House of Commons (2001e) *Hansard*, 21 November 2001. The United Kingdom Parliament. Available from: www.publications.parliament.uk/pa/cm200102/cmhansrd/vo011121/debindx/11121-x.htm (accessed 30 July 2013).

House of Commons (2002a) *Hansard*. 24 September 2002. The United Kingdom Parliament. Available from: www.publications.parliament.uk/pa/cm200102/cmhansrd/vo010914/debindx/10914-x.htm (accessed 1 July 2013).

132   *Comparing decision processes on use of force*

House of Commons (2002b) Hansard, 25 November 2002. The United Kingdom Parliament, Available from: www.publications.parliament.uk/pa/cm200102/cmhansrd/vo010914/debindx/10914-x.htm (accessed 1 July 2013).

House of Commons (2003a) *Hansard*, 17 March 2003. The United Kingdom Parliament. Available from: www.publications.parliament.uk/pa/cm200203/cmhansrd/vo030317/debtext/30317-33.htm (accessed 1 July 2013).

House of Commons (2003b) *Hansard*, 18 March 2003. The United Kingdom Parliament, Available from: www.publications.parliament.uk/pa/cm200102/cmhansrd/vo010914/debindx/10914-x.htm (accessed 1 July 2013).

House of Commons (2003c) *Hansard*, 26 February 2003. The United Kingdom Parliament. Available from: www.publications.parliament.uk/pa/cm200102/cmhansrd/vo010914/debindx/10914-x.htm (accessed 1 July 2013).

House of Lords (2004) Judgements – A (FC) and others (FC) (Appellants) v. Secretary of State for the Home Department (Respondent). UK Parliament. Available from: www.publications.parliament.uk/pa/ld200405/ldjudgmt/jd041216/a&oth-1.htm (accessed 25 July 2013).

House of Lords Constitution Committee (2009) *Fast-Track Legislation: Constitutional Implications and Safeguards*. UK Parliament. Available from: www.publications.parliament.uk/pa/ld200809/ldselect/ldconst/116/11602.htm (accessed 26 July 2013).

ICM Research/Guardian (2001) ICM Research/Guardian Poll September 2001. Available from: www.icmresearch.com/pdfs/2001_september_guardian_september_poll.pdf (accessed 23 July 2013).

Ipsos MORI/Reuters (2011) Reuters/Ipsos MORI International Poll on Libya. Available from: www.ipsos-mori.com/researchpublications/researcharchive/2763/ReutersIpsos-MORI-International-poll-on-Libya.aspx (accessed 24 February 2014).

Kampfner J (2004) *Blair's Wars*. New edition. New York: Free Press.

MacAskill E and White M (2001) "Bold Blair Takes the Zealous Road to War". *Guardian*, 29 September. Available from: www.guardian.co.uk/politics/2001/sep/29/uk.september11 (accessed 12 April 2013).

Mandelson P (2003) "The Day of Reckoning Has Arrived. The UN Must Act: The Real Battle in the Security Council is about a New World Order". *Guardian*, London, 10 March.

Meyer CO (2007) *The Quest for a European Strategic Culture: Changing Norms on Security and Defence in the European Union*. London: Palgrave Macmillan.

Monbiot G (2001) "The Need for Dissent: Attack on America Voices from Britain and the US Highlight the Risks of a Hasty Response". *Guardian*, London, 18 September.

New York Times (2001) Text of Prime Minister Tony Blair's Remarks. *New York Times*, 7 October. Available from: www.nytimes.com/2001/10/07/international/07BLAIR-TEXT.html (accessed 22 May 2013).

Norton-Taylor R (2001) "This Is Britain's Moment: Whitehall officials Have Long Been Sceptical of the US's Line on the Middle East. Now Is the Time to Say So Openly". *Guardian*, London, 13 September.

Pew Global Attitudes Project (2002) Thinking about possible war with Iraq, would you favor or oppose (survey country's) joining the US and other allies in military action in Iraq to end Saddam Hussein's rule? *Pew Global Attitudes Project Question Database*, Available from: www.pewglobal.org/question-search/ (accessed 13 August 2013).

Riddell P (2004) *Hug Them Close: Blair, Clinton, Bush and the 'Special Relationship'*. London: Politico's.

Ridley J (2013) *Lord Palmerston*. Sydney: Pan Macmillan.

Righter R (2001) "The US Has to Move into More Visible Action Soon or Risk Losing Impotent". *The Times*, London, 5 October.

Analysing British decision processes 133

Seldon A, Snowdon P and Collings D (2008) *Blair Unbound*. London; New York: Pocket Books.

Sun (2001a) "Last Hours". *Sun*, London, 19 September.

Sun (2001b) "Top Team". *Sun*, London, 15 September.

Sun (2002a) "Brits 45 mins from Doom". *Sun*, London, 25 September.

Sun (2002b) "He's Got 'em. Let's Get Him, PM Warns on Saddam". *Sun*, London, 25 September.

The Times (2001) "Still a Haven – Terrorists Are Still Using London to Plot Evil Overseas". *The Times*, London, 15 September.

Toynbee P (2001) "Bush is on a Steep Learning Curve, Just Like the Rest of Us: Since September 11 the World Has Changed with Astonishing Speed". *Guardian*, London, 26 September.

Travis A (2001) "2 in 3 Back Air Strikes". *Guardian*, London, 18 September.

UK Government (2002) "Iraq's Weapons of Mass Destruction – The Assessment of the British Government". The Stationary Office. Available from: www.archive2.official-documents.co.uk/document/reps/iraq/cover.htm (accessed 10 August 2013).

UK Government (2003) "Iraq-its Infrastructure of Concealment, Deception and Intimidation". Guardian News and Media. Available from: http://image.guardian.co.uk/sys-files/Guardian/documents/2003/02/07/uk0103.pdf (accessed 10 August 2013).

Webster P, Watson R and Dynes M (2001) "We Are at War with Terrorism". *The Times*, London, 17 September.

Williams PD (2006) *British Foreign Policy under New Labour*. London: Palgrave Macmillan.

Wintour P (2001) "Blunkett Rejects 'Airy Fairy' Fears. *Guardian Online*, London, 12 November. Available from: www.theguardian.com/politics/2001/nov/12/uk.september11 (accessed 30 July 2013).

Woollacott M (2001) "Don't Inflate the Size of the Enemy to Fit the Crime: As in the Cuban Missile Crisis, the President Still Has Choices". *Guardian*, London, 14 September.

YouGov/BBC (2003) YouGov Survey Results: A Possible War in Iraq. Available from: http://cdn.yougov.com/today_uk_import/YG-Archives-ira-dim-ShowdownIraq-030317.pdf (accessed 13 August 2013).

Young H (2001) "The Free World Must Decide How Its Values Are Protected: September 11 Marked the End of American Isolationism". *Guardian*, London, 13 September.

7 Analysing German decision processes on the use of force

Looking at the trajectory of German state behaviour regarding the use of force since 1990, it is tempting to conclude, as many scholars have, that the country underwent a process of 'normalisation' (cf., inter alia, Berger, 1998; Dalgaard-Nielsen, 2006; Duffield, 1998; Longhurst, 2004). This could lead to the assumption that Germany's immediate reaction to 9/11 would not differ substantially from that of its European partners. However, the analysis conducted in Chapter 5 also showed that at least on the level of the wider public a convergence of norms towards a level of proclivity to the use of force more similar to that of the other four countries' strategic cultures stalled since the turn of the century. One can therefore expect German strategic culture to condition securitisation processes into 'milder' forms, which also entail more intense debates, scrutiny and controversy over the use of force in their resonance.

Analysing the German decision process regarding the use of force in Afghanistan

Germany participated in OEF with a maximum of 3,900 soldiers, 100 of which were Special Forces of the *Kommando Spezialkräfte* (Special Forces Command) deployed to Afghanistan while the remainder were marines deployed to the horn of Africa to patrol shipping routes and NBC weapons defence forces deployed to Kuwait for the protection of American troops and civilians from possible attacks by Iraq (Dalgaard-Nielsen, 2006: 86; Hellmann *et al.*, 2006: 200–201).

The decision to use force in Afghanistan

The securitisation process leading up to Germany's deployment of troops after 9/11 initially resembled that in the UK in many respects but then proceeded in a significantly more protracted way. This is already discernible in the time frame of the decision to use force after 9/11. The *Bundestag* gave its final approval for troop deployments on 16 November and the first German troops, *KSK* Special Forces, arrived in Afghanistan by mid-December 2001 (Rauss, 2004; Scholzen, 2004: 48). It was "the first occasion in history when *Bundeswehr* ground forces were sent into a combat area" (Wagener, 2006: 87). Yet the German government's immediate reaction to 9/11 did not differ substantially from that in the UK. Then Federal Chancellor Gerhard Schröder released a short statement on

Analysing German decision processes 135

11 September, repeated in parliament the next day, in which he declared that this was a "declaration of war against the entire civilised world" (Schröder, 2006: 164–165). The statement was unequivocal in establishing a terrorist threat to his audience. He declared that the terrorist violence of 9/11 "...directly threatens the principles of human coexistence in peace and security, therefore all that which has been built over generations" (Deutscher Bundestag, 2001c: 18293).

Crucially, Schröder famously stated that while he was talking to Bush the day before he offered the US president not only his condolences but also "the unrestricted – I emphasise: the unrestricted – solidarity of Germany". He then pledged that the people of Germany would stand firmly on America's side in this hour of need and later added that "Of course we offer the citizens and authorities of the United States of America any help desired, of course also in investigating and chasing the initiators and masterminds of these despicable attacks" (Deutscher Bundestag, 2001c: 18293). These statements conveyed the message that if the US planned to use military force in reaction to the terrorist events, Germany would also do so alongside the US. But Schröder was careful to consult as broad an array of political actors as possible rather than autonomously assuming a lead role in forming an international anti-terror coalition. After hearing of the terrorist events on 11 September, Schröder consulted his Foreign Minister Joschka Fischer, his Minister of the Interior Otto Schily, the Federal President Johannes Rau, his cabinet's Federal Security Council and several European and extra-European heads of government before holding a meeting with the heads of all parliamentary groups in the *Bundestag* and the parties they represented.

In his memoires, Schröder revealed that his key concern was that Germany acted cohesively after 9/11. Therefore he thought "It was essential to convince the cabinet, the coalition and the opposition of the necessity of unrestricted solidarity" (Schröder, 2006: 164). Schröder and Fischer sought to achieve this aim not only through extensive domestic consultations but also through their efforts at consulting allies and forging a common European response in which they could then embed their own policies. The Special Summit of the European Council in Tampere on 21 September can largely be seen as having been convened at the behest of Fischer and Schröder (Görtemaker, 2009: 133; Longhurst, 2004: 83). Fischer and Schröder also had no hesitation to support NATO Secretary-General George Robertson's decision to invoke Article 5 on 12 September (Fischer, 2011: 6–7).

On the surface, the German government then seemed on course toward military action. On 19 September, Schröder clarified that his proclamation of unrestricted solidarity included a German military contribution to US-led military action, but not under any condition. He stressed that "Germany is prepared to take risks, also in military regards, but not to take part in adventures" (Deutscher Bundestag, 2001d: 18302). He added that a fixation exclusively on military measures would be fatal and that instead, a comprehensive concept was needed for the fight against terrorism as well as for crisis prevention and relief, which was to be based on political, economic, cultural and security cooperation (Deutscher Bundestag, 2001d: 18302). While firm on the need for military action, the German chancellor therefore also considered those among his

136   *Comparing decision processes on use of force*

coalition and the public who are concerned about Germany getting drawn into an American military overreaction in his proscriptions for an appropriate German response to 9/11.

Yet it was not before 6 November, after repeated consultations with Washington over its concrete demands from Germany, that Schröder's cabinet passed a motion to the *Bundestag* in which it outlined the details of Germany's military contribution and sought its approval (Bannas, 2001). The mandate also contained several important restrictions, including a maximum troop number of 3,900; regular parliamentary review of the deployment; clear definitions of the various missions' tasks; and, most importantly, the requirement of consent from the countries to which troops were to be deployed. The latter might have been designed in order to prevent *Bundeswehr* deployments to a possible war with Iraq on the basis of the mandate for OEF (Hellmann *et al.*, 2006: 201).

On 16 November, more than a month after the initial attacks on Afghanistan and as coalition forces were about to drive the Taliban out of Kabul, the *Bundestag* eventually authorised the deployment of 3,900 soldiers to various missions at various locations of OEF in Afghanistan and elsewhere. Not only this relatively long time frame but also the restricted mandate and the important fact that on 11 November Schröder decided to combine the vote over Germany's participation in OEF to a vote of confidence for his government show that "the domestic political scene created the most direct danger to the Schröder government" (Erb, 2003: 193; Spiegel Online, 2001a). The government was aware that many MPs especially among the Greens and the SPD did see a need to capture and arrest the perpetrators of 9/11 but also saw military action as only increasing civilian casualties and instability in a region whose destitution already provided ample ground for fanaticism (Erb, 2003: 194).

One month after the Bundestag passed the government's motion, the first German Special Forces arrived in Afghanistan. While ultimately successful, the scope, as well as the restrained and reactive nature of the securitisation process show that there was some contention about this process of proclaiming a terrorist threat and establishing the legitimacy of countering this threat through the use of military force. In part, it lay in the nature of Germany's decentralised constitution that more actors got involved in driving the securitisation process and that more efforts were required for this process to be ultimately successful than in the UK, for example. But to a large extent this also reflects awareness among those actors of a strategic culture demanding more deliberation over the use of military force and more exploration of non-military alternatives while at the same time demanding alliance loyalty, as Chapter 4 has shown. As Schröder and Fischer have acknowledged themselves, these preferences for a milder securitisation process do not only arise from strategic calculations about the collective expectations and cultural underpinnings of one's electorate but they also derive in part from actors adhering to these cultural traits themselves. While in the UK the use of force in Afghanistan after 9/11 was largely a matter of course, Schröder had to pull together a more dispersed strategic culture which did contain norms supportive of the use of force in this case but which also retained some significant recalcitrance towards it especially among the left wing of the political spectrum.

Analysing German decision processes 137

Resonance of the decision to use force in Afghanistan

The long time span in which the securitisation process took place allowed for a lively debate over the use of force on several fronts. As the extensiveness of the process itself already suggests, the resonance was mostly positive but also inter-mixed with criticism and scepticism towards the government's course of action.

After Schröder's proclamation of unrestricted solidarity with the US on 12 September 2001, the heads of all parliamentary groups in the *Bundestag* expressed their condolences in short statements delivered on behalf of their party. All state-ments reaffirmed Schröder's expression of solidarity and his description of 9/11 as an attack on the fundamental values of society the world over. Friedrich Merz (CDU), Wolfgang Gerhard (FDP) and Rezzo Schlauch (Greens) indicated that the task of defending universal values from attack now lay ahead, while still leaving open how this defence was going to take place. Only Roland Claus, head of socialist PDS in the Bundestag, urged the parliament to remain in its moment of solemn reflection for a little while longer and then to act prudently, which can be interpreted as an early signal of his party's fundamental opposition to the use of force (Deutscher Bundestag, 2001c: 18296).

The *Bundestag* debated the use of force in Afghanistan on 19 September and once more on 11 October 2001. Aside from the PDS, all parties' senior parliament-arians expressed their general support for Schröder's course. There was therefore only little debate. Some dispute existed between the government and opposition parties about whether the government showed enough support for the American administration so far and whether Germany's constitutional ban on the domestic use of military force (unless in support of other domestic state security services) needed to be overhauled. Angela Merkel (CDU), for example, criticised Schröder for only visiting the United States as late as the current week and disagreed with Schröder's call to maintain the distinction between domestic and international security (Deutscher Bundestag, 2001f: 18684). Yet there was a general consensus that the US reacted appropriately and that Schröder was right in arguing that Germany had a special responsibility to support the US, as it helped Germany in overcoming the aftermath of two world wars, which included help through military means (Deutscher Bundestag, 2001f: 18682). But one can also discern that the German defence minister sought to make the impending German military inter-vention more palatable to his sceptical audience by disassociating himself from more bellicose Anglo-Saxon rhetoric. Scharping explained in the October debate that:

> the use of the military against terrorism and against those states which afford support or a haven to terrorists is not, say, classical warfare but at its core it is actually a police operation with the means of the military.
>
> (Deutscher Bundestag, 2001f: 18697)

This way of reasserting the government's portrayal of military action in Afghani-stan again points to underlying tensions between norms of alliance solidarity and norms of restraint in the use of military force contained in German strategic culture, which surfaced not only during the German securitisation process after 9/11 but also in its resonance.

138   *Comparing decision processes on use of force*

The next and final parliamentary debate before German troops were deployed took place in the *Bundestag* on 16 November 2001. Since Schröder gave MPs a single vote on both the decision to deploy German troops and on whether the government should stay in power through a vote of no confidence or *Vertrauensfrage*, this crucial debate received significant attention both in the media and in the scholarly literature on German strategic culture, as it brought forth once more the various strands of norms on the use of force in Germany (Erb, 2003: 198–203; cf. Longhurst, 2004: 85–86). However, the debate on the use of force in Afghanistan was not as controversial as it may seem from the eventual vote alone. Altogether 336 MPs voted in favour while 326 voted against the government's motions (Deutscher Bundestag, 2001f: 19893). The government thus won the *Vertrauensfrage* by two votes more than the required absolute majority of 334 votes.

Yet the CDU and FDP opposition made clear in its statements that it only voted against the government's motion because it could not declare its confidence in the Red–Green coalition government, although it firmly supported military action. Inversely, many of the written statements which 70 MPs chose to attach to the parliamentary record in order to explain their vote came from SPD or Green Party members, who qualified that they had severe doubts about the military campaign but chose to vote 'yes' in order to keep the government in power (Deutscher Bundestag, 2001f: 19897–19912). Furthermore, many other statements also expressed that their approval only extended to the government's plan for restrictive military action under a carefully deliberated mandate. Ultimately, only the 36 MPs of PDS and four Greens MPs voted against the government's motion because they opposed the use of force outright. There was therefore relatively broad support from the centre-right and the centre-left of the *Bundestag* for the government's plan for restrictive military action, but Schröder's decision to link the issue to a vote of no confidence in order to force orthodox pacifists within his coalition to support him drew heavy criticism from all sides.

Defence minister Struck (SPD) outlined five areas in which the *Bundeswehr* was to get involved. These were first, paramedics for the evacuation and rescue of wounded civilians or soldiers; second, the supply of airlift capacity for military personnel and cargo as well as humanitarian goods; third, NBC reconnaissance vehicles and troops preventatively deployed "in the hope that they will never have to be applied"; fourth, marine assets deployed to protect civilian maritime shipping along the Horn of Africa; and fifth, the provision of 100 Special Forces troops which he deemed "... particularly well-suited to arrest identified terrorists or Taliban-criminals in Afghanistan through police-like raid methods" (Deutscher Bundestag, 2001i: 19863). He started his outlines of the first four measures with the repeated suggestion that the measures described left little room for serious objections by couching his descriptions of the proposed actions in rhetorical questions such as "Who wants to seriously object, when..."; "Who can have concerns, if..."; "Who can mind, that..."; and "What is supposed to be bellicose about ..." Struck, akin to Scharping in the prior debate, thus utilised a particularly alleviative rhetoric in his strenuous efforts to throw his weight behind the government's distinctively mild securitisation efforts. It illustrates that

Analysing German decision processes 139

in this debate German strategic culture challenged the government's endeavours to generate positive resonance in parliament, especially among the governing coalition's own ranks.

When Kerstin Müller later spoke on behalf of the Green Party, it became apparent that such efforts bore fruit. She defended her party's diffidence about the decision on the grounds that "Our party-internal debate is also an expression of the many doubts, worries and fears of the entire society" (Deutscher Bundestag, 2001i: 19869). A critique of this debate therefore denounced all those striving to draw the right lessons from Germany's Nazi past. Yet crucially, she stated that the government's specification of scope, composition and location of the planned mandate convinced a large majority in her faction that the deployment was morally justifiable. After all, the government clarified that German troops would neither be involved in aerial bombardments nor in combat action on the ground but instead, the German military contribution would largely serve civilian purposes and the Special Forces had "quasi police-military tasks" (Deutscher Bundestag, 2001i: 19868).

There was hardly any criticism of the late and confined nature of Germany's planned involvement from speakers of the opposition. A notable exception was Michael Glos of the CDU/CSU faction, who argued that people in Afghanistan could only be helped now because the US liberated the country's capital from the Taliban with the help of the British and the French, adding: "While our friends acted, the old Left in Germany once again only cultivated fear" (Deutscher Bundestag, 2001i: 19874). Erb (2003: 200) therefore rightly argued that the arguments brought forward in this debate "were interesting both in what was said and what was not said." A closer look at the arguments brought forward and the language used in this debate reveals that the government's securitisation efforts received largely positive resonance in parliament, but this resonance reflected the same cultural norms of restraint in the use of force as identified in Chapter 4 that also shaped the government's securitisation process. Especially the circumvention of the term 'war' and the restrictive interpretation of the mission's mandate showed in this debate that the positive resonance was highly conditional and did not extend much further beyond the levels of force envisaged by the government.

In order to evaluate the resonance of Schröder's securitisation process in the German print media, this section will analyse commentaries in three German newspapers between 12 September and 17 November 2001. These are the more conservatively oriented *Frankfurter Allgemeine Zeitung* (FAZ), which had a circulation of around 500,000 in the third quarter of 2001; the more left-of-centre *Süddeutsche Zeitung* (SZ), which had a circulation of around 537,000 issues in 2001; and the tabloid *Bild*, which had a circulation of around 5,500,000 issues in 2001 (Informationsgemeinschaft zur Feststellung der Verbreitung von Werbeträgern e.V., 2013).

The *Frankfurter Allgemeine Zeitung* featured 40 commentaries which were identified as addressing the issue of military force in response to 9/11 between 12 September and 17 November 2001. Of these, 18 articles could be classified as strongly supportive of the use of military force against terrorism after 9/11, 13 as moderately supportive, seven as neutral and two as moderately critical. However, several factors complicate a simple classification of newspaper commentaries

140 *Comparing decision processes on use of force*

along a binary spectrum from strong support to strong criticism towards the use of force in the case of the German *FAZ*. Many articles which are nominally commentaries and which address the issue of military force after 9/11 express surprisingly little opinion on this issue (cf. Falkenberger, 2001b, 2001c, 2001e, 2001f, 2001g; Kohler, 2001; Lerch, 2001; Wieland, 2001). There is also surprisingly little commentary on the German government's action or inaction among the few opinions expressed on the moral grounds of military action (cf. Falkenberger, 2001a, 2001b, 2001c, 2001f; Nonnenmacher, 2001a, 2001b, 2001d). Commentators thus seemingly conferred this detached position to the German government. One can assume that the FAZ would have also endorsed a stronger securitisation process and an earlier, more forceful military contribution by the German government. But since there was little opinion expressed in this direction one can also assume that there was a general awareness, if not acceptance, of the presence of widespread reservations towards the use of force in Germany as well as the constraints this imposes on any German government. However, this acceptance stopped short of displaying sympathy for those advocating a more critical German engagement within NATO. Alliance loyalty rather than proactive engagement appears to be the overriding normative concern for most German conservatives.

In the *Süddeutsche Zeitung*, on the other hand, editorials were slightly more pronounced on the issue of war in Afghanistan after 9/11 and commented more directly on the plans of the American and German governments for conducting war there and elsewhere. Altogether, the analysis determined that of the 36 articles identified, in 12 articles the arguments presented were, on balance, moderately critical of the use of military force after 9/11, in 14 articles they were moderately supportive, six articles were strongly supportive, three were strongly critical and one article discussed its implications for domestic party politics rather than expressing an opinion on the issue of war. It was therefore classified as neutral. The newspaper's commentators were thus divided but not polarised on the issue of military force after 9/11. Almost all articles drew careful, moderate conclusions after weighing several arguments against each other, but a majority of 20 over 15 articles still supported the government's course of providing a limited military contribution.

The *Bild* newspaper, meanwhile, was significantly more vocal and more unison in its commenting. Of the 28 articles, 18 were classified as strongly supportive, nine as moderately supportive and only one as moderately critical of the use of military force after 9/11. In the first days after the attacks, commentators clearly positioned themselves firmly behind the Bush administration, rallied for solidarity with the US and condemned what they perceived as anti-Americanism in parts of the political left. However, *Bild*'s commentators also did not write much with regards to the German government's activity or inactivity in the first weeks after 9/11. Besides calls for demonstrating solidarity with Germany's strongest ally, applause for Schröder's unequivocal demonstration of loyalty to the US and warnings that Germany will not be able to avoid a military contribution through a financial contribution to the war effort, as it did regarding the 1991 Gulf War (Henkel, 2001b), there were no calls for a more active engagement by the Schröder government in forging an alliance against terrorism. The

Analysing German decision processes 141

tabloid newspaper was therefore significantly more forthcoming than the other two German newspapers in providing positive resonance to the Schröder government's mild securitisation process and its cautious decision to use force in Afghanistan after 9/11, but it also did not push the government into stronger action. Although strongly pro-American, the paper did not exhibit the same patriotic and militaristic fervour as the British *Sun* in the aftermath of 9/11, possibly in order not to alienate its readership.

Weighted public opinion polls conducted in the months after 9/11 also reveal limited public support for German military action against terrorism in the weighted opinion polls conducted after 9/11. The polls also show that this support is lower than in France or the UK and that it is largely restricted to a non-combative role for German forces. The Gallup poll taken shortly after 9/11 on 14 and 15 September revealed that 53 per cent of German respondents, compared with 73 per cent of French and 79 per cent of British respondents agreed that their country "should take part in military actions against terrorists with the United States", after having been informed that "Some countries and all NATO member states have agreed to participate in any military action against the terrorists responsible for the attacks or against those countries harbouring the terrorists" (and archived version by Canadian Centres for Teaching Peace Inc., 2001; Gallup International poll of 14/15 September 2001; see Gordon, 2001).

Table A4 (see Appendix) shows that at the beginning of October a wide majority of 71 per cent supported Schröder's promise of unrestricted solidarity. Against the backdrop of German troop commitments, this support dropped to 51 per cent at the beginning of November. Furthermore, the table shows that there are wide differences across regions and party support. Around 20 per cent more West German than East German respondents supported the chancellor's pledge in November. Among the major political parties, the CDU and the SPD, there are similar levels of support and disapproval for Schröder's plans for military action but these are slightly lower among supporters of the liberal FDP and significantly lower among supporters of the Green Party and the PDS. This suggests that the majority of the general public supported Schröder in his rally for a German troop contribution to the US-led war on terror. But there was a sizeable minority opposed to this, especially as the war in Afghanistan continued into November and especially among a still staunchly pacifist left wing of the public. This was also discernible in the parliamentary and media resonance as well as the general findings on German strategic culture.

A survey by Infratest dimap for the German television network ARD conducted in mid-September and from 27 September to 2 October asked respondents whether Germany should provide military support to the US now that it announced it would vigorously pursue the masterminds of international terrorism (Infratest dimap/ARD, 2001b: 3–5). The survey revealed that support for German military action increased from 58 per cent to 64 per cent from mid-September to the beginning of October. However, there was widespread opposition among both East and West German respondents on the question of German troops engaging in combat activities. When asked in October what shape the envisaged German contribution should take, 32 per cent supported the

142 *Comparing decision processes on use of force*

Bundeswehr's participation in combat activities whereas 60 per cent wanted to see this contribution restricted solely to logistic and paramedical support (Infratest dimap/ARD, 2001b: 3–5). Overall, the public opinion surveys show that the public provided positive resonance to Schröder's mild securitisation process, but the surveys also show that there was a general reticence towards the idea of using German military force in Afghanistan, which was strongest among left-leaning members of the public and in East Germany.

Analysing the German decision to introduce counterterrorist legislation after 9/11

There is a relative aversion towards the use of force by the state in norms contained in German strategic culture which applied both to the external and to the domestic application of force, although to a lesser degree in the latter case. This also leads to the assumption that 9/11 triggered a comparatively milder securitisation process receiving a mixed resonance in debates regarding domestic counterterrorist legislation in Germany that highlights the controversy surrounding the use of force in Germany. The milder securitisation process is also expected to allow for a higher cross-conditioning impact of strategic culture on security policy decision-making within the less reclusive securitisation process during the phase of agential social interaction. But one can also expect the distinct impact of prior strategic cultural conditioning on the securitisation process itself to be less strongly pronounced than in cases of the external application of state force through the military.

The German counterterrorism laws passed pursuant to 9/11 extended the reach of existing anti-terrorism provisions in the German penal code to include the membership or support of foreign terrorist associations, increased the funds available to various security agencies, introduced new anti-money laundering provisions and lifted the exemption of religious associations from the law on associations. As such, this legislative action represents a comparatively minor expansion of the state's coercive capacities.

The decision to introduce counterterrorist legislation after 9/11

The process of decision-making regarding the domestic exercise of force by the state in response to 9/11 through new anti-terrorism legislation proceeded incrementally in individual sequences that each followed a series of proposals, arguments and counterarguments by various political actors in Germany. In contrast to the British case, there was not as much of an immediate consensus over which state capacities now urgently needed enhancement in order to counter the new domestic security challenges brought about by 9/11. In lieu of such a suspension of debates on how to enable effective threat prevention, the event much rather modified and expedited existing debates over issues such as immigration, intelligence cooperation, and state surveillance powers as preventive measures against a perceived growing risk of terrorism. The debate involved a multitude of proposals and topics which gradually accumulated over the course of the debate. In some cases, the government introduced these ideas, in other

Analysing German decision processes 143

cases it picked up on the opposition's proposals or rejected these. The process can therefore not be readily described as a securitisation process, as the remainder of this section will show.

Otto Schily of the SPD stressed before the press on the day of the attacks that German security agencies received no indications of an imminent terrorist threat for Germany or another EU member state (Käppner, 2001). Nevertheless, Schily called for a readjusted security concept on 13 September. This included a special meeting of the EU's interior ministers to discuss additional security measures, a strengthening of Germany's intelligence services in some areas, and a reconceptualisation of the strict separation between the military and domestic security services (*Frankfurter Allgemeine Zeitung*, 2001). The next day, Schily added that he would put radical-Islamic groups under closer scrutiny and step up air space surveillance. At the same time, he stressed that he would not abandon the *Rechtsstaat* (constitutional state) (Grassmann and Viering, 2001). Conceding that the military might assist the police in some areas, he added that this was in line with existing clauses in Germany's constitution and hence rejected the opposition's calls for reforming constitutional restrictions on deploying the military domestically (*Süddeutsche Zeitung*, 2001d). While members of the CDU and also some prominent SPD politicians demonstratively backed the government's proposals for increased security measures but also vied for more far-reaching proposals of their own, members of the Green Party and others from the SPD as well as from the PDS and the FDP showed little enthusiasm for any proposals potentially curtailing civil liberties (Höll, 2001).

This debate over enhanced domestic security legislation also reinvigorated an ongoing debate between the governing coalition and the CDU-led opposition on an overhaul of Germany's immigration law. Three days after 9/11 the CDU's deputy faction leader Wolfgang Bosbach demanded stronger consideration of the aspect of domestic security in the bill, which was to include provisions making it easier to deport foreigners convicted of crime. Schily countered that his pre-9/11 bill already contained a clause suspending the ECHR's ban on deportation in cases where this implied torture or death if the foreigners in question were found to pose a grave threat to Germany's security (*Süddeutsche Zeitung*, 2001a).

This flurry of proposals, counterproposals and arguments over domestic counterterrorist measures continued in a similar vein until Schröder's cabinet presented a first comprehensive set of measures to be included in new anti-terrorism legislation on 19 September, the so-called '*Sicherheitspaket I*' ('Security Package I') (Grassmann, 2001c). One of these measures in the security package was the extension of laws governing private associations to religious associations, a measure which the government had already considered in the spring since special legal privileges for religious groups hitherto prevented the government from banning radical-Islamic groups supporting terrorism (Glaessner, 2003: 49). Other measures included regulations for increased airport security and the introduction of a new paragraph (§129b StGB) in the penal code allowing for members of terrorist organisations operating abroad to be prosecuted in Germany (Grassmann, 2001c). The government therefore settled for introducing relatively moderate and not entirely new enhancements of the state's capacities for security provision, at least as a first step. Indicative for this moderation is the

144   *Comparing decision processes on use of force*

preservation of pre-charge detention time of arrested suspects at 48 hours maximum, instead of extending it mildly or heavily – as the other four countries under discussion did – in the area of terrorism-related charges.

While the *Bundestag* debated the issue of laws governing private associations again on 9 November and it became law on 12 December 2001, criminalising association with terrorist organisations from abroad (§129b StGB) was not discussed again in parliament until 24 April 2002 and only became law on 30 August 2002 (Deutscher Bundestag, 2001a, 2002). According to Kirstin Hein (2004: 147–148), this is attributable to disputes within the SPD and among the parties in parliament. Christian Ströbele of the Green Party may have voiced the main concern causing the dispute, which may have halted the legislative process, when he remarked in the *Bundestag* on 11 October 2001 that §129b might criminalise residents of Germany who associate themselves with liberation movements in other countries which consider such movements terrorist organisations (Deutscher Bundestag, 2001f: 18717). The killing of 14 Germans in an Al Qaeda attack in Tunisia in April 2002 then re-triggered the legislative process of §129b (Hein, 2004: 147–148). This process is exemplary of the scope and nature of the German government's decision process regarding Security Package 1 because it shows that in Germany, 9/11 as a triggering event did not initiate a strong securitisation process resulting in radically new domestic security measures being enacted in an exceptionally short period of time. Rather, and in strong contrast to its UK counterpart, it can be described as a very mild securitisation process that corresponds to the characteristics of German strategic culture as identified in Chapters 4 and 5, especially regarding norms of the state's domestic coercive capacities versus civil liberties.

These characteristics in scope and nature can also be observed in the decision process surrounding the so-called '*Sicherheitspaket II*' ('Security Package II'). On 28 September Schily announced to the press that a second package of new laws and amendments of existing laws was necessary to enhance the state's preventive counterterrorism capacities. (*Süddeutsche Zeitung*, 2001c). Schröder then announced in his statement delivered to the Bundestag on 11 October 2001 that the government planned to pass a second legislative package by the end of the month. This package would enhance the competencies and data accessibility of Germany's security and criminal investigation agencies for terrorism and crime prevention. This might entail fingerprints and other biometric data being added to identity cards, passports and visa applications. Schröder then immediately emphasised that such measures would in no way undermine the Rechtsstaat, but that they would only enhance the quality and efficiency of the state's counterterrorism agencies (Deutscher Bundestag, 2001f: 18681).

Nevertheless, by mid-October the first rifts had already appeared within the Red–Green coalition over first drafts of Security Package II, with some within the SPD and most of the Green Party arguing that elements in the set of measures now nicknamed the 'Otto catalogue' in reference to the famous mail-order house or 'Schily's wish list' was too much of an intrusion into fundamental rights to privacy and put citizens under general suspicion (*Die Welt*, 2001; Schulte, 2008: 184; *Süddeutsche Zeitung*, 2001b). Only after a 30 hour 'negotiation marathon' between Schily and representatives of the Green Party could

Analysing German decision processes   145

the coalition reach a compromise on 28 October and introduce a first bill to both chambers of parliament on 8 November (Bruns, 2001; Grassmann, 2001a; Schulte, 2008: 182–183).

The compromise bill contained decrees for altogether 200 changes to 20 existing laws and decrees mostly concerning an extension of the competencies of intelligence and security agencies (Grassmann, 2001b; Hein, 2004: 148–149; Roell, 2003; Schulte, 2008: 184–185). The only measure which directly related to the domestic use of force by the state concerned stipulations allowing the federal police to use force as *ultima ratio* on board civilian aircraft (Hein, 2004: 149). The main points of contention during the negotiations, which Schily then agreed to drop, were the German Federal Office of Criminal Investigation's (*Bundeskriminalamt*, BKA) competency to initiate investigations on its own, the re-introduction of chief witness protection laws and stipulations easing the legal requirements for the deportation of asylum seekers suspected of terrorism (Bruns, 2001; Drobinski, 2001; Schulte, 2008: 184).

Nevertheless, the compromise anti-terrorism bill continued to be a source of contention both within the coalition and with other parties once it was debated in parliament. The SPD's spokesperson for interior affairs, Dieter Wiefelspütz, functioned as the bill's chief proponent in the *Bundestag*. In his statements, he placed particular emphasis on the notion of the *Rechtsstaat*, which stood for a state that placed particularly high value on civil liberties and the rule of law. He repeatedly emphasised that Germany was both a liberal and highly secure state, and that the bill would not do anything to change that (Deutscher Bundestag, 2001h: 19665, 2001a: 20748). In fact, on 14 December he explicitly referred to the way in which the same discussion was held in the UK to support his argument that by contrast, there was not in the least a fundamental critique to be levied against the bill regarding its *Rechtsstaatlichkeit*, meaning its compatibility with a liberal, constitutional state (Deutscher Bundestag, 2001j: 20749). This indicates that notions of Germany's identity as a *Rechtsstaat* emanated strong norms emphasising restraint in the use of force by the state to provide security domestically, which shaped the relatively mild securitisation process concerning domestic counterterrorist legislation in Germany after 9/11. Overall, one could not observe as much of a 'rally around the government'-effect in the decision processes regarding post-9/11 counterterrorist legislation in Germany as one would expect from a hard securitisation process. From a comparative perspective the draft legislation was less intrusive into civil liberties in respect to the state's coercive powers as was counterterrorist legislation in the Anglophone countries covered here.

Resonance of the decision to introduce counterterrorist legislation after 9/11

The relatively mild securitisation process with which the government took the decision to overhaul counterterrorist legislation after 9/11 already displayed the characteristics of a strategic culture with low conduciveness to the domestic use of state force against international terrorism. Yet this process is also the product of the particular constellation of political forces in power at that time. An

146 *Comparing decision processes on use of force*

analysis of the decision's resonance can shed further light on the extent to which this particular expression of norms in strategic culture was shared by and therefore resonated positively with various sectors of German politics, the media and the public at large.

The first reactions to Schröder's announcement of measures to enhance Germany's counterterrorism capacities stood in the light of immediate impressions after 9/11. Nevertheless, subtle differences in each party's appraisal of the relationship between security and liberty already surfaced in the first debates on this subject. On 19 November, after Schröder's statement before the *Bundestag*, Friedrich Merz spoke for the CDU and demanded new and comprehensive security policies both domestically and internationally since there could be no liberty without its foundation of security (Deutscher Bundestag, 2001d: 18306). This conceptualisation of the relationship between the two concepts as a complementary rather than a conflicting one was to become a major source of contention both between the CDU and the CSU on the one hand and the SPD, the Green Party, the PDS and the FDP on the other hand as well as between the parties, especially the left wing parties, themselves.

But Schily's first security package still received mostly positive resonance from all parties. When the *Bundestag* voted on the issue of changing the law on associations to include religious associations, only a few members of the PDS voted against the amendment or abstained (Deutscher Bundestag, 2001g: 19551). This broad consensus dwindled somewhat during the debates on the second security package in the *Bundestag*. Speaking for the CDU, Wolfgang Bosbach sharply criticised Schily for compromising too much with the Green Party and therefore not delivering the far-reaching reforms of Germany's domestic security architecture that were now needed. He therefore described the second security package as necessary but insufficient and only going half the distance required (Deutscher Bundestag, 2001h: 19669). But the CDU's criticism did also not translate into specific demands for drastic extensions of the state's powers to use force domestically. This was illustrated e.g. by Bosbach's criticism that the bill did not contain stipulations allowing criminal investigation authorities to request connection data from telecommunications providers beyond 31 December 2001 as well as that fingerprints will not be stored on identity cards and passports, and that principal witness regulations will not be reintroduced (Deutscher Bundestag, 2001h: 19667–19668). In general, the CDU and CSU backed Schily's efforts to overhaul Germany's counterterrorism capacities. While the Conservatives favoured more far-reaching measures to be included in the amendments passed through parliament, they did not actively push for any particularly drastic proposals themselves. The Union parties were generally less concerned about a potential conflict between civil liberties and counterterrorism as they saw security and liberty more as complementary than conflicting aims of statecraft.

Volker Beck spoke for the Greens in both major debates. He concurred with Wiefelspütz of the SPD that through the proposed measures the government was sufficiently careful to both provide adequate means to fight terrorism and not to overreact to terrorism and thereby bring efforts to achieve security in the face of terrorism in conflict with its duty to safeguard hard-won civil liberties. Underscoring this argument, he referred to the many proposals that the coalition did not include in the bill, such as the right to deport foreigners on the basis of a mere suspicion of involvement in terrorist activities, certain rights of the BKA to start investigations without official warrants, and rights of the Federal Office for the Protection of the Constitution (*Bundesamt für Verfassungsschutz*, BfV) to request information from banks as well as transport or telecommunications services providers without parliamentary control and reporting duties (Deutscher Bundestag, 2001h: 19670, 2001j: 20753). These examples demonstrate the meticulous, legalistic and detailed arguments on the rights and duties of the state that characterised the parliamentary debates over Schily's counterterrorism legislation. Ultimately, a broad majority of parliamentarians in the *Bundestag* provided positive resonance to the government's mild securitisation efforts regarding domestic counterterrorism legislation after 9/11.

Of the 22 commentaries on the subject of post-9/11 counterterrorist legislation in the *Frankfurter Allgemeine Zeitung*, 14 were classified as supporting the government's plans. Eight of these were classified as strongly supportive and six as moderately supportive. Another six articles were found to be moderately critical of these and two were categorised as neutral since they dealt with the subject of Schily's counterterrorist legislation but did not express an opinion that falls into either category. From these figures one can already discern that the newspaper's editorial staff was divided on the subject but a majority supported the measures. However, for a number of reasons many FAZ commentaries once again did not fit into these categories straightforwardly. Many articles commented on a host of other related subjects such as the coalition's general performance in government, immigration policy, or party politics. Others criticised Schily's proposals for not going far enough but thereby actually expressed strong support for those measures that were eventually agreed on. Nevertheless, one can conclude that most commentators supported the government's domestic security policies after 9/11 and many advocated for more drastic measures. Overall, there was widespread yet no unequivocal endorsement of an expansion of state powers for the purpose of counterterrorism. Some fears of civil liberties being compromised too much through Schily's perceived post-9/11 counterterrorist frenzy persisted.

In the *Süddeutsche Zeitung* there was a strong current of opinions against expanding state powers among the commentaries. This opinion was expressed near-exclusively by the newspaper's editor-in-chief for domestic affairs, Heribert Prantl. Prantl wrote 20 out of the 21 articles analysed, all of which were critical of the government's actions. Eleven of these were classified as strongly critical. The articles made frequent references to Germany's earlier experience with terrorism in the 1970s and the country's history of state encroachments into civil liberties in times of perceived insecurity. A left-leaning liberal, Prantl was unequivocal in his opinion and vividly recalled West Germany's vitriolic debate over internal security in the 1970s in the face of terrorism and the associations this raised with Germany's totalitarian past.

The tabloid *Bild* was similarly unequivocal in its views but argued largely in the opposite direction. All of the seven opinion pieces on the topic of counterterrorism legislation are supportive of the government's decisions in this regard and all but one supported it strongly. While its commentators concurred with the *Süddeutsche* that one must not succumb to fear in the face of terrorism, they

148 *Comparing decision processes on use of force*

drew the opposite conclusion in arguing that the country must therefore be brave enough to allow the state to confront terrorism through far-reaching new counterterrorism powers (Lambeck, 2001; Quoos, 2001). Consequently, *Bild*'s editors held an unfavourable opinion of the Greens and criticised Schily for making too many concessions during the coalition-internal negotiations over the second security package (Henkel, 2001a; Koch, 2001). But the second security package eventually received a highly favourable commentary in which Rolf Kleine rhetorically asked: "Why can't politics always act this fast?" (Kleine, 2001). Insofar as these comments reflect the opinions of large parts of *Bild*'s readers, they suggest that the general population was not as concerned about civil liberties being curtailed after 9/11 as the country's left-leaning liberal elites.

Although the available data on public opinion polls on the subject of post-9/11 counterterrorist legislation in Germany is scarce, one can discern a general acceptance of the measures implemented. According to a weighted TNS Emnid poll for the German news television network N-TV of 5 October 2001, 66 per cent of all 1001 respondents polled in the week of 24–30 September 2001 supported drawing on the *Bundeswehr* in domestic efforts to fight terrorism, even if this required changes to Germany's constitution. The poll also showed that 75 per cent favoured curtailing the protection of data privacy in order to facilitate counterterrorism efforts and a further 84 per cent supported extending the powers of undercover agents to fight terrorism (Rheinische Post Online, 2001b; TNS Emnid/N-TV, 2001). Another weighted poll by Forsa for the weekly *Die Woche*, which asked 1002 respondents on 25 and 26 October for their opinion on the second security package, showed that 59 per cent supported the measures contained in the package while only 31 per cent thought it was too much of an intrusion into civil liberties. Yet while a majority of supporters of the SPD, the CDU and the PDS favoured the measures, supporters of the Greens rejected the compromise negotiated between the SPD and its party's leadership by 61 per cent, with only 28 per cent supporting it (Rheinische Post Online, 2001a). With some exceptions, the general public therefore generally provided positive resonance to the government's mild securitisation moves resulting in moderate enhancements of the state's security and intelligence capacities.

Analysing the German decision process regarding the use of force in Iraq 2003

Germany's decision not to participate in this war may already at first glance appear as the product of its strategic culture. But this correlation alone does not reveal whether a widely shared strategic culture indeed expresses itself in the resonance or whether some actors sought to securitise the situation and bring about an active military participation, yet various circumstantial factors and constellations of decision-makers led to the outcome at hand. After all, there is strong potential for a conflict between German norms of alliance solidarity and German norms of restraint in the range of goals for which military force can be legitimately applied. The potential triggering event for the securitisation of Iraq's WMD programme, however, emanated from the US administration's securitisation moves. An analysis of the decision process leading to the relative absence of

Analysing German decision processes   149

securitisation and its resonance regarding the threat nexus between Iraq's weapons of mass destruction programme, terrorism and the Iraqi regime can therefore shed further light on the question of the extent to which the particular expressions of Germany's strategic culture can explain the German government's decision to refrain from joining the war on Iraq after 9/11.

The decision not to use force in Iraq

There are numerous scholarly analyses and descriptions of the German decision regarding the Iraq War (Buras and Longhurst, 2004; Dettke, 2009; Erb, 2003; Harnisch, 2004; Longhurst, 2004; cf. Meyer, 2007; Szabo, 2004). Much of this attention emanated from the unprecedented discord that this decision stirred up between some European states and the US as well as, to a lesser degree, among European states themselves. From the sequence of the decision process described in these analyses one can derive that the German position regarding the question of military intervention in Iraq solidified at a relatively early point in time. Already at the annual Munich Security Conference in February 2002, Germany's defence minister Rudolf Scharping expressed strong disagreement with the American administration over the idea of extending the war on terror to Iraq and that it was naïve to believe Europeans would support this (Baltrusaitis, 2008: 269–270; Harnisch, 2004: 8; Longhurst, 2004: 87).

The German government therefore already signalled its reluctance towards the idea of extending the war on terror to Iraq in early 2002. But at this stage the government had not yet ruled out the possibility. Over the summer of 2002, Schröder stressed repeatedly that he would only contemplate such action if it had the UN's authorisation and that for the moment Iraq posed no threat to the US or its allies since the policy of containment was still effective (Harnisch, 2004: 12). In late July, a government spokesperson still evaded the question of whether Germany would participate in military action against Iraq by stating that as long as there were no specific requests for military support from the US, there was no need for a decision by the German government (cited in Harnisch, 2004: 12).

But as the next *Bundestag* elections of 22 September 2002 moved closer, the German position became more articulate. On 5 August, Schröder stated at an election rally in Hannover that Germany was not available for military adventures and that *Spielereien* (playing games) with war and military intervention would happen "without us" (quoted in Szabo, 2004: 23). Over the remainder of the election campaign Schröder became increasingly outspoken in his criticism of the US administration's rhetoric concerning Iraq and rallied for a 'German way' in foreign policy (Baltrusaitis, 2008: 272–273; Longhurst, 2004: 88; Szabo, 2004: 23–27). On 5 September, in an interview with the *New York Times*, Schröder then argued that the case against a war with Iraq was so strong that he would oppose it even if it had UN Security Council authorisation (see also Baltrusaitis, 2008: 273–274; Erlanger, 2001; Szabo, 2004: 26).

Thus, as US war rhetoric intensified in August and September 2002, Schröder presented himself as a staunch opponent of military action in Iraq during the election campaign and thereby provided an antithesis of US securitisation efforts.

150   *Comparing decision processes on use of force*

In a sense, he almost securitised American securitisation in warning against what he saw as a 'military adventure' and a 'huge mistake' since it brought further instability to the Middle East, distracted from the fight against terrorism in Afghanistan Thus it only helped Al Qaeda and added tension to relations between the Islamic world and the West (Erlanger, 2001; see also Longhurst, 2004: 88–89). During the election campaign, Schröder therefore presented himself as the only guarantor of a foreign policy that would keep Germany secure from a US-led military campaign that was bound to bring more insecurity to Germany and the world at large.

Schröder's direct opponent, candidate for Chancellor Edmund Stoiber of the CSU, accused him of opportunistically damaging US–German relations to an unprecedented extent by prematurely answering a question over which the US administration still deliberated, which in turn only reduced the pressure on Saddam Hussein's regime to comply with the international community's demands (Erb, 2003: 204–205). However, Stoiber did not securitise the issue of Iraqi WMDs himself and attack Schröder for failing to realise the presence of an existential threat, but he accused Schröder of opportunism in the face of the upcoming election.

After turning a 10 per cent lag one month before polling day into a narrow win, Schröder stood by his decision to rule out any German involvement. On 13 February 2003, Schröder delivered a statement before the *Bundestag* in which he defended his position once more on the grounds that Iraq did not pose a threat to international peace and security that was sufficient in the sense of the UN Charter to allow for military action, and that such action against Iraq could even be counterproductive to the fight against terrorism (Deutscher Bundestag, 2003: 1876). Most importantly, Schröder argued that the international community had not exhausted all means to resolve the conflict through peaceful alternatives. He emphasised that the most noble cause of international politics was to prevent wars, that the policy of his government was a policy of peace [*Friedenspolitik*], that the use of military force always had to be subjected to the strictest confinements and that there must never be a process of gradual acclimatisation to the thought that war was an ordinary means of politics (Deutscher Bundestag, 2003: 1875). He therefore saw it as his distinct responsibility to ensure that every opportunity to disarm Iraq by peaceful means was given a chance before the UN Security Council could authorise the use of force (Deutscher Bundestag, 2003: 1878).

The relatively short time frame within which Schröder made the decision to rule out any military contribution to a war in Iraq, the arsenal of arguments which he could mobilise to defend this position and the vigour with which he pursued his stance during the election campaign all indicate that it was not a decision that involved careful deliberation of the various risks involved for the chancellor. Much rather, this was a decision which almost forced itself on the chancellor given the normative context or, in other words, strategic culture in which German politics operated. This normative context bore a very low conduciveness to any attempts at securitising the situation in Iraq but it presented ample opportunities for political actors to gain political capital from reconstituting Germany's identity in opposition to the US.

Analysing German decision processes 151

Resonance of the decision not to use force in Iraq

As mentioned, Schröder caught up from a 10 per cent gap in pre-election polls during August and September 2002, elevating the issue of a possible war with Iraq to one of the main issues in the campaign. This alone already indicates that his clear stance on the issue was widely popular and encountered little contestation. Nevertheless, it was the subject of intense debate. After all, there was no precedent to the decision to openly oppose US plans in the history of the Federal Republic's foreign policy. Strong sentiments of gratitude for America's support in the past forged the maxim that even in cases of disagreement over foreign policy, Germany would quietly abstain from direct action rather than openly argue against the US government. Schröder's move therefore proved to be popular yet also controversial. Although less the subject of debates in parliament, his decision received extensive commentary in the media and was the subject of numerous public opinion polls.

A major debate over Germany's position on the issue of war with Iraq took place in the *Bundestag* on 13 February 2003. Schröder first delivered a statement in which he reiterated his aforementioned arguments against a war with Iraq and defended himself against accusations of disloyalty towards the US by highlighting Germany's commitments to Operation Enduring Freedom in Afghanistan and elsewhere as well as German contributions to peacekeeping missions worldwide. He then attacked the CDU as being part of the "coalition of the willing" (Deutscher Bundestag, 2003: 1879).

This accusation seemingly infuriated Angela Merkel of the CDU. She declared at the outset that "The people in this country do not want war. Those who sit in this chamber also do not want war" (Deutscher Bundestag, 2003: 1880). She then accused Schröder of seeking to vilify her party as warmongers, which only showed that he was under pressure and on the wrong track. In her view, his openly declared intent that he would work to prevent the implementation of Resolution 1441, irrespective of what UN weapons inspections in Iraq concluded, actually made war more likely by alleviating international pressure on the Iraqi regime (Deutscher Bundestag, 2003: 1880). Her arguments against Schröder therefore mirrored Stoiber's during the election campaign in that she did not accuse Schröder of refusing to commit to an increasingly unavoidable war, but she accused him of pursuing the wrong strategy to prevent the current situation from escalating into war.

This similarity with Stoiber also transpired when she accused Schröder of opportunistically damaging Germany's ties with the US as well as weakening the EU, the UN, NATO and the work of the weapons inspectors by not communicating his position with the American administration in advance. In her view, all chancellors of the Federal Republic had thus far and above all domestic political disputes pledged themselves to the higher aim of "Never again war! In its implementation this means: never again a German *Sonderweg* (separate path)" (Deutscher Bundestag, 2003: 1880). She found strong words to express her criticism of Schröder's diplomatic handling over Iraq but ultimately she criticised the nature in which he expressed his opposition to US policy rather than criticising this opposition per se and defending the US position regarding Iraq's threat

152   *Comparing decision processes on use of force*

potential. This suggests that many centre-right conservatives of Germany's political spectrum placed more emphasis on norms of alliance solidarity while sharing
norms imposing strict constraints on the use of military force. This presented
Germany's centre-right parties with a particularly delicate situation in the run-up
to the Iraq War. These were torn between opposing Schröder's blunt stance
against military action regardless of what further efforts by UN weapons inspectors might conclude, and America's drive for war regardless of such further
efforts might conclude. The CDU's resonance was therefore negative towards
the government's open confrontation with the US but positive towards the government's refraining from a German participation in a war.

Wolfgang Schäuble of the CDU voiced similar disconcertment about the
currently frosty relationship with the US administration. His criticism centred
on his observation that there was no need to take a stand and confront the US
over its Iraq policy since there were no US demands for a German military
contribution. Schäuble clarified that the CDU also never vied for a substantial
German military contribution to the eventuality of war. More importantly,
Germany owed the US its "political solidarity" (*politische Solidarität*) (Deutscher
Bundestag, 2003: 1902). The CDU's motion put before the *Bundestag* in the
debate merely called upon the German government to support provisions such
as aerial reconnaissance, medical evacuation, NBC reconnaissance, Patriot-
defence systems, granting overflight rights, protecting US military bases in
Germany and patrolling the Persian Gulf, together with its European partners
and within the confines of its capabilities and constitutional capacities (Deutscher Bundestag, 2003: 1902). Some of these assets, such as NBC reconnaissance teams, were already deployed to the Kuwaiti border with Iraq under
Operation Enduring Freedom. Guido Westerwelle of the FDP faction also
refrained from attacking Schröder's non-securitisation per se, but mainly criticised Schröder for instrumentalising the issue for personal political gain by
depicting the opposition as warmongers and the ruling coalition as *Friedensfre-
unde* (friends of peace) even though in his view the opposite was the case
(Deutscher Bundestag, 2003: 1888). The vote on the CDU's parliamentary
motion revealed the disunity within the opposition over the question of war
with Iraq. Besides all members of the Red–Green coalition, two parliamentarians each from the CDU and the FDP also voted against the motion while
another CDU parliamentarian and 35 FDP members, including Westerwelle,
abstained (Deutscher Bundestag, 2003: 1916).

The coalition, accordingly, rejected the opposition's harsh yet ambiguous critiques as exaggerated and irrelevant to the question at hand. The Greens' Joschka
Fischer, for instance, replied to Merkel that her accusations of the Schröder government pursuing a *Sonderweg* and breaking with Germany's traditional transatlanticism were merely "questions of style" (*Stilfragen*) distracting from the actual
question at hand: how to resolve the Iraq crisis peacefully (Deutscher Bundestag,
2003: 1885). Fischer argued that the Iraqi regime's obstructions diminished and
that weapons inspections had already made Iraq less dangerous. The right
strategy to resolve the crisis by peaceful means was therefore to intensify inspections whilst maintaining international pressure rather than to abort inspections
and start a war. He further argued that the latter strategy had no public backing

Analysing German decision processes 153

and that even the CDU did not dare to publicly support this strategy before the *Bundestag* in this debate (Deutscher Bundestag, 2003: 1885). One can interpret this to imply that Fischer complained about the opposition harshly attacking the coalition whilst actually providing positive resonance to its anti-war stance. All parties ostensibly agreed that at this stage a war with Iraq was still avoidable and had to be avoided at all costs. The debate took place over the right strategy on how to achieve this goal.

Schröder declared his intention to oppose a war with Iraq during the election campaign in September 2002 and stood by this decision until the war broke out in March 2003. Correspondingly, the German media's commentaries on this decision are more sparsely scattered over a wider time horizon and are concentrated at the time when he announced this decision during the election campaign and as the Iraq crisis intensified in the three months leading up to the outbreak of war. In order to capture a more complete picture of the media's resonance to this decision it is therefore necessary to look at the broader time span in September 2002, when Schröder announced his decision, and from January 2003 until the war broke out on 21 March.

Within this time frame, the *Frankfurter Allgemeine Zeitung* featured 56 commentaries on the Iraq War. Of these, 22 can be considered to be moderately supportive of the German government's decision to oppose it, six articles did not express a clear opinion on this and are therefore classified as neutral, and 24 are considered to be critical of the decision, with six of these being strongly critical. The newspaper's editorialists therefore once again held mixed and not particularly strong opinions on the decision, but a majority provided negative resonance. Initially, most editorialists echoed the CDU in condemning Schröder's decision as an opportunistic and populist election campaign strategy which damaged Germany's ties to its closest allies and isolated it internationally. But this line of criticism did not address the decision to refrain from committing German troops to a possible war with Iraq. Editorialists such as Berthold Kohler, Eckart Lohse and Karl Feldmayer merely argued that it was unrealistic of the German government to believe its stance could have any effect on the United States, therefore it was not worth the potential costs.

From January 2003 onwards, opinions became more varied and some editorialists changed their views, especially after the US administration's criticism of European opposition became increasingly articulate. Some FAZ editorialists such as Günther Nonnenmacher, Karl Feldmayer and Volker Zastrow ultimately took a more sympathetic view of the German government's firm position on a war with Iraq as based on real and irreconcilable differences in opinion with the US. The ambiguity of the FAZ's commentaries demonstrates the difficult position in which German conservative political forces found themselves in early 2003. Most rejected an open confrontation with the US while simultaneously disagreeing with its rationale for war.

In the *Süddeutsche Zeitung*, commentaries were once again more in unison. Of the 50 editorials identified to be on the subject of a possible Iraq War, 40 were considered to support the German government's course, although only moderately. In another nine articles, criticism outweighed support for Schröder's stance and another editorial did not take a clear side. As in the case of the FAZ, the

154 *Comparing decision processes on use of force*

criticism was strongest during the election campaign in September 2002. However, the result of the analysis shows that an overwhelming majority of four-fifths stood behind the German government's decision to oppose the Iraq War. This result does not imply that the SZ's authors did not criticise the Schröder government in their editorials. On the contrary, many commentators such as Nico Fried, Wolfgang Koydl, Christoph Schwennicke and Stefan Kornelius expressed near outrage at his absolute stance against a war expressed at a relatively early point in time. They saw Schröder's absolute stance in this regard as a disingenuous, politically motivated move which incurs heavy costs on Germany by weakening its alliances. But as the debate over a possible war intensified and concrete evidence of an Iraqi threat became the subject of debate internationally, the SZ's editorialists supported the German government's opposition to the case for war in near unison. With the exception of Stefan Kornelius, the argument that the German government should not openly oppose the US on grounds that a war lacked legitimacy because the German government could not prevent the war in any case, and therefore the damages this incurs to European and NATO's cohesion were not justified, did not find any supporters. Kurt Kister summed up the reason given by most SZ editorialists for their rejection of this argument: "Whoever demands from the Schröder government to affiliate itself with a policy identified to be wrong, supports a lack of principles" (Kister, 2003). Overall, the SZ's commentaries in the selected time frame displayed close to no positive resonance at all to any potential securitisation processes of Iraqi WMDs.

The *Bild*'s editorials underwent a transformation similar to that in the other newspapers within the selected time frame, with the notable difference that its editorialists were initially critical of Schröder's categorical 'no' but then became less assertive in their commentaries. Of 18 editorials on the issue, eight contained moderate criticisms of the Schröder government's decision, four criticised it strongly, one showed moderate support for his stance and the last five editorials were classified as neutral. But in contrast to the other two newspapers, the Bild's editorialists Herbert Kremp, Klaus Naumann and Hugo Müller-Vogg supported American securitisation efforts as well as humanitarian and strategic rationales for war in early February 2003. Yet by the second half of February, the tone changed again. The *Bild*'s editorials expressed more neutral opinions such as the need to address domestic economic problems again despite the Iraq crisis (Henkel, 2003), the need for Europe and America to overcome its differences and cooperate in Iraq's post-war reconstruction despite its current differences in opinion (Loewe, 2003), the need for those who opposed war to also hope for a short war and American victory (Kremp, 2003), or the need for the international community to start a wider debate on legitimate forms of government at the United Nations (Martin, 2003). *Bild* thus first provided negative resonance to Schröder's decision not to securitise the threat case of Iraqi WMDs but then provided only little resonance. This indicates that a stronger securitisation effort had little potential of finding positive resonance in Germany, which supports the findings in Chapter 5 that broadly shared strategic cultures provide different preconditions for such efforts.

Both members of the *Bundestag* and editorialists often referred to public opinion polls in the German case to either support or criticise the German

Analysing German decision processes 155

government's position on the issue of a possible war with Iraq. They either depicted Schröder as a chancellor who was in touch with his voters or a chancellor who instrumentalised public opinion for political gain rather than leading the public on the basis of principle. In both cases polls were invoked to demonstrate that the German public overwhelmingly opposed the war. The polls indeed show that consistently wide majorities of respondents, ranging from 66 per cent to 85 per cent and even 95 per cent in one poll, were opposed to American military action against Iraq in the months before and after its start (see Table A5, Appendix). Although there are not many disaggregated figures available, Infratest dimap added to its March 2003 survey that the figures indicating an overwhelming rejection of military action are similar across population groups such as age, gender and party affiliations (Infratest dimap/ARD, 2003: 3). Only a poll for the TV network ZDF of 24–27 March 2003 revealed that of 85 per cent overall, 77 per cent of all men and 89 per cent of all women did not think it was right of the US and its allies to act militarily against Iraq. (Forschungsgruppe Wahlen/ZDF, 2003).

Table A6 (see Appendix) shows that a comparatively strong rejection among the German public of the idea of a war on Iraq also applies to various hypothetical conditions under which such a war could take place. Opposition to war approached 90 per cent in questions concerning military action without a UN mandate and remained at a comparatively strong 52 per cent and 46 per cent even in the scenarios of a UN Security Council mandate and the discovery of WMDs, respectively. The general public in Germany therefore showed a distinctly low predisposition for positive resonance to a German securitisation process of Iraqi WMDs resulting in German support for a war on Iraq, especially when compared with the case of the UK.

The ZDF poll conducted shortly after the outbreak of war also showed that 75 per cent agreed with the Schröder government's policy towards a war with Iraq, including 57 per cent of all respondents affiliated with the CDU, while only 20 per cent of all respondents and only 39 per cent of all CDU supporters agreed with the CDU's position in this regard, whereas 68 per cent of all respondents and also 49 per cent of all CDU supporters did not agree (Forschungsgruppe Wahlen/ZDF, 2003). This shows that the CDU did not propose an attractive alternative position regarding the war on Iraq. The strong accusations of populism and recklessness levelled against Schröder in parliament and the media for his categorical position towards the US seemingly did not encounter much criticism among the electorate.

Differences along party affiliations can also be discerned in the Politbarometer Survey of early March 2003. It shows that 62 per cent overall and three-quarters of all SPD-aligned respondents rejected any form of German contribution to US military action against Iraq. However, a slim majority of 50 per cent of CDU supporters favoured a German contribution to US military action against Iraq either through material and financial support or through troops, while 48 per cent rejected any form of contribution. Furthermore, SPD and Greens supporters were significantly more inclined to support Germany openly opposing a second resolution authorising the use of force against Iraq in the UN Security Council. This indicates that those among the German public with a more

156 *Comparing decision processes on use of force*

conservative political orientation were less staunchly opposed to military action and showed some potential for accommodating the German government taking a position resembling that of the Dutch government, which, in its own words, supported the war "politically, but not militarily" (Everts and Isernia, 2005: 11). While this policy might incur higher costs to Germany's decision-making elites, one cannot claim on the basis of public opinion polls that it would be entirely outside the range of possible state actions supported by German strategic culture.

One can therefore conclude that German strategic culture contained very little room for a hard securitisation process of Iraqi WMDs as pursued by the Blair government in the UK. On the contrary, it even provided some political incentive to mildly securitise – and seek an open confrontation with – the US government. However, a soft securitisation process as envisaged by the CDU, in which the German government provided political support and some rudimentary military contributions, might have also encountered some positive resonance. This applies especially to Germany's more conservative segments of the population, which share a normative aversion to use of force with the rest of the population, though theirs is slightly less strongly pronounced, but which also feels a stronger normative attachment to the transatlantic alliance. Yet a German government authorising a sizeable German troop contribution to the Iraq War would, in all likelihood, find itself far outside the confines of German strategic culture.

Conclusion and outlook

The three analyses of German decision processes on the use of force by the state after 9/11 conducted in this chapter showed that the shapes of the securitisation or not-securitisation processes leading up to these decisions correspond to the findings on strategic culture previously elaborated in Chapters 4 and 5. The first two instances of security policy decisions can be described as the products of a relatively mild securitisation process, and the third decision represents an instance of not-securitisation bordering counter-securitisation of the US's securitisation process.

The decision processes analysed in this chapter are largely reflective of the modern centre-left strand within German strategic culture, which holds norms that are more conducive to the use of military force and enhanced domestic security measures than the more orthodox left-wing strand, but which also conform less to demands by Western allies and the domestic security bureaucracy than the more conservative right-wing strand. But the criticisms levied and alternative policies discussed in the debates during which actors from across the political spectrum voiced their resonance to the government's course of action showed that the spectrum of opinions on specific security policy decisions mirrors the confines of German strategic culture in general as identified in Chapters 4 and 5. Through their securitisation processes, actors largely positioned themselves close to the centre of gravity of German strategic culture.

The ensuing largely positive resonance during the phase of agential social interaction across all three instances indicates that these actions by and large brought about morphostasis in German strategic culture. While the 1990s can be argued to have seen a slight and gradual adjustment of German strategic culture towards a more proactive strategic culture commensurate to Germany's new position in the post-Cold War context, the analysis of the three post-9/11 instances of security policy and practice in this chapter suggests that these have largely stalled this process. During the extended phase of structural elaboration, new information, events and experiences are likely to have reinforced this morphostasis. This applies especially to the non-discovery of WMD in Iraq and the country's deteriorating security situation after the fall of the regime. These are likely to have further discredited the original Anglo-Saxon position, and reinforced those norms within German strategic culture that caused reluctance and scepticism during the decision process both on the side of elites and of the public. The protracted and inconclusive campaign in Afghanistan, on the other hand, is likely to have called the original decision into question (cf. Löfflmann, 2008). The recent news reports about US-led global surveillance programmes, meanwhile, are likely to have reaffirmed norms within German strategic culture demanding restraint in the state's coercive capacities for the provision of security.

The opinion polls addressed in Chapter 5 even suggest that the proclivity towards the use of force within German strategic culture diminished somewhat since 2003. Another clue of morphostasis can be found in the adoption of the notion of a *Kultur der militärischen Zurückhaltung* [culture of military restraint] as a *Leitmotiv* of the foreign and security policy of the former German Foreign Minister Guido Westerwelle between 2009 and 2013 (Auswärtiges Amt, 2012). He applied this notion in his decisions to refrain from a significant German military involvement in the French- and British-led military interventions in Libya in 2011 and Mali in 2012 (Nass, 2013). When a new government took over in 2013, it announced its intention to abandon this *Leitmotiv* and heed the call launched in a speech by German Federal President Joachim Gauck in January 2014 to allow for a more proactive involvement and the assumption of more global responsibilities by Germany in international security affairs, including through a stronger military engagement worldwide (Monath, 2014). The new Minister of Defence, Ursula von der Leyen, then announced that she would seek a stronger involvement of *Bundeswehr* forces in international peace operations. Tellingly, an opinion poll conducted for the German public television channel ZDF then revealed on 31 January 2014 that only 32 per cent of respondents supported this idea while 62 per cent rejected it (Forschungsgruppe Wahlen/ZDF, 2014). Far from being in the process of passing the threshold to a 'proactive-robust' type, German strategic culture is therefore likely to remain in the 'reactive-proactive' category for the foreseeable future.

Bibliography

Auswärtiges Amt (2012) "Die Kultur der militärischen Zurückhaltung ist zeitgemäßer denn je". (Interview). German Foreign Ministry. Available from: www.auswaertiges-amt.de/DE/Infoservice/Presse/Interviews/2012/120330-BM_WAZ.html (accessed 23 February 2014).

Baltrusaitis DF (2008) *Friends Indeed? Coalition Burden Sharing and the War in Iraq.* Ann Arbor, MI: ProQuest.

158   Comparing decision processes on use of force

Bannas G (2001) "Eine amerikanische Anfrage und eine deutsche Antwort". *Frankfurter Allgemeine Zeitung*, Frankfurt am Main, 7 November.

Berger TU (1998) *Cultures of Antimilitarism: National Security in Germany and Japan*. Baltimore: JHU Press.

Bruns T (2001) "Kompromiss nach 30 Stunden Verhandlung". *Die Welt*, Berlin, 29 October. Available from: www.welt.de/print-welt/article484008/Kompromiss-nach-30-Stunden-Verhandlung.html (accessed 10 October 2013).

Buras P and Longhurst K (2004) "The Berlin Republic, Iraq, and the Use of Force". *European Security*, 13(3), 215–245.

Canadian Centres for Teaching Peace Inc. (2001) Gallup International poll on terrorism in the US. Available from: www.peace.ca/galluppollonterrorism.htm (accessed 23 July 2013).

Dalgaard-Nielsen A (2006) *Germany, Pacifism and Peace Enforcement*. Manchester: Manchester University Press.

Dettke D (2009) *Germany Says 'No': The Iraq War and the Future of German Foreign and Security Policy*. Washington DC: Woodrow Wilson Center Press.

Deutscher Bundestag (2001a) Basisinformationen über den Vorgang Erstes Gesetz zur Änderung des Vereinsgesetzes (G-SIG: 14019763). Available from: http://pdok.bundestag.de/extrakt/ba/WP14/570/57099.html (accessed 10 October 2013).

Deutscher Bundestag (2001b) Plenarprotokoll 14/186 (12 September 2001). Available from: http://dip21.bundestag.de/dip21/btp/14/14186.pdf (accessed 21 August 2013).

Deutscher Bundestag (2001c) Plenarprotokoll 14/187 (19 September 2001). Available from: http://dip21.bundestag.de/dip21/btp/14/14187.pdf (accessed 23 August 2013).

Deutscher Bundestag (2001d) Plenarprotokoll 14/192 (11. October 2001). Available from: http://dip21.bundestag.de/dip21/btp/14/14192.pdf (accessed 22 August 2013).

Deutscher Bundestag (2001e) Plenarprotokoll 14/199 (9 November 2001). Available from: http://dipbt.bundestag.de/doc/btp/14/14199.pdf (accessed 22 August 2013).

Deutscher Bundestag (2001f) Plenarprotokoll 14/201 (15 November 2001). Available from: http://dipbt.bundestag.de/doc/btp/14/14201.pdf (accessed 22 August 2013).

Deutscher Bundestag (2001g) Plenarprotokoll 14/202 (16 November 2001). Available from: http://dip21.bundestag.de/dip21/btp/14/14202.pdf (accessed 22 August 2013).

Deutscher Bundestag (2001h) Plenarprotokoll 14/209 (14 December 2001). Available from: http://dipbt.bundestag.de/doc/btp/14/14209.pdf (accessed 10 October 2013).

Deutscher Bundestag (2002) Basisinformationen über den Vorgang Vierunddreißigstes Strafrechtsänderungsgesetz – § 129b StGB (34. StrÄndG) (G-SIG: 14019764). Available from: http://pdok.bundestag.de/extrakt/ba/WP14/558/55887.html (accessed 10 October 2013).

Deutscher Bundestag (2003) Plenarprotokoll 15/25 (13 February 2003). Available from: http://dip21.bundestag.de/dip21/btp/15/15025.pdf#site=6 (accessed 18 October 2013).

Die Welt (2001) Grüne streiten mit Schily über innere Sicherheit. *Die Welt*, Berlin, 17 October, Available from: www.welt.de/print-welt/article481838/Gruene-streiten-mit-Schily-ueber-innere-Sicherheit.html (accessed 10 October 2013).

Drobinski M (2001) Schneller abschieben. *Süddeutsche Zeitung*, Munich 7 November.

Duffield JS (1998) *World Power Forsaken: Political Culture, International Institutions, and German Security Policy after Unification*. Palo Alto, CA: Stanford University Press.

Erb S (2003) *German Foreign Policy: Navigating a New Era*. Boulder: Lynne Rienner Pub.

Erlanger S (2001) "German Leader's Warning: War Plan Is a Huge Mistake". *New York Times*, New York, 5 September. Available from: www.nytimes.com/2002/09/05/world/traces-of-terror-perspectives-german-leader-s-warning-war-plan-is-a-huge-mistake.html (accessed 17 October 2013).

Everts P and Isernia P (2005) "The War in Iraq". *Public Opinion Quarterly*, 69(2), 264–323.

Analysing German decision processes   159

Falkenberger KD (2001a) "Die Zeit ist abgelaufen". *Frankfurter Allgemeine Zeitung*, Frankfurt am Main, 8 October.

Falkenberger KD (2001b) "Druckwelle". *Frankfurter Allgemeine Zeitung*, Frankfurt am Main, 13 September.

Falkenberger KD (2001c) "In Kabul". *Frankfurter Allgemeine Zeitung*, Frankfurt am Main, 19 September.

Falkenberger KD (2001d) "Reaktionen". *Frankfurter Allgemeine Zeitung*, Frankfurt am Main, 10 October.

Falkenberger KD (2001e) "Zielkonflikt". *Frankfurter Allgemeine Zeitung*, Frankfurt am Main, 25 September.

Falkenberger KD (2001f) "Zwischenbilanz". *Frankfurter Allgemeine Zeitung*, Frankfurt am Main, 13 October.

Fischer J (2011) *'I am not convinced': der Irak-Krieg und die rot-grünen Jahre*. Cologne: Kiepenheuer & Witsch.

Forschungsgruppe Wahlen/ZDF (2003) ZDF-Politbarometer II im März 2003. Available from: www.presseportal.de/pm/7840/433270/zdf-pressemitteilung-zdf-politbarometer-ii-im-maerz-2003-ueberwaeltigende-mehrheit-gegen-irak-krieg (accessed 21 October 2013).

Forschungsgruppe Wahlen/ZDF (2014) ZDF-Politbarometer January II 2014. Available from: https://presseportal.zdf.de/aktuelles/mitteilung/zdf-politbarometer-januar-ii-2014/772/ (accessed 23 February 2014).

Frankfurter Allgemeine Zeitung (2001) "Schily fordert neues Sicherheitskonzept". *Frankfurter Allgemeine Zeitung*, Frankfurt am Main, 13 September.

Glaessner GJ (2003) "Internal Security and the New Anti-Terrorism Act". *German Politics*, 12(1), 43–58.

Gordon PH (2001) "NATO after 11 September". *Survival*, 43(4), 89–106.

Görtemaker M (2009) *Die Berliner Republik: Wiedervereinigung und Neuorientierung*. Berlin: bebra.

Grassmann P (2001a) "Schilys Balance-Akt". *Süddeutsche Zeitung*, Munich, 29 October.

Grassmann P (2001b) "Sicherheitspaket II komplett". *Süddeutsche Zeitung*, Munich, 12 December.

Grassmann P (2001c) "Strengere Regeln für Sicherheit an Flughäfen". *Süddeutsche Zeitung*, Munich, 20 September.

Grassmann P and Viering J (2001) Schily: "Der Rechtsstaat wird nicht abgeschafft". *Süddeutsche Zeitung*, Munich, 15 September.

Harnisch S (2004) "German Non-Proliferation Policy and the Iraq Conflict". *German Politics*, 13(1), 1–34.

Hein K (2004) "Die Anti-Terrorpolitik der rot-grünen Bundesregierung". In: Harnisch S, Katsioulis C, and Overhaus M (eds), *Deutsche Sicherheitspolitik: Eine Bilanz der Regierung Schröder*, Baden-Baden: Nomos, pp. 145–171.

Hellmann G, Baumann R and Wagner W (2006) *Deutsche Außenpolitik: Eine Einführung*. 2006th edn. Wiesbaden: VS Verlag für Sozialwissenschaften.

Henkel HO (2001a) "Der Kanzler sieht Roth". *Bild*, Berlin, 16 October.

Henkel HO (2001b) "Es braucht Taten und das Scheckbuch". *Bild*, Berlin, 18 September.

Henkel HO (2003) "Der Kanzler schaut nach innen". *Bild*, Berlin, 24 February.

Höll S (2001) "Lob und ein paar Hintergedanken". *Süddeutsche Zeitung*, Munich, 19 September.

Informationsgemeinschaft zur Feststellung der Verbreitung von Werbeträgern e.V. (2013) "Werbeträgerdaten – Presseerzeugnisse". Available from: http://daten.ivw.eu (accessed 27 September 2013).

Infratest dimap/ARD (2001) "DeutschlandTrend Oktober 2001". Available from: www.infratest-dimap.de/uploads/media/dt0110.pdf (accessed 1 October 2013).

160   *Comparing decision processes on use of force*

Infratest dimap/ARD (2003) "DeutschlandTrend März 2003". Available from: www. infratest-dimap.de/uploads/media/dt0303.pdf (accessed 21 October 2013).

Käppner J (2001) "Beschwichtigende Worte, makabre Scherze". *Süddeutsche Zeitung*, Munich, 13 September.

Kister K (2003) "Deutschland und der Krieg". *Süddeutsche Zeitung*, Munich, 21 March.

Kleine R (2001) "Sicherheit im Paket". *Bild*, Berlin, 15 December.

Koch E (2001) "Otto, finden wir nicht so gut . .". *Bild*, Berlin, 29 October.

Kohler B (2001) "Amerika im Krieg". *Frankfurter Allgemeine Zeitung*, Frankfurt am Main, 22 September.

Kremp H (2003) "Dramatische Stunden". *Bild*, Berlin, 17 March.

Lambeck MS (2001) "Angst ist ein schlechter Ratgeber". *Bild*, Berlin, 19 September.

Lerch WG (2001) "Was tun gegen den Terror?" *Frankfurter Allgemeine Zeitung*, Frankfurt am Main, 16 October.

Loewe L (2003) "Stunde der Wahrheit". *Bild*, Berlin, 18 March.

Löfflmann G (2008) *Verteidigung am Hindukusch? Die Zivilmacht Deutschland und der Krieg in Afghanistan.* Hamburg: Diplomica-Verl.

Longhurst K (2004) *Germany and the Use of Force.* Manchester: Manchester University Press.

Martin PC (2003) "Demokraten und Tyrannen". *Bild*, Berlin, 19 March.

Meyer CO (2007) *The Quest for a European Strategic Culture: Changing Norms on Security and Defence in the European Union.* London: Palgrave Macmillan.

Monath H (2014) "Steinmeier und Leyen wollen mehr militärisches Engagement". *Der Tagesspiegel Online*, 30 January. Available from: www.tagesspiegel.de/politik/aufraeumen-mit-westerwelles-erbe-steinmeier-und-leyen-wollen-mehr-militaerisches-engagemen t/9404918.html (accessed 23 February 2014).

Nass M (2013) "Außenminister: Westerwelles 'Kultur der militärischen Zurückhaltung'". *Die Zeit*, Hamburg, 9 February, Available from: www.zeit.de/2013/06/Westerwelle-Aussenminister-Portrait/seite-3 (accessed 23 February 2014).

Nonnenmacher G (2001a) Koalition der Interessen. *Frankfurter Allgemeine Zeitung*, Frankfurt am Main, 7 October.

Nonnenmacher G (2001b) "Krieg in der Krise". *Frankfurter Allgemeine Zeitung*, Frankfurt am Main, 31 October.

Nonnenmacher G (2001c) "Westlicher Gleichklang". *Frankfurter Allgemeine Zeitung*, Frankfurt am Main, 9 October.

Quoos J (2001) "Keine Angst vor mehr Sicherheit". *Bild*, Berlin, 25 October.

Rauss U (2004) "Kommando Spezialkräfte: Die Profis – S.2 – Politik | STERN.DE". *Stern*, Hamburg, 12 November.

Rheinische Post Online (2001a) "Mehrheit der Deutschen unterstützt Anti-Terror-Paket". *Rheinische Post Online.* Düsseldorf, 30 October, Available from: www.rp-online.de/politik/mehrheit-der-deutschen-unterstuetzt-anti-terror-paket-1.2249494 (accessed 16 October 2013).

Rheinische Post Online (2001b) "Politumfrage: SPD legt zu in der Wählergunst". *Rheinische Post Online*, Düsseldorf, 5 October. Available from: www.rp-online.de/politik/politumfrage-spd-legt-zu-in-der-waehlergunst-1.2249404 (accessed 16 October 2013).

Roell P (2003) "Deutschlands Beitrag zur internationalen Terrorismusbekämpfung". In: Hirschmann K and Leggemann C (eds), *Der Kampf gegen den Terrorismus: Strategien und Handlungserfordernisse in Deutschland*, Berlin: Berliner Wissenschafts-Verlag, pp. 125–142.

Scholzen R (2004) *Das Kommando Spezialkräfte der Bundeswehr KSK.* Stuttgart: Motorbuch.

Schröder G (2006) *Entscheidungen: mein Leben in der Politik.* Hamburg: Hoffmann und Campe.

Schulte PH (2008) *Terrorismus- und Anti-Terrorismus-Gesetzgebung: eine rechtssoziologische Analyse.* Muenster: Waxmann Verlag.

Spiegel Online (2001) "Koalitionskrise: Schröder stellt die Vertrauensfrage". *Spiegel Online*, 13 November. Available from: www.spiegel.de/politik/deutschland/koalitionskrise-schroeder-stellt-die-vertrauensfrage-a-167540.html (accessed 20 August 2013).

Süddeutsche Zeitung (2001a) "Kabinett verschiebt Entscheidung über Zuwanderungsgesetz". *Süddeutsche Zeitung*, Munich, 14 September.

Süddeutsche Zeitung (2001b) "Katastrophen-Warnung aus dem All". *Süddeutsche Zeitung*, Munich, 15 October.

Süddeutsche Zeitung (2001c) "Schily: Militär könnte der Polizei helfen". *Süddeutsche Zeitung*, Munich, 15 September.

Süddeutsche Zeitung (2001d) "Schily will zweites Sicherheitspaket vorlegen". *Süddeutsche Zeitung*, Munich, 29 September.

Szabo SF (2004) *Parting Ways: The Crisis in German-American Relations*. Washington DC: Brookings Institution Press.

TNS Emnid/N-TV (2001) "Emnid-Umfrage: Mehrheit für Diplomatie gegen Terror". *N-TV*, 5 October, Available from: www.n-tv.de/politik/Mehrheit-fuer-Diplomatie-gegen-Terror-article135944.html (accessed 16 October 2013).

Wagener M (2006) "Normalization in Security Policy? Deployments of Bundeswehr Forces Abroad in the Era Schröder, 1998–2004". In: Maull H (ed.), *Germany's Uncertain Power: Foreign Policy of the Berlin Republic*, Basingstoke: Palgrave Macmillan, pp. 79–92.

Wieland L (2001) "Amerika stellt sich um". *Frankfurter Allgemeine Zeitung*, Frankfurt am Main, 1 October.

8 Analysing French decisions on the use of force

French strategic culture's strong drive for self-assertiveness coupled with generally high regard for the institution of a centralist state with the presidency at its epitome afford the French state significant autonomy as regards domestic authorisation requirements. At the same time, this drive also generates strong attachment to those international institutions in which France can play a major role. Regarding norms on the range of goals for which the use of force is considered legitimate, an ambivalent relationship with the US-dominated Western security architecture entails a relative aversion towards the use of force beyond clear self-defence and alliance rationales or its use on humanitarian and idealistic grounds such as missions nominally intended to spread freedom and civilisation or to re-establish order. Domestically, the high regard for the institution of the state on the one hand imbues a relatively high tolerance of intrusive measures to protect the state while on the other hand a strong sense of pride in the achievement of civil liberties implies that the executive must hold these in high regard, at least towards one's own citizens. From this 'proactive-robust' strategic culture that stands close to the 'proactive' end of this range one can deduce that for securitisation processes to be successful these must generally live up to high public expectations of their intended actions to further enhance France's status.

This element of self-assertiveness in French strategic culture and its corresponding ambivalence in France's relationship to its transatlantic alliance became particularly discernible in the months prior to 9/11. At that time, Jacques Chirac had served his first of two terms as president of France since 1995. He was a member and the founder of the centre-right and Gaullist political party 'Rally for the Republic' (*Rassemblement pour la République*, RPR). The RPR stood in the tradition of de Gaulle's principles of social conservatism, economic *dirigisme* and national independence (Bell, 2002: 92). When Bush succeeded Bill Clinton as US president in January 2001, these principles became likely to come in conflict with the Bush administration's discounting of multilateralism and the concerns of allies, as signalled by its early policies on climate change and the International Criminal Court (Vernet and Cantaloube, 2004: 53–54).

In addition, Chirac had to share power over foreign and security policy with a government headed by Lionel Jospin of the *Parti Socialiste* (PS, Socialist Party), France's main centre-left political party, in an arrangement known as *cohabitation*. Jospin was equally concerned about the Bush administration's veering towards unilateralism. The PS led a majority in the *Assemblée Nationale* (National Assembly), the lower house of France's parliament. It had formed a 'Plural Left' coalition together with smaller left-wing, communist and environmentalist parties. This coalition held 320 of all 577 seats in the National Assembly, while the right was split between Chirac's RPR, which held 139 seats, and the centrist Union for French Democracy (*Union pour la démocratie française*, UDF), which held 112 seats.

Analysing the French decision process to use force in Afghanistan after 9/11

With these insights on French strategic culture and the political constellations surrounding the events of 11 September, one can assume that the French government had an interest in participating in military actions pursuant to 9/11 with rather great fanfare so as to demonstrate that it showed solidarity with its allies in the face of tragedy and attack, but also played a decisive role within this alliance. The theoretical model therefore leads to the assumption that French strategic culture, prompted by the relatively straightforward rationale for military action in response to 9/11, allowed for a rather strong securitisation process leading to a robust and prominent military commitment to Operation Enduring Freedom. France's deployment of several fighter and support aircraft, Special Forces, ground troops and an air craft carrier was indeed sizeable.

The decision to use military force in Afghanistan

Soon after 9/11, Chirac made clear that France would participate in military action, but on its own terms. On 18 September, during a state visit to Washington planned long before 9/11, Chirac expressed "the total solidarity of France and the French people" and pledged that France was "completely determined to fight by your side this new type of evil, of absolute evil, which is terrorism" (The White House, 2001). According to *Le Monde*, Chirac had already announced ahead of the meeting that France could not evade demonstrating its solidarity with the US because history, morality and the national interest demanded it and because France was also a potential target. Yet he qualified that this did not imply one should strike blindly but one needed to be sure of the objectives (Jarreau *et al.*, 2001). In Washington, he stated: "Of course military cooperation is conceivable, but in the manner that we have previously agreed on the objectives and modalities of an operation whose goal is the elimination of terrorism" (Jarreau *et al.*, 2001). Chirac thus made clear at the outset that a French contribution was only possible under the condition that France was involved in formulating the goals and means of an intervention.

This concern for achieving and maintaining influence on the overall operation against terrorism through military cooperation with the US also transpired when a journalist asked Chirac during the visit if he considered France to be at war against terrorism alongside the US. He replied:

> I don't know whether we should use the word "war", but what I can say is that now we are faced with a conflict of a completely new nature. It is a conflict which is attempting to destroy human rights, freedom, the dignity

164   *Comparing decision processes on use of force*

of man. And I believe that everything must be done to protect and safe-guard these values of civilization.

(The White House, 2001)

As one could hypothesise from the insights on French strategic culture, Chirac therefore fully securitised the events of 9/11 as an attack on universal values and called for a robust French contribution but sought to retain full control for France over the interpretation of the events as well as the precise extent and objectives of military action. This was to ensure that the response would be multilateral and that France was recognised internationally as well as domestically as a leading country in the fight against the common threat of terrorism.

Prime Minister Jospin and other cabinet ministers used a similar logic in their securitisation rhetoric. On 3 October, the National Assembly debated the situation after the events of 11 September. In his government address delivered at the start of the session, Jospin expressed the French people's complete solidarity with the US and declared the events as an attack on the most deep-seated values of respect for life, democracy and liberty, which required a clear and determined response from all nations (Assemblée Nationale, 2001a: 5377). But he also refrained from framing this situation as a war. While he conceded that "Some spoke of war, because the attacks were conducted like acts of war, because the response can imply the use of military means", he argued that in this case there were "neither nations attacked nor regular armies in sight nor are peace treaties conceivable" (Assemblée Nationale, 2001a: 5377).

Instead, Jospin made clear that besides the direct interest in fighting a threat that was also directed at France, Paris had an important role to play in providing a counterweight to the US approach and in thereby transforming the international fight against terrorism into one that is narrower in its objective to fight terrorists and one to which all nations sharing the values under attack can subscribe, independent of their relationships to the US. Jospin thus stated:

> Our ambition must be to give the coalition against terrorism a universal character. This coalition will not make the tensions of the world disappear. It does not seek to impose on people who suffer to forget their sufferings or frustrations, to take away their identity in order to submerge it into a mono-lithic struggle. But we must also not accept that a critical view of the United States' responsibilities in recent history is invoked as a pretext to say "this fight is not ours": this is a mistake. The struggle against terrorism is a common imperative of democracies and must become one for all nations. *It is not another one's war in which we are being dragged along, it is a necessary and methodical operation to which we freely dedicate all our efforts.*
>
> (Assemblée Nationale, 2001a: 5377; emphasis added)

By critically disassociating himself from the American rhetoric of a 'war on terror' and calling for a specifically French role of making the response more universally acceptable and more targeted in its objectives, Jospin thus supported Chirac's rhetorical efforts to stress that France showed its full solidarity with the US while maintaining its critical engagement within the transatlantic alliance. As

Analysing French decisions 165

Davidson (2011: 118) points out, these efforts to highlight the prestige gained through the operations continued after Chirac announced his positive reply to American troop requests and the impending start of operations on 7 October. (Chirac, 2001). Jospin, for instance, stated to the National Assembly on 21 November 2001 that the government would continue, alongside the president, to affirm its solidarity and to "make France's voice heard" (quoted from Davidson, 2011: 118). And Chirac pointed out in February 2002 that "the French involvement is, like that of Great Britain, the most important to have been put in place at the United States' request" (quoted from Davidson, 2011: 118).

Chirac and Jospin thus both made securitisation efforts that were succinct in scope and proactively self-assertive in nature. Both stressed that France freely chose to acquire a lead role in the international coalition against terrorism through full-scale involvement rather than following the US lead entirely. This was because it was in France's interest to demonstrate its full solidarity with the US and to defeat the common threat of terrorism but in the process France also had to achieve an influence on the campaign's outlook and to enhance its international standing rather than merely contribute military assets. One can therefore discern that a strategic culture in which norms on the range of goals for the use of force take precedence over norms on alliance ties, which in turn derives from identity narratives that stress the pursuit of *rang* and *grandeur* and a *mission civilisatrice*, expressed itself in the French securitisation process on the use of force abroad after 9/11.

Resonance of the decision

The National Assembly did not debate the use of force after 9/11 until 3 October 2001. In this short debate, the president and the government received near-unanimously positive resonance as most deputies rallied behind their decision to commit French forces to international military operations against terrorism. However, as *Le Monde* pointed out, while none of the seven speakers in the debate challenged the government's decision to support the American response, each posed their conditions (Chemin and Clarisse, 2001). In formulating these conditions, the different political factions inadvertently resonated positively with the position adopted by the government in its post-9/11 securitisation process, which *Le Monde* fittingly summarised as "*Aux côtés des Etats-Unis, pas derrière*" ("Alongside the United States, not behind" Chemin and Clarisse, 2001). Most deputies appeared to share the government's and president's concern for demonstrating France's solidarity with the US whilst asserting its independence of action. The speakers therefore also heeded or reiterated Jospin's call for national unity behind the ensuing fight against terrorism.

Speaking for the UDF, former president of the Republic Valéry Giscard d'Estaing stated at the outset that he did not see the current parliamentary session as a debate but rather an occasion to express the sense of horror felt by all deputies following the images of 9/11. He argued that "This horror called for an immediate and unanimous demonstration of solidarity, without reservation or second thought, to the American people, who were attacked on their soil for

166   *Comparing decision processes on use of force*

the first time, and who are paralysed with shock" (Assemblée Nationale, 2001a: 5385). On behalf of his party he then applauded the president's and the government's actions as having done so in a perfect manner.

However, Giscard d'Estaing did not argue that this solidarity automatically extended to the American government but chose to speak of solidarity with the American people instead. Although this is a minor semantic difference, it may well be an expression of the determination to preserve France's independence of action despite the resounding demand for solidarity in the situation at hand. This became more pronounced when he consequently argued that "Emotional solidarity must extend into solidarity of action" but then also clarified that "In the emotional climate that followed the attacks, there was talk of war. But there will be no head-on collision between two armies, or fight between two groups of nations" (Assemblée Nationale, 2001a: 5385). He then stated that while one could not rule out that states were complicit in preparing for the attacks, using the term 'war' at this stage was to fall into the trap set by the terrorists and therefore he chose to avoid it (Assemblée Nationale, 2001a: 5385). He then cautioned that the allies should settle for a short-term mission on the ground and withdraw once the terrorist networks had been effectively destroyed without trying to solve the internal problems of Afghanistan, which should be left to humanitarian and international organisations instead (Assemblée Nationale, 2001a: 5385).

Édouard Balladur of the RPR voiced similar tones of solidarity and sympathy paired with clearly formulated ideas about France's role and contributions. Balladur was also explicit about his belief that a certain obstinacy had always been an element of France's proper role in the world, which did not naturally stand in the way of its loyalty to its alliance with the US:

> As she has already shown during the Berlin Crisis or the Cuba Crisis, at the times of Géneral de Gaulle, France is an at times cumbersome and demanding ally, but she is, and the United States know this, an ally who knows how to fulfil her responsibilities.

Accordingly, Balladur declared his party's consent to France living up to its responsibility once again. He agreed that the government should supply anything that will be asked of France, yet he also stressed that this should not be done under any condition and not without due influence on the process and objectives of military action:

> A special responsibility may thus weigh on our country. Its course shall be adapted to what shall be asked of her [France] as well as to the nature of the operations. Likewise, the objectives and means to be implemented shall be the subject of thorough prior consultation between the United States and France. *Thus, whilst maintaining our freedom of judgement* [emphasis added], we are prepared to partner in a response of which we assume *a priori* that it will be proportionate and avoid leading to a humanitarian disaster for the civilian populations.

Analysing French decisions 167

This notion of guarding France's *liberté d'appréciation*, which can be roughly translated as 'freedom of judgement' or 'discretion', characterised the government's response and, as shown above, also found positive resonance in parliament as most speakers reiterated this notion, although in various terms, while most also reaffirmed the imperative to demonstrate absolute solidarity to the US. Even the notoriously Eurosceptic and America-critical deputy Jean-Pierre Chevènement of the smaller yet vocal left-wing party *Mouvement des Citoyens* (Citizens' Movement) joined the ranks of deputies affirming action and voicing conditions:

> the United States exercise a legitimate right in seeking to overthrow the Taliban regime.... But insofar as France is neither associated with the definition of the objectives nor with a direct intervention ... it is natural that she should determine herself the forms of its support ... and that she continues to preserve to herself, in the interest of all mankind, her freedom of judgement, counsel and action.
>
> (Assemblée Nationale, 2001a: 5396)

Reportedly, of all speeches held that day, Jospin was most concerned about Chevènement's speech but as he left the podium, a visibly relieved Jospin muttered *"très bien, Jean-Pierre, très intéressant"* ("very well, Jean-Pierre, very interesting") (Chemin and Clarisse, 2001). From the self-confident nature and the short scope of the debate, one can therefore discern that a strategic culture with the characteristics previously identified as pertaining to French strategic culture indeed pervaded both the securitisation process regarding the use of force after 9/11 and its largely positive parliamentary resonance. In contrast to its Anglo-Saxon counterparts, this strategic culture contains norms which emphasise slightly more restraint and multilateralism in the use of force than their Anglo-Saxon counterparts. But above all, these emphasise independence of action in the use of force.

For the analysis of print media commentaries, *Le Figaro* was selected as France's most authoritative quality newspaper with a conservative editorial stance, *Le Monde* as its pendant with a centre-left editorial stance and *Le Parisien/Aujourd'hui en France* as France's most widely read national daily and one that comes closest to the style of a tabloid paper in France. In 2006, for which the oldest figures are available, the three papers had average daily circulations of 338,269 copies, 355,017 copies and 517,965 copies respectively (OJD – Association pour le Contrôle de la Diffusion des Médias, 2006: 12).

The opinion pieces of *Le Figaro* mirrored the debate in the National Assembly insofar as commentators expressed heartfelt sympathy with the US and support for the American-led war on terror but also advocated the French government or Europeans in general to adopt the role of a moderating influence on the US within the coalition. In this respect, many commentators used the term 'Manichaean' to describe the American outlook on the impending military campaign against terrorism in contrast to a more nuanced European outlook. Consequently, most opinion pieces supported France's involvement in the war but many articles simultaneously struck notes of caution. Of all 20 articles analysed,

168 *Comparing decision processes on use of force*

11 could hence be classified as moderately supportive while eight are considered to be strongly supportive and one lone dissenting voice as strongly critical. The following extract from an editorial by Charles Lambroschini best sums up the arguments and opinions expressed in *Le Figaro* in the immediate aftermath of 9/11:

> If ... the United States manages to organise a military coalition to decapitate the terrorist Hydra, French, British or even German contingents thus must be at the forefront. This would be the best way to educate an America which, blinded by its own strength, risks succumbing to a Manichaeism with terrible consequences.... This European commitment would also open up the right to participate in the definition of a new world order. It would give France and its 14 partners more arguments to convince Washington to renounce a unilateralism that has done too much damage. Thanks to its activism, Europe could afford to remind Americans that, against terrorism, the purpose of war must be peace.
>
> (Lambroschini, 2001)

In *Le Monde*, on the other hand, an unequivocal outpouring of sympathy and solidarity as epitomised by the world-renowned headline "*Nous sommes tous Américains*" ("We are all American") was followed by speculations about the American response, which tellingly involved little mentioning of possible French roles within it, and concerns about the US overreacting to the events through military means. As plans for an attack on Afghanistan became more concrete, editorialists increasingly called on its readers, Europe and the French government to assume the role of a voice of reason counterbalancing the overly bellicose American rhetoric and plans for action. The initially strong and emotional expressions of solidarity gradually gave way to the more critical tones that are usually associated with French left-wing intellectuals. These did not shy away from offering bleak pessimism and scepticism, especially regarding prospects for a measured, reasonable American response. Hence, the 20 articles analysed varied in opinion, with strong support intermixed with increasingly strong criticism. Five articles were categorised as strongly supportive, six as moderately supportive, five as moderately critical and four as strongly critical.

Le Parisien (called *Aujourd'hui en France* outside Paris) does not appear to have specifically designated opinion pages or editorials. Its articles are generally concise and at times sensationalistic but they do not reveal a clear editorial stance. However, during the period under analysis the paper featured several interviews with outside experts from the military, academia, politics and journalism. Many of these express concrete opinions on the use of military force against terrorism after 9/11. All but one of the nine interviews analysed could be considered supportive of the use of military force after 9/11.

Public opinion also resonated positively with the French government's decision to participate in the war in Afghanistan with a noticeable contingent. A poll taken by TNS and Gallup International on 14 and 15 September 2001 showed that similar to the British public, 73 per cent of respondents backed a French participation in American military action against terrorism following the attacks

(Soulé, 2001). Another poll by Ifop, taken shortly after the first strikes were launched on 11 and 12 October 2001 among 934 adults, also showed that 75 per cent viewed a French military intervention against terrorism favourably. The poll also showed that the strongest divergence in public opinion existed between left-leaning respondents, who supported this by 56 per cent to 58 per cent, and right-leaning supporters, whose support surpassed 80 per cent (Ifop/Le Figaro, 2001). *Le Figaro* also pointed out that in the same poll only 52 per cent of those supporting military intervention also supported targeting other states complicit in terrorism, which showed that the French public supported military action against terrorism but did not want to get drawn into the "wheelworks of a generalised war" that Jospin spoke of in the National Assembly (Ifop/Le Figaro, 2001). Overall, public opinion polls therefore concur with the other findings on the French resonance to the post-9/11 securitisation process leading to military intervention abroad. There was widespread support and a wave of sympathy for the US but this did not entirely suspend sceptical reflexes towards US-led military interventions and the desire to assume a distinct role, especially among those on the left in France.

Analysing the French decision to implement counterterrorist legislation after 9/11

French identity narratives entail both a high regard for the institution of the French state and for the civil liberties attained through persistent revolutionary struggle. Public opinion polls also show divergent positions, with respondents showing strong support for the protection of civil liberties in general but in some cases also showing relatively strong support for infringements on civil liberties when queried on specific state measures. Furthermore, one can discern a weaker institutional linkage between political elites and the public in France relative to other liberal democracies. Norms within French strategic culture are also conducive to lower authorisation criteria for the domestic and international use of force.

This all allows for the assumption that within French strategic culture, the protection of the institution of the French republic takes normative precedence over the specific degrees of civil liberties enjoyed within a republican form of government. Paradoxically, French security policy making elites therefore have significant leeway in the expansion of the state's coercive powers through securitisation processes, as long as these processes depict the measures as a temporary means to protect the Republic from a direct threat rather than a permanent erosion of the Republic. One can therefore expect the domestic post-9/11 securitisation process in France to be swift in scope and drastic in nature but moderated by the requirement that the republican constitution remains unscathed.

Yet in evaluating the process leading up to post-9/11 anti-terror laws in France one needs to consider that France already had a robust counterterrorism regime in place prior to 9/11. Furthermore, 9/11 did not initiate a legislative process for new laws but only accelerated a process already before the National Assembly since 14 March 2001. Through this process, named *Projet de Loi Relatif à la Sécurité Quotidienne* (Bill on Everyday Security), the Jospin

170 *Comparing decision processes on use of force*

government sought to overhaul and enhance police powers as well as measures to prevent small weapons proliferation in response to increasing crime in suburban areas (Assemblée Nationale, 2001c; Monjardet, 2004: 136–137). The bill passed on 15 November as the *Loi Relatif à la Sécurité Quotidienne* (Law on Everyday Security) expanded the government's authority in order to further increase French capabilities to combat terrorism but this did not constitute a wholesale reordering of existing counterterrorist policies and practices due to the already extensive regime in place. Like Germany, France also left pre-charge detention times unchanged. However, the police can detain a suspect for six days, which is three times the time span allowed in France's eastern neighbour.

The decision to implement counterterrorist legislation after 9/11

Taking these factors into account, one can nevertheless discern a remarkable speediness in the French domestic post-9/11 securitisation process. The day after 9/11, the government took a number of immediate security measures under its national security alert system named *Vigipirate*. On 3 October, Jospin then announced before the National Assembly that the government would introduce a number of further legislative measures to prevent future terrorist attacks. On 16 and 17 October, the Senate then debated new anti-terror laws introduced by the government into the existing Bill on Everyday Security. The final debate on this bill already took place on 31 October in the National Assembly and on 15 November, before any of the other four countries introduced new anti-terror laws, the bill became the Law on Everyday Security. This remarkably short scope demonstrates the urgent need perceived by the government and the legislative to expedite the bill through parliament.

During the National Assembly debate on 3 October, Jospin announced in his opening statement that the fight against terrorism would include a number of legislative measures designed to prevent and combat terrorism more effectively, which the government would soon introduce to parliament with urgency. After announcing these measures, he called for national unity behind both the government's measures to ensure the security of its citizens and behind measures to prepare France for its participation in the fight against terrorism, adding that "In the present circumstances, we must pay more attention than ever to maintaining our national unity around the republican pact" (Assemblée Nationale, 2001a: 5381–5382). One can therefore see that in Jospin's securitisation rhetoric, he emphasised that the institution of the republic as a guarantor of civil liberties rather than civil liberties themselves needed protection. This potentially allowed for more far-reaching security legislation to be implemented.

Minister of the Interior Daniel Vaillant reiterated these arguments and pleas for national unity behind the government's plans when he outlined the post-9/11 anti-terrorism amendments to the Bill on Everyday Security before the Senate on 16 October and again before the National Assembly on 31 October. Similar to Jospin, he argued that not only the acute terrorist threat but also the public demanded swift action as individual freedoms needed to be protected by safeguarding the institutional order that preserves these. As he stated:

Robert Badinter expressed what we all think by reminding us that "the rule of law is not the rule of weakness". Our citizens expect us to be forceful. Forceful meaning capable to act fast and to surpass our traditional cleavages since security is a republican value that must unite us all.

(Assemblée Nationale, 2001b: 6914)

This invocation of republican values, or a republican pact in the threat frames employed within securitisation processes related to the domestic use of state force in France, marks a minor yet crucial difference from the parallel processes in the other four countries. It mirrors the prior analysis on French identity conceptions, which found that the specific institution of the French Republic plays a central role in these. This notion of republican values may at first glance not differ much from notions such as the values of freedom and democracy employed in all cases. But it is more specific in its proscriptions for action. The latter notions leave open whether they demand restraint in the domestic use of force by the state, as in the cases of Canada and Germany, or whether they proscribe the robust defence of the state through far-reaching coercive powers by the state, as in the cases of Australia and the UK. The notion of republican values, on the other hand, refers more directly to an institutional order rather than individual rights. It thereby engenders norms conducive to the robust use of force in defence of these values but which also demand that this use does not negate but that it credibly reconstitutes such republican values, i.e. by upholding the constitution.

Similar to the prior case of the use of military force against terrorism, one can therefore position France's securitisation process close to, yet slightly below, Australia's and the UK's in terms of the intensity of force against terrorism which it proscribes. On the one hand, the government prioritised collective security over individual freedoms by invoking the defence of the republican institutional order rather than the freedoms enjoyed within it. On the other hand, this order itself cannot credibly exist without constitutionally guaranteed individual freedoms. In this regard, it should be noted that only the French government included an automatic expiry date of 31 December 2003 in its anti-terrorism bill. Vaillant stressed this fact when he concluded his speech:

The government does not ask for a blank cheque from you, but for wide support for a balanced text as it is limited to the fight against terrorism and the traffic that sustains it; a text limited in time and which fosters the judiciary's authority in its role as the guardian of individual liberty; in brief: a text which offers all the guarantees against the excesses which some might fear.

(Assemblée Nationale, 2001b: 6914)

Resonance of the decision

The concluding debate on the Bill on Everyday Security showed that the government's arguments for the measures proposed in the bill did not encounter much opposition. The debate concerned the bill in its entirety rather than anti-terrorism legislation exclusively. But tellingly, most of the debate revolved around various everyday security issues rather than the bill's anti-terrorism

172   *Comparing decision processes on use of force*

provisions. In both respects most parliamentarians concurred with the government that the state must defend itself and maintain its security robustly. For example, following Vaillant's speech, RPR deputy Thierry Mariani stated:

> the survival of our democracy depends not only on its ability to thwart the destructive plans of terrorist groups. It also depends on its commitment to upholding the respect for republican values within it, starting with the rule of law.
>
> (Assemblée Nationale, 2001b: 6918)

This exemplifies how deputies from the right invoked the notion of 'republican values' or of a 'republican pact' (*pacte républicaine*) in support of arguments for a strong state in their resonance to the government's securitisation processes. While the opposition thus resonated mostly positively with the proposed measures, it also accused the socialists of not having paid enough attention to security issues in the past and on still being too lax on security, including anti-terrorism, in the present bill. At a later stage of the debate, Mariani thus lamented that:

> A certain rhetoric of "security, this too often ignored republican value" has now entered all the speeches of the left. But this rhetoric does not base itself on any conviction, as the law which we will all vote on in a few minutes shows. For four years, crime rates increase and this is the result of your policies; you must take responsibility.
>
> (Assemblée Nationale, 2001b: 6926)

Similarly, Michel Herbillon of the Group of Liberal Democrats and Independents accused the left of having dealt with issues of national security with idealism and laxity but now seemed to have realised "to what extent insecurity puts a strain our society and undermines the foundations of our Republic", although he added the left still had "a long way to go" (Assemblée Nationale, 2001b: 6924). In order to demonstrate both its commitment to national security and its opposition to the government, the centre-right group voted in favour of the anti-terrorism amendments to the bill but voted against the bill in its entirety (Roger, 2012).

Within the Plural Left majority group in the National Assembly, one can also discern widespread support for the government's anti-terrorism provisions. Socialist Party deputies largely followed their government's plea for national unity and even the Communist Party did not vote against the bill but abstained. According to Communist deputy Jean Vila:

> The insecurity reflects the weakening of our republican pact.... This is the price paid for deficiencies of education, solidarity and social diversity. Of course, the state must firmly fulfil its obligation to provide security, but punishment must be accompanied by a reaffirmation of the rights and duties of each and the principles of justice and solidarity on which our Republic rests. The 13 government amendments to strengthen our fighting against terrorism must also be assessed on the basis of our republican pact.
>
> (Assemblée Nationale, 2001b: 6932)

The far left thus shared this republican consensus on a strong state in security affairs, including anti-terrorism, but argued that this must be accompanied by extensive social policies. The anti-terrorism provisions of the Bill on Everyday Security ultimately won the support of all political parties but the Greens, who voted against the bill, and the Communists, who abstained (Roger, 2012). The relatively short scope and consensual nature of the debate shows that identity-derived notions of 'republican values' or a 'republican pact' generated norms conducive to robust anti-terrorism policies within French strategic culture.

In the French print media, the issue of new legal provisions against terrorism after 9/11 caught only little attention by editorialists and commentators. In *Le Figaro*, most commentaries discussed domestic counterterrorism legislation together with the new anti-crime laws and argued that new, tougher legislation was overdue. Commentators also lauded France's expertise in domestic anti-terrorism measures. Overall, most commentators endorsed the government's arguments in favour of robust domestic state action against terrorism. Of five articles, four supported new anti-terror laws. Even the otherwise critical *Le Monde* did not appear to see much controversy in the government's plans. Of the four opinion pieces identified to discuss the anti-terrorism legislation, three arrived at a conclusion that narrowly supported the government. In *Le Parisien*, the three interviews on the subject of new security laws with parliamentarians from both sides and a security official of the city administration of Paris expressed opinions largely in favour of the new anti-terror provisions.

An absence of controversy surrounding the new anti-terrorism provisions also expresses itself in the absence of public opinion polls on the specific provisions in question, at least to the author's knowledge. But a poll of October 2002 on another set of exceptional security legislation can provide a remedy. After crime rates and rioting in suburban areas continued over the course of 2002, then-Minister of the Interior Nicolas Sarkozy proposed another set of further expanded surveillance, search and arrest powers by state security forces in August 2002. In a public opinion poll by Ipsos for *Le Figaro* of 4 and 5 October 2002, 72 per cent of respondents thought that the proposed law on domestic security was justified in light of the current situation of insecurity, while only 22 per cent thought they constituted a curtailing of individual liberties (Ipsos/Le Figaro, 2002). This suggests that the general public also largely supported the government's anti-terrorism provisions implemented after 9/11.

Overall, this section shows that French strategic culture provides norms that are conducive to a strong state resorting to robust security measures in situations of heightened perceptions of insecurity, as presupposed in Chapter 5. A general consensus on 'republican' values discernible in politics, the media and to a lesser extent in opinion polls allows the state to resort to exceptional measures in exceptional circumstances in France.

Analysing the French decision process regarding the use of force in Iraq

So far, we have seen that there is a prevalent self-conception in France of a strong, self-assertive state that does not see itself as the junior partner to a hegemon in a

174 *Comparing decision processes on use of force*

unipolar world but as a major power in a multipolar world managed through the primacy of the Security Council. This self-conception generates norms that support the robust use of force as long as it advances French interests or prestige and as long as it is in accordance with 'republican' principles of rules-based conduct in international affairs and of sovereignty in decision-making. In the case of the Iraq War one can therefore postulate that the decision not to participate in military action was taken autonomously by the French executive based on an independent assessment of French interests regarding Iraq and that this absence of factoring the concerns of allies into this decision found positive resonance in French politics, the media and the general public. Since the government changed after general elections in June 2002 to a centre-right government headed by Prime Minister Jean-Pierre Raffarin of the UMP, Chirac no longer faced *cohabitation* and could play a greater role in this decision.

The decision regarding the use of force in Iraq

France's opposition to a second Security Council resolution authorising the use of force against Iraq, announced by Chirac on 10 March 2003, caught worldwide attention and represented a major crisis in transatlantic relations. Despite consequent widespread scholarly attention to this decision, there is no consensus on the point at which Chirac and his government made the decision to openly oppose France's closest allies in the Security Council. Yet a closer examination of the events leading up to this decision suggests that this decision was not an erratic diplomatic move but the product of a coherent policy pursued at least since September 2002.

This policy differed substantially from Germany's early and determined stance against military action in Iraq. In fact, Chirac is said to have behaved quite condescendingly towards Germany after Schröder advanced his position in 2002 (Gaffney, 2004: 250). He repeatedly stated on 10 March that France was neither a pacifist, nor an anti-American country (Styan, 2004: 382). Instead, one can describe his position as one that proactively endorsed a policy of containment and peaceful disarmament through enhanced UN weapons inspections. Chirac first outlined this policy in a *New York Times* interview on 9 September 2002. He stated that he condemned the Iraqi regime "for all the dangers that it puts on the region and the tragedy it constitutes for the Iraqi people who are being held hostage by it" (*New York Times*, 2002). When his interviewer asked about the Bush administration's "doctrine of pre-emption", Chirac replied that he had already told Bush he had great reservations about this doctrine. Regarding the best way to deal with Iraq, Chirac stated:

> I am totally against unilateralism in the modern world ... if a military action is to be undertaken, it must be the responsibility of the international community, via a decision by the Security Council. Now, the Security Council has decided that Iraq must not have weapons of mass destruction; it did not say that a regime change was necessary there. So if the objective is to prevent Iraq from having weapons of mass destruction, we have to go along with what the United Nations has done, that is, impose the return of

inspectors in Iraq without restrictions or preconditions.... If it refuses, then it's up to the Security Council to deliberate and decide what must be done and notably whether a military operation should be undertaken or not.

(*New York Times*, 2002)

Chirac's policy thus rejected regime change and pre-emptive action based on the presupposition that Iraq concealed WMDs and intended to use these against the US or its allies. But his policy did not rule out the use of military force should inspections lead to clear signs of a major WMD arsenal which the Iraqi regime failed to disclose or destroy, but only if the Security Council then collectively arrived at the conclusion that this arsenal posed an immediate threat and therefore explicitly authorised military action through a second resolution (cf. Styan, 2004: 379–380).

Chirac's policy thus rejected regime change and pre-emptive action based on the presupposition that Iraq concealed WMDs and intended to use these against the US or its allies. But his policy did not rule out the use of military force should inspections lead to clear signs of a major WMD arsenal, which the Iraqi regime failed to disclose or destroy, but only if the Security Council then collectively arrived at the conclusion that this arsenal posed an immediate threat and therefore explicitly authorised military action through a second resolution (cf. Styan, 2004: 379–380).

On 8 October 2002, Raffarin reiterated this policy before the National Assembly. He stated that Iraq was certainly a threat to the security of the region and although it was not the only country where the question of WMD proliferation posed itself, Iraq's past behaviour made clear that this situation could not last (Assemblée Nationale, 2002: 3049). Hence, the international community was legitimately preoccupied with Iraq and demanded its acceptance of renewed inspections, its renouncement of WMDs as well as the destruction of those in its possession. Raffarin proudly proclaimed that the president of the Republic placed France at the heart of international diplomatic efforts to resolve the current crisis and that:

France has a clear vision of its challenges and responsibilities. Faithful to its history, it seeks to be a force of proposals and initiatives, in particular alongside its European partners, amidst the international community and at the heart of the Security Council.

(Assemblée Nationale, 2002: 3049)

Like Chirac, Raffarin also stressed that the Security Council should be determined to take further measures, without excluding any option, in the case of an Iraqi failure to comply with these demands. But Raffarin also insinuated his disagreement with US policy by warning of the effects regime change would have on Iraq's internal stability and the region's security:

It is a fact: young countries tend to underestimate the history of old countries. The assumptions surrounding regime change are still marked by uncertainty and France is not alone in advancing major questions on this subject.

176   *Comparing decision processes on use of force*

> The debates at the UN have shown that our concerns are widely shared, notably by our European partners.
>
> (Assemblée Nationale, 2002: 3049)

The French president and government thus securitised Iraqi WMD in a slightly milder form than their Anglo-Saxon counterparts. France acknowledged a regional threat requiring the international community as embodied by the Security Council to be united in its determination to ensure the rapid return of weapons inspectors and the destruction of WMDs. Only the failure to comply with these basic demands would allow for the consideration of military force, and this was to be done only multilaterally through the Security Council. At the same time, notions of 'responsibility' and a drive for self-assertiveness obliged France to play a central role in international efforts to secure these objectives.

This policy, now firmly in place through the government's securitisation process, enabled the government to see Resolution 1441 and the return of weapons inspectors as a major success. France contributed to this resolution not only through intensive cooperation with American diplomats but also through its numerous diplomatic engagements with Arab countries, including Syria and Saudi Arabia, in order to ensure their support for a multilateral approach and for pressuring Baghdad into compliance. While the US and the UK then grew increasingly dissatisfied with the results of weapons inspections by January 2003, the opposite was true for France. On 20 January, French Foreign Minister de Villepin stated that "today, nothing justifies envisaging the use of military force" and that France would consider using its veto should the US insist on the "military short-cut" in the Security Council (quoted from Styan, 2004: 382). On 5 February, France then proposed significantly intensified weapons inspections as a compromise. But the French government continued to make clear that it would use its veto against another resolution legitimising the use of force at this stage now that inspections as a means to peacefully disarm Iraq were making progress, as Raffarin declared before the National Assembly on 26 February (Assemblée Nationale, 2003: 1417).

This sequence of events shows that France arrived at a coherent policy towards Iraq leading to proactive diplomatic efforts to disarm Iraq at a relatively early point of the Iraq crisis. This short scope and the proactive and self-assertive yet still comparatively mild nature of the French securitisation process reflects the characteristics of French norms on the use of force contained in its strategic culture as previously identified. As in the previous instances, French norms on the use of force were conducive to a robust securitisation process which went beyond German and to some extent Canadian reserves but fell short of the UK's or Australia's proclivities to use force. One can also discern that the normative preferences for modes of cooperation within French strategic culture generated collective expectations for proactive international engagement as a major power pulling its weight among its equals in multilateral fora, notably the Security Council, in the tradition of Gaullist republicanism.

Analysing French decisions 177

Resonance of the decision

In the National Assembly, the left-wing opposition largely concurred with the government's position but criticised the US more explicitly and demanded that the government positioned itself more clearly against pre-emptive military action. Speaking for the Socialist group, Jean-Marc Ayrault stated at the outset that he saw the Iraqi regime as a threat to regional stability, and he saw it as a necessity to prevent Saddam Hussein from obtaining WMDs as well as to continue the fight against international terrorism. But Ayrault also soberly assessed that there was neither any compelling evidence of a link between Al Qaeda and Iraq, nor of Saddam pursuing a major WMD armaments programme at this time. Furthermore, in his view international pressure had already produced a first result in the shape of renewed weapons inspections, and this route needed to be continued with great vigilance. Ayrault thus denied being complacent about Saddam's regime or Saddam himself. However, he added that "As long as he [Saddam Hussein] accepts to submit himself to international law, nothing authorises America to dictate war. Yet this is about to happen" (Assemblée Nationale, 2002: 3051). He then outlined indications that Bush was willing to resort to the use of force at any cost and without any regard for the international community. Ayrault then attacked the government for failing to position itself more clearly against this development. Unsurprisingly, the opposition then did not criticise the government for its threat to use France's veto in the Security Council during the debate on 26 February 2003. In fact, the Socialists' speaker François Hollande commended the government on this and called for national unity behind the president's and the government's position:

> France is strong every time it is united behind a clear line. Since today we can, with the approval of public opinion, with a majority of the French, defend certain positions together, let us not deprive ourselves of this opportunity.
>
> (Assemblée Nationale, 2003: 1427)

These relatively short and uncontroversial debates at the National Assembly therefore show that the government's policy of securitising Iraq as a regional threat requiring intensified inspections while rejecting the evidence brought forward by the US and the UK as sufficiently compelling to justify military action received largely positive resonance in parliament. This also indicates that the decision widely adhered to the norms of French strategic culture.

In French print media, however, one can discern more divergence of opinions. *Le Figaro* debated the issue extensively and allowed a great variety of viewpoints to be expressed in its opinion pieces featured between 20 February and 20 March. There was also not a singular editorial stance discernible. While some journalists and most guest commentators supported Chirac's threatened invocation of France's veto power, a few commentators wished for a less confrontational stance towards the US or were critical that France adopted a pacifist stance while the rationale for war was compelling. Yet critics of military action far outweighed its supporters with 30 articles classified to be moderately critical, nine to be strongly critical and the remaining 13 articles to be moderately supportive.

178 *Comparing decision processes on use of force*

Le Monde again mostly followed the tradition of French left-wing intellectualism and discussed the question of war with Iraq from a mostly philosophical and critical perspective. Apart from a few dissenting guest commentaries highlighting the humanitarian cause for war, the paper's editorials and commentaries argued overwhelmingly against the Iraq War. Of 34 articles analysed, 27 were moderately critical, four were strongly critical, and only three were moderately supportive of the idea of military action against Iraq. However, unlike the articles in *Le Figaro*, this critical stance did not equate to pacifism but endorsed France's proactive engagement in the Iraq crisis while rejecting the US's and the UK's rational for the war. At times, articles therefore also criticised the German position as immature or opportunistic. Chirac's wielding of France's veto power, meanwhile, met widespread approval in *Le Monde*. 14 out of 18 interview partners of *Le Parisien* were also critical of military action. Most supported Chirac's decision on the basis that France should not endorse the impending military campaign since it does not endorse the rationale for war in this case. Overall, the arguments brought forward in the French media thus correspond to the assumption that French strategic culture provided for norms on the use of force which fully supported Chirac's decision.

Public opinion polls indicate that the French public was also opposed to military action by a large and growing majority of between 58 per cent in August 2002 and 83 per cent in February 2003. This opposition was equally strong across different gender and age groups as well as different political orientations. Strong support grew across these groups in January 2003 for Chirac's threat to veto a resolution authorising the immediate use of force against Iraq. The French public, the media and parliament thus provided largely positive resonance to the French leadership's proactive yet sober securitisation process regarding Iraq.

Conclusion and outlook

As in the previous French decisions analysed in this section, this resonance indicates the structurally conditioning workings of a more 'proactive' than 'robust' strategic culture with a moderately high proclivity to support the use of force by the state and a high proclivity to assert the state as an independent, potent and principled actor internationally and domestically. In the alignment of their actions with these structurally conditioning factors of French strategic culture, the French government under Chirac, as well as first Jospin and then Raffarin, are likely to have conditioned a largely morphostatic structural elaboration of French strategic culture, with only minor shifts in its centre of gravity through societal evaluations of the wider repercussions of the wars in Afghanistan and Iraq across the West. A moderately 'proactive-robust' strategic culture is therefore also likely to have informed French policies regarding international military interventions in Libya in 2011 and in Mali in 2013 as well as the relatively relaxed reactions of the French government to allegations of global US-led surveillance efforts under the aegis of the US National Security Agency (NSA) (Tagesanzeiger, 2014).

Bibliography

Assemblée Nationale (2001a) "Compte rendu intégral des séances du Mercredi 3 Octobre 2001". Journaux Officiels de la République Française. Available from: www.assemblee-nationale.fr/11/cri/pdf/20020005%201re%20s%C3%A9ance%20du%20mercredi%203%20octobre%202001.pdf (accessed 19 December 2013).

Assemblée Nationale (2001b) "Compte rendu intégral des séances du Mercredi 31 Octobre 2001". Journaux Officiels de la République Française. Available from: www.assemblee-nationale.fr/11/cri/html/20020042.asp (accessed 19 December 2013).

Assemblée Nationale (2001c) No. 2938 – Projet de loi relatif à la sécurité quotidienne. *Projets de loi*, Documents parlementaires. Available from: www.assemblee-nationale.fr/11/projets/pl2938.asp (accessed 8 January 2014).

Assemblée Nationale (2002) "Compte rendu intégral des séances du Mardi 8 Octobre 2002". Journaux Officiels de la République Française. Available from: www.assemblee-nationale.fr/12/pdf/cri/2002-2003/20030009.pdf (accessed 19 December 2013).

Assemblée Nationale (2003) "Compte rendu intégral des séances du Mercredi 26 Février 2003". Journaux Officiels de la République Française. Available from: www.assemblee-nationale.fr/12/pdf/cri/2002-2003/20030149.pdf (accessed 19 December 2013).

Bell DS (2002) *French Politics Today*. Manchester: Manchester University Press.

Chemin A and Clarisse F (2001) "Les leaders politiques français approuvent un soutien limité aux Américains". *Le Monde*, Paris, 5 October.

Chirac J (2001) Discours de M. Jacques Chirac, Président de la République, sur les opérations militaires américaines en Afghanistan en représailles des attentats terroristes commis par les musulmans intégristes contre New York et Washington et la coopération de la France dans la lutte contre le terrorisme, Paris, le 7 octobre 2001. *République Française, Direction de l'information légale et administrative*, Discours publics. Available from: http://discours.vie-publique.fr/notices/017000222.html (accessed 19 December 2013).

Davidson JW (2011) *America's Allies and War: Kosovo, Afghanistan, and Iraq*. New York: Palgrave Macmillan.

Gaffney J (2004) "Highly Emotional States: French–US Relations and the Iraq War". *European Security*, 13(3), 247–272.

Ifop/Le Figaro (2001) "Selon un sondage Ifop-Le Figaro, 55% des Français sont pour un engagement militaire plus important aux côtés des Etats-Unis". *Le Figaro*, Paris, 15 October.

Ipsos/Le Figaro (2002) "SONDAGE L'opinion soutient le ministre de l'Intérieur mais se montre plus réservée sur ses mesures réprimant la prostitution et le squat des halls d'immeubles; Les Français approuvent le projet Sarkozy". *Le Figaro*, 7 October.

Jarreau P, Bacque R and McCormack S (2001) "Jacques Chirac réaffirme à Washington l'offre de coopération de la France". *Le Monde*, Paris, 20 September.

Lambroschini C (2001) "Un nouveau rôle pour l'Europe". *Le Figaro*, Paris, 15 September.

Monjardet D (2004)" Le Terrorisme International et la Cage d'Escalier – La Securite Publique dans le Debat Politique en France, 2000–2003". *Canadian Journal of Law and Society*, 19, 135–151.

New York Times (2002) Interview With Jacques Chirac. *New York Times*, 9 September. Available from: www.nytimes.com/2002/09/09/international/europe/09CTEX.html (accessed 17 January 2014).

OJD – Association pour le Contrôle de la Diffusion des Médias (2006) *Book 2006 Presse Payante GP*. Paris: OJD. Available from: www.ojd.com/books (accessed 23 December 2013).

Roger P (2012)" En 2001, quand droite et gauche s'accordaient sur l'antiterrorisme". *Le Monde*, Paris, 27 March, Available from: www.lemonde.fr/election-presidentielle-2012/

180 *Comparing decision processes on use of force*

article/2012/03/27/en-2001-la-droite-avait-bien-approuve-les-mesures-anti terroristes_1676175_1471069.html (accessed 14 January 2014).

Soulé V (2001) "L'opinion occidentale determine". *Libération*, Paris, 19 September. Available from: www.liberation.fr/evenement/2001/09/19/l-opinion-occidentale-determinee_377489 (accessed 3 January 2014).

Styan D (2004) "Jacques Chirac's 'non': France, Iraq and the United Nations, 1991–2003". *Modern & Contemporary France*, 12(3), 371–385.

Tagesanzeiger (2014) "Ziemlich beste Freunde". *Tagesanzeiger*, Zurich, 11 February. Available from: www.tagesanzeiger.ch/ausland/amerika/Ziemlich-beste-Freunde/story/16538276 (accessed 24 February 2014).

The White House (2001) President Chirac Pledges Support. Press Release, Available from: http://georgewbush-whitehouse.archives.gov/news/releases/2001/09/20010918-8.html (accessed 18 December 2013).

Vernet H and Cantaloube T (2004) *Chirac contre Bush: l'autre guerre*. Paris: JC Lattès.

9 Analysing Australian decisions on the use of force

Australian identity conceptions and norms concerning the use of force by the state make up a 'proactive-robust' strategic culture which bears great similarities to British strategic culture. Despite Australia's geographic remoteness, prevailing identity narratives appear to have engendered strong normative ties to the West as well as widespread normative support for the robust use of force by the state in defence of the West and the values which purportedly underpin it, both at home and abroad. One can therefore presuppose that in all three policy areas investigated in the case studies, the aftermath of 9/11 prompted strong securitisation efforts leading to proactive and robust state action, which encountered largely positive resonance during the phase of agential social interaction in parliament, the media and public opinion in Australia.

From 1996 to 2007, John Howard served as prime minister of Australia. A member of the centre-right Liberal Party, Howard headed a government comprised of members of the Liberal-National Coalition, commonly known as 'the Coalition', which is a formal alliance dating back to 1922 between Australia's two main centre-right parties, the Liberal Party and the National Party, as well as two smaller, regional centre-right parties, the Country Liberal Party and the National Liberal Party. Throughout the time period under analysis, the Coalition held a majority of between five and seven seats in the 150 seat Australian House of Representatives, the lower house of the bicameral Parliament of Australia. The Australian Labour Party (ALP) held all other seats. In the upper house, the Senate, the Coalition did not hold a majority but had to rely on so-called Crossbenchers, which are independent senators and representatives from smaller parties such as the Australian Greens or the social-liberal Australian Democrats. Centre-right parties thus formed the government while a centre-left party formed the opposition in the Australian case.

Analysing the Australian decision process to use force in Afghanistan after 9/11

When analysing Australia's behaviour in the immediate aftermath of 9/11, one needs to take into account the structural factor that, as White (2006a: 19–20) argues, Australian debates over the meanings and implications of 9/11 were "somewhat different from the debates in Europe and North America" because by September 2001, a series of regional crises such as the Sandline

182   *Comparing decision processes on use of force*

Affair in Papua–New Guinea, the East Asian financial crisis of 1997, the conflict in East Timor and the Tampa crisis already engendered a "heightened sense of insecurity" in Australia. With security and defence issues thus being central to Australian politics at the turn of the century, the Howard government announced significant expansions in defence spending in its Defence White Paper short-titled Defence 2000. (Australian Department of Defence, 2000) Second, it needs to be taken into account that Prime Minister Howard was on a state visit to the US in Washington DC on the day of the attacks. This experience is highly likely to have affected his decisions on Australia's response to 9/11. This section will now assess to what extent, beyond these circumstantial factors, the characteristics of Australian strategic culture provided a formal, structural conditioner to Howard's securitisation process and to what extent this is reflected in the ensuing resonance. The Australian involvement in the war in Afghanistan consisted of a Special Forces Task Group of the Australian Special Air Service Regiment (SAS) as well as air force and navy assets such as major fleet units operating in the Persian Gulf, fighter jets and support personnel, two air-to-air refuelling aircraft and transport aircraft.

The decision to use military force in Afghanistan

Perhaps unsurprisingly, given his personal presence in Washington on the day of the attacks, one can discern a particularly bellicose note in Howard's statements delivered immediately after the events. At a press conference held in Washington DC on the day of the attacks, he expressed his hope that those responsible "will be hunted down and meted out the justice that they so much deserve" and then already declared that:

> we will support actions they [the US] take to properly retaliate in relation to these acts of bastardry against their citizens and against what they stand for.... The resolution of the American people will be evident and they will respond and they will respond in accordance with the courageous traditions of their country.
>
> (US Reference Service, Embassy of the United States in Canberra, Australia, 2001b)

These remarks indicate that already at this stage Howard anticipated impending US military action and wished to see Australian forces involved in it, although he did not state this explicitly.

As in the British and German cases, Howard was quick to express his country's emotional solidarity with the US and to securitise the attacks by implicating his country not only on the basis of Australian loss of life but more importantly because it represented an attack on shared ideals of freedom, democracy and civilisation. He already indicated this in his press conference on 11 September and stressed this more explicitly in another press conference on 12 September, where he stated that "Australia will provide all support that might be requested of us by the United States in relation to any action that might be taken" (US Reference

Analysing Australian decisions 183

Service, Embassy of the United States in Canberra, Australia, 2001a). At a press conference on 14 September, Howard announced that Australia invoked the ANZUS common defence treaty and re-emphasised his prior pledge:

> Australia stands ready to cooperate within the limits of its capability concerning any response that the United States may regard as necessary in consultation with her allies ... at no stage should any Australian regard this as something that is just confined to the United States. It is an attack upon the way of life we hold dear in common with the Americans.
>
> (Australian Government, Department of the Prime Minister and Cabinet, 2001b)

Jack Holland (2012) argues that Howard's emphasis on 9/11 being an attack on 'shared values' represents a subtle but crucial difference to the way in which Blair implicated the UK by portraying 9/11 as an attack on 'democracy' or 'civilisation', which indicated subtle differences in 'foreign policy culture' between Australia and the UK. One might claim that the former is more exclusionary and less cosmopolitan in character and that it therefore reflects Australia's drive for belonging to a more restrictive 'Anglosphere' that Chapter 4 identified in Australian strategic culture.

However, these subtle differences stand alongside many commonalities between Howard's and Blair's immediate post-9/11 rhetoric and behaviour. Howard's statement before the House of Representatives in its first session after 9/11 showed that these commonalities included a shared emphasis on the universality of the values under attack. Howard stated that 9/11 "represents a massive assault on the values not only of the United States of America but also of this country – the values of free men and women and of decent people and decent societies around the world" (House of Representatives, 2001: 30739). Later in his statement he repeated this characterisation of 9/11 as an attack on universal values:

> This attack has brought home to us many things. It has brought home to us the global character of our world.... When you think about it, it was an outrage to attack buildings in a city which is a monument to inclusion. There is no more multiracial city in the world; there is no city in the world that has more generously welcomed people from around the globe than the city of New York.
>
> (House of Representatives, 2001: 30739)

Nevertheless, the short time frame and the vigour with which Howard expressed sympathy with the US and pledged his country's military support is a striking feature of the Australian securitisation process after 9/11. As Holland and McDonald (2010: 187–188) point out, he established a striking linkage "from sorrow to emotional and then practical solidarity". His remarks suggest a strong motivation to demonstrate Australia's loyalty and value as an ally. Indeed, Holland and McDonald point out that already the day after 9/11, Howard declared in an interview with the Australian radio station 2UE:

184   *Comparing decision processes on use of force*

> I think it is important that countries like Australia play a role in identifying ourselves with the Americans. I mean, just because you are big and strong doesn't mean that you can't feel lonely.... And I think that is [*sic*] very important, therefore, that Americans know that they have got some really good, reliable friends.
>
> (quoted from Holland and McDonald, 2010: 188)

This strong determination to show not only emotional but also practical solidarity also transpired in Howard's address to the House of Representatives on 17 September. He remarked that "These events do bear very much upon the relationship between our two great societies" and that it was "with symbolic as well as practical resonance that any response that is undertaken, if we are asked and within the limit of our capability, will have the involvement of Australia" (House of Representatives, 2001: 30739). He added later on: "But, in the process of responding, we must do so with care as well as with lethal force" (House of Representatives, 2001: 30739). One can therefore discern a strong post-9/11 securitisation process in Australia, which centred heavily on the head of government and which declared a fundamental threat requiring a robust military response within a remarkably short time frame. This not only bears similarities to the British case but also validates the theoretical assumptions generated on the basis of the findings on Australian identity and strategic culture.

Resonance of the decision

Through a glance at the resonance which this process received in Parliament, in the media, and among the general public, this section will now analyse to what extent Howard's forceful rhetoric reflects his individual experience of 9/11 or whether his rhetoric and action represented a widespread sentiment in Australia.

The statement of the leader of the opposition, Labour MP Kim Beazley, suggests the latter. His remarks were similarly patriotic and bellicose in their expression of loyalty and sympathy for the US. Beazley repeatedly praised the United States for its willingness to "accept responsibility", reminding his audience that:

> We in Australia owe our freedom to the United States. In our darkest hour in 1941, our wartime prime minister called on the Americans, and they did not let us down. In the Battle of the Coral Sea and in the Battle of Midway they were there for us and fought valiantly, with many lives lost, to halt the progress of the enemy. And we were there too: we saved ourselves at the same time that we were helped by them.
>
> (House of Representatives, 2001: 30742)

He went on to argue that during the Cold War the United States was unselfishly "prepared to see its people as a target, perhaps of nuclear devastation, in order to defend values of freedom and the security of the nations who were its allies in World War II and those who subsequently emerged" (House of Representatives, 2001: 30742). Beazley thus reiterated Howard's pledge of emotional and practical solidarity to the US, and he also underpinned this pledge with narratives

Analysing Australian decisions 185

of common values, historical experiences, military operations and long-lasting protection provided by the US against threats to the established democratic order in Australia and the freedoms that it guarantees. These narratives of particularly close association with Anglo-Saxon values therefore appear to be indeed central to Australian identity, as argued in Chapter 4. This identity appears to engender a strategic culture containing strong normative attachment to Australia's alliance with the US as well as norms providing strong conduciveness to the use of force by the state in defence of perceived threats to the values on the basis of which its national identity is constructed.

Beazley then explicitly inferred from this narrative of past experiences that Australia must participate in military action alongside the US in this situation. He argued that the US continued to accept responsibility and must be supported in doing so. Furthermore:

> We show our support for the United States in this fight because the fight against international terrorism is our fight. This is not only because of those Australians missing, believed killed, but also because of our belief in freedom, a belief we hold in common with the United States. It was an attack on all of us and all of ours.
>
> (House of Representatives, 2001: 30742)

He also argued for an active military involvement in the fight against terrorism because Australia already supported the US during the Gulf War in 1991:

> If it turns out to have been the bin Laden group that was responsible for this act of terrorism, then there is a direct link between that conflict, in which we as a Parliament approved our active engagement, and these events. There are many reasons why we should stand with the United States in this particular hour, and that is one of those reasons.
>
> (House of Representatives, 2001: 30742)

At various other times during his speech Beazley repeated this call for Australia to join "the strong international coalition to fight terrorism wherever it threatens democratic and peaceful nations" including through "providing appropriate military and police support to international counterterrorist operations" (House of Representatives, 2001: 30742). The opposition leader's rhetoric therefore matched entirely Howard's prior expressions of emotional solidarity and an explicit need for an active participation in any military action.

One can therefore discern in Beazley's statement a very acute sense of freedom and democracy requiring the active and united defence by all states which support these principles whenever they come under attack. The resonance to Howard's securitisation move as expressed by the leader of the opposition in the House of Representatives did not display any signs of disagreement, rivalry or dispute with the government but re-emphasised the need for determined action and a united stance both internationally and domestically against threats to the freedoms and national security of Australia or its allies. A brief analysis of the resonance in Australia's print media confirms this impression at first. With a circulation of 130,378

186 *Comparing decision processes on use of force*

in 2002, (Australian Press Council, 2007) the Murdoch-owned *The Australian* is the country's largest and most established centre-right national newspaper. It commented on the decision to use military force in Afghanistan in 23 opinion pieces between 12 September and 23 October 2001, when the first Australian troops departed. Most commentaries shared the government's strong opinions on the necessity for decisive military action and the importance of an Australian contribution. Nine articles were classified as strongly supportive, another nine as moderately supportive and five as moderately critical.

However, the commentaries featured in the left-leaning *Sydney Morning Herald*, which had a circulation of 228,800 in 2002 (Australian Press Council, 2007), reveal a different picture. Of the 16 opinion pieces on the issue of military force against terrorism that were analysed, three were strongly critical, nine moderately critical, and the other four were moderately supportive. The paper's opinion pieces showed great similarities with the *Guardian*'s line of argumentation in the UK. Its editorialists viewed America's past military actions and Australia's involvement in these considerably more critically and were therefore also considerably more critical of the American and Australian governments' plans for military action in the aftermath of 9/11.

Many commentaries criticised Howard for running a 'khaki election' campaign by exaggerating and exploiting Australia's modest military contribution, with the media "prepared to play along", even though his opponent Beazley was in full agreement on the extent of the commitment (Henderson, 2001). The articles also criticised the US for having shown indifference to world poverty and for having ignored warnings about terrorism emanating from Afghanistan before 9/11. Yet these arguments show that the paper criticised the government as much as it sought to criticise, and thereby acknowledge, a prevailing public mood that enabled the government's hard securitisation move. Rather than showing the absence of norms bearing a relatively high proclivity to use military force in Australian strategic culture, the commentaries show that there is a substantial countercurrent to these prevalent norms in Australia, as was postulated in Chapter 4. The numerous references to common historical experiences suggest that this strong normative attachment to the US and the sense of urgency for state action to defend one's closest ally from perceived attacks on the alliance's fundamental values are embedded in dominant identity narratives and therefore constitute a broadly shared Australian strategic culture.

A brief analysis of the resonance in Australia's print media confirms this impression at first. With a circulation of 548,764 in 2002, (Australian Press Council, 2007) the Melbourne-based tabloid *Herald-Sun* is Australia's highest-circulating newspaper. Of the ten articles that directly expressed an opinion on this issue, only one could be classified as moderately critical and one as moderately supportive while the rest were strongly supportive. Although the tabloid's opinion pieces did not quite match the British *Sun* in their patriotic fervour and although they were more at length, the articles were similarly vocal in their call for support of American and Australian military force in Afghanistan. One can therefore see many parallels between the British and the Australian print media landscape just as there are similarities in the proclivity to use force between British and Australian strategic culture.

Analysing Australian decisions 187

A poll by Newspoll among 1,200 respondents asked between 14 and 16 September 2001 shows that 69 per cent favoured, and 50 per cent even strongly favoured, "America retaliating with force against those it believes responsible for the terrorist attacks" (quoted from Goot, 2006: 260–261). This support was highest among conservative, older and male respondents. These polls indicate that the public at large also provided positive resonance to the government's relatively strong securitisation process after 9/11. This supports the theoretically generated assumptions about Australian state behaviour after 9/11 based on the analysis of its strategic culture conducted in Chapter 4.

Analysing the Australian decision to implement anti-terror legislation after 9/11

Australian norms on the use of force by the state bear a similar proclivity to deem the use of force legitimate when exercised domestically against proclaimed threats as when exercised internationally. According to the theoretical model of this book one should therefore observe a similarly strong post-9/11 securitisation process in Australia regarding its domestic counterterrorist measures as one could observe regarding the use of military force abroad.

The decision to implement counterterrorist legislation after 9/11

Yet a first glance at the scope of the legislative process involving the decision to expand the state's coercive capacities after 9/11 reveals that this decision involved a significantly longer time frame than the cases of British and German counterterrorist legislation did. Not until 12 March did the government introduce its first main package of anti-terrorism bills into Parliament. The most controversial of these bills was the *Security Legislation Amendment (Terrorism) Bill 2002 [No. 2]*, which received royal assent and became the *Terrorism Act 2002* on 5 July 2002 (Parliament of Australia, 2002). However, one needs to consider that the Australian Parliament did not meet between 27 September 2001 and 11 February 2002 as it was dissolved for the Federal Election on 10 November 2001. When taking this into account, one can discern several indications of a 'strong' securitisation process in which the government passed a large volume of far-reaching legislation within as little debate and time as possible. This seems to be confirmed when regarding, inter alia, the introduction of a pre-detention period of up to 12 days: It means that persons suspected of potentially perpetrating or supporting the preparation of terrorist acts can be held for nearly two weeks without a mandatory ruling by a custodial judge. Of the five countries investigated here, only the UK went even further in this regard.

Prime Minister Howard and his cabinet minister responsible for domestic security, the Australian Attorney-General Daryl Williams, addressed the need for new anti-terror laws only briefly in the first session of the House of Representatives after 9/11 on 17 September, as their statements mostly focused on expressing sympathy and the need for international action. But on 2 October, after the Labour opposition had accused the government of acting slowly on the issue of domestic security, the Howard cabinet announced that it had

188   *Comparing decision processes on use of force*

decided on a number of anti-terrorism measures to be implemented immediately and on new anti-terror legislation to be introduced into the next Parliament if it was re-elected (Grattan and Metherell, 2001). The immediate measures mostly concerned aviation security and some extended police powers to question and investigate, whereas the new legislation would mostly include new terrorism offences modelled after the UK's Terrorism Act 2000 (Grattan and Metherell, 2001).

However, the government did not reveal the precise contents of the new anti-terrorism bills until shortly before it introduced the bills to Parliament in March 2002. The government introduced the Terrorism Bill along with bills related to Criminal Code amendment, terrorism financing, border security and telecommunications interception on the evening of 12 March 2002, in the last week of the Parliament's autumn session. Despite their "complexity and significant implications", the House of Representatives debated and passed the bills one day later on 13 March 2002 "after a rushed and heavily criticised trajectory during which the government gagged the debate which lasted barely a few hours", as Jenny Hocking (2004: 196) comments.

In their First Reading on 12 March, Williams outlined the details of the bills. Drawing on the British Terrorism Act 2000, the Terrorism Bill proposed giving the Attorney General the power to proscribe without trial any organisations considered a threat to security, which made membership or support of such organisations punishable by law (Hocking, 2004: 195–196). Furthermore, it proposed a broad range of new terrorism offences punishable by life imprisonment and it proposed to change the existing offence of treason so that, as Williams argued, it reflected "the realities of modern conflict, which do not necessarily involve a declared war against a proclaimed enemy that is a nation-state" (House of Representatives, 2002a: 1041). He justified these new measures on the grounds that there had been "a profound shift in the international security environment" since 9/11 (House of Representatives, 2002a: 1040). Although there was "no known specific threat of terrorism in Australia at present", Williams argued that "We must direct all available resources, including the might of the law, at protecting our community and ensuring that those responsible for threatening our security are brought to justice. And we must do so as swiftly as possible" (House of Representatives, 2002a: 1043).

Yet while the House of Representatives complied with Williams' urge to move swiftly, the bills received more scrutiny in various committees of the Senate. Between 23 March and 5 April, the Liberal chairwoman of the Senate's Constitutional Legal Committee invited interested parties to make final submissions to the Terrorism Bill. Despite this short time frame, which also coincided with the Easter holiday period, the committee received 431 submissions (Hocking, 2004: 197). In June the Senate then considered these submissions and introduced a number of changes to the Terrorism Bill, such as a narrower scope for the offence of treason so that it would exclude e.g. humanitarian aid, or reduced penalties for many new terrorist offences from life imprisonment to various lesser terms, all of which the House of Representatives agreed to.

The government also introduced the *Australian Security Intelligence Organisation (ASIO) Legislation Amendment Bill 2002* to the House of Representatives on 21

Analysing Australian decisions   189

March 2002. This bill proposed expanding ASIO's powers to include the detention without trial or access to legal representation of anyone, including non-suspects and children, for the purpose of interrogation. Refusal to answer any questions put during detention would carry a maximum penalty of five years imprisonment (Hocking, 2004: 195). However, the two Houses of the Australian Parliament could not reach an agreement over the ASIO Bill, despite an all-night sitting of both Houses on 12 and 13 December 2002, and the bill had to be re-introduced in March 2003 before it was passed into law on 17 December 2003. This shows that the government's hard securitisation process did not deter the non-Coalition-controlled Senate from scrutinising all anti-terrorism bills. Nevertheless, the Senate also eventually agreed to afford the state remarkably broad and far-reaching new coercive powers. Overall, the government's far-reaching proposals for counterterrorist legislation as well as the rhetoric and speed with which these were enacted to bear the characteristics of a hard securitisation process. One also needs to consider that in the Australian case the first post-9/11 anti-terror laws only represented the beginning of a constant stream of new laws, which totalled 54 pieces of anti-terror legislation enacted between 9/11 and 11 September 2011 (Roach, 2011: 309; Williams, 2011: 1144–1145).

Resonance of the decision

The debate in the House of Representatives on the Terrorism Bill on 13 March 2002 contained a lively argument between the governing Coalition and the Labour opposition. However, this argument centred not as much on disagreements over the contents of the bill as it centred on the manner in which the bill was to be passed. The Leader of the Opposition, Simon Crean, stated at the outset of the debate: "Legislation to more effectively counter terrorism is essential and we support it. But what we strongly object to is the abuse of parliamentary process by which this legislation is being introduced and progressed through the Parliament" (House of Representatives, 2002b: 1142). He made clear that his party did not oppose the bills and that it believed "that as a nation, we must be tough on terrorism" (House of Representatives, 2002b: 1142). But Crean argued that

> Careful consideration of the bills is particularly important. After having waited a full six months for this legislation to be drawn up, we have to ask why the government has taken until now to introduce the legislation. They have taken six months to consider this legislation and they have given us 16 hours to consider their consideration.
>
> (House of Representatives, 2002b: 1143)

Tellingly, Crean's announcement that his party would closely examine the bills in the Senate invoked strong words of criticism from the Coalition. The next speaker in the debate, Alan Cadman of the Liberal Party, argued that Crean's actions belied his "commitment to urgency" and "the suggestion that the Australian Labour Party is really serious about any attempt to deal with terrorism today" (House of Representatives, 2002b: 1148). He further denounced the ALP as being:

190 *Comparing decision processes on use of force*

anti–Australian in every action they have taken today here.... Not patriotic, not committed, not anti–terrorist – just prepared to let things roll along and just hope that there are no terrorist actions in Australia that we have to deal with.

(House of Representatives, 2002b: 1149)

ALP MP Graham Edwards, on the other hand, later wanted to have put on record his "disgust over the government's treatment of this House regarding ... the raft of bills which the government gagged debate on today." From these heated exchanges one can recognise that the opposition complained about being sidelined despite having signalled its support of the far-reaching pieces of legislation, while the Coalition criticised this protest as a lack of commitment to an urgent matter of security. Yet both sides shared a remarkably strong commitment to expanding the state's counterterrorist capacities as a matter of urgency. The opposition thereby provided largely positive resonance to the government's strong securitisation move.

Judging by the following brief analysis, this bipartisan consensus on extensive new anti-terrorism powers for the state received a noticeably restrained echo in the Australian print media. In the wide time frame between 12 September 2001 and 10 July 2002, when the Terrorism Act became law, one can only find five opinion pieces on the subject in *The Australian*, of which one strongly criticised the government's plans, another one supported these strongly and the other three showed moderate support. At first, the commentaries deemed new anti-terror laws as necessary and urged the government to act faster on this issue. Once the government revealed the first details of the laws the commentaries still supported new laws in principle but also welcomed the Senate's scrutiny and amendments. The paper thus provided scarce and varied but generally positive resonance.

The *Sydney Morning Herald*, however, presents an exception to the otherwise more reticent media coverage of counterterrorist legislation. At least ten commentaries appeared on the subject between September 2001 and July 2002. Six of these can be classified as being moderately critical of the government's plans, three were considered to be strongly critical and only one commentary was classified as moderately supportive. The paper not only consistently criticised the government's plans for being too intrusive on civil liberties but it also criticised the ALP for not opposing these plans more strongly as the party's leadership "remains paranoid about being accused of aiding and abetting terrorist sentiment and activity, even to the point of civil dissent". The paper thus appears to reflect the views of the sizeable critical counter current to an otherwise high level of supportiveness for extensive expansions of the state's coercive capacities against terrorism.

The *Herald Sun*, meanwhile, again commented more scarcely and more supportively on new anti-terror laws, although its commentaries also became more critical as the legislative process progressed. Two out of its seven commentaries were classified as strongly supportive, another two as moderately supportive and three as moderately critical. This brief media analysis therefore shows that despite their far-reaching nature, the government's proposals did not draw much media attention and received relatively positive, if scarce, resonance. Kent Roach argues that "There was relatively little journalistic coverage and criticism of the original security proposals in contrast to the situation in Canada" (Roach, 2011: 317). This contrast will be further examined in the next section.

The parliamentary debates and the media content analysed so far suggest that there was widespread, though not universal, public support for most of the government's proposals for anti-terror legislation after 9/11. Although there seem to be no opinion polls on the specific proposals analysed, later and more generic polls support this claim. A poll by IpsosMackay of 16–17 July 2005 showed that 62 per cent of all 1,000 respondents supported "the powers given to police and ASIO officers to question and arrest suspects, that were increased following the September 11 2001 attacks in the US" being "increased further to prevent a terrorist attack on Australian soil" (quoted from Goot, 2006: 268).

As was discussed in Chapter 5, generic polls on popular attitudes towards counterterrorism measures also show a particularly high level of supportiveness for various anti-terrorism measures in Australia. Opinion polls conducted by ACNielsen among 1,409 respondents in July and October 2005, for example, have shown that 66 per cent of those interviewed supported "life imprisonment for giving funds to a terrorist organisation" and allowing "terrorist suspects to be detained for two weeks without charge" (quoted from Goot, 2006: 266–268). Furthermore, the 2007 Australian Survey of Social Attitudes found that among 2,522 adults, 73 per cent agreed with the statement that "If a man is suspected of planning a terrorist attack in Australia, the police should have the power to keep him in prison until they are satisfied he was not involved" (quoted from Pietsch and McAllister, 2012). A further 54 per cent thought that if "the government suspected that a terrorist act was about to happen", then "the authorities should have the right to detain people for as long as they want without putting them trial" (quoted from Pietsch and McAllister, 2012).

These polls suggest that the relatively strong securitisation process leading up to particularly sweeping anti-terror laws in Australia after 9/11 was carried by the particular expressions of norms on domestic coercive powers by the state contained in Australian strategic culture, although some pieces of legislation appear to have moved close to the limits of its carrying capacity. Parliament, the media and public opinion showed some apprehension towards the most drastic measures, such as the ASIO bill, requiring the government to backtrack on them.

Analysing the Australian decision process to use force in Iraq

Australia committed SAS troops, air-to-air refuelling aircraft, maritime patrol aircraft, transport aircraft, fighter jets, naval ships and clearance drivers. Altogether, this contribution involved around 2,200 personnel, or 4 per cent of the Australian military's full-time personnel (White, 2006b: 180, 186). Altogether, this constituted a "modest but useful contribution from the operational perspective" (White, 2006b: 186). But the deployment to Iraq also represents another departure from Australia's role as a regional power. An analysis of its preceding decision process can therefore shed further light on the effects of Australian strategic culture on its state behaviour.

192   *Comparing decision processes on use of force*

The decision to use military force in Iraq

The securitisation process in the run-up to Australia's participation in the Iraq War is indicative of a relative causal impact of the particular characteristics of Australian strategic culture and its underlying identity narratives. While the Australian government openly committed itself to military action in Iraq only by late 2002, it repeatedly reaffirmed its strenuous backing of the US in the war on terror throughout the time period since 9/11. This did not change as the US increasingly included Iraq in its terror threat portfolio from January 2002 onwards. When reaffirming its commitment, the Australian government, in contrast to the British case, placed more emphasis on the cultural commonalities, the friendship and the common values rather than a vocation to be a 'force for good in the world' or common security interests.

Holland (2012: 159–167) describes in detail how Howard continued and transformed his post-9/11 rhetoric from one of justifying military action in Afghanistan to one which makes a case for Australia's participation in the Iraq War. On 26 September 2001, Howard delivered a speech at the opening ceremony of Canberra's Magna Carta Monument. His speech used the opportunity to stress the "common values that are shared by the people of Britain, the people of Australia and the people of the United States and indeed the people of many lands in the twenty-first century", which "find their origin in the Magna Carta" and which Australia was "prepared to stand for and defend" (Australian Government, Department of the Prime Minister and Cabinet, 2001a; also quoted in Holland, 2012: 160). This statement already exemplifies how Howard invoked Australian identity narratives which provide for particularly Anglocentric alliance attachments and the robust application of military force.

In his address to the US Congress on 12 June 2002, Howard reminded his American and Australian audiences of their countries' parallel histories and resultant shared values. Both countries had a "pioneer past" and left "the divisions and prejudices of the Old World far behind" (Australian Government, Department of the Prime Minister and Cabinet, 2002b; also quoted in Holland, 2012: 160–162). This common culture implied that "Most of all, we value loyalty given and loyalty gained. The concept of mateship runs deeply through the Australian character. We cherish and where necessary we will fight to defend the liberties we hold dear" (ibid.). After outlining the long history of joint military interventions since the First World War, Howard then argued that with 9/11, "America was under attack. Australia was immediately there to help" (ibid.). Consequently, Australia would remain committed "to the constant struggle to preserve democracy and freedom around the world" and "no matter what happens", both countries "travel through the century in the constant company of a true and great friend" (ibid.). Even though Howard did not mention Iraq, the notion of 'mateship', a term which Howard even tried to include in the Australian constitution's preamble in 1999, signalled that any securitisation by the US was likely to be followed by Australia. The speech exemplifies Howard's explicit invocation of Australian identity narratives in the war on terror.

Two days after the Bali bombings of 12 October 2002, the House of Representatives then reaffirmed "Australia's commitment to continue the war against

Analysing Australian decisions   193

terrorism in our region and in the rest of the world" (House of Representatives, 2002c: 7497). Within this climate of heightened alert to terrorism and Howard's strong association with the US increasingly incorporating Iraq into its 'war on terror' rhetoric, Howard then declared on 20 November in a speech delivered to the Australian Committee for Economic Development of Australia:

> In the current international climate made so stressful by the almost constant terrorist threats, the ultimate nightmare must surely be the possibility of weapons of mass destruction falling into the hands of terrorist groups. That is a powerful additional reason why a country such as Iraq, which has previously been willing to maliciously use weapons of mass destruction, should have those weapons denied to it.
>
> (Australian Government, Department of the
> Prime Minister and Cabinet, 2002a)

While not yet ruling out the possibility of a peaceful solution at this stage, Howard thus fully endorsed the American threat nexus between rogue states, weapons of mass destruction and terrorism. He repeated this in Parliament on 4 February 2003, when he justified the government's decision to pre-deploy Australian forces to the Persian Gulf two weeks earlier:

> I have no doubt that the driving force behind American policy towards Iraq now is that, in the wake of the events of 11 September, they have a justifiable concern that the twin evils of weapons of mass destruction, in the hands of rogue states, and international terrorism will come together with horrific consequences.
>
> (House of Representatives, 2003a: 10650)

Howard outlined at length the claims laid against Iraq as he made the case for participating in pre-emptive action. But he also spoke at length about the shared values, the long history of mutual sacrifice and the common interests regarding Iraq between the US and Australia before stating that "Australia's alliance with the United States has been and will remain an important element in the government's decision-making process on the Iraqi issue" (House of Representatives, 2003a: 10650). He then stated that Australia preferred a new Security Council resolution authorising war but it did not believe that this was required by international law (House of Representatives, 2003a: 10651).

Howard largely repeated these arguments in the final debate on the Iraq War on 18 March. He lauded America's "strong leadership to the world on the issue of Iraq" and expressed his extreme disappointment with the Security Council (House of Representatives, 2003b). Overall, Howard drove a strong and concise securitisation process in the run-up to the Iraq War. While only addressing the threat posed by Iraq relatively late in this process, he signalled early on that Australia was firmly committed to any pre-emptive action deemed necessary by the US. The language he used shows that Australian identity narratives, especially the ANZAC legend, were highly conducive to this securitisation process. While they present a unique and distinct identity conception, these have shown to

194 *Comparing decision processes on use of force*

imply norms on the use of force with similar expressions to those found in British strategic culture, particularly as regards their remarkably strong normative attachments to alliances and the wide range of goals for which the use of force is considered legitimate. As was theoretically assumed, the securitisation processes in both countries therefore resembled each other in character and outcome, despite their different contents.

Resonance of the decision

Despite Howard's strong securitisation efforts involving frequent invocations of Australian identity narratives, his decision to commit Australian forces to the Iraq War stirred significant controversy in the House of Representatives. In the debate on 4 February, the leader of the Labour opposition, Simon Crean, strongly criticised Howard for pre-deploying Australian forces without a UN mandate, "knowing all along that, having committed them, you cannot pull them out" (House of Representatives, 2003a: 10652). He repeatedly demanded from Howard to tell the American president that Australia will only participate in war if it has the explicit approval of another UN Security Council resolution. However, Crean also stated that his party concurred with the government over Iraq having to be disarmed. As Peter Jennings (2013) argues:

> Simon Crean's speech … makes it clear that the Opposition accepted the view that Iraq was concealing WMD and indeed would have supported the commitment of Australian forces had a further UNSC resolution authorising the conflict been passed. This was a position structured around a preference for UN procedure, not opposition to war.

The opposition's fierce opposition to a war not explicitly sanctioned by the UN also became apparent in the debate on 18 March. Crean called the government's decision "a reckless and unnecessary act" borne out of "subservience" to the US (House of Representatives, 2003b: 12512). Again he made clear that "Labour does support the disarmament of Iraq – but it says that that must happen through the United Nations, not through unilateralism. We agree on the objective but not the means (House of Representatives, 2003b: 12513). The debate exposed the ALP's different reading of Australian history and the resultant alternative identity conception of Australia as a regionally involved country strongly believing in multilateralism:

> What we do not want is a country that is cowed in fear. We do not want a country that only responds to aggression. We want a country that is prepared to stand proud, prepared to understand its history of engagement with the region, and prepared to understand its history of involvement through the United Nations – to understand the circumstances in which, despite the strength of our alliance with the United States, we have been prepared to carve out an independent foreign policy for this country. That is what Labour believes in, but it is not what the Liberals believe in.
>
> (House of Representatives, 2003a: 10661)

Analysing Australian decisions 195

The spirited debate ended on 20 March 2003 with 79 MPs voting for the government's motion and 62 against it (House of Representatives, 2003c: 13155). The Australian Parliament's resonance to the government's securitisation move was therefore mixed and displayed the polarised nature of Australian strategic culture.

This also applies to the Australian print media's resonance. Of the 23 editorials on the decision to join the war in Iraq identified in *The Australian* in the month leading up to the war, the author classified 17 as moderately supportive while two articles each pertain to the categories strongly supportive, strongly critical and moderately critical. The paper thus responded widely positively to Australia's participation in the war. It largely followed Howard's line of argumentation but emphasised humanitarian arguments more strongly and saw the absence of another UN resolution more as a cause for criticism of the Security Council than an argument against the war.

In the *Sydney Morning Herald*, on the other hand, there were 27 opinion pieces identified to be on the subject of war with Iraq, of which 21 were critical of the decision, 12 even strongly so, and only six were moderately supportive. The paper's commentators were particularly critical of Howard's perceived submissiveness towards the US and his perceived disregard for the views of other allies and the UN. The opposition's stance was also viewed critically. Some commentators, such as Alan Ramsey or Paul Sheehan, saw Crean's insistence on a second UN resolution as an opportunistic attempt to capitalise on anti-war sentiment whilst avoiding a firm anti-war stance.

Commentaries in the *Herald Sun* were surprisingly mixed for a tabloid paper, although they were again supportive on balance. Of the 22 articles that were found, eight are classified as moderately critical, one as strongly critical, four as moderately supportive and nine as strongly supportive. This relatively slim majority of supportive opinions, even though these were particularly vocal, indicate that notwithstanding Howard's strong securitisation process, there was a substantial polarisation of opinions on the Iraq War among the general population in Australia. Peter FitzSimons of the *Sydney Morning Herald* expressed this aptly when he commented on 20 March:

> There will come a time ... when historians will look back on this day and try to gauge just what the mood of the Australian people was on the eve of the invasion. To those historians I say, "Welcome to our nightmare". For the short answer is that there is no one mood which can be ascribed to the nation as a whole, and as a matter of fact none of us can remember a time when ... we were ever less united and more at each other's throats.
>
> (FitzSimons, 2003)

A divided Australian public is also discernible from public opinion polls. As in the case of the UK, the issue of a possible war with Iraq was as contentious as it was the subject of intensive polling. Their results also reveal a picture very similar to that of the British case. Public opinion was at first divided over an American attack on Iraq and then supported it once the war began. A poll conducted in December 2002 showed that 49 per cent approved "of the use of an

196 *Comparing decision processes on use of force*

American military force against Iraq to depose Saddam Hussein" while 43 per cent disapproved, which shifted to a 52:41 split on 19–20 March 2003 (Roy Morgan Research, 2003b; sample size: 408). Furthermore, in a poll conducted between 31 January and 2 February 2003, 75 per cent of respondents thought Saddam Hussein was "hiding weapons of mass destruction" and 65 per cent thought he was "a threat to global security" (Newspoll Market Research/The Australian, 2003a; sample size: 1,000).

When it comes to an Australian participation, opinion was more opposed. Yet although many public commentators claimed that polls showed the majority of Australians to be opposing Howard's decision to join the war, this can be said for most but not for all relevant polls. Murray Goot (2006: 268–274) compiled all professional, large-scale opinion polls on general support for Australian or Australian and US military action against Iraq since August 2002. The pre-war poll results ranged from 26 per cent supporting and 57 per cent opposing such action in a poll of 27–29 September 2002 (UMR Research, 2002; sample size: 1,000) to 53 per cent supporting and 40 per cent opposing such action in a poll of 22–23 January 2003 (Roy Morgan Research, 2003a; sample size: 604).

In international comparison the level of support for participation was comparatively strong in Australia. A Gallup International survey conducted in 39 countries in January 2003 showed that with 53 per cent thinking their "country should support military action against Iraq" Australian respondents came second only to the US in supporting military action, closely followed by British respondents with 44 per cent supporting this (Roy Morgan Research, 2003a). However, the question of UN backing had a particularly strong effect on poll results in Australia. In polls conducted in early February and mid-March 2003, 57 per cent and 61 per cent of respondents supported an Australian involvement in military action if the UN supported it, while only 18 per cent and 25 per cent did so without UN backing, respectively (Newspoll Market Research/*The Australian*, 2003b; sample size: 1,200). But as in the British case, opinion nonetheless swung around to support the government once the war broke out. By April 2003, 59 per cent of respondents thought Australia made "the right decision to use military force in Iraq" (Pew Global Attitudes Project, 2003; sample size: 774).

Conclusion and outlook

This brief analysis shows that the Howard government ultimately received narrowly positive resonance for its decision to participate in the Iraq War. However, even though "the ANZAC legend was mined to an unprecedented degree under the prime ministership of John Howard" (Holland, 2012: 165), he could only rally little more than half the population behind himself in the run-up to the Iraq War. This shows that on the one hand, the idiosyncratic Australian identity narratives generated norms that comprise a 'proactive-robust' strategic culture similar in kind to British strategic culture, with comparatively strong proclivities to the use of force by the state even as regards pre-emptive warfare. On the other hand, these norms had strong contenders within Australian strategic culture, which are based on identity conceptions more closely resembling those commonly ascribed to Canada, which entail a middle-power

Analysing Australian decisions   197

role conception with strong attachments to multilateralism. As Blair did in the British case, Howard therefore moved perilously close to exceeding the carrying capacity of Australian strategic culture with the decision to join the Iraq War. The fact that he could still sway public opinion can be attributed to Australian strategic culture. But this particular decision regarding Iraq was one among several decisions potentially within the margins of Australian strategic culture.

The formal conditioning cause of strategic culture can thus only explain Australia's non-participation when seen in combination with the particularly bold agency of the Howard government's securitisation move as an important final cause of the decision. In the long run, the latter is likely to have effected a lasting structural readjustment of Australian strategic culture, i.e. morphogenesis, in a slightly more 'proactive' and slightly less 'robust' direction during the extended period of structural elaboration, especially in light of later developments in Iraq. However, continuing restrictive border security and asylum practices suggest that Australian strategic culture nonetheless largely retained its 'robust' mark both regarding norms on the domestic and on the international use of force.

Bibliography

Australian Department of Defence (2000) Defence White Paper. Available from: www. defence.gov.au/publications/wpaper2000.PDF (accessed 11 October 2011).

Australian Government, Department of the Prime Minister and Cabinet (2001a) Transcript of the Prime Minister The Hon John Howard MP, Address at the Opening of the Magna Carta Monument, Canberra. *PM Transcripts.* Available from: http://pm transcripts.dpmc.gov.au/browse.php?did=12382 (accessed 18 November 2013).

Australian Government, Department of the Prime Minister and Cabinet (2001b) Transcript of the Prime Minister the Hon John Howard MP Press Conference 14 September. *PM Transcripts.* Available from: http://pmtranscripts.dpmc.gov.au/browse. php?did=12308 (accessed 31 October 2013).

Australian Government, Department of the Prime Minister and Cabinet (2002a) Address to the Committee for Economic Development of Australia: Strategic Leadership for Australia – Policy Directions in a Complex World. *PM Transcripts.* Available from: http:// pmtranscripts.dpmc.gov.au/browse.php?did=12934 (accessed 19 November 2013).

Australian Government, Department of the Prime Minister and Cabinet (2002b) Transcript of the Prime Minister the Hon John Howard MP, Address to Joint Meeting of the US Congress. *PM Transcripts.* Available from: http://pmtranscripts.dpmc.gov.au/ browse.php?did=12906 (accessed 18 November 2013).

Australian Press Council (2007) *State of the News Print Media in Australia.* Available from: www.presscouncil.org.au/uploads/52321/state-of-the-news-print-media-2007.pdf (accessed 7 November 2013).

FitzSimons P (2003) "From Relaxed and Comfortable to Bitterly Divided". *Sydney Morning Herald*, Sydney, 20h March.

Goot M (2006) "Neither Entirely Comfortable nor Wholly Relaxed: Public Opinion, Electoral Politics, and Foreign Policy". In: Cotton J and Ravenhill J (eds), *Australia in World Affairs 2001–2005: Trading on Alliance Security*, South Melbourne: Oxford University Press, pp. 253–304.

Grattan M and Metherell M (2001) "PM Takes War to Terrorists". *Sydney Morning Herald*, Sydney, 3 October.

Henderson G (2001) "Campaign Issues Hidden in the Fog of War". *Sydney Morning Herald*, Sydney, 23 October.

198 *Comparing decision processes on use of force*

Hocking J (2004) *Terror Laws: ASIO, Counter-Terrorism and the Threat to Democracy.* Sydney: University of New South Wales Press.

Holland J (2012) *Selling the War on Terror: Foreign Policy Discourses after 9/11.* Abingdon: Routledge.

Holland J and McDonald M (2010) "Australian Identity, Interventionism and the War on Terror". In: Siniver A (ed.), *International Terrorism Post-9/11: Comparative Dynamics and Responses*, Abingdon: Routledge. Available from: http://epubs.surrey.ac.uk/235577/2/SRI_deposit_agreement.pdf (accessed 4 November 2013).

House of Representatives (2001) *Hansard*, 17 September 2001. United States of America: Terrorist Attacks. Parliament of Australia. Available from: parlinfo.aph.gov.au (accessed 4 November 2013).

House of Representatives (2002a) *Hansard*, 12 March 2002. Security Legislation Amendment (Terrorism) Bill 2002. First Reading. Parliament of Australia. Available from: parlinfo.aph.gov.au (accessed 4 November 2013).

House of Representatives (2002b) *Hansard*, 13 March 2002. Security Legislation Amendment (Terrorism) Bill 2002. Second Reading. Parliament of Australia. Available from: http://parlinfo.aph.gov.au/parlInfo/download/chamber/hansardr/2002-03-13/toc_pdf/1620-2.pdf;fileType=application%2Fpdf#search=%22chamber/hansardr/2002-03-13/0074%22 (accessed 13 November 2013).

House of Representatives (2002c) *Hansard*, 14 October 2002. Indonesia: Terrorist Attacks. Parliament of Australia. Available from: http://parlinfo.aph.gov.au/parlInfo/search/display/display.w3p;db=CHAMBER;id=chamber%2Fhansardr%2F2002-10-14%2F0004;query=Id%3A%22chamber%2Fhansardr%2F2002-10-14%2F0000%22 (accessed 19 November 2013).

House of Representatives (2003a) *Hansard*, 4 February 2003. Ministerial statements – Iraq. Parliament of Australia. Available from: http://citeseerx.ist.psu.edu/viewdoc/download?doi=10.1.1.125.9933&rep=rep1&type=pdf (accessed 19 November 2013).

House of Representatives (2003b) *Hansard*, 18 March 2003. Iraq. Parliament of Australia. Available from: http://parlinfo.aph.gov.au/parlInfo/search/display/display.w3p;query%3DId%3A%22chamber/hansardr/2003-03-18/0000%22 (accessed 19 November 2013).

House of Representatives (2003c) *Hansard*, 20 March 2003. Iraq. Parliament of Australia, Available from: http://parlinfo.aph.gov.au/parlInfo/genpdf/chamber/hansardr/2003-03-20/0049/hansard_frag.pdf;fileType=application%2Fpdf (accessed 20 November 2013).

Jennings P (2013) "The Iraq War Decision Ten Years On". *The Strategist: The Australian Strategic Policy Institute Blog*, Available from: www.aspistrategist.org.au/the-iraq-war-decision-ten-years-on/ (accessed 19 November 2013).

Newspoll Market Research/*The Australian* (2003a) Iraq Poll. Available from: www.newspoll.com.au/opinion-polls-2/opinion-polls-2/ (accessed 21 November 2013).

Newspoll Market Research/*The Australian* (2003b) Iraq Poll. Available from: http://polling.newspoll.com.au.tmp.anchor.net.au/image_uploads/cgi-lib.26256.1.0303war.pdf (accessed 21 November 2013).

Parliament of Australia (2002) Security Legislation Amendment (Terrorism) Bill 2002 [No. 2]. Available from: www.aph.gov.au/Parliamentary_Business/Bills_Legislation/Bills_Search_Results/Result?bId=r1517 (accessed 10 November 2013).

Pew Global Attitudes Project (2003) On the subject of Iraq, did (survey country) make the right decision or the wrong decision to use military force against Iraq? *Pew Global Attitudes Project Question Database.* Available from: www.pewglobal.org/question-search/ (accessed 21 November 2013).

Pietsch J and McAllister I (2012) "Terrorism and Public Opinion in Australia". In: Pietsch J and Aarons H (eds), *Australia: Identity, Fear and Governance in the 21st Century*, Canberra: ANU E Press, pp. 79–95.

Analysing Australian decisions 199

Roach K (2011) *The 9/11 Effect: Comparative Counter-Terrorism.* 1st edn. Cambridge University Press.

Roy Morgan Research (2003a) Americans and Australians Lead World with Support for Military Action Against Iraq – Roy Morgan Research. Available from: www.roymorgan.com.au/findings/finding-3593-201302282302 (accessed 21 November 2013).

Roy Morgan Research (2003b) Australians Approve Action Against Iraq: Believe UN Should Have Supported Military Action – Roy Morgan Research. Available from: www.roymorgan.com.au/findings/finding-3616-201302282259 (accessed 21 November 2013).

UMR Research (2002) Hawker Britton Omnibus Survey Results: September 2002. Available from: www.hawkerbritton.com/hawker-britton-publications/umr_polling/oct02results.pdf (accessed 21 November 2013).

US Reference Service, Embassy of the United States in Canberra, Australia (2001a) Transcript of the Prime Minister the Hon John Howard MP Press Conference – Ambassador's Residence, Washington DC. *U.S.–Australia Relations*, U.S.–Australia Archive. Available from: http://usrsaustralia.state.gov/us-oz/2001/09/12/pm1.html (accessed 31 October 2013).

US Reference Service, Embassy of the United States in Canberra, Australia (2001b) Transcript of the Prime Minister the Hon John Howard MP Press Conference, Australian Embassy, Washington DC, USA. *U.S.–Australia Relations*, U.S.–Australia Archive. Available from: http://usrsaustralia.state.gov/us-oz/2001/09/11/pm1.html (accessed 31 October 2013).

White H (2006a) "Old, New or Both? Australia's Security Agendas at the Start of the New Century". In: McDougall D and Shearman P (eds), *Australian Security after 9/11: New and Old Agendas*, Hampshire, UK: Ashgate Publishing, pp. 13–27.

White H (2006b) "Security, Defence, and Terrorism". In: Cotton J and Ravenhill J (eds), *Australia in World Affairs 2001–2005: Trading on Alliance Security*, South Melbourne: Oxford University Press.

Williams G (2011) "A Decade of Australian Anti-Terror Laws. *Melbourne University Law Review*, 35, 1136–1197.

10 Analysing Canadian decisions on the use of force

Traditional Canadian identity conceptions, underpinned by legends of the War of 1812, 'benevolent mounties' or the 'golden era of Canadian diplomacy' under Lester Pearson, foster pride in the country's multiculturalism, its openness towards immigration, its strong involvement in multilateral institutions and its expertise in peacekeeping. This traditional notion of Canada being a 'peace-keeper rather than a war-fighter' or the counterpart to its more powerful and belligerent southern neighbour sits alongside the notion of a proud record of contributing to the defence of first the Commonwealth in both world wars and then NATO during the Cold War. The analysis of public opinion polls conducted in Chapter 5 showed that these identity conceptions appear to engender norms with a slightly lower proclivity to use state force towards a slightly narrower range of modes compared with the findings for British or Australian strategic culture. Besides a strong normative attachment to the US and NATO, there also appears to be high value placed on multilateralism in Canadian strategic culture. This leads to the assumption that Canadian strategic culture pertains to the 'reactive-proactive' range and that securitisation processes triggered in response to 9/11 are therefore likely to take a slightly milder and more deliberative shape in comparison with the British and Australian cases.

Yet these different nuances of Canadian strategic culture, the traditional one which emphasises multilateralism, multiculturalism and a 'middle power' role conception on the one hand, and the more 'anglocentric' strand, which stresses the track record of mutual defence within first the Commonwealth and then the NATO alliance with the US, are also shared to varying degrees among Canada's main political forces. The Liberal Party of Canada, which used to be commonly referred to as Canada's 'natural governing party', dominated Canadian politics for much of the twentieth century and the early 2000s as it "functioned very effectively as a unifying centrist national force within a multi-party system" (Behiels, 2010: 118–119). The party espoused bilingualism, civil liberties, multilateralism, peacekeeping, and human security as a guiding principle in security policy (Clarkson, 2011).

From November 1993 to December 2003, Jean Chrétien served as Canada's prime minister and the Liberal Party's leader. During this time, the Liberal Party's dominance reached its apogee, while its traditionally strongest opponent, the centre-right Progressive Conservative Party of Canada, was rivalled by two sectional movements: the western Canadian Reform Party, which renamed itself

Democratic Alliance in 2000, and the secessionist Bloc Québécois (Behiels, 2010: 119). From January 2001 to May 2004, the Liberal Party held between 170 and 172 out of the 301 seats of the House of Commons and also held a majority in the upper house of the Parliament of Canada, the Senate. The strongest opposition party was the Canadian Alliance with 66 seats followed by the Bloc Québécois with 33 to 38 seats, the centre-left New Democratic Party with 13 seats and the Progressive Conservatives with 12 seats (Parliament of Canada, 2013). In December 2003 the Canadian Alliance and the Progressive Conservatives merged to form the Conservative Party of Canada.

Analysing the Canadian decision process to use force in Afghanistan after 9/11

Given the prior findings on the norms of Canadian strategic culture and the political circumstances at the time period under analysis, one can theoretically assume that to some degree, norms calling for drastic action in defence of one's closest allies came in conflict with norms supporting a restrained and reactive response in order to display a distinctly Canadian role after 9/11. However, since the decision to commit troops to the war in Afghanistan occurred under the immediate impression of the terrorist events in the US, one can expect the former norms dimension to have overridden the latter in favour of determined action. The theoretical model therefore leads to the assumption that the government justified military action more on grounds of defending universal values rather than allied states alone within a moderately strong securitisation process receiving largely positive resonance from other parties, the media and the public. Between October 2001 and January 2002 Canada's deployment to Operation Enduring Freedom, code-named Operation Apollo, involved six warships involving 1,500 navy personnel as well as four airlifters, long-range patrol aircraft and helicopters altogether involving around 500 air force personnel, and 850 ground troops, including Special Forces (Bouldin, 2003: 269–270).

The decision to use military force in Afghanistan

The initial reaction of the Canadian government to the events in Washington and New York on 11 September 2001 did not differ substantially from those of other US allies in that it did not fall short of expressions of sympathy and solidarity. Nonetheless, one can discern traits of distinctly Canadian restraint and reactiveness in the government's immediate reaction. On the day of the attacks, Canadian Prime Minister Jean Chrétien issued a short statement to the press in which he deplored the "cowardly and depraved assault upon thousands of innocent people" and in which he expressed all Canadians' "deepest sympathies ... to the American people", called the attacks "an assault not only on the targets but an offense against the freedom and rights of all civilised nations", and offered "any assistance that our American friends may need at this very, very difficult hour and in the subsequent investigation" (Office of the Prime Minister of Canada, 2001). He therefore did not immediately invoke notions of mutual defence and military sacrifice between close allies

202 *Comparing decision processes on use of force*

but framed the events in more cosmopolitan terms. Chrétien also only gave one brief public appearance on 11 September, in which he thanked "all Canadians who have kept their calm in these last four hours" and expressed his "hope that the situation will come to a little bit more normality" (Kennedy, 2011). As he stated later in Parliament and in interviews, his primary concern on that day was to stay calm so as to avoid alarming Canadians and "public grandstanding" (CTVNews.ca Staff, 2011; House of Commons, 2001c: 1429). The Canadian journalist Mark Kennedy (2011) fittingly described the contrast between Chrétien's reaction and that of his international colleagues as he commented that the Canadian government consciously decided on a "low key public approach" while "Others such as British Prime Minister Tony Blair called emergency cabinet meetings and appeared anxious on TV, seemingly feeding the media frenzy..."

The academic Grant Dawson (2003: 181–182) concurs that "In contrast to the United Kingdom and Australia, which both promptly put troops at Washington's disposal, Ottawa held back and avoided high-profile moves like visiting 'ground zero'", which was in his view "because Chrétien wanted to encourage the US to proceed with a controlled and measured military response". Reportedly, Chrétien was indeed worried about a hasty American overreaction after 9/11 and he was also critical of Tony Blair, whom he even once referred to as "Tory Blair", for being overly eager to go to war (Dawson, 2003: 182; Laghi, 2001a; McCarthy, 2001). Chrétien's immediate reaction therefore reflects norms calling for restraint in the use of force and a consequently reactive style of security policy decision-making.

When the Canadian House of Commons first met on 17 September, Chrétien continued to speak in a reactive, moderate tone stressing the universality of the values under attack more than the way in which these values bind together Canada's particular alliances. At the same time, however, he gave the first signals that there would be a military response with Canadian participation. The Canadian government thereby securitised 9/11 by proclaiming universal values being under attack. This is already discernible in the motion which the government tabled for the debate. Besides expressing its horror at the attacks and its condolences to the victims and the American people, Chrétien moved that the House of Commons "reaffirms its commitment to the humane values of free and democratic society and its determination to bring to justice the perpetrators of this attack on these values and to defend civilization from any future terrorist attack" (House of Commons, 2001c: 1105). At the outset of the debate, Chrétien again implicated Canada in the attacks by stressing the global nature of the values under attack and Canada's duty to contribute to their defence by virtue of its identity:

> This was not just an attack on the United States. These cold-blooded killers struck a blow at the values and beliefs of free and civilized people everywhere. The world has been attacked. The world must respond. Because we are at war against terrorism and Canada, a nation founded on a belief in freedom, justice and tolerance, will be part of that response.
>
> (House of Commons, 2001c: 1115)

The conclusion of Chrétien's speech again signalled that there will be a military response, but that this response should also display the features of Canadian identity:

> We are all Canadians. We are a compassionate and righteous people.... We have never been a bystander in the struggle for justice in the world. We will stand with the Americans as neighbours, as friends, as family. We will stand with our allies. We will do what we must to defeat terrorism. However, let our actions be guided by a spirit of wisdom and perseverance, by our values and our way of life. As we go on with the struggle, let us never, ever, forget who we are and what we stand for. Vive le Canada.
>
> (House of Commons, 2001c: 1120)

Accordingly, Chrétien assured MPs in the ensuing question-and-answer session that Canada "will be participating with the Americans and our allies to make sure that we defeat terrorism" but that it would not give a "carte blanche" to any state for any action but consult Parliament beforehand, and that his government would work towards involving the United Nations, the International Criminal Court and as broad an international coalition as possible in the international response to terrorism (House of Commons, 2001c: 1425–1435). Chrétien thus sought to strike a careful balance in his securitisation move between the conflicting expectations of what constituted an appropriate Canadian response emanating from both sides of the political spectrum. He sought to provide a response that would demonstrate Canada's commitment to the fight against terror to its allies, but also one that would "reflect Canadians' comfort with peace operations and discomfort with war, and ensure that the country's engagement was consistent with its multilateral interests", as Dawson (2003: 180) put it.

When Chrétien followed an invitation to the White House in Washington to meet President Bush on 24 September 2001, he travelled amid a "consuming national debate over what to give Washington" between those on the left who "want Canada to resist automatically following the United States into any kind of war" and conservatives who "want a firm military commitment abroad", as Barbara Crossette (2001) of the *New York Times* observed.

This observation and the fact that Bush omitted Canada from his 20 September congressional address while acknowledging the actions of the UK or El Salvador suggest that this debate did not fail to be noticed in the US (Dawson, 2003: 183). In his statement delivered after his meeting with Bush, Chrétien therefore reaffirmed his commitment to the alliance:

> This problem of terrorism is a problem that concerns all the nations of the world. And we're working together to build a coalition that will defeat that, because it will disrupt the societies around the world. And I think that you know you have the support of Canadians. When you will need us, we will be there.
>
> (The White House, 2001)

However, his statement shows that Chrétien pursued a more reactive securitisation process which was in part driven by American pressure and which referred

204 Comparing decision processes on use of force

to the universal nature of the threat affecting all humanity in order to legitimise military action.

After the US formally requested Canadian military contributions on 5 October, Chrétien gave a televised address to the nation on 7 October in which he announced that the government made available a number of units, without going into further detail. Interestingly, he called 9/11 "an act of premeditated murder on a massive scale", hence a crime, rather than an act of war, as well as "an attack not just on our closest friend and partner, the United States, but against the values and the way of life of all free and civilized people around the world", as he had done before (Corbett, 2012: 50–51). The following day, Defence Minister Art Eggleton specified in a press conference that Canada's contribution, named Operation Apollo, involved naval and air support assets but no ground or combat troops aside from Special Forces,[1] although he added that if the US requested them, he would consider making these available, too (Corbett, 2012: 51).

In mid-November, the Canadian government followed a US request and put a 750-person battle group on short notice for deployment to defuse tensions and protect relief-supplies in Northern Alliance-held territory (Dawson, 2003: 190). Chrétien famously commented to much criticism in the House of Commons on 19 November that "Of course, we do not want to have a big fight there. We want to bring peace and happiness as much as possible" (House of Commons, 2001e: 1419). This deployment eventually did not occur because the situation stabilised but on 4 January 2002 the US requested the same battle group again to help fight Taliban and Al Qaeda remnants, which the government happily complied with as it was a "visible and identifiably Canadian" task (Dawson, 1989: 192). Eggleton stressed in an interview on 7 January 2002 that Canada was "good at peacekeeping, but if we have to be involved in combat we can do that too. We've demonstrated that time and time again in history. Canadians know how to fight when they have to fight" (quoted from Dawson, 2003: 192).

Canada thus ultimately delivered a robust and sizeable contribution to OEF but the protracted and reactive decision process involving a strong but comparatively restrained securitisation move shows that much of this contribution came in reaction to external requests and after much careful deliberation over what military actions would best represent 'Canadianness', i.e. the country's identity. As theoretically anticipated, the government appeared to struggle between competing norms within Canadian strategic culture, which concerned relative restraint in the use of force, a preference for peacekeeping in the range of goals for the use of force and multilateralism on the one hand and a robust commitment to the defence of one's closest allies against an immediate threat on the other.

Resonance of the decision

The resonance from Parliament, the media and public opinion also reflected a certain indeterminacy of what constitutes an appropriately Canadian response which 9/11 appears to have prompted to many Canadians. Indeed, the debate revealed a certain discomfort with the established identity conceptions and

Analysing Canadian decisions 205

norms on the use of force by Canada as hitherto propagated predominantly by the Liberal Party and to a lesser extent the Progressive Conservatives. This discomfort may have been latently present for some time already, especially among those of a more centre-right wing or conservative political orientation, as the rapid rise in the 1990s of the Reform Party of Canada, renamed in 2000 as Canadian Alliance, already indicates. This party was opposed to the notion that Canada's main divisions lie between and needed to be redressed between its two language groups, as this justified government intervention that neglected the rapidly growing economies and populations of Western Canada and privileged Eastern Canada, especially Quebec. Instead, the party advocated less federal government intervention and more autonomy for all provinces (see Manning, 1992).

As leader of the opposition, Stockwell Day of the Democratic Alliance followed Chrétien in the 17 September debate in the House of Commons. His statement gave an indication that his party's agenda to reconceptualise Canadian identity also aimed at some of the hitherto dominant strands of Canada's strategic culture. After associating his party with the prime minister's condolences and calls for solidarity regarding 9/11 and the US, he then directly addressed dominant notions of Canadian identity and its resultant strategic culture, and outlined his criticism of these in the light of 9/11. It needs to be quoted at length:

> Canadians do not dwell often on thoughts of war. We are thankful for having enjoyed a long season of peace. When we consider our role in the world, we are more likely to think of Canadians keeping peace than waging war.
>
> Some in this country have already begun to say that talk of war is overblown and irresponsible and that we must instead address the root causes of terrorism. This is true. Root causes must be addressed, but it is sheer folly, let there be no mistake, when we say that the root cause of terrorism is the terrorists themselves. The hatred that moves them to massacre the innocent can never be negotiated with or reasoned with.
>
> This is not a time for moral ambiguity. It is a moment of moral clarity. As Canadians ... we did not seek this conflict, but however much we might tell ourselves that we are not targets, that we really are not involved and that this is not our war, the reality is that we cannot avoid it. As I said last week, there are no rearguard positions in the struggle against terrorism, only front lines. Canada is on the front line whether we want to be there or not.
>
> (House of Commons, 2001c: 1135–1139)

Day then reminded his audience of the Canadian war effort in both world wars, the Korean War and the Gulf War in order to provide his reading of their implications for the present:

> We joined with our allies and did our share, sometimes at great cost. Now it is no different. The war on terrorism will require real sacrifices and new priorities. Now we must face the difficult question of whether Canada is ready to face this new struggle. Canada is a free and democratic society. It

206 *Comparing decision processes on use of force*

is precisely because we are a free and democratic society with values and desires to protect our way of life that we cannot avoid the awful responsibility of joining the war on terrorism.

(House of Commons, 2001c: 1139)

These remarks signify that 9/11 heralded a slight shift in the centre of gravity of Canadian strategic culture away from norms demanding restraint in the use of military force beyond peacekeeping and towards a more proactive involvement in military operations within NATO. This change was borne out of a change in the Canadian political landscape, which in turn is the product, among many factors, of demographic and economic dynamics within Canada, especially its four provinces west of Ontario. To some extent, the political forces representing these dynamics, on whose behalf Day spoke, saw 9/11 as having discredited Canada's traditional preference for restraint in the use of force and the goals for which it is used.

In contrast to this push for change, the leader of the New Democratic Party Alexa McDonough stood to the left of Chrétien's Liberals and urged these to stand firm on Canada's orthodox norms on the use of force. After expressing revulsion about the terrorist events and demanding that "the perpetrators of these heinous crimes be tracked down and punished" on behalf of her party, she went on to argue:

In these extremely dangerous times it is essential that we reaffirm our commitment to pursuing peaceful solutions to the tensions and hostilities that breed such mindless violence in our world. In the immediate aftermath of the horrific death and destruction, people were driven understandably to demand instant, massive military retaliation to these terrorist atrocities. However, as freedom loving citizens have grasped the complexity and magnitude of what has happened, *the imperative of a more measured response, more multilateral response and more informed response must form the basis of our actions....* Canadians know that we have a very special relationship with the United States of America and we value that relationship with our neighbour to the south but *we also have a special role internationally. If there were ever a time that both our neighbours to the south and the world needed to hear the voice of Canada, it is now.*

(House of Commons, 2001c: 1205–1210, emphasis added)

This demand for a measured response to a large-scale crime displaying what McDonough purported to be the typically Canadian characteristics of multilateralism and restraint rather than a robust military response to an act of war committed against an ally, as the Canadian Alliance did, thus represents the other side of an extensive debate which 9/11 catalysed in Canada. The Canadian government sought to make a meaningful contribution to the war on terror but it did not automatically follow from Canadian identity conceptions and strategic culture what such a contribution would entail in the special circumstances of the 9/11 terrorist attacks. Canada's participation in the war in Afghanistan therefore represents a 'special case' (Dawson, 2003) as it was Canada's first combat mission in 49 years (Corbett, 2012: 56).

Analysing Canadian decisions 207

Print media commentaries also reflected this debate about Canada's proper role in the war on terror. *National Post*, one of Canada's most well-known daily national newspapers with a conservative editorial stance and an average daily circulation of around 200,000 in 2008 (Newspapers Canada, 2013), featured opinion pieces which advocated for a decisive military commitment to the war on terror but which were also deeply critical, if not cynical, about the Canadian government's willingness and ability to provide such a commitment. Hence, of the 13 editorials analysed between 12 September and 31 December 2001, nine strongly supported and three moderately supported the idea of a war on terror against Al Qaeda and Taliban forces in Afghanistan with Canadian participation while only one dissenting column was moderately critical of this. Editorials criticised the government particularly heavily over its perceived indecisiveness regarding ground troops in mid-November and December 2001.

The traditionally more left wing *Globe and Mail*, one of Canada's largest national newspapers with a daily circulation of around 330,000 (Newspapers Canada, 2013), was substantially more critical of US foreign policy as well as its proclamation of a war on terror, and more supportive of the Canadian government's initial restraint after 9/11. Of 18 articles analysed, eleven supported the government moderately and one supported it strongly in its decisions on the war on terror while four articles were moderately critical and two were strongly critical of these.

With a circulation of 336,000 in 2008 (Newspapers Canada, 2013), the *Toronto Star* has a tradition as Canada's most widely circulated newspaper. Originally a left-wing, nationalist 'yellow press' paper writing in eye-catching font, it no longer prints in tabloid-style but retained its both left-wing and patriotic editorial stance. Its editorialists thus shared the *Globe and Mail*'s critical stance on US foreign policy but also applauded the Chrétien government for its measured response and initial restraint. Hence, of 15 editorials analysed, only one is classified as moderately critical while nine are strongly supportive and five are moderately supportive. On 20 September the paper's editorial board wrote:

> Prime Minister Jean Chrétien has promised, rightly, that Canada will be with the Americans every step on the way as they bring bin Laden to justice. Canadians demand no less. No one proposes to hand the Bush administration a blank cheque. Canadians want a focused, measured, international police action to bring the culprits to justice, with minimal grief being visited on third parties.
>
> (Toronto Star, 2001)

These lines best sum up the *Toronto Star*'s stance on Canada's role in the war on terror.

Public opinion polls also indicate positive resonance to the Canadian government's balanced approach after 9/11. However, the table also shows that there are high regional disparities, with support being strongest in Alberta and weakest in Quebec. Furthermore, the same poll found that this support dropped to 43 per cent if this were to provoke a terrorist attack leading to civilian casualties in Canada. Another poll among 800 adults conducted by the Canadian Alliance

208 *Comparing decision processes on use of force*

between 21 and 23 September 2001 found that 66 per cent supported Canada contributing ground troops to the war on terror but only 48 per cent approved of this if it led to hundreds of military casualties (Dawson, 2003: 182; Laghi, 2001b). Besides Parliament and the media, the public therefore also showed largely positive resonance to Chrétien's relatively cautious securitisation process after 9/11. This reflects the ambivalence harboured in Canadian strategic culture towards the use of military force and Canada's relationship with the US. As Darrell Bricker of Ipsos-Reid commented: "Mr. Chrétien has read the public mood quite well" (quoted from Ipsos-Reid/*Globe and Mail*, 2001).

Analysing the Canadian decision to implement anti-terror legislation after 9/11

After 9/11 Canada found itself in a special situation as it shares a long border with the US and was the subject of erroneous claims that terrorists may have entered the US through Canada. The case of a convicted terrorist who travelled to the US on a fake Canadian passport in 1999 already heightened awareness in Canada that the US was worried over relatively lax domestic security, immigration and border protection arrangements within its northern neighbour (Roach, 2011: 374). As before, the government therefore found itself under domestic and international pressure to demonstrate its commitment to the fight against terrorism. At the same time, the prior findings induce the assumption that the norms on domestic security provision of Canada's strategic culture demand as much restraint in the use of force as do norms on the use of force abroad.

The decision to implement counterterrorist legislation after 9/11

The Canadian government indeed acted with relative restraint in its securitisation process leading to enhanced domestic counterterrorism legislation, especially in comparison to the parallel processes in Australia and the UK. Once again, Chrétien sought to strike a careful balance between complying with pressure to demonstrate commitment in the fight against terrorism and upholding values he deemed central to Canadian identity. After Chrétien declared in the House of Commons on 17 September that 9/11 was an attack not only on the US but on "the values and beliefs of free and civilized people everywhere", he later added:

> Our actions will be ruled by resolve but not by fear. If laws need to be changed they will be. If security has to be increased to protect Canadians it will be. We will remain vigilant but will not give in to the temptation in a rush to increase security to undermine the values that we cherish and which have made Canada a beacon of hope, freedom and tolerance in the world. We will not be stampeded in the hope, vain and ultimately self-defeating, that we can make Canada a fortress against the world. Finally, I want to make another very important point. Canada is a nation of immigrants from all corners of the globe, people of all nationalities, colours and religions. This is who we are. Let there be no doubt. We will allow no

Analysing Canadian decisions 209

one to force us to sacrifice our values or traditions under the pressure of urgent circumstances. We will continue to welcome people from the whole world. We will continue to offer refuge to the persecuted.... Today more than ever we must reaffirm the fundamental values of our charter of rights and freedoms: the equality of every race, every colour, every religion and every ethnic origin.

(House of Commons, 2001c: 1115–1120)

Chrétien's heavy emphasis on multiculturalism and the Canadian bill of rights in this securitisation move mirrors the prior findings on traditional Canadian identity conceptions and its resultant strategic culture, but it also foreshadows their ensuing contestation by newly invigorated societal forces for which 9/11 discredited these traditional norms. In this first statement on domestic security after 9/11 before Parliament, Chrétien ostensibly saw the need to declare his refusal to partake in any major contestation of traditional Canadian norms on the use of force by the state in the light of 9/11.

The further process of drafting counterterrorism legislation also indicates that adherence to norms within Canadian strategic culture demanding restraint in the domestic use of force by the state for the provision of security moderated the government's securitisation process. On 18 September, the second day that the House of Commons met after 9/11, the Canadian Alliance tabled a motion calling upon the government to introduce anti-terrorism legislation similar to the UK's Terrorism Act, 2000, thus challenging the government's commitment to national security. In response, Minister of Justice Anne McLellan of the Liberal Party highlighted Canada's commitment to complying with UN counterterrorism conventions and bilateral agreements with the US. She pledged to bring legislation before Parliament on time to enable Canada to further comply with these agreements (House of Commons, 2001d: 1040–1045). In this justification of counterterrorism actions on the basis of UN conventions she avoided resemblances to the Canadian government's much-criticised invocation of the consequently repealed War Measures Act in response to kidnappings by separatist groups known as the 'October Crisis' of 1970 (Roach, 2011: 375).

After accelerated work within the Canadian Department of Justice, McLellan introduced Bill C-36, the draft *Anti-Terrorism Act* (ATA), to the House of Commons on 15 October 2001 (cf. Mazer, 2003). During the bill's Second Reading debate the following day, McLellan highlighted the government's commitment to the fight against terrorism before outlining the bill's main provisions. Amongst other things, the ATA would introduce a definition of terrorism for the first time, amend Canada's criminal code with regards to this definition, and extend the powers of government agencies to investigate and prosecute terrorist activity. Although the bill was far-reaching, it stopped short of some elements contained in the anti-terror legislation of the UK or Australia, such as a proscription regime (Roach, 2011: 363).

Nevertheless, McLellan noticeably strived to assure her audience of the bill's compatibility with what she considered Canadian core values of multiculturalism and civil liberties, as enshrined in the 1982 Canadian Charter of Rights and Freedoms. She made clear that;

210　*Comparing decision processes on use of force*

> Canadians can rest assured that we kept in mind the rights and freedoms guaranteed in the charter when drafting our proposals. The bill reaffirms the equal right of every citizen of whatever religion, race or ethnic origin to enjoy the security, protections and liberties shared by all Canadians.
>
> > (House of Commons, 2001b: 1015)

Akin to Chrétien's earlier statement, she also vociferously countered calls to now abandon traditional norms demanding restraint:

> They [terrorists] aimed to frighten us, disrupt our lives and force us to question our most basic democratic values of freedom and liberty. They did not succeed. Our commitment to democracy is stronger than ever. Together all Canadians are committed to increasing public security while maintaining our core values. Bill C-36 represents an appropriate legislative balance to reflect Canadian values.
>
> > (House of Commons, 2001b: 1030–1035)

As these remarks show, one can describe the Canadian government's securitisation process driven to introduce domestic counterterrorist legislation as relatively mild in nature.

The scope of debate that took place over the bill also indicates a relatively mild securitisation process. The government was strongly motivated to meet a deadline set by Security Council resolution 1373 of 28 September 2001, which required states to adopt certain anti-terror measures by the end of December (Roach, 2011: 363). Although this deadline condensed the legislative process, it still allowed for ample scrutiny of the bill in debates taking place in various committees and on the floor of both the House of Commons and the Senate as well as in parliamentary hearings from altogether 140 expert witnesses (Mazer, 2003: 22). During this process, the government accepted a number of substantive changes to the bill, including inter alia a narrower definition of terrorism that excluded expression of political and religious views and various forms of protest, the requirement of guilty intent for criminal responsibility of terrorist offences, a non-discrimination clause to protect minorities from discriminatory treatment and five-year sunset clauses for the police's new powers of preventive arrest for up to 72 hours as well as of investigative hearing (Mazer, 2003: 24; Roach, 2011: 363). In continuing to limit pre-charge detention strictly, Canada was showing a level of restraint similar to that in Germany, with both countries standing in contrast to the other three. Both the language employed and the scrutiny applied during the legislative process therefore confirm that a high regard for norms on multiculturalism and civil rights, which are enshrined in Canadian identity conceptions and thereby central to its strategic culture, induced the government's relatively mild securitisation process leading to comparatively restrained counterterrorism legislation in Canada after 9/11.

Resonance of the decision

As in the previous case of military action in response to 9/11, the Canadian government thus observed established norms on the domestic use of force within Canadian strategic culture despite domestic and international pressure to

Analysing Canadian decisions   211

demonstrate its commitment to the fight against terrorism. But as in the previous case, expanding societal forces called into question the viability of such established norms, especially in the light of the new terrorist threat that unfolded with 9/11. Already in the first House of Commons debate after 9/11, Canadian Alliance leader Stockwell Day criticised the government's attitude towards domestic security:

> For several years the official opposition has consistently raised issues of border security, the integrity of our refugee identification system and the need for more resources for military, security and intelligence purposes. We have drawn attention to terrorist activity within Canada. In our view the government unfortunately has not always responded as fully as it should have to these concerns, but the world has changed since September 11, 2001, and what was an important if sometimes overlooked concern before September 11 has now become an absolute moral imperative since September 11. Addressing these issues of national security must now become the single highest priority of the Parliament and the Government of Canada.
> (House of Commons, 2001c: 1135–1140)

Day consequently voiced anti-terrorist legislation as a central demand of his statement.

Throughout the remainder of the legislative process, Canadian Alliance MPs reiterated their perceived neglect of domestic security issues in the past and demanded more far-reaching measures than those proposed by the government, such as the Terrorism Act 2000 in the UK, the US Patriot Act or legislation in Australia and France. Speaking on behalf of the Canadian Alliance on 25 October, MP Vic Toews complained that his party was accused of racism whenever it raised issues of immigration and refugee system abuse by terrorists and that Canada "let down our American allies who suffered a terrible tragedy in New York City" by failing to deal with these issues prior to the events of 9/11 (House of Commons, 2001a: 1110–1115). On 16 October, during the Second Reading debate, Stockwell Day raised a number of measures that the bill omitted in his party's view, especially regarding preventive detention powers for immigration officers and judges, on which he commented: "This happens in the United Kingdom. It happens in the United States. It happens in Australia. It happens in other freedom loving democracies. It should happen here" (House of Commons, 2001b: 1555–1560). The Democratic Alliance therefore sought to break with past practices guided by traditional norms and pursue more robust domestic security policies akin to the US, the UK or Australia.

The other parties represented in the House of Commons did not share this desire for drastic change. The Bloc Quebecois was mostly concerned with the bill going too far, especially as regards the rights of associations, possibly in consideration of Quebecois independence movements. Speaking for the BQ on 16 October, Pierrette Venne conceded that terrorism must be fought effectively but also demanded close scrutiny of the bill despite its urgency. She warned her audience about not repeating the mistakes of the harsh War Measures Act implemented during the October Crisis of 1970, which in her view was

212   *Comparing decision processes on use of force*

"undoubtedly the worst case of abuse of power ever known in Quebec" (House of Commons, 2001b: 1114). She therefore affirmed on behalf of her Quebecois electorate that the government should not let anti-terror measures interfere with established norms of multiculturalism and civil liberties, which proscribe restraint by the state in its domestic exercise of force.

Bill Blakie of the New Democratic Party also saw a need for new anti-terror legislation per se. He added that this not only arose out of legitimate fears and concerns after 9/11 but also out of the demands of United Nations resolutions passed after 9/11. However, he also expressed his party's strong concerns about the bill, urging that "We need to respect Canadian values as set out in the Canadian Charter of Rights and Freedoms" (House of Commons, 2001b: 1125). He also expressed pride in the traditionally strong standing of civil liberties in Canada, for instance in stating:

> In fairness to the government and to the charter, the charter has already had its effect on this legislation. My understanding is that the bill does not go as far as the British anti-terrorism legislation. This is because we have a Canadian Charter of Rights and Freedoms and Britain does not.
>
> (House of Commons, 2001b: 1140)

This pride in the norms of Canadian strategic culture on the domestic use of force can also be discerned in the frequent use of the term 'Canadian values' in calls for the safeguarding of multiculturalism and civil liberties from state power. NDP and Liberal Party MPs used this term altogether 11 times during the debate on 16 October.

The Progressive Conservatives also did not share the Canadian Alliance's strong dissatisfaction over the purportedly restrained nature of the bill. On behalf of his party, MP Peter McKay declared he was "generally supportive of this legislation and enthusiastically supportive of the need to bring about changes in our internal security measures and the way in which we deal with terrorism in this country" (House of Commons, 2001b: 1150). In contrast to the Liberals and the NDP, the Progressive Conservatives therefore supported the bill's robustness rather than its restraint. Overall, the parliamentary resonance to the government's securitisation process on domestic security was generally supportive but revealed a polarised Canadian strategic culture in which an established consensus over norms demanding restraint in the use of force by the state became increasingly challenged, especially in the light of 9/11.

An analysis of print media commentaries also reveals a polarised debate. Of the 16 *National Post* editorials of September to December 2001 that were analysed, 13 can be described as strongly supportive of an expanded domestic fight against terrorism while one article was considered to be moderately supportive of this idea and two articles were moderately critical and demanded caution towards too much compromise on civil liberties for the sake of security. But the overall editorial stance was highly sceptical of the government's ability to confront the terrorist threat domestically with the purportedly necessary determination and robustness. Most editorialists also saw Canada as having been too soft on terrorism in the past, to the grave concern of the US.

The 13 articles analysed from the *Globe and Mail* contrasted sharply with the *National Post*'s editorials. The authors stated at the outset that they understood the need for new legislation but showed themselves deeply concerned about civil liberties in Canada. Notably, the paper lobbied persistently for sunset clauses in its editorials throughout the legislative process. Nine of the 13 articles were moderately critical of the government's plans, one was strongly critical and only two were considered to be moderately supportive of the new anti-terror laws on balance. The *Toronto Star* was also wary of calls for enhanced anti-terror legislation at first and warned that basic freedoms must not be surrendered to terrorism. Once the government unveiled its first drafts and the parliamentary process ensued, however, the paper raised a few concerns but generally endorsed the bill. Its editorialists welcomed the government's and parliament's consideration of its concerns and deemed the bill tough but balanced. Seven out of nine editorials were moderately supportive of the new laws while two were moderately critical.

The analysis thus far shows that Parliament and the media generally provided positive resonance to the government's relatively mild securitisation process in Canada, although a fractious debate took place with vociferous demands for more far-reaching measures on the one hand and wariness towards the measures put forward on the other. Public opinion polls also indicate that there was generally positive resonance but also strong reservation towards the government among the general public. A survey taken by Ipsos-Reid among 1,000 Canadians for the *Globe and Mail* between 17 and 20 September showed that a narrow majority of 53 per cent of respondents "would be prepared to see police and security services get more power to fight terrorism" even if this entailed interceptions of one's telephone, email and postal communications, while 46 per cent disagreed (Ipsos-Reid/*Globe and Mail*, 2001). Another poll among 1,000 Canadians taken by Ipsos-Reid for the *Globe and Mail* on 2 and 4 October shows that 52 per cent of respondents thought it would be necessary to give up some of one's civil liberties currently protected in law in order to curb terrorism in Canada, while 46 per cent disagreed nationwide and 62 per cent disagreed in Quebec (Leblanc, 2001).

The analysis in this section therefore showed that as Chapter 4 derived from a reading of Canadian identity conceptions and strategic culture based on the theoretical model composed of the strategic culture and securitisation approaches, norms on the use of force by the state demanded greater restraint in Canada both as regards military force and as regards the domestic use of force. Canadian strategic culture was therefore conducive to a relatively mild securitisation process regarding anti-terror measures taken after 9/11, which received generally positive, although contentious, resonance in Parliament, the media and the public.

Analysing the Canadian decision process regarding the use of force in Iraq

In the run-up to the war on Iraq Canada again found itself under considerable and conflicting domestic and international pressures. In contrast to other US

214   *Comparing decision processes on use of force*

allies, Canada can consider itself America's closest friend and ally in a literal sense. Perceptions and the realities of Canada being a relatively small country sharing a long border with the world's superpower played an important role in discussions on the question of a Canadian participation in the war on Iraq. After all, the US accounts for 87 per cent of Canada's trade volume (Fawn, 2008: 528). The option to oppose the US on the question of war therefore stirred some speculation and anxiety about possible implications arising out of Canada's many disproportionate dependencies on the US.

On the other hand, incidents related to Canada's military involvement in Afghanistan contributed to a decline in pro-American sentiments in Canada as the debate over the Iraq War unfolded. Many Canadians took pride in the accomplishments of the Canadian ground forces which Canada contributed to allied combat operations in Afghanistan, but already by the first half of 2002 many also felt that this contribution went unacknowledged in the US. For instance, a major uproar emerged in January 2002 when Canadian troops captured Taliban soldiers, but the US imprisoned these as criminals rather than treating them as prisoners of war under the Geneva Convention. Also, on 17 April, four Canadian soldiers died in 'friendly fire' when US fighter jets accidentally bombed Canadian artillery. Subsequent investigations discovered that the US high command in complicity with the Canadian Defence Minister attempted to cover up facts related to the incident (Thompson, 2003: 10–11).

These two factors formed the country-specific backdrop against which the Canadian government needed to decide on the question of a war with Iraq. They exemplify the potential dilemmas surrounding this question, which arise from the centrality of contrast with the US to traditional Canadian identity on the one hand and the undeniable importance of good neighbourly relations on the other. The Canadian government decided not to participate in the Iraq War. Given these dilemmas and the polarised nature of Canadian strategic culture, one can hypothesise that this decision largely fell in line with the traditional preferences and norms of Canadian strategic culture but also drew sturdy domestic opposition.

The decision regarding the use of force in Iraq

The process leading up to the decision not to participate in the US-led Operation Iraqi Freedom reveals that the Canadian government encountered its predicament towards the US by only fully revealing its ultimate decision not to participate at a very late stage of the Iraq War's prelude. However, the Chrétien government also did not follow the US in fully securitising the threat of Iraqi WMDs but instead called for a vigorous weapons inspections regime and full Security Council backing for military action in order to subject American threat claims to multilateral scrutiny and decision (Barry, 2005: 215). The Canadian government thus signalled scepticism about the American case for war and aversion to US unilateralist impulses, which did not reconcile with traditional Canadian norms on multilateralism and international law guiding decisions on the use of force.

The Bush administration's international campaign to securitise Iraqi WMD claims, which gained momentum from Bush's famous January 2002 "axis of

Analysing Canadian decisions 215

evil" speech onwards, largely passed without comment in Canada throughout the first half of 2002 (Barry, 2005: 217). Only by August 2002, the Canadian government entered the debate. Drawing on Canada's long experience with UN weapons inspections, Canada's foreign minister Bill Graham commented on 7 August that although Saddam Hussein was "extremely dangerous" his offer to allow weapons inspectors back into the country should be followed up. Urging the Bush administration to give the regime "an opportunity to cooperate", Graham warned: "If we say we are just going to attack him, he is clearly going to take defensive measures, and that could lead to a very dangerous situation.... I would encourage the Americans to make the UN system work" (quoted from Sallot, 2002). Graham further stated that there was no evidence at this time of an Iraqi possession of WMDs or of an intention to use them and without clear evidence of an imminent threat or UN authorisation Canada would be loath to participate in any military action (Barry, 2005: 217–218; Sallot, 2002). This mild securitisation calling for a multilateral solution and for the averting of unilateral military action mirrors Canada's traditional preferences generated by a strategic culture that emphasises multilateralism and restraint in the use of force.

In September, Chrétien met Bush and reiterated Graham's remarks about the need for more inspections, clear evidence and UN involvement regarding Iraq, adding that Canada would be involved in any action against Iraq if the Security Council approved (Barry, 2005: 218). On 1 October, the House of Commons debated the Iraq issue. Graham stated that "Canada, and much of the world, welcomed President Bush's commitment to the UN General Assembly that the United States would work with the Security Council in resolving this serious threat", but he also reaffirmed Canada's rejection of unilateral action, adding:

> Canadians are proud of our longstanding tradition in foreign policy which has been to pursue and promote dialogue and understanding among the peoples of the world and to seek political and diplomatic solutions even in the face of imminent conflict. By continuing to act consistently with these values, world peace and security will be enhanced and international institutions strengthened.
>
> (House of Commons, 2002: 1835–1840)

Graham therefore made clear that the government saw a threat in the Iraqi regime, but that it would proudly allow its actions to be constrained by strategic cultural norms stemming from a traditional identity conception which contrasted with perceived American attributes. This message was also targeted at the opposition, which Graham referred to as "those who call upon us to follow blindly whenever and wherever the United States would lead, even if such actions would threaten the multilateral system we have built together with our American partners so painstakingly over the past 50 years…" (House of Commons, 2002: 1835–1840).

In the following months the Chrétien government continued to frame Iraq's intransigence towards the international community as a serious threat while at the same time asserting its independence from the US on the question of using force against Iraq and pushing for a multilateral solution. For instance, when

216 *Comparing decision processes on use of force*

Chrétien met Bush again in late January, he again made clear that Canada would not participate in military action without a clear UN mandate. Chrétien stated to the press that he would support war "only if the Americans or the Brits have great evidence that Saddam Hussein, who is no friend of mine, is not following the instructions of the United Nations..." Asked about concerns over the implications of opposing the US, he replied: "If I have to say no, I will. If I have to say yes, I will. We are an independent country" (Barry, 2005: 224–225; quoted in Sallot, 2003).

Throughout February and March, Canada then made several attempts to forge a compromise between the members of the Security Council. Canada's ambassador to the UN, Paul Heinbecker, unveiled a plan to the public in a speech to the Security Council on 19 February that would bridge the growing divide between the French and Anglo-American positions by establishing key disarmament tasks monitored by UN inspectors and a firm deadline for compliance (Barry, 2005: 224). Chrétien, meanwhile, endorsed the build-up of American and British forces around Iraq as it increased pressure on Saddam Hussein to cooperate with UN inspectors. But on 9 March, in an American television debate inter alia with US National Security Advisor Condoleeza Rice, he argued that such international pressure and the revived inspections programme had now successfully contained Iraq as its regime showed improved compliance with UN disarmament resolutions (Barry, 2005: 227). After negotiations at the Security Council failed, Chrétien then stated before the House of Commons on 17 March that "If military action proceeds without a new resolution in the Security Council, Canada will not participate" (House of Commons, 2003: 1415–1420).

The Canadian government thus drove a relatively mild, protracted and reactive securitisation process in which it proclaimed a threat but also advocated a multilateral solution through UN inspections backed up by military pressure. From this, one can discern that the government adhered to the traditional norms of Canadian strategic culture and thereby sought to reconstitute Canadian identity in a recognisable manner, as was previously deduced.

Resonance of the decision

Despite Chrétien's cautiously deliberative approach to the Iraq crisis, his government attracted criticism from both sides of the political spectrum. The two sides were united in their criticism of the lateness of the decision and the lack of a clear stance beforehand (Fawn, 2008: 520). On the decision itself, opinions naturally diverged and again revealed the polarised and contested nature of Canadian strategic culture but generally, Chrétien's decision again resonated positively with supporters of all parties except for those on the new right.

In the House of Commons debate on 1 October 2002, the Canadian Alliance's new leader of the opposition Stephen Harper, who became prime minister in 2006, declared that his party wanted Canada "to pledge support to the developing coalition of nations, including Britain, Australia and the United States..." which saw military action as already sanctioned by existing UN Resolutions (House of Commons, 2002: 1900). All other parties supported the

Analysing Canadian decisions 217

government's call for further diplomatic action through the UN. Francine Lalonde of the Bloc Quebecois warned that "this notion of pre-emptive strikes takes us well back into the nineteenth century" and insisted that any future military action by Canada should first be debated and voted on in the House of Commons (House of Commons, 2002: 1925–1950).

Alexa McDonough of the left-wing NDP joined the BQ in calling on the government to play a more active diplomat role in peacefully resolving the crisis. Regarding the Canadian Alliance's position, she commented: "Their gung ho approach to attacking Iraq, circumventing the legitimate role of the United Nations and the absolute necessity for a multilateral approach is downright scary." Her statement revealed how the Canadian left perceived the Canadian Alliance's stance as further indication of a radically new and provocative development rather than a stance which one would routinely expect from a conservative opposition. It is also telling in this regard that the former Prime Minister Joe Clark, who spoke for the Progressive Conservatives, Canada's traditional conservative counterpart to the Liberal Party, struck a much milder tone in the debate than the Canadian Alliance did. He argued that the positions of the US, the UK and Australia were helpful in making Saddam Hussein understand the seriousness of the situation but argued that "the position of Canada ... is far better and more effectively exercised trying to make the authority of the United Nations as respected as possible." He therefore urged the government "to be making the case to the United States of how contagious and dangerous the idea of regime change can be" (House of Commons, 2002: 2025–2035).

MPs largely reiterated these positions in the debate that took place after Chrétien announced his final decision on 17 March to thunderous applause of Liberal MPs and their supporters (see video *Harper's Conservatives Wanted Canada to Join the War in Iraq*, 2008). The Bloc Quebecois and the NDP criticised the lack of parliamentary debate and Chrétien's lack of clarity on the question of war with Iraq but expressed relief that the government did not adopt the position that Resolution 1441 was justification enough for Canada to participate (House of Commons, 2003: 1815–1920). The Progressive Conservatives also did not see Resolution 1441 as sufficient justification and lamented the failure of Canadian diplomacy to influence the US and achieve a consensus at the UN in order to avert war (House of Commons, 2003: 1930–1945). In contrast, the Canadian Alliance decried the government for estranging Canada from its most important ally, opposing the enforcement of Resolution 1441 and for playing no role in the "historic liberation of the Iraqi people" and the disarming of Saddam Hussein (House of Commons, 2003: 1850–1910).

A similarly fractious resonance can be discerned in Canadian print media. Within the time frame of 1 to 31 March 2003, the *National Post* featured 15 editorials on the Iraq War, of which 14 are strongly supportive of military action in Iraq and one is moderately supportive. In stark terms the paper commented that Canada's abstention "while similarly situated nations such as Australia and Britain fight shoulder to shoulder with the United States brings shame to this country" ("On to War", 2003). The paper thus endorsed the stance of the Canadian Alliance in arguing that Canada's traditional norms guiding security policy were obsolete, not least since 9/11. For instance, its editorialists described

218 *Comparing decision processes on use of force*

Chrétien and Graham as "still living in a lost age – when theories like 'soft power' were still taken seriously, people believed everlasting peace could be achieved through multilateral treaties, and Lloyd Axworthy circled the globe, soaking up praise from America's critics" ("Cellucci's Message", 2003). Hence, the *National Post* advocated for a wholesale overhaul of Canadian strategic culture in the run-up to the Iraq War as it did in the prior cases.

Surprisingly, the *Globe and Mail*'s official editorial stance was one of reluctant support for the war on Iraq after efforts to attain a second UN resolution failed as well as of criticism of Chrétien's belated and allegedly incoherent decision to refuse Canada's participation in it. Editorials were critical that Chrétien did not support his insistence on a second resolution with arguments against the war itself, as he seemingly endorsed threat claims regarding Iraqi WMDs and as Chrétien could not explain why failure to abide by Resolution 1441 was not already justification enough for war. Akin to arguments brought forward by Germany's opposition parties, editorialists argued for Canada to declare its support for the war without providing military contributions beyond post-war reconstruction and peacekeeping assets.

At the same time, the paper also published numerous internal and external commentaries criticising the official case for war against Iraq as inherently flawed and lauding Chrétien's decision as courageous. Hence, of the 18 opinion pieces analysed, nine can be considered as moderately critical of the use of military force in Iraq, three as strongly critical, and six as moderately supportive. The paper's mixed resonance indicates that part of the Canadian Left struggled with the seeming contradiction between Chrétien's mild securitisation rhetoric regarding Iraq and his eventual categorical refusal to take part in military action against the purported threat, while others refuted claims about the threat of Iraqi WMDs necessitating war as implausible. Canadian strategic culture therefore did not automatically lend itself to a position of outright opposition to war but it generated stronger scepticism towards calls for the pre-emptive use of military force in Canada.

The 16 opinion pieces analysed in the *Toronto Star* further indicate this. All were moderately critical of a war on Iraq. The paper's editorialists did not see such war as a necessary and lawful measure taken after all peaceful means had been exhausted, and therefore endorsed Chrétien's belated but in their views nonetheless correct decision not to participate. One can deduce from the commentaries that the decision instilled some pride in Canadians for being more insistent on these criteria than the US. The paper's widely positive resonance can thus be seen as representing the adherents of traditional Canadian identity conceptions and the norms stemming from these.

In public opinion polls, one can read a similar divergence of opinions over the war on Iraq. Generally, the polls show that Chrétien's decision resonated positively with large parts of the Canadian public. For instance, in mid-January 2003, an Ipsos-Reid poll among 1,005 adults in Canada showed that 62 per cent thought Canada should contribute to taking military action against Iraq "only if the United Nations, not just the United States, decides that military action is required", while only 15 per cent thought Canada should provide military assistance "If the United States decides to take military action

Analysing Canadian decisions   219

against Iraq on its own without UN authorization" (Ipsos-Reid/ *Globe and Mail*, 2003a). Immediately after Chrétien's announcement, a poll taken on 18–20 March 2003 among 1,000 Canadians reveals that 69 per cent of respondents thought Canada should stay out of the conflict and 52 per cent opposed US military action (Ipsos-Reid/ *Globe and Mail*, 2003b). However, one can again discern strong regional variations in the polls. In the Democratic Alliance stronghold-province of Alberta, only 39 per cent disagreed with US action and only 51 per cent thought Canada should stay out of the war (Ipsos-Reid/ *Globe and Mail*, 2003b). On the other hand, another Ipsos-Reid poll taken on 25 to 27 March 2003 among 1,000 Canadians showed that while 83 per cent of Quebecers said they were glad that Canada opted out of the war, only 52 per cent of non-Quebecers and 59 per cent of respondents overall did so (Ipsos-Reid/ *Globe and Mail*, 2003c).

Conclusion and outlook

The poll data therefore tends to reaffirm the conclusion that in the decades after the Second World War, traditional Canadian identity narratives and norms guiding foreign and security policy secured a fragile consensus between French and English speaking Canadians over what constitutes Canadianness as opposed to Americanness. Elites therefore had a long-standing interest in maintaining and nurturing the strategic culture that emanated from these identity narratives, as was manifest in Lester Pearson's and Lloyd Axworthy's foreign policies. But 9/11 served as a catalyst for the expression of increasing disenfranchisement with this consensus by new political forces growing 'bottom-up' out of economic and demographic developments taking place mainly in Canada's western provinces. While the effects of traditional Canadian strategic culture were discernible in the decision processes analysed in this section, one could also discern that it was heavily contested as many Canadians saw 9/11 as having discredited the traditional norms of Canadian strategic culture and called for a more assertive stance, including through the more robust use of military force.

Such endogenous change in Canadian strategic culture appears to have continued beyond the post-9/11 period and to have had further repercussions during the premiership of current (as of 2014) Canadian Prime Minister Stephen Harper, who assumed office in 2006 after electoral success despite his earlier vocal support for the Iraq War and the hindsight that its threat was overestimated. Besides economic and demographic developments within Canada, the melting of the polar ice caps might also have contributed to an endogenous shift in Canadian strategic culture. This has opened up the possibility of a Russian military encroachment, which the Harper government seeks to pre-empt through an expanded military presence in the north (Torobin, 2011; on the wider implications of these developments in the Arctic Ocean theatre, see Seidler, 2009). Yet a detailed analysis of further developments within strategic culture would be required to establish whether it indeed progresses towards a more 'robust' category due to factors largely independent of agency or whether Canadian society as a whole has become more polarised and its strategic culture is undergoing a process of segmentation.

220 *Comparing decision processes on use of force*

Note

1 On 19 December 2001 Eggleton clarified that around 40 of Canada's Special Forces troops were deployed in Afghanistan in early December to assist US, British and Australian Special Forces as well as local fighters. The naval assets, however, were already deployed in Afghanistan on 17 October, ten days after Chrétien's announcement (Corbett, 2012: 53–55).

Bibliography

Barry D (2005) "Chrétien, Bush, and the War in Iraq". *American Review of Canadian Studies*, 35(2), 215–245.

Behiels MD (2010) "Stephen Harper's Rise to Power: Will His 'New' Conservative Party Become Canada's 'Natural Governing Party' of the Twenty-First Century?" *American Review of Canadian Studies*, 40(1), 118–145.

Bouldin M (2003) "Keeper of the Peace: Canada and Security Transition Operations". *Defense & Security Analysis*, 19(3), 265–276.

Cellucci's message (2003) *National Post*, Toronto, 26 March.

Clarkson S (2011) *The Big Red Machine: How the Liberal Party Dominates Canadian Politics*. Kelowna, British Columbia: University of British Columbia Press.

Corbett R (2012) *First Soldiers Down: Canada's Friendly Fire Deaths in Afghanistan*. Toronto: Dundurn.

Crossette B (2001) "A Nation Challenged: Canada; Chrétien Under Pressure From Right and Left Over What to Give Washington". *New York Times*, New York, 23 September. Available from: www.nytimes.com/2001/09/23/world/nation-challenged-canada-chretien-under-pressure-right-left-over-what-give.html (accessed 26 November 2013).

CTVNews.ca Staff (2011) "Ten years later, Chretien remembers 9–11". *CTVNews*. Available from: www.ctvnews.ca/ten-years-later-chretien-remembers-9-11-1.693180 (accessed 24 November 2013).

Dawson G (2003) "'A Special Case': Canada, Operation Apollo, and Multilateralism". *Canada Among Nations 2003: Coping with the American Colossus*, 180–199.

Dawson PF (1989) "Canadian Military Mobilization". *Armed Forces & Society*, 16(1), 37–57.

Fawn R (2008) "No Consensus with the Commonwealth, No Consensus with Itself? Canada and the Iraq War". *The Round Table: The Commonwealth Journal of International Affairs*, 97(397), 519–533.

Harper's Conservatives Wanted Canada to Join the War in Iraq (2008) Available from: www.youtube.com/watch?v=iPVOhva_cwI&feature=youtube_gdata_player (accessed 13 December 2013).

House of Commons (2001a) *Hansard*, 15 October 2001. Parliament of Canada. Available from: www.parl.gc.ca/HousePublications/Publication.aspx?Language=E&Mode=1&Parl=37&Ses=1&DocId=1227567#Int-55925 (accessed 24 November 2013).

House of Commons (2001b) *Hansard*, 16 October 2001. Parliament of Canada. Available from: www.parl.gc.ca/HousePublications/Publication.aspx?Language=E&Mode=1&Parl=37&Ses=1&DocId=1226580#SOB-56586 (accessed 24 November 2013).

House of Commons (2001c) *Hansard*, 17 September 2001. Parliament of Canada. Available from: www.parl.gc.ca/HousePublications/Publication.aspx?Language=E&Mode=1&Parl=37&Ses=1&DocId=653212#SOB-47885 (accessed 24 November 2013).

House of Commons (2001d) *Hansard*, 18 September 2001. Parliament of Canada. Available from: www.parl.gc.ca/HousePublications/Publication.aspx?Language=E&Mode=1&Parl=37&Ses=1&DocId=1236607#Int-48998 (accessed 24 November 2013).

House of Commons (2001e) *Hansard*, 19 November 2001. Parliament of Canada. Available from: www.parl.gc.ca/HousePublications/Publication.aspx?Language=E&Mode=1&Parl=37&Ses=1&DocId=1245722 (accessed 24 November 2013).

Analysing Canadian decisions 221

House of Commons (2002) *Hansard*, 1 October 2002. Parliament of Canada, Available from: www.parl.gc.ca/HousePublications/Publication.aspx?Language=E&Mode=1&P arl=37&Ses=2&DocId=509870#SOB-297684 (accessed 24 November 2013).

House of Commons (2003) *Hansard*, 17 March 2003. Parliament of Canada. Available from: www.parl.gc.ca/HousePublications/Publication.aspx?Language=E&Mode=1&P arl=37&Ses=2&DocId=755432 (accessed 24 November 2013).

Ipsos-Reid/Globe and Mail (2001) "Canadians Reject War If Civilians Put at Risk". *Globe and Mail*, Toronto, 22 September.

Ipsos-Reid/Globe and Mail (2003a) "Canadians Oppose War in Iraq Without UN". *Globe and Mail*, Toronto, 18 January.

Ipsos-Reid/Globe and Mail (2003b) "PM's Iraq Call Backed by 66%, Poll Reveals". *Globe and Mail (Canada)*, 22 March.

Ipsos-Reid/Globe and Mail (2003c) "Support for PM's War Stand Sags". *Globe and Mail (Canada)*, 29 March.

Kennedy M (2011) "Canada's 9/11, Part 1: Chretien Urged Calm Amid Chaos". *Postmedia News, Canada.com*, 1 September. Available from: www.canada.com/Canada+Part+Chretien+urged+calm+amid+chaos/5347551/story.html (accessed 24 November 2013).

Laghi B (2001a) "Blair Captains Team Coalition". *Globe and Mail*, Toronto, 6 October.

Laghi B (2001b) "Support for Forces Funding Limited, Alliance Poll Finds". *Globe and Mail*, Toronto, 2 October.

Leblanc D (2001) "80 per cent Would Back National ID Cards". *Globe and Mail*, Toronto, Ont., Canada, 6 October.

Manning P (1992) *The New Canada*. Toronto, Ont., Canada: Macmillan Canada.

Mazer A (2003) "Debating the Anti-Terrorism Legislation: Lessons Learned". *Canadian Parliamentary Review*, 26(2), 21–32.

McCarthy S (2001) "PM Plans Trip to US to Discuss United Force". *Globe and Mail*, Toronto, 19 September.

Newspapers Canada (2013) Daily Newspaper Circulation Data. Available from: www.newspaperscanada.ca/daily-newspaper-circulation-data (accessed 1 December 2013).

Office of the Prime Minister of Canada (2001) News Release. Government of Canada. Available from: www.patriotresource.com/wtc/intl/alpha2.html (accessed 24 November 2013).

"On to War" (2003) *National Post*, Toronto, 18 March.

Parliament of Canada (2013) Members of The House Of Commons. Available from: www.parl.gc.ca/parlinfo/Lists/Members.aspx (accessed 23 November 2013).

Roach K (2011) *The 9/11 Effect: Comparative Counter-Terrorism*. 1st edn. Cambridge: Cambridge University Press.

Sallot J (2002) "Give Iraqi Leader a Chance to Co-operate, Graham Says". *Globe and Mail*, Toronto, Ont., Canada, 8 August.

Sallot J (2003) "PM to Bush: Hold Off on War". *Globe and Mail*, Toronto, Ont., Canada, 24 January.

Seidler C (2009) *Arktisches Monopoly der Kampf um die Rohstoffe der Polarregion*. Munich: Dt. Verl.-Anst.

The White House (2001) Canadian PM: "We Will Be There". Press Release. Available from: http://georgewbush-whitehouse.archives.gov/news/releases/2001/09/20010924-7.html (accessed 18 December 2013).

Thompson JH (2003) "Playing by the New Washington Rules: the US–Canada Relationship, 1994–2003". *American Review of Canadian Studies*, 33(1), 5–26.

Torobin J (2011) "Military Plans a show of Force in High Arctic". *Globe and Mail*, Toronto, 3 July. Available from: www.theglobeandmail.com/news/politics/military-plans-a-show-of-force-in-high-arctic/article586436/ (accessed 24 February 2014).

Toronto Star (2001) "Don't Blame America for Global Terror". *Toronto Star*, Toronto, 20 September.

11 Conclusion

This book claimed that the differences in the extent to which Western liberal democracies resorted to the use of force within the two-year period after the terrorist events of 11 September 2001 can be explained largely on the basis of differences in societies' identity-derived norms on the legitimate use of force by the state against perceived existential threats. To test this claim, this book chose to compare a range of factors which, according to existing theories of international relations, could presumably contribute to differences in behaviour regarding the use of force by the state against perceived threats. It chose to compare these on the basis of five Western liberal democracies which differed in the extent to which they resorted to the use of force as a result of three major security policy decisions that presented themselves to most Western liberal democracies within the period after analysis. These concerned the question of whether and to what extent to contribute to the war in Afghanistan, whether and how to expand the state's domestic coercive powers to fight against terrorism, and whether or to what extent to contribute to the Iraq War. In all three respects, these countries took differing decisions. The conclusion will now seek to recapture the main insights and reflect on the various implications of the attempt by this book to explain these differences.

Revisiting the results

Through analyses of literature on identity conceptions and comparative public opinion polls, this book discerned that there are significant differences in the proclivities to the use of force of the five countries chosen as cases. It found that one can generally categorise German strategic culture as more reactive, Canadian and French strategic cultures as more proactive, and Australian and British strategic culture as more robust. After 9/11, the governments of these countries drove securitisation processes in the run-up to the wars in Afghanistan and Iraq as well as the enactment of domestic anti-terror measures which largely corresponded to each country's respective strategic culture. German and to a lesser extent Canadian and French securitisation processes were consistently 'milder' than the 'stronger' Australian and British securitisation processes. As a result, the securitisation processes largely received positive resonance across wider society, although the Australian and the British securitisation process in the run-up to the Iraq War already came close to bringing about dissonance.

Conclusion 223

The results show that strategic culture provides an important formal cause of a state's behaviour regarding the use of force. The agency of securitisation provides an important final cause of the precise nature of particular instances of state behaviour. This agency usually adheres to the confines of strategic culture, but it can potentially deviate from these and thereby affect strategic culture in the long run, as the book discussed in the conclusion and outlook of each country analysis. Power capabilities and institutions, meanwhile, were found to be material and formal causes that also structurally condition securitisation processes and their outcomes, but these mostly become relevant when comparing countries with vast differences in these factors.

Revisiting the first research step

At the outset, the introduction showed that Australia and Canada on the one hand and France, Germany and the UK on the other, resemble each other in the total size of their populations and economies. The five countries chosen, namely Australia, Canada, France, Germany and the UK, are all liberal democracies, to varying but negligible degrees; are all aligned to the US in some way or another, and all have vaguely similar potential power capabilities relative to the size of their populations. However, the countries displayed consistent differences in behaviour not only but especially in the period immediately after 9/11. Across all three policy domains, irrespective of the internal or external dimension of the use of force in question, a pattern emerged. Whereas Australia and the UK contributed rapidly and sizeably to both the wars in Afghanistan and in Iraq, and enacted far-reaching legislation expanding the state's coercive capacities to a considerable degree, Germany played a minor role in the invasion of Afghanistan, enacted moderate new anti-terror laws and decided early on that it would not participate in military action against Iraq. Canada and France, meanwhile, assumed a position in the middle ground by participating readily in military action in Afghanistan but enacting more moderate anti-terror provisions than the UK and Australia, and by eventually opting out of plans for an invasion of Iraq. The countries translated their potential power capabilities into actual power capabilities to varying degrees, but this only adds to the question of why they differed in behaviour after 9/11 besides these similar contextual factors.

Part II turned to the prime suspect in this empirical puzzle: strategic culture, defined as comprising the widely shared, identity derived norms, ideas and beliefs about the legitimate use of force by the state for the provision of security against perceived existential threats. It was analysed in three steps. First, the foundation of a strategic culture, i.e. national identity conceptions, were analysed on the basis of secondary literature. Although this exercise was inherently simplifying and generalising given the vastness and broadness of literature on countries' respective identity conceptions, it could establish that one can once again recognise a pattern. While Germany and to some extent also Canada had more 'Kantian' conceptions of international relations and their role within these; depictions of British, Australian and French identity conceptions tended to infer a more 'Hobbesian' perspective. On this basis, one could formulate assumptions about the content of a strategic culture, which are its norms on the legitimate

224 Comparing decision processes on use of force

use of force by the state. It was assumed, in very generalising terms, that the more 'Kantian' the identity conception, the more robust were the norms on the legitimate use of force by the state.

These assumptions were then once again tested through international comparative public opinion polls which related to the use of force by the state in some way or another. Chapter 5 thus evaluated polls which surveyed samples of the public on questions such as whether the respondent would defend their country in case of war, whether war was sometimes necessary to obtain justice and whether the respondent would support the death penalty. Although these polls are inherently problematic, hence one would go too far in claiming that they provide solid evidence of clear-cut expressions of different strategic cultures, and although their results also present a somewhat diffuse picture, they were nonetheless insightful since one could once again discern a pattern across the five states in this analysis.

The polls indicated that the poll results tended to differ coherently between those states with a more 'Hobbesian' identity conception, i.e. Australia and the UK, and those with a more 'Kantian' identity conception, i.e. Germany, with France and Canada assuming a position in the middle ground, with regards to various norms dimensions concerning both norms on the external and on the internal application of force by the state. On this basis, the chapter proceeded to classify German strategic culture in the 'reactive-proactive' category of proclivity to the use of force, and Australian as well as British strategic culture within the 'proactive-robust' category. Canada and France were categorised as pertaining to the former and the latter category, respectively, but in close proximity to the 'proactive' demarcation along a spectrum of proclivity to the use of force ranging from passivity to aggressiveness.

Revisiting the theoretical model

With these insights, the case was far from solved. The book established that the five countries in question resemble each other in many respects but differ in the expressions of their strategic cultures largely in accordance with the observed differences in behaviour, both as regards the use of force abroad and domestically. This provides a strong indication about the explanatory power of strategic culture but in this point the analysis cannot prevail in the courtroom of academia. After all, international relations theory presents another prime suspect. Through the concept of securitisation, the theory convincingly argues that in the realm of security policy and practice, where existential threats are involved, those in a position of authority sufficient for making key decisions on how to encounter those threats enjoy a particular autonomy in making such decisions. In contrast to issues of ordinary politics, which often end up being 'politicised' in liberal democracies, security issues can become 'securitised' and thereby become the exclusive preserve of key decision-makers. The concept of securitisation thus describes a distinguishing feature of decisions on the use of force by the state against perceived threats.

Yet all along, while pondering on the concept of strategic culture, this book came to the realisation that since differences in norms as well as differences in

Conclusion 225

behaviour are relatively coherent across internal and external policy domains, it must be the use of force which renders the concept of strategic culture its particular explanatory relevance within the domain of security studies. Furthermore, it is also because the concept refers to the use of force by the state against threats, both at home and abroad, that it is required to be conceptualised as one that involves wider society rather than the views and opinions of an elite cast of security policy experts, at least in liberal democracies. What distinguishes strategic culture from other domains of political culture or other applications of the concept of culture in the social sciences is that it describes the particular features of a society's relationship to the use of force by the state, which is a state's most recognisable, ultimate resort for the performance of its most elementary task. As such it describes an action that is particularly strongly tied to national identity.

A central claim of this book is that these two at first glance contradictory prime suspects were, as they often are, complicit in bringing about the observed differences in state behaviour. Neither strategic culture nor securitisation can by themselves afford to treat the other concept as epiphenomenal. Both therefore need to be seen as having their own, distinct roles to play in shaping the outcomes of decisions on the use of force. One provides the formal cause of structural conditioning, while the other provides the final cause of a particular expression of the use of force by the state. But what reasons would the two have for working together and taking each other into consideration rather than claiming the full ransom themselves? In other words, to what extent can strategic culture be said to have a discernible impact on the course and outcome of securitisation processes? To what extent do the Australian and British decisions to join the war on Iraq come down to Australian and British strategic culture rather than Howard and Blair?

This is where a morphogenetic approach becomes particularly relevant. On the basis of sequentially dialectical ontology and Aristotelian epistemology as provided by critical realism, we can assess the relative impact of strategic culture and securitisation by addressing the two in turns. First, we examine a strategic culture's attributes and formulate assumptions about its structural conditioning capacities. We can then hypothesise about in which country an actor will find it easier to opt for a certain option than in another, as we can stipulate the consequences that are likely to follow from each option. By examining the scope and nature of securitisation processes we can then examine to what extent actors took these structural conditioning factors into account when positioning their securitisation move. Broadly speaking, one can assume that more robust strategic cultures lend themselves to stronger securitisation processes, while more reactive strategic cultures are likely to generate milder securitisation processes. Yet while their own cultural embedding and an interest in attaining public admiration rather than hostility make it likely that securitisation actors align with strategic culture, other factors such as biography or exposure to international socialisation effects and pressures imply that this need not always be exactly the case. In unlikely cases, actors can even unwittingly or errantly deviate very far from the confines of strategic culture through securitisation processes.

We can then retrospectively single out the relative conditioning impact of strategic culture among the various other factors by analysing the resonance of a

226   *Comparing decision processes on use of force*

securitisation process among wider society during the period of agential social interaction. The more aligned that the strength of a securitisation process is with the analytically pre-existent normative proclivity of a strategic culture towards the use force, the more positively it will resonate with most segments and spheres of society as expressed through parliamentary debates, the media and public opinion. During the phase of structural elaboration, this is likely to bring about morphostasis in strategic culture, i.e. reaffirm the pre-existent norms. Within the confines of strategic culture, actors can also bring about morphogenesis through minor misalignments that challenge the appropriateness of established norms in the given situation. In cases of severe misalignment, alienation and loss of trust in political leadership can lead to a rapid backlash through public dissonance during agential social interaction and structural elaboration, which leads to morphogenesis in the opposite direction. Securitisation processes therefore bear some potential for transforming strategic cultures, but only when this process occurs within moderate distance to the strategic cultural context within which it occurs.

Revisiting the second research step

The cross-national comparison of this book allowed us to examine this sequentially dialectical interplay in detail up until the passing of a decision within the phase of agential social interaction. The five chapters of Part III analysed decision processes and debates related to three instances of the state wielding force for the provision of security in response to the same triggering events in five countries. Despite the same triggering events and similarities between the five countries in their institutional and material contexts, the different governments drove widely differing securitisation processes as regards their nature, scope and outcome in the shape of specific security policy decisions. These differences largely corresponded to the theoretical expectations derived beforehand on the basis of the findings on each country's strategic culture along four norms dimensions as outlined in Chapters 4 and 5. Furthermore, the analysis of the resonance to the government's securitisation processes from actors across the political spectrum as expressed in parliamentary debates, the media and opinion polls showed that the spectrum of opinions on specific security policy decisions took place within confines that mirror the boundaries of each strategic culture as identified in Chapters 4 and 5. This applied to instances of the external use of force by the state as well as to instances of the domestic use of force for the provision of security.

The relative confines to which strategic culture subjected the options and arguments circulated in the securitisation processes and resonant debates over the use of force by the state in the three instances analysed become particularly well discernible when compared across countries. For instance, in all three instances of decision-making, political forces on the left and the right of the political spectrum in the UK and Australia vied for stronger securitisation processes than their German counterparts and in some cases also their natural opponents in Germany. This corresponds to the consistently higher proclivity to the use of force identified in all norms dimensions of Australian and British strategic culture in comparison to their German counterparts. France and Canada, meanwhile, assumed a position in-between these two camps in all three instances, just as the analysis conducted in Chapters 4 and 5 identified their strategic cultures to assume positions in the middle ground in all four norms categories.

Figure 11.1 below graphically illustrates this observation. The grey bars depict the range of prevalent opinions on the decision in question that were observable in parliamentary debates, media commentaries and public opinion polls in Australia, Canada, France, Germany and the UK.

The bars cover different lengths of the spectrum of norms on the legitimate use of force by the state because the different expressions of these norms within their respective norms dimensions of different strategic cultures have generated different sets of opinions and collective expectations of a legitimate response by the state to the triggering event in question. The grey bars thus represent the structural conditioning effect of strategic culture as expressed through the resonance in the respective instance of security policy decision-making.

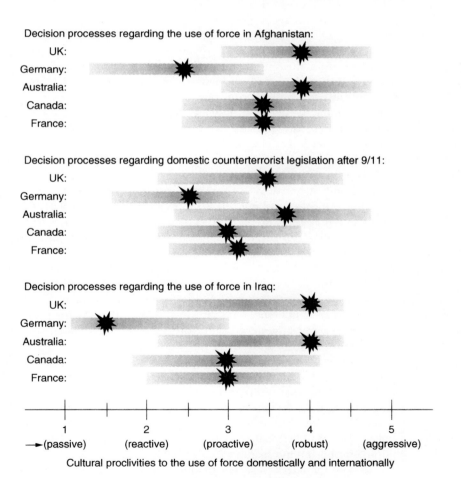

Figure 11.1 Overview of findings on conduciveness to securitisation.

228 *Comparing decision processes on use of force*

The black blot signifies the position of the government's agency within this spectrum of opinions. It may lie at the spectrum's centre of gravity illustrated by a darker shade of grey, or it may lie at the margins of prevalent opinions generated by the confines of strategic culture, as was the case in the British and Australian decisions to robustly apply military force against Iraq, for instance. If it lies further outside the confines of the structurally conditioning formal cause of a pre-existent strategic culture, the phase of agential social interaction between securitisation processes and strategic culture is marked by widespread dissonance among parliament, the media and other spheres of the public at large, which has severe political repercussions and can also halt or revert a securitisation process. As was expected on the basis of assumptions generated through the theoretical model and prior analyses of the respective strategic cultures, this did not occur in the cases analysed here. However, the extended phase of structural elaboration is likely to have generated some shifts especially in Australian and British strategic culture towards a slightly lower proclivity to the use of force. Yet this claim only constitutes a preliminary assessment that merits further empirical analysis.

Figure 11.1 thus illustrates the main observation of Chapters 6–10. They showed that different strategic cultures provide the contextual determinants for different degrees of securitisation pursued by different democratic governments. The results confirmed prior theoretical assumptions that in countries with strategic cultures comprising a comparatively higher proclivity to the use of force, such as the UK or Australia, securitisation processes are likely to be comparatively strong and to result in the comparatively extensive use of force by the state, whereas in countries with strategic cultures comprising a comparatively low proclivity to the use of force, such as Germany, Canada and to some extent also France, securitisation processes are likely to be relatively mild and result in the restrained use of force by the state.

The book thus found that strategic culture was a critical formal cause in all cases of security policy decision-making across the five countries. Crucially, the different securitisation processes all received largely positive resonance from across society. Even in the cases of Australian and British decisions to join the war in Iraq, the instantaneous resonance during the agential social interaction phase was still positive by and large. The assumptions of this theoretical model would not hold if one discerned a similar constellation of opinions across countries, only varying by societal sub-groups of political orientation, gender, age or class. But to a certain degree differences in strategic culture were reflected in the constellation of opinions and arguments in national debates as a whole. One could discern that countries such as Australia and the UK, which harbour more 'robust' strategic cultures and which experienced 'strong' securitisation moves in all three instances, also saw a higher normative proclivity towards the use of force expressed in the relative proportions of arguments and opinions as expressed during the resonance. One can therefore claim with some confidence that strategic culture therefore had a discernible impact on state behaviour in the cases of Australian, British, Canadian, French and German security policy and practice both domestically and internationally after 9/11.

Despite the autonomy inherent in securitisation processes, these do not cause behaviour independently of conditioning causes. Since the use of force is intimately linked with identity, strategic culture provides a particularly strong conditioning cause for state behaviour involving the use of force. This link became particularly apparent through the coherent national patterns of the sequential and dialectical interplay between securitisation actors and strategic culture across policy domains. For each state, one could discern similar expressions of strategic culture, securitisation and resonance across their sequence in each policy domain. Despite its intangibility, strategic culture is therefore, at least ontologically, a very 'real' cause of particular state actions in the sense that its pre-conditioning effects become discernible in the securitisation processes and their resonance across policy domains. Although it is materially unobservable, strategic culture brings about real world effects.

A simple summary of the central insight that can be gained from this book would therefore probably amount to the simple claim that people care about the actions of their state conducted in their name. Through the use of force either at home or abroad, the state displays its good or bad behaviour, either towards the citizen or towards others, most distinctly. And perceptions about what constitutes good or bad behaviour vary across countries through distinct strategic cultures. The state, however, normally wants to leave a good impression with its citizens in a liberal democracy. It is for this reason that decisions on who the state should kill or capture in the name of its citizens and for the sake of their security cannot be examined independently of these perceptions despite the state wielding the gun and having to react fast when under threat. In turn, demonstrations of good or bad behaviour cannot be expected to be necessarily without consequences on future perceptions of how the state should behave, either through the citizen harbouring disdain or through the demonstration of a positive innovation in thought. In the realm of security policy, the concept of culture thus deserves particular attention as it stands out as a particularly relevant conditioning cause in this field as opposed to other fields of politics in which cultural causes are one minor factor among many other, structural causes of behaviour.

Implications for theory and research in IR

This book sought to make the case for a conception of strategic culture as a broader societal phenomenon rather than one pertaining exclusively to a society's political elites. It also sought to make the case for conceiving of this concept as one that relates to the use of force against perceived existential threats domestically as well as internationally, rather than military force alone. From the perspective of literature on strategic culture, this implies that the concept needs to be seen as a causal factor operating on the level of structure, where it is in a position to condition behaviour but it is similarly in a position to be conditioned by it. While this poses challenges to more comprehensive theorising it also provides the opportunity to combine the concept with a suitable agential 'soul mate' rather than expanding the concept itself towards adopting the role of agency.

From the perspective of scholarship on securitisation, it also appears more fruitful to acknowledge the concept for what it essentially is, namely a process-oriented description of the special role and relevance of language in security policy. As such, it needs to be seen in conjunction with other concepts describing how this agency

230 *Comparing decision processes on use of force*

is conditioned by various contextual factors, rather than searching for ways in which the concept can adopt this task by itself. Overall, these theoretical insights should provide an encouragement of more comprehensive theory building and of attempts to create synergies between the various and diverse constructivist approaches to IR, security studies and foreign policy analysis.

The ontological and epistemological assumptions advanced by the philosophical school of 'critical realism' provide a particularly promising framework within which such efforts at theoretical aggregation can be pursued. Especially the sequentially dialectical approach advanced by Archer deserves more attention by IR theorists dealing with culture. The Aristotelian conception of causation also provides ample opportunities for drawing together various theories and methodologies from different paradigms in a pragmatic fashion. This can potentially counteract a trend towards ever further disaggregation and divide in IR theory and thereby allow for more 'common-sensically' explanations and enhanced insights into security policy and practice.

Implications for policy

The insight that culture has a particularly strong conditioning impact in the realm of security policy as opposed to other policy fields begs the both inevitable and uncomfortable question of how one should critically evaluate the respective strategic cultures that were analysed. Criticising cultures is an uncomfortable task but not expounding their respective problems on the basis of the insights gained through the analyses of this book would be a major omission. Famously, the European Security Strategy (ESS) of 2003 declares that Europe needs to "develop a strategic culture that fosters early, rapid and when necessary, robust intervention" (European Union, 2003: 11). One can interpret this to imply that European strategic cultures should converge towards a coherent, European 'proactive-robust' strategic culture, hence one that is akin to British strategic culture.

This is perhaps unsurprising when considering that reportedly, one of the main authors of the ESS was Robert Cooper, who was also one of Tony Blair's main foreign policy advisors (Brown, 2004). And yet especially the premiership of Tony Blair provides a perhaps rather tragic example of how a particularly 'robust' strategic culture can also be overly permissive and uncritical towards state actions involving the use of force, which can thereby lead to hubris on the part of its decision-makers. Considering the successes of British interventions in Sierra Leone, Kosovo and Afghanistan, one could indeed speak of Britain as a 'force for good in the world' during the first years of Blair's premiership. But in the case of Iraq there was an absence of scrutiny and scepticism towards the use of military force. Calls for 'early and rapid' intervention should thus not trump calls for carefully planned and executed intervention that comes about as a result of intensely scrutinising decision processes and debates, even when professed to be intended for the most noble, humanitarian purposes.

On the other hand, one needs to consider that security is a public good. A more 'reactive' strategic culture such as that of Germany runs the risk of free-riding on the security provided by its allies through controversial measures such as drone strikes, counterinsurgency operations and mass surveillance. These

Conclusion 231

might well have foiled and prevented a good number of terrorist acts. Hence, just as overly 'robust' strategic cultures can be overly permissive of the use of force and come to regard it as a panacea, more 'reactive' strategic cultures can lead to complacency and passive bystanding to major humanitarian atrocities or aggression. The ideal is therefore arguably a 'proactive' strategic culture that allows for the state to acknowledge and confront threats to itself or others but which nonetheless retains a healthy dose of scepticism towards the efficacy of the use of force and the overemphasis of threats.

A shift towards this ideal requires leadership that does not shy away from honest and transparent debate over what the use of force can realistically achieve in a given situation and at what point one needs to concede that the danger or atrocity needs to be counteracted by other means because the use of force would do more harm than good. This requires the realisation by actors in liberal democracies cooperating through international institutions that a united stance on a certain issue should not be an ends in itself. Instead, such institutions can greatly benefit from a diversity of opinions among its members. When debates focus on questions of alliance loyalty and symbolism rather than the substance of the danger at hand and the available means to counter it, an overly consensus-seeking perspective can emerge which leads to an oversimplifying and over-optimistic view of coercive state action. Similarly, a more transparent and exhaustive public debate surrounding what the use of force can realistically achieve can avoid an escalation of countermeasures against increasingly diffuse threats, and thereby provide a democratic corrective to overambitious state security agendas.

Avenues for further research

What the theoretical model proposed in this book highlights is that the public and security actors are engaged in an ongoing process of interaction and re-evaluation. However, the book stopped short of further elaborating on how exactly the causal impact of agency on structural elaboration and long-term change in strategic culture takes place. Instead, it placed the primary research focus on examining the interplay between strategic culture and agency in the run up to specific decisions on the use of force within the period of structural elaboration and agential social interaction. A particular interesting case for analysis in this regard could be the wider repercussions of the wars in Afghanistan and Iraq on the strategic cultures of the liberal democracies involved in these conflicts, and to what extent these impacted on recent security policy debates surrounding humanitarian interventions in the Middle East region subsequent to the Arab Spring. This could also shed further light on how the experience of the use of force for humanitarian purposes attained during the 1990s morphed into changed norms regarding the efficacy of military force for such purposes. This, in turn, could be critically evaluated with regards to more recent conflicts such as the Syrian civil war, in which the international community largely refrained from intervening even for the purpose of securing the supply of humanitarian goods.

Another promising avenue of further research could be the examination of critical cases of misalignment between strategic culture and securitisation. This

232   *Comparing decision processes on use of force*

could provide further insights into how, when and to what extent structural elaboration takes place. The case of the Spanish government's decision during President Jose Aznar's term to join the US-led coalition against Iraq despite staunch domestic opposition might provide one such rare case of misalignment bringing about a 'backlash' within strategic culture during the structural elaboration phase. Besides such 'rebound' effects, one could also examine more closely cases in which agency brought about changes in strategic culture as a result of positive evaluations of securitisation processes despite some misalignment with strategic culture. Such closer examinations of processes of morphogenesis within strategic culture could provide for insights into which actions came to be regarded as more legitimate, and which were gradually delegitimised over the course of recent security policy and practice.

One could also research instances of misalignment and change, either in the direction opposite to agency through alienation or towards agency through inspiration and leadership, which achieve a shift in strategic culture towards a higher proclivity to the use of force. Instances of upward shifts could also be compared with instances of downward shifts in strategic culture within the same country over time. For instance, to the extent permitted by data availability, one could trace the interaction between culture and agency in relation to US security policy behaviour over the last century, which fluctuated between low levels of the use of force during periods of isolationism and high levels of the use of force during periods of interventionism. Comparative analyses of the effects of the Vietnam War and the Iraq War on American strategic culture also spring to mind in this regard. Ideally, such a longitudinal analysis could also be applied to an increasingly influential non-Western country such as China. Through applications of the theoretical model proposed by this book, one could better grasp the direction in which both Chinese strategic culture and the security policy shaped by its elites are headed. Prior to that, however, the model would need to be adapted to non-democratic countries.

Overall, this book sought to make the case for the sequential analysis of the dialectical interplay between those in charge of deciding on the use of force and wider society, because this interrelationship goes to the heart of international politics. At the same time, this perpetual interrelationship demonstrates that one cannot claim to possess knowledge of an ideal mode of behaviour that can inform all decisions. This interrelationship persists precisely because there are no blueprints for achieving perfect peace and security. In a sense, the dialectic between strategic culture and securitisation represents a perpetual search for both.

EH Carr argued in *The Twenty Years' Crisis* that no order can rest on either power or morality alone. The variance of strategic cultures demonstrates that there are different perceptions across states of the extent to which the existing order rests on either. Ultimately, the perpetual re-evaluation of the use of force that is inherent in this interrelationship might imply that these two spheres incrementally move closer with each experience that is accumulated through societal evaluations of the use of force by the state against perceived threats. After all, Carr also argued: "That human affairs can be directed and modified by human action and human thought is a postulate so fundamental that its rejection seems scarcely compatible with existence as a human being" (Carr, 2001: 87).

Conclusion 233

This should apply especially to collective thoughts and experiences accrued through encounters with violence over the course of history. These inescapably drive the search for a global order that provides security through morality rather than power.

This book proposes that every instance of liberal states using force against perceived existential threats is accompanied by intense wider societal reflections about whether this action corresponds to one's conception of the nature of global order and the state's role within it. Such reflections then feed into subsequent decisions on the use of force. This allows for some measure of confidence that international relations are ultimately destined towards the achievement of a just and peaceful global order. As Immanuel Kant put it:

> Perpetual peace is guaranteed by no less an authority than the great artist Nature herself (*natura daedala rerum*). The mechanical process of nature visibly exhibits the purposive plan of producing concord among men, even against their will and indeed by means of their very discord. This design, if we regard it as a compelling cause whose laws of operation are unknown to us, is called fate."

> (quoted from Brown *et al.*, 2002: 443)

Scholarly attempts to grasp this mechanical process by which we can progress towards such concord among men can perhaps provide a modicum of acceleration towards this ultimate goal.

Bibliography

Brown C (2004) "Britain and the European Security Strategy". *European Foreign Policy Research Network Working Paper* (6).

Brown C, Nardin T and Rengger NJ (eds) (2002) *International Relations in Political Thought: Texts from the Ancient Greeks to the First World War*. Cambridge: Cambridge University Press.

Carr EH (2001) *The Twenty Years' Crisis 1919–1939: An Introduction to the Study of International Relations*. Basingstoke: Palgrave Macmillan.

European Union (2003) "A Secure Europe in a Better World". Available from: www.consilium.europa.eu/uedocs/cmsUpload/78367.pdf (accessed 25 February 2014).

Appendix

Table A1 International military interventions since 1990

Australia	Canada	France	Germany	UK
Gulf War 1990–1991 1,820 personnel	Gulf War 1990–1991 more than 4,000 armed forces personnel	Gulf War 1990–1991 18,000 troops		Gulf War 1990–1991 around 45,000 troops
Maritime Interception Force; Persian Gulf, Gulf of Oman, Red Sea 1990– up to 3 vessels and 600 personnel	UNMIH, Haiti 1993–1997 750 personnel		UNAMIC, Cambodia 1991–1992 140 paramedics	Operation Warden, Iraq, 1991–2003 Air force assets to patrol no-fly-zones
UNOSOM I, UNITAF, UNOSOM II, Somalia 1992–1995 1,100 troops	UNOSOM I, UNITAF, UNOSOM II, Somalia 1992–1995 1,400 personnel	UNITAF, UNOSOM II, Somalia 1992–1993 2,400 troops	UNOSOM II, Somalia 1993–1994 1,640 troops	
UNTAC, Cambodia 1992–1993 550–700 troops	Peacekeeping missions in former Yugoslavia 1992–1995 Up to 2,000 personnel	Peacekeeping missions in former Yugoslavia 1992–1995 Up to 4,500 troops	Peacekeeping missions in former Yugoslavia 1992–1995 Up to 4,000 troops	Peacekeeping missions in former Yugoslavia 1992–1995 Up to 13,000 troops
UNAMIR, Rwanda 1994–1995 300 paramedics	UNAMIR, Rwanda 1993–1994 Up to 400 troops	Operation Turquoise, Rwanda 1994 2,500 troops		Operation Chantress/ UNAVEM III 650 troops
Operation Lagoon, Papua New Guinea 1994 800 troops		Operation Azalée, Comoros 1995 1,070 troops		

Truce Monitoring Group and Peace Monitoring Group, Papua New Guinea 1997–2003 260 troops		Operations Almandin I & II, Central African Republic 1996–1997 2,500 troops		
		Operation Pelican, Congo Brazzaville 1997 1,300 troops		
		Operation Cigogne, Central African Republic 1997–1998 1,800 troops		Operation Desert Fox, Iraq 1998 Combat aircraft flying 250 strike sorties
	OAF, Kosovo 1999 69 pilots and 250 ground crew, 684 combat sorties	OAF, Kosovo 1999 84 combat aircraft, 2,414 sorties	OAF, Kosovo 1999 14 fighter jets, 500 sorties	OAF, Kosovo 1999 48 aircraft flying 1,950 sorties
	KFOR, Kosovo 1999– 1,500 troops	KFOR, Kosovo 1999– 7,000 troops	KFOR, Kosovo 1999– 8,000 troops	KFOR, Kosovo 1999– 10,500 forces
INTERFET, East Timor 1999 5,000 personnel	INTERFET, East-Timor 1999 650 personnel			INTERFET, East-Timor 1999 290 troops
UNTAET, East Timor 2000–2001 2,000 troops	UNTAET, East Timor 2000–2001 650 troops			Operations Palliser and Baras/UNAMSIL, Sierra Leone 2000 1,300 troops
	UNMEE, Ethiopia & Eritrea 2000 450 troops	Operation Licorne/ ONUCI, Cote d'Ivoire 2002–2011 Up to 4,000 troops	Operation Essential Harvest, Macedonia 2001 600 troops	Operation Essential Harvest, Macedonia 2001 1,500 troops

continued

Table A1 Continued

Australia	Canada	France	Germany	UK
Initial invasion of Afghanistan, 2001 Special Forces Task Group, air force and navy assets	OEF, Afghanistan 2001–2003 750 ground troops, 1,500 naval forces, strategic airlift, long-range patrol aircraft	OEF, Afghanistan 2001–2003 Special Forces, combat aircraft, refuelling aircraft, 2,900 troops	OEF, Afghanistan 2001–2003 100 Special Forces	OEF, Afghanistan 2001–2003 1,700 troops, submarines, aircraft carrier, assault ship, combat aircraft and refuelling aircraft
Operation Slipper (stabilisation mission to Afghanistan), 2002– Up to 1,550 personnel	ISAF, Afghanistan 2003–2011 Up to 2,300 troops	ISAF, Afghanistan 2003– Up to 4,000 troops	ISAF, Afghanistan 2003– Up to 5,000 troops	ISAF, Afghanistan 2003– Up to 10,000 troops
Iraq War 2003–2009 Up to 2,050 troops				Iraq War 2003–2009 Up to 46,000 troops
UNMISET, East Timor 2002–2005 Up to 1,600	Operation HALO/ Multinational Interim Force in Haiti, February–July 2004 500 armed forces personnel	Operation Artemis/ MONUC 2003 1,070 troops	EUFOR, DR Congo 2006 780 troops	
International Stabilisation Force for East Timor (ISF), 2006– 2,600 troops		UNIFIL, Lebanon 2006– Up to 1,400 troops	UNIFIL, Lebanon 2006– Naval patrol contingent with up to 2,400 soldiers.	
RAMSI,SolomonIslands2003– 1,650 personnel	Operation Unified Protector, Libya 2011 650 armed forces personnel	Operation Unified Protector, Libya 2011 50 aircraft flying 4,500 sorties	Operation Unified Protector, Libya 2011 4,500 sorties	Operation Unified Protector, Libya 2011 4,000 personnel, four ships, 37 aircraft flying 3,000 sorties

Sources: Australian Department of Defence, 2012; Australian Government, Department of Defence, 2012a, 2012b; Australian Government, Department of Veterans' Affairs, 2009; Australian War Memorial, Military History Section, 1999, 2011; Bensahel, 2003; Bundeswehr, 2012; Charbonneau, 2008; Davidson, 2011; Granatstein and Oliver, 2010; Griffin, 2009; Hellmann et al., 2006; Keohane, 2000; Londey, 2008; Mangold, 2002; NATO – International Security Assistance Force (ISAF), 2012; Palazzo, 2008; Rottman, 1993; Self, 2010; UK Ministry of Defence, 2000, 2008, 2011a, 2011b; Veterans Affairs Canada, 2011a, 2011b, 2011c, 2011d, 2011e, 2011f, 2011g.

Table A2 Military expenditure in total, per capita and as percentage of GDP

Year	1985	1990	1995	2000	2005	2010
Total military expenditure (current US$ and exchange rates)[1]						
Australia	4,668	4,306	8,544	7,384	15,550	23,634
Canada	7,566	7,064	9,004	8,320	12,828	20,240
France	20,780	18,113	48,002	34,053	53,128	52,005
Germany	19,992	16,940	41,815	27,924	38,004	44,057
UK	23,791	19,574	34,154	35,655	51,696	57,796
Military expenditure per capita (current US$ and exchange rates)[2]						
Australia	296	256	468	386	774	1,098
Canada	298	265	320	273	391	600
France	377	321	826	575	876	803
Germany	262	281	509	341	462	540
UK	421	346	586	601	855	927
Military expenditure as percentage of current GDP						
Australia	3.0	2.3	2.5	1.9	2.2	1.9
Canada	2.2	1.7	1.6	1.2	1.1	1.3
France	4.0	2.8	3.1	2.6	2.5	2.0
Germany	3.2	2.2	2.0	1.5	1.4	1.3
UK	5.2	3.7	3.1	2.5	2.3	2.6

Source: International Institute for Strategic Studies, 1992: 218, 220; 1996: 306, 308; 2002: 332, 334; 2007: 406, 408; 2012: 467, 469.

Table A3 Guardian/ICM Poll of 14–16 September 2001

"The USA, with the backing of NATO (including the UK) has said it will conduct military strikes against terrorist organisations responsible for this week's aeroplane attacks on the World Trade Centre in New York and the Pentagon in Washington DC. Would you yourself support or oppose taking military action against the terrorist groups responsible?" (in %)

	All	Labour	Conservative	Liberal Democrat	Aged 25 to 34	Over 65	Men	Women
Support	66	76	69	59	74	60	74	58
Oppose	14	n/a	n/a	22				
Don't know	20	n/a	n/a	n/a				

"Would you support or oppose the United States and NATO taking military action against countries that assist or harbour terrorists who carry out such attacks?"

	All	Labour	Conservative
Support	59	68	68
Oppose	21	n/a	n/a
Don't know	20	n/a	n/a

"Would you support or oppose military action against such countries if it meant that the United States and NATO (including the UK) got into a war?"

	All	Men	Women
Support	49	55	43
Oppose	31	n/a	32
Don't know	20	n/a	n/a

"Would you support or oppose British troops, ships and planes taking part in such military action?"

Support	Oppose	Don't know
63	22	15

"How close to the Americans do you think Tony Blair has been during the crisis? Do you think he has got too close to the Americans, not close enough, or has he got it about right?"

Too close	Got it about right	Not close enough	Don't know
14	76	3	7

"How well do you think George W. Bush, the American President, has handled the crisis? Do you think he has handled it very well, quite well, not very well, or not well at all?"

Very well	Quite well	Not very well	Not well at all	Don't know
23	53	12	4	9

Sample size: 1,007 adults

Sources: Ipsos MORI, 2001; Travis, 2001.

240   *Appendix*

Table A4 "The American government requested the supply of 3,900 German soldiers for the Afghanistan crisis. Do you support, against this backdrop, the 'unrestricted solidarity' with the US, which Chancellor Schröder promised?" (in %)

| | 01/October | 6–8 November | | | | | | | |
	All	All	West	East	SPD	CDU	Greens	FDP	PDS
Yes	71	51	55	36	62	62	24	58	11
No	23	43	40	58	35	35	76	42	89
n/a	6	6	5	6	3	3	0	0	0

Source: TNS Forschung, 2001; *Der Spiegel*, 2001.

Table A5 Opinion polls on the legitimacy of a US attack on Iraq

EMNID/n-TV: Do you think that a military attack of the United States against Iraq would be justified, or not?

Infratest Dimap 1: the American President Bush argues that Iraq produces weapons of mass destruction and wants to prevent it from using these weapons through a preemptive attack on Iraq. Do you think that this situation justifies an attack on Iraq by the United States?

Infratest dimap 2: do you consider presently a war against Iraq to be justified or unjustified?

Allensbach: did you think the Iraq war was justified or were you opposed?

Date	Poll	Yes (%)	No (%)	No opinion (%)	Sample size
21–26/02/2002	Infratest dimap 1	27	66	7	1,300
07–13/08/2002	Emnid/n-TV	29	61	10	1,000
08/2002	Emnid/n-TV	19	74	7	1,000
09–12/09/2002	Infratest dimap 1	17	79	4	1,300
26–29/09/2002	GEWIS/TV Hören und Sehen	n/a	95	n/a	1,051
27/09/2002	Emnid/n-TV	34	59	7	1,000
01/2003	Forsa	10	85	5	1,300
04–05/03/2003	Infratest dimap 2	13	85	2	1,300
06/–07/03/2003	Forsa	12	84	4	1,300
18–24/03/2003	Emnid/n-TV	18	79	3	1,000
25–31/03/2003	Emnid/n-TV	18	79	3	1,000
27/03/2003	Infratest dimap 2	12	83	5	1,300
31/3–02/4/2003	Infratest dimap 2	14	80	6	1,300
04/04/2003	Infratest dimap 2	14	80	6	1,300
28/6–12/7/2003	Allensbach	12	76	12	n/a

Source: Everts, 2007: 152–153.

Appendix 241

Table A6 EOS Gallup International Crisis Survey 21–27 January 2003 (%)

The United States should intervene militarily in Iraq even if the United Nations does not give its formal consent

	Agree	*Disagree*
Germany	13	87
UK	29	68

Do you consider that it would be (justified/unjustified) that our country participates in a military intervention in Iraq …

(a) if the United States intervenes militarily in Iraq without a preliminary decision of the United Nations?

	Justified	*Unjustified*
Germany	10	89
UK	27	68

(b) if the United Nations security council decides on a military intervention in Iraq?

Germany	45	52
UK	79	15

(c) if the Iraqi regime does not cooperate with the United Nations inspectors?

Germany	32	64
UK	61	32

(d) the United Nations inspectors discover weapons of mass destruction in Iraq?

Germany	51	46
UK	81	16
Sample size: 500		

Source: EOS Gallup Europe, 2003: 4–9.

Notes

1 Except for 1990 values, for which data is only available in deflated 1985 prices.
2 Ibid.

Bibliography

Australian Department of Defence (2012) "Australia's Commitment in Afghanistan". Available from: www.defence.gov.au/op/afghanistan/info/factsheet.htm (accessed 21 August 2012).

Australian Government, Department of Defence (2012a) "Operations in East Timor". Available from: www.defence.gov.au/op/eastTimor/general.htm (accessed 26 August 2012).

Australian Government, Department of Defence (2012b) "Operations in the Solomon Islands". Available from: www.defence.gov.au/op/solomonislands/general.htm (accessed 26 August 2012).

242   *Appendix*

Australian Government, Department of Veterans' Affairs (2009) "Preliminary Gulf War Nominal Roll". Available from: www.dva.gov.au/commems_oawg/nominal_rolls/gulf/Pages/index.aspx (accessed 21 August 2012).

Australian War Memorial, Military History Section (1999) "Australian Military History, First Gulf War, 1990–1991". Available from: www.awm.gov.au/atwar/gulf.asp (accessed 14 August 2012).

Australian War Memorial, Military History Section (2011) "Australians and Peacekeeping". Available from: www.awm.gov.au/atwar/gulf.asp (accessed 14 August 2012).

Bensahel N (2003) *The Counterterror Coalitions: Cooperation with Europe, NATO, and the European Union.* Rand Corporation. Available from: http://books.google.com/books?-hl=en&lr=&id=HVLpiPopsBEC&oi=fnd&pg=PP2&dq=THE+COUNTERTERROR+COALITIONS+rand&ots=rWqZYdla45&sig=KYbCwPv8O8ArmAfZLEEyXb RdFZU (accessed 20 September 2012).

Bundeswehr (2012) "Bundeswehr im Einsatz". Available from: www.einsatz.bundeswehr.de/portal/a/einsatzbw (accessed 21 February 2012).

Charbonneau B (2008) *France and the New Imperialism.* London: Ashgate.

Davidson JW (2011) *America's Allies and War: Kosovo, Afghanistan, and Iraq.* New York: Palgrave Macmillan.

Der Spiegel (2001) "Abmarsch in die Realität". *Der Spiegel,* Hamburg, 12 November.

EOS Gallup Europe (2003) International Crisis Survey. Available from: www.paks.uni-duesseldorf.de/Dokumente/International-Crisis-Survey_Rapport-Final.pdf (accessed 16 August 2013).

Everts P (2007) *Public opinion on 'Iraq': International Comparative Polls and Countries outside USA (up to August, 2004).* Leiden: Leiden University, Department of Political Science. Available from: http://media.leidenuniv.nl/legacy/Poll%20Data%20War%20against%20 Iraq%20(outside%20the%20US).pdf (accessed 16 August 2013).

Granatstein JL and Oliver DF (2010) *The Oxford Companion to Canadian Military History.* Oxford: Oxford University Press.

Griffin CW (2009) *French Grand Strategy in Africa in the Fifth Republic.* Online Publication: University of Southern California. Available from: http://digitallibrary.usc.edu/assetserver/controller/item/etd-Griffin-2665.pdf (accessed 14 September 2012).

Hellmann G, Baumann R and Wagner W (2006) *Deutsche Außenpolitik: Eine Einführung.* 2006th edn. Wiesbaden: VS Verlag für Sozialwissenschaften.

International Institute for Strategic Studies (1992) *The Military Balance 1992–93.* London: Brassey's.

International Institute for Strategic Studies (1996) *The Military Balance 1996–97.* Oxford: Oxford University Press.

International Institute for Strategic Studies (2002) *The Military Balance 2002–03.* Oxford: Oxford University Press.

International Institute for Strategic Studies (2007) *The Military Balance 2007.* Abingdon: Routledge.

International Institute for Strategic Studies (2012) *The Military Balance 2012.* Abingdon: Routledge.

Ipsos MORI (2001) "Support for War in Afghanistan – Trends 2001". Available from: www.ipsos-mori.com/researchpublications/researcharchive/poll.aspx?oItemId=2399 (accessed 23 July 2013).

Keohane D (2000) *Security in British Politics 1945–99.* Basingstoke: Palgrave Macmillan.

Londey P (2008) "Australia and Peacekeeping". 2nd edn. In: *The Oxford Companion to Australian Military History,* Melbourne: Oxford University Press, pp. 412–417.

Mangold P (2002) *Success and Failure in British Foreign Policy: Evaluating the Record, 1900–2000.* London: Palgrave Macmillan.

NATO – International Security Assistance Force (ISAF) (2012) Troop Numbers & Contributions. Available from: www.isaf.nato.int/troop-numbers-and-contributions/index.php (accessed 22 February 2012).

Palazzo A (2008) "The Australian Deployment to Afghanistan". 2nd edn. In: *The Oxford Companion to Australian Military History*, Melbourne: Oxford University Press, pp. 7–9.

Rottman G (1993) *Armies of the Gulf War*. Oxford: Osprey Publishing.

Self PR (2010) *British Foreign and Defence Policy Since 1945: Challenges and Dilemmas in a Changing World*. Basingstoke: Palgrave Macmillan.

TNS Forschung (2001) "TNS Infratest – Quartalsumfrage Spiegel". Available from: www.tns-forschung.com/spiegel_umfragen.asp?search=2001 (accessed 1 October 2013).

Travis A (2001) "2 in 3 Back Air Strikes". *Guardian*, London, 18 September.

UK Ministry of Defence (2000) *Kosovo – Lessons from the Crisis*. Online Publication: UK Ministry of Defence.

UK Ministry of Defence (2008) "Operations in Afghanistan: Background Briefing 1". *Factsheets*. Available from: www.blogs.mod.uk/defence_news/files/factsheets.htm (accessed 11 October 2012).

UK Ministry of Defence (2011a) "LIBYA: Operation ELLAMY: Questions and Answers". Available from: www.mod.uk/DefenceInternet/FactSheets/MilitaryOperations/Libya-OperationEllamyQuestionsAndAnswers.htm (accessed 12 November 2012).

UK Ministry of Defence (2011b) "Operations in Iraq: Facts and Figures". Available from: www.mod.uk/DefenceInternet/FactSheets/OperationsFactsheets/OperationsInIraq-FactsandFigures.htm (accessed 5 November 2012).

Veterans Affairs Canada (2011a) "The Canadian Forces in Afghanistan". Available from: www.veterans.gc.ca/eng/history/canadianforces/factsheets/afghanistan (accessed 30 August 2012).

Veterans Affairs Canada (2011b) "The Canadian Forces in East Timor". Available from: www.veterans.gc.ca/eng/history/canadianforces/factsheets/easttimor (accessed 30 August 2012).

Veterans Affairs Canada (2011c) "The Canadian Forces in Ethiopia and Eritrea". Available from: www.veterans.gc.ca/eng/history/canadianforces/factsheets/ethiopia (accessed 30 August 2012).

Veterans Affairs Canada (2011d) "The Canadian Forces in Haiti". Available from: www.veterans.gc.ca/eng/history/canadianforces/factsheets/haiti (accessed 29 August 2012).

Veterans Affairs Canada (2011e) "The Canadian Forces in Rwanda". Available from: www.veterans.gc.ca/eng/history/canadianforces/factsheets/rwanda (accessed 29 August 2012).

Veterans Affairs Canada (2011f) "The Canadian Forces in Somalia". Available from: www.veterans.gc.ca/eng/history/canadianforces/factsheets/somalia (accessed 29 August 2012).

Veterans Affairs Canada (2011g) "The Canadian Forces in the Balkans". Available from: www.veterans.gc.ca/eng/history/canadianforces/factsheets/balkans (accessed 29 August 2012).

Index

Page numbers in *italics* denote tables, those in **bold** denote figures.

2UE (radio station) (Australia), interview with John Howard 183–4

Afghanistan, use of force in 1, 3, 12; and Australia 13, 15, 181–7, **227**, *236*; and Canada 13, 58, 201–8, 214, 220n1, **227**, *236*; and France 163–9, **227**, *236*; and Germany 134–42, 157, **227**, *236*, *240*; and UK 105–14, 129, 183, 202, **227**, 230, *236*, *239*
'aggressive/suppressive' strategic culture 34, 46, *47*, *75*, 100, **101**, **227**; Australia *75*, **101**, **227**; UK *75*, **101**
Al-Qaida, attacks against *see* Afghanistan, use of force in
ALP (Labour Party) (Australia) 181, 184–90, 194
Anti-Terrorism, Crime and Security Act 2001 (ATCSA) (UK) 114–17
Anti-Terrorism Act 2001 (ATA) (Canada) 209–12
anti-terrorism measures *see* counterterrorism
ANZAC (Australian and New Zealand Army Corps), legend of 53–4
ANZUS Treaty (Australia, New Zealand and United States Security Treaty) 15
Arab Spring, research options 231
Archer, Margaret 11, 25–31
ARD (broadcaster) (Germany), opinion poll 141–2
Aristotle, and causality 11, 26, 29–31, *31*, 225
ASIO (Australian Security Intelligence Organisation), Legislation Amendment Bill 2002 188–9
Assemblée Nationale see National Assembly *(Assemblée Nationale)* (France)
ATA (Anti-Terrorism Act 2001) (Canada) 209–12

ATCSA (Anti-Terrorism, Crime and Security Act 2001) (UK) 114–17
Attlee, Clement 70
Aujourd'hui en France see Parisien, Le/ Aujourd'hui en France (newspaper) 167, 168
Australia 1, 12–15; and Afghanistan 13, 15, 181–7, **227**, *236*; and authorisation of state force 97–101, *99*, **101**; counterterrorism 13, 187–91, **227**; and international cooperation 93, 96–7, *96–7*, *99*, 100; and Iraq 13, 15, 191–7, 222, 225, **227**, *236*; and legitimate use of force *79*, 79–81, 100; military expenditure 14, *237*; military interventions *234–6*; national identity 53–5, 73, 74, 222–5; state security competency 81–93, *82–5*, *87*, *89–92*, 100; strategic culture demarcation 55, *74–5*, 81, 100–1, **101**, 181, 184, 194–7, 222–4, **227**
Australia, New Zealand and United States Security Treaty (ANZUS Treaty) 15
Australian, The (newspaper): on Afghanistan 186; on counterterrorism 190; on Iraq 195
Australian and New Zealand Army Corps (ANZAC), legend of 53–4
Australian Security Intelligence Organisation (ASIO), Legislation Amendment Bill 2002 188–9
Axworthy, Lloyd 58
Ayrault, Jean-Marc 177
Aznar, Jose 232

Bali bombings 192–3
Balladur, Édouard 166–7
Balzacq, Thierry 9
Basic Law 1949 (Germany) 64–5, 67–8
BBC (British Broadcasting Corporation): and counterterrorism 119; interview

Index   245

with Tony Blair 115; YouGov opinion
poll, on Iraq 128–9
Beazley, Kim 184–6
Beck, Volker 146–7
'Benevolent Montie' myth (Canada) 56–7
Biehl, H. 8
Bild (newspaper) (Germany): on
Afghanistan 139–41; on
counterterrorism 147–8; on Iraq 154
Bill C-36 (Canada) 209–12
BKA (*Bundeskriminalamt*) (Federal
Criminal Police Office) (Germany) 147
Blair, Tony 71–2; Afghanistan, decisions
on 106–7, 109, 129, 183, 202, *239*; and
Bush, George W. 121–2, *239*; and
counterterrorism 115, 117–18, 129; and
Iraq 72, 121–7, 129, 225, 230, *239*;
media interviews 106, 115
Blakie, Bill 212
Bloc Québécois (BQ) (Canada) 201,
211–12, 217
Blunkett, David 115–20
Bosbach, Wolfgang 143, 146
BQ (Bloc Québécois) (Canada) 201,
211–12, 217
Breakfast with Frost (BBC radio
programme), interview with Tony Blair
115
British Government Communications
Headquarters (GCHQ) 130
Buckley, Walter 28
Bundeskriminalamt (BKA) (Federal
Criminal Police Office) (Germany) 147
Bundestag (German parliament): on
Afghanistan 134–9; on counterterrorism
144, 146–8; on Iraq 149–53, 156
Bundeswehr (German military) 134, 138,
142, 148, 152, 157
Bush, George W.: and Blair, Tony 121–2,
239; and Chirac, Jacques 162, 174; and
Chrétien, Jean 203, 215–16; and
Schröder, Gerhard 135, *240*
Buzan, B. 8

Cadman, Alan 189–90
Cameron, David 72
Canada 1, 12–15; and Afghanistan 13, 58,
201–8, 214, 220n1, **227**, *236*; and
authorisation of state force 97–101, *99*,
101; counterterrorism 13, 208–13, **227**;
and international cooperation 93, 96–7,
96–7, *99*, 100; and Iraq 13, 58, 213–19,
227, *236*; and legitimate use of force *79*,
79–81, 100; military expenditure 14,
237; military interventions *234–6*;
national identity 56–9, 73, *74*, 222–5;

peacekeeping 57–8, *234*; state security
competency 81–93, *82–5*, *87–92*, 100;
strategic culture demarcation 57–9,
74–5, 101, **101**, 200–6, 211–12, 216,
219, 222–8, **227**
Canadian Alliance 201, 205, 209, 211,
212, 216–17
Carlsnaes, W. 26
Carr, E.H.: *The Twenty Years' Crisis* 232
CDU (Christian Democratic Union)
(Germany) 137–9, 141, 143–8, 151–6,
240
Chamberlain, Neville 70
Chevènement, Jean-Pierre 167
China, research options 232
Chirac, Jacques 162–3; and Afghanistan
163–5; and Iraq 122, 125, 127, 174–8;
media interviews 174–5
Chrétien, Jean 200; and Afghanistan
201–4, 207–8; and counterterrorism
208–9; and Iraq 58, 214–18
Christian Democratic Union (CDU)
(Germany) 137–9, 141, 143–8, 151–6,
240
Christian Social Union in Bavaria (CSU)
(Germany) 139, 146, 150
Churchill, Winston 70
Citizens' Movement (*Mouvement des
Citoyens*) (France) 167
Clark, Joe 217
Claus, Roland 137
Clinton, Bill 127
CNN (TV network): interview with
Tony Blair 106
Coalition (Australia) *see* Liberal-National
Coalition (Australia)
Communist Party (France) 172–3
Conradt, D.P. 66
Conservative Party (UK) 105, 108–9,
113–14, 118–19, 123, 125–7
Conservative Party of Canada 201
Cook, Robin 124–5, 127
Cooper, Robert 230
Copenhagen School (CS) 7–10, 40
counterterrorism 1, 3, 12–13, 38, 223;
Australia 13, 187–91, **227**; Canada 13,
208–13, **227**; France 13, 169–73, **227**;
Germany 13, 142–8, **227**; UK 13,
114–20, 129, **227**
Crean, Simon 189, 194–5
Crossette, Barbara 203
CSU (Christian Social Union in Bavaria)
(Germany) 139, 146, 150

Dalgaard-Nielsen, A. 45
Dalyell, Tam 124

246   *Index*

Davidson, Jason W. 107, 165
Dawson, Grant 202, 203
Day, Stockwell 205–6, 211
de Gaulle, Charles 62
de Villepin, Dominique 176
Democracy Index, Economist Intelligence
    Unit (EIU) 15
Democratic Alliance (Canada) 201, 205,
    211, 219
Democrats (Australia) 181
Duncan Smith, Iain 108, 109, 117, 123, 125

ECHR *see* European Convention on
    Human Rights (ECHR)
Eden, Anthony 70
Edwards, Graham 190
Eggleton, Art 204, 220n1
ESS (European Security Strategy) 230
European Convention on Human Rights
    (ECHR): and Germany 143; UK
    derogation 115–19
European Security Strategy (ESS) 230
European Union, Common Security and
    Defence Policy 15

Falklands War 71
FDP (Free Democratic Party of Germany)
    137, 138, 143, 146, 152
Federal Office for the Protection of the
    Constitution (*Bundesamt für
    Verfassungsschutz*, BfV) (Germany) 147
Figaro, Le (newspaper) (France): on
    Afghanistan 167–8, 169; on
    counterterrorism 173; on Iraq 177–8
First World War 53–6, 60, 69–70, 192
Fischer, Joschka 135, 152–3
Fisher, Mark 118
FitzSimons, Peter 195
France 1, 12–15; and Afghanistan 163–9,
    227, *236*; and authorisation of state
    force 97–101, *98, 99*, **101**;
    counterterrorism 13, 169–73, **227**; and
    international cooperation 93–7, *93–9*,
    100; and Iraq 122, 125, 127–9, 173–8,
    227, *236*; and legitimate use of force *79*,
    79–81, *80*, 100; military expenditure
    14, *237*; military interventions *234–6*;
    national identity 59–63, 73, *74*, 222–5;
    state security competency 81–93, *82–5*,
    87–92, 100; strategic culture
    demarcation 57, 59, 62–3, *74–5*, 81,
    100–1, **101**, 162–4, 171–8, 222–8, **227**
Frankfurter Allgemeine Zeitung (FAZ)
    (newspaper) (Germany): on Afghanistan
    139–40; on counterterrorism 147; on
    Iraq 153

Free Democratic Party of Germany (FDP)
    137, 138, 143, 146, 152
Frost, David 115

Gauck, Joachim 157
GCHQ (British Government
    Communications Headquarters) 130
Gerhard, Wolfgang 137
Germany 1–2, 5, 12–15, 230–1; and
    Afghanistan 134–42, 157, **227**, *236,
    240*; and authorisation state force
    97–101, *98, 99*, **101**; counterterrorism
    13, 142–8, **227**; and international
    cooperation 93–7, *93–9*, 100; and Iraq
    136, 148–56, 174, **227**, *236*; and
    legitimate use of force *79*, 79–81, *80*,
    100; military expenditure 14, *237*;
    military interventions *234–6*; national
    identity 63–8, 73, *74*, 222–5;
    peacekeeping 157, *234*; state security
    competency 81–93, *82–5*, 87–92, 100;
    strategic culture, demarcation 66–7, *75*,
    81, 101, **101**, 136, 140, 156–7, 222–8,
    227
GESIS Leibniz Institut für
    Sozialwissenschaften surveys: National
    Identity 78, *82, 83, 96, 97, 99*; Role of
    Government *85, 87, 89, 90, 91, 92*
Giddens, Anthony 23–7
Giscard d'Estaing, Valéry 165–6
Globe and Mail (newspaper) (Canada): on
    Afghanistan 207; on counterterrorism
    213; on Iraq 218
Glos, Michael 139
'Golden Era of Canadian diplomacy'
    (Canada) 57–8
Gove, Michael 111, 120, 127
Graham, Bill 215, 218
Great Britain *see* United Kingdom
Green Party (Germany) 137–9, 141,
    143–8, 152–3, 155
Greens (Australia) 181
Greens (France) 173
Guardian, The (newspaper) (UK): on
    Afghanistan 107, 110–12, 113–14; on
    counterterrorism 120; on Iraq 127;
    opinion polls *238–9*
Gulf War (1990–1991) 13, 121, 140, 185,
    205, *234*

Hagmann, Jonas 25, 26, 30, *31*, 31n1
Harper, Stephen 58, 216, 219
Hauge, William 125
Hein, Kirstin 144
Heinbecker, Paul 216
Herald Sun (newspaper) (Australia): on

Index 247

Afghanistan 186; on counterterrorism 190; on Iraq 195
Herbillon, Michel 172
Hobbs, Thomas, 'Hobbesian' identity 1, 45, 73, *74*, 223–4
Hocking, Jenny 188
Holland, Jack 183–4, 192
Hollande, François 177
Hoon, Geoffrey 108
House of Commons (Canada) 201; on Afghanistan 202–6; on counterterrorism 208–12; on Iraq 215–17
House of Commons (UK): on Afghanistan 106–10; on counterterrorism 115–20; on Iraq 122–6; on Syria air strikes (2013) 129–30
House of Representatives (Australia) 181; and Afghanistan, use of force in 183–5; and counterterrorism 187–90; and Iraq, use of force in 192–5
Howard, John 54–5, 181; and Afghanistan 182–6; and counterterrorism 187–8; and Iraq 54, 192–7, 225; media interviews 183–4
Hughes, Kevin 118
Hughes, Simon 118
"Human Rights Act 1998 (Designated Derogation) Order 2001" (UK) 116
Hume, David and 'Humean' causality 11, 26, 29–30
Hume, Mike 120

identity, national *see* national identity
international relations (IR) theory 4–10, 23–31, *31*, 229–33; *see also* theoretical model
International Security Assistance Force (ISAF) 13, 106, *236*
Ipsos MORI surveys *88*, *238–9*
Iraq, use of force in 1, 3, 12–13, *240*; and Australia 13, 15, 191–7, 222, 225, **227**, *236*; and Canada 13, 58, 213–19, **227**, *236*; and France 122, 125, 127–9, 173–8, **227**, *236*; and Germany 136, 148–56, 174, **227**, *236*; and UK 120–9, 222, 225, **227**, *236*
"Iraq – Its Infrastructure of Concealment, Deception and Intimidation"/'Iraq Dossier' (UK Government) 123–5
"Iraq's Weapons of Mass Destruction: The Assessment of the British Government" (UK Government) 122–5, 127
ISAF (International Security Assistance Force) 13, 106, *236*

Jasper, U. 26

Jeanneney, J.N. 60–1
Jennings, Peter 194
Joffe, Josef 66
Johnston, A.I. 4
Jospin, Lionel 162–3, 178; on Afghanistan 164–5, 167, 169; on counterterrorism 169–70

Kaletsky, Anatole 127
Kampfner, John 72, 107, 121–3, 125
Kant, Immanuel, 'Kantian' identity 45–6, 73, *74*, 223–4, 233
Katzenstein, P.J. 6
Kaufman, Gerald 110
Kennedy, Charles 108, 110, 117, 123–5
Kennedy, Mark 202
Kilfoyle, Peter 125
Kingdon, J.W. 38–9
Kirchner, E.J. 45
Kister, Kurt 154
Kleine, Rolf 148
Kohl, Helmut 64
Korean War 205
Kornelius, Stefan 154
Kosovo 67, 122, 230, *235*
Kumar, Krishan 69
Kurki, M. 26, 29–30, *31*

Labour Party (ALP) (Australia) 181, 184–90, 194
Labour Party (UK) 105–10, 113–14, 118–19, 123–6, 129; *see also* Blair, Tony
Lalonde, Francine 217
Lambroschini, Charles 168
Law on Everyday Security 2001 (*Loi Relatif à la Sécurité Quotidienne 2001*) (France) 170
Legislation Amendment Bill 2002, Australian Security Intelligence Organisation (ASIO) 188–9
Letwin, Oliver 118
liberal democratic states *see* states, liberal democratic
Liberal Democrats (UK) 105, 108, 110, 114, 118–19, 124–6
Liberal Party (Australia) 181, 189–90
Liberal Party of Canada 200–1, 205, 209, 212; *see also* Chrétien, Jean
Liberal-National Coalition (Australia) 181; *see also* Howard, John
Liberty 114
Libya, interventions in 72, 130, 157, 178, *236*
Loi Relatif à la Sécurité Quotidienne 2001 (Law on Everyday Security 2001) (France) 170

248   *Index*

MacAskill, Ewen 107
McDonald, Matt 9, 183–4
McDonough, Alexa 206, 217
McKay, Peter 212
McLellan, Anne 209–10
Mali, interventions in 13, 72, 157, 178
Mandelson, Peter 127
Mariani, Thierry 172
Martin, Michael 124
Massie, J. 58
media coverage 49–50; Australia 186, 190, 195; Canada 203, 207, 212–13, 217–18; France 163, 165, 167–9, 173, 177–8; Germany 139–41, 147–8, 153–4; UK 107, 110–14, 119–20, 126–8
Merkel, Angela 137, 151–2
Merz, Friedrich 137, 146
Meyer, Christoph O. 5, 45, *47*, 60
Middle East, research options 231
military expenditure 14, *237*
military interventions *234–6*
Mitterrand, François 64
Monbiot, George 111, 112
Monde, Le (newspaper) (France): on Afghanistan 163, 165, 167, 168; on counterterrorism 173; on Iraq 178
'morphostasis'/'morphogenesis' 11–12, 16, 25–6, 28–9, 34, 38–42; and case studies 129, 156–7, 178, 197, 225–6, 232
Mouvement des Citoyens (Citizens' Movement) (France) 167
Müller, Kerstin 139
Munich Security Conference (2002) 149

N-TV (TV network) (Germany), opinion poll 148
narratives *see* national identity
National Assembly (*Assemblée Nationale*) (France) 163–4; on Afghanistan 164–7, 169; on counterterrorism 169–72; on Iraq 175–7
national identity 4–6, 35, 45–6, 53, 73, *74*, 222–5; Australia 53–5, 73, *74*, 222–5; Canada 56–9, 73, *74*, 222–5; France 59–63, 73, *74*, 222–5; Germany 63–8, 73, *74*, 222–5; UK 68–73, *74–5*, 222–5
National Identity surveys, GESIS Leibniz Institut für Sozialwissenschaften 78, *82, 83, 96, 97, 99*
National Party (Australia) 181
National Post (newspaper) (Canada): on Afghanistan 207; on counterterrorism 212–13; on Iraq 217–18
NATO (North American Treaty Organisation): Article 5, invocation of

135; case studies, as member states 15; opinion surveys on *94*, 94–6, *238–9*
NDP (New Democratic Party) (Canada) 201, 206, 212, 217
New Democratic Party (NDP) (Canada) 201, 206, 212, 217
New York Times (newspaper): on Canada 203; Chirac, Jacques, interview 174–5; Schröder, Gerhard, interview 149
New Zealand 3, 15
newspapers *see* media coverage
North American Treaty Organisation *see* NATO (North American Treaty Organisation)
Norton-Taylor, Richard 111

OAF (Operation Allied Force) 13, *235*
OEF *see* Operation Enduring Freedom (OEF), participation
Operation Allied Force (OAF) 13, *235*
'Operation Apollo' (Canada) 201, 204
Operation Enduring Freedom (OEF), participation 13, *236*; Canada 201, 204, *236*; France 163, *236*; Germany 134, 136, 151, 152, *236*; UK 110, *236*
opinion polls *see* public opinion on state force
'oppressive' strategic culture *see* 'aggressive/suppressive' strategic culture
'Otto catalogue' (Germany) 144–8

Palmerston, Henry John Temple, 3rd Viscount 130
Parisien, Le/Aujourd'hui en France (newspaper): on Afghanistan 167, 168; on counterterrorism 173; on Iraq 178
parliamentary debates 49; *see also Bundestag* (German parliament); House of Commons (Canada); House of Commons (UK); House of Representatives (Australia); National Assembly (*Assemblée Nationale*) (France)
Party of Democratic Socialism (PDS) (Germany) 137, 138, 141, 143, 146, 148
'passive' strategic culture 34, 46, *47*, *75*, 231; and Canada *75*; and Germany *75*, **101**, **227**
PDS (Party of Democratic Socialism) (Germany) 137, 138, 141, 143, 146, 148
peacekeeping 13, *234*; Canada 57–8, *234*; Germany 157, *234*
Pearson, Lester 57
Pew Research Center Global Attitudes Project (GAP) surveys 78, *94*
Prantl, Heribert 147

Index 249

Prevention of Terrorism Act 2005 (UK) 115

'proactive' strategic culture 36, 46, *47*, **101**, 222, 224, **227**, 230–1; and Australia 55, *74–5*, 100, **101**, 181, 196–7, 224, **227**; and Canada 57, 59, *74–5*, 101, **101**, 200, 222, 224, **227**; and France 57, 59, *74–5*, 101, **101**, 162, 174–8, 222, 224, **227**; and Germany 66–7, 75, 101, **101**, 140, 157, 224, **227**; and UK 72, *75*, **101**, 106–7, 109, 129, 224, **227**

Progressive Conservative Party of Canada 200–1, 205, 212, 217

Projet de Loi Relatif à la Sécurité Quotidienne (Bill on Everyday Security 2001) (France) 169–73

PS (*Parti-Socialiste*) (Socialist Party) (France) 162–3, 172, 177

public opinion on state force 78, 100–1, **101**, 222–4, *238–41*; on authorisation requirements 97–101, *98, 99*; on international cooperation 93–7, *93–9*, 100; on legitimate use *79*, *79*–81, *80*, 100; on state security competency 81–93, *82–5*, *87–92*

Raffarin, Jean-Pierre 174–6, 178

Rassemblement pour la République (RPR) (France) 162–3, 166–7, 172; *see also* Chirac, Jacques

Rau, Johannes 135

'reactive' strategic culture 34, 46, *47*, 225, 230–1; and Canada 58–9, *75*, 101, **101**, 200–4, 216, **227**; and France *75*, 101, **101**, **227**; and Germany 67, *75*, 81, 101, **101**, 136, 157, 222, **227**

Reform Party of Canada 200–1, 205

Rice, Condoleeza 216

Roach, Kent 190–1

Robertson, George 135

'robust' strategic culture 13, 46, *47*, 81, 93, **101**, 222–5, **227**, 228, 230–1; and Australia 55, *75*, 81, 100–1, **101**, 181, 184, 194, 197, 222, **227**; and Canada 204–6, 211–12, 219, **227**; and France 62–3, *75*, 81, 100, **101**, 163–4, 171–4, 178, **227**; and UK 71–2, *75*, 81, 100, **101**, 105, 110, 120, 129, 222, **227**

Role of Government, GESIS Leibniz Institut für Sozialwissenschaften surveys *85, 87, 89, 90, 91, 92*

RPR (*Rassemblement pour la République*) (France) 162–3, 166–7, 172; *see also* Chirac, Jacques

Russia, and Canada 219

Sarkozy, Nicolas 173

Scharping, Rudolf 137, 149

Schäuble, Wolfgang 152

Schily, Otto 135, 143–8

Schlauch, Rezzo 137

Schröder, Gerhard: and Afghanistan 134–41, *240*; and Bush, George W. 135, *240*; and counterterrorism 143–6; and Iraq 149–55, 174; media interviews 149

Second World War 57, 60–2, 64–6, 70, 72

Security Legislation Amendment (Terrorism) Bill 2002 [No. 2] (Australia) 187–90

Seldon, Anthony 122

'September Dossier' (UK Government) 122–5, 127

'*Sicherheitspaket I*' ('Security Package I') (Germany) 143–4, 146–7

'*Sicherheitspaket II*' ('Security Package II') (Germany) 144–8

Sierra Leone, interventions in 106, 122, 230, *235*

Smith, Chris 125

Snowden, Edward 130, 178

Social Democratic Party of Germany (SPD) 138, 141, 143–6, 148, 155; *see also* Schröder, Gerhard

Socialist Party (PS) (*Parti-Socialiste*) (France) 162–3, 172, 177

Spain, and Iraq 232

SPD (Social Democratic Party of Germany) 138, 141, 143–6, 148, 155; *see also* Schröder, Gerhard

Speech Act theory 7–10

Sperling, J. 45

states, liberal democratic 1–4, 222–3; case studies 12–15; *see also* Australia; Canada; France; Germany; theoretical model; United Kingdom

Stoiber, Edmund 150, 151

strategic culture demarcation 34–6, 46, *47*, *75*, 100, **101**, **227**; *see also* 'aggressive/ suppressive' strategic culture; 'passive' strategic culture; 'proactive' strategic culture; 'reactive' strategic culture; 'robust' strategic culture

Straw, Jack 108

Ströbele, Christian 144

Struck, Peter 138

Stunde Null ('zero hour') (Germany) 64–5, 67, 73

Süddeutsche Zeitung (SZ) (newspaper) (Germany): on Afghanistan 139–40; on counterterrorism 147; on Iraq 153–4

Suez Crisis 57, 61, 70–1

250   *Index*

Sun, The (newspaper) (UK): on Afghanistan 110–11, 112–13; on counterterrorism 120; on Iraq 127–8
'suppressive' strategic culture *see* 'aggressive/suppressive' strategic culture
Sydney Morning Herald (newspaper) (Australia): on Afghanistan 186; on counterterrorism 190; on Iraq 195
Syria: air strikes, and UK (2013) 129–30; research options 231

Taliban, attacks against *see* Afghanistan, use of force in
Taylor, M. 25
terrorism *see* counterterrorism
Terrorism Act 2000 (UK) 114, 188
Terrorism Act 2002 (Australia) 187–90
Thatcher, Margaret 64, 71
theoretical model 10–12, 33–43, **33**, **35**, **40**, 224–6; demarcation of strategic culture 34–6, 46, *47*, *75*, 100, **101**, **227**; and international relations (IR) theory 4–10, 23–31, *31*, 229–33; methodology and strategy 15–17, 44–50, *47*
Thucydides, Melian Dialogues 2
Times, The (newspaper) (UK): on Afghanistan 110–11; on counterterrorism 119–20; on Iraq 126–7
Today (BBC radio programme), and counterterrorism 119
Toews, Vic 211
Toronto Star (newspaper) (Canada): on Afghanistan 207; on counterterrorism 213; on Iraq 218
Toynbee, Polly 111–12
Transatlantic Trends surveys 78, *80*, *95*, *98*
Treacher, A. 59, 61–2

Union for a Popular Movement (UMP) (France) 174
Union pour la démocratie française (UDF) (Union for French Democracy) (France) 163, 165–6, 172
United Kingdom 1–2, 12–15; and Afghanistan 105–14, **227**, 230, *236*; and authorisation of state force 97–101, *98*, *99*, **101**; counterterrorism 13, 114–20, **227**; and international cooperation 93–7, *93–9*, 100; and Iraq 120–9, 222, 225, **227**, *236*; and legitimate use of force *79*, 79–81, *80*, 100; military expenditure 14, *237*; military

interventions *234–6*; national identity 68–73, *74–5*, 222–5; state security competency 81–93, *82–5*, *87–92*; strategic culture demarcation 71–2, *75*, 81, 100, **101**, 105–7, 109–10, 120, 129–30, 222–4, **227**
United Nations Security Council (UNSC): and Australia, on Iraq 193–6; and Canada 210, 212; and Canada, on Iraq 215–19; and France, on Iraq 174–7; and Germany, on Iraq 149–52, 154, 155, *241*; public opinion polls *93*, 93–4, 98, *98*, *241*; resolution 1373; and UK, on Iraq 124–6, 128, *241*

Vaillant, Daniel 170–2
Venne, Pierrette 211–12
Vertrauensfrage (vote of no confidence) (Germany) 138
Vietnam War 54, 61
Vila, Jean 172
Von der Leyen, Ursula 157

Walser, Martin 66
War Measures Act 1914 (Canada) 209, 211
War of 1812 56
Weizsäcker, Richard von 66
Wendt, A. 23, 25, 27
Wenger, A. 38
Westerwelle, Guido 152, 157
White, H. 181, 191
White, Michael 107
"Who Rules the World?", Bertelsmann Foundation survey 78, *93*
Wiefelspütz, Dieter 145, 146
Williams, Daryl 187–8
Woche, Die (newspaper) (Germany), opinion poll 148
Woolf, Harry, Baron, (Lord Chief Justice) 115
Woollacott, Martin 111, 112
World Values Survey (2015) 78, *79*, *84*
World War One 53–6, 60, 69–70, 192
World War Two 57, 60–2, 64–6, 70, 72

YouGov/BBC opinion poll, on Iraq 128–9
Young, Hugo 111, 112

ZDF (TV network) (Germany), opinion poll 155, 157
Zimmermann, D. 38